Ut

D1600996

The Father

Countless children throughout the world grow up without fathers. *The Father* studies the reasons for this and assesses the contribution of this phenomenon to social and psychological problems.

Using images of the father from classical antiquity to the present day, Luigi Zoja views the origins and evolution of the father from a Jungian perspective. He argues that the father's role in bringing up children is a social construction that has been subject to change throughout history. The author examines the consequences of this, and considers the crisis facing fatherhood today.

Covering these issues from historical, sociological and psychological points of view, *The Father* will be welcomed, both by people from a wide variety of disciplines, including practitioners and students of psychology, sociology and anthropology, and by the educated general reader. This book fills an important gap as no other existing book faces the subject of fatherhood from such a broad and multi-disciplinary perspective.

Luigi Zoja is a Jungian Analyst and is the President of the International Association for Analytical Psychology. From 1984 to 1993, he was President of CIPA (Centro Italiano di Psicologia Analitica).

The Father

Historical, psychological
and cultural perspectives

Luigi Zoja

English translation by Henry Martin

First published in English 2001
by Brunner-Routledge
27 Church Road, Hove, East Sussex BN3 2FA

Simultaneously published in the USA and Canada
by Taylor & Francis Inc
325 Chestnut Street, Philadelphia PA 19106

Originally published in Italian as *Il gesto di ettore: Preistoria, storia, attualità e scomparsa del padre*, Bollato Boringhieri, Torino 2000 by Luigi Zoja

Brunner-Routledge is an imprint of the Taylor & Francis Group

English Edition © 2001 Luigi Zoja

Typeset in Times by M Rules
Cover design by Sandra Heath
Printed and bound in Great Britain by
Biddles Ltd, Guildford and King's Lynn

British Library Cataloguing in Publication Data
A catalogue record for this book is available from the British Library

Library of Congress Cataloging-in-Publication Data
Zoja, Luigi.
  [Gesto di Ettore. English]
  The father: historical, psychological, and cultural perspectives/Luigi Zoja.
    p. cm.
  Includes bibliographical references and index.
  ISBN 1 58391 106 5 (hbk) – ISBN 1 58391 107 3 (pbk)
    1. Fatherhood–History. 2. Fatherhood–Psychological aspects.
  I. Title.

HQ756.Z65 2001
306.874'2–dc21   2001018065

ISBN 1 58391 106 5 (hbk)
ISBN 1 58391 107 3 (pbk)

For Giorgio and Marinella

Contents

Figures

Acknowledgments

My thanks must go to Andrea Camperio Ciani for his help with zoological considerations, to Nini Buccheri and Maria Grazia Ciani for their assistance on questions of classical antiquity, to Patricia Michan for her information on Mexico, to Hechmi Dhaoui for his guidance on the Arab countries, to Giovanna Carlo, Franco Livorsi, Giuditta Lo Russo, Stanislao Nievo and Luisa Passerini for their reading of the text at various stages of its composition, and to Maria Tresoldi for her editorial assistance and the organization of the illustrations. Special thanks are also due to a number of persons whose native language is not my own, but who were nonetheless able to read the original Italian text and to help to free it of provincialism, in the light of their experience of the cultural coordinates of other countries: Carole Beebe and Henry Martin (USA), Christian Gaillard (France and Switzerland), Roberto Gambini (Brazil), Manfred Kuder (Germany), Martin Mumelter (Austria). Finally I have to thank Eva Pattis for her contribution not only to my research on the father, but also to my life as a father.

Permissions

The following copyright holders have given their kind permission for use of their artwork.

Museo di Brera, Milan.
Soprintendenza per i beni artistici e storici (Ministry of culture), Rome.
Bildarchiv Preussischer Kulturbesitz, Berlin.
Chiesa di San Donato, Genoa.
Réunion des Musées Nationaux (Louvre), Paris.
The Imperial War Museum, London.
Carl Hanser Verlag, Munich.
Olympia Publifoto, Milan and Rome.
Wallraf-Richartz Museum, Koln, Germany.
VG Bild-Kunst, Bonn.
Petit Format, Paris.
Urban & Fischer Verlag, Munich.
Jan Saudek, Prague.

Introduction

The universal principle that [Freud] discovered, and for which discovery his unconscious Jewish antireligious affect was partly responsible, was the psychic significance of the father image (the patriarchate) for Western man. . . . Freud's heroic struggle with the father archetype of Judaism . . . is not Freud's personal affair, nor is it simply a problem of Jewry itself; Western culture (religion, society, and morals) is mainly formed by this father image and the psychic structure of the individual is partly damaged by it.

E. Neumann, *Freud und das Vaterbild*, 1956

Jakob Freud was a cloth merchant whom history remembers as the father of Sigmund Freud. Well dressed, and wearing a new fur hat, he was taking a walk one Saturday through the streets of the city of Freiberg, and on rounding a corner found another man blocking his path. The situation was embarrassing. Sidewalks at the time were often no more than a narrow track that allowed pedestrians to avoid the mud in the streets. Jakob Freud began to take another step forward, but timidly, since he found no question of honor or principle in demanding or allowing precedence. The other man, however, was quicker, and eager to assert his sense of superiority: he knocked the hat from Jakob Freud's head and into the mud, shouting, "Get down from the sidewalk, you Jew!"

On telling his son about the incident, this was the point at which he stopped. But the little Sigmund wanted to hear more, since this, for him, was where the story began to grow interesting. He asked, "So, what did you do?"

His father replied, in perfect calm, "I stepped down from the sidewalk and picked up my hat."[1]

According to Ernest Jones, Sigmund Freud's first biographer, this was one of the essential events in the shaping of the character of the founder of psychoanalysis. This utter lack of heroism in the man he had formerly seen as an absolute and perfect model fell like a bludgeon on his mind, and decided its future course.

If no such episode had taken place, psychoanalysis might have developed in a somewhat different way. Freud wouldn't have thought of the son as the father's inevitable rival, and he wouldn't have criticized monotheism and its institution of God the Father.

At a later date, Freud was to read the *Aeneid* and was finally to understand: his father had found himself at the same fork in the road which Aeneas had had to negotiate while fleeing Troy. The encounter with the enemy demands a decision: is it better to fight for one's honor and run the risk of death, or to turn one's thoughts to the future and the continuance of the existence of one's people and family? Freud was so grateful to the *Aeneid* as to head *The Interpretation of Dreams* (1900) with one of its verses (VII, 312): *Flectere si nequeo Superos Acheronta movebo* – "If I cannot bend the gods of heaven, I will move the gods of hell." We'll lend attention to Aeneas in a subsequent part of this book, and for the moment we'll also take leave of Freud, alone with the loss of his illusions.

This story, however, tables a central question: what do children expect from their fathers? In the patriarchal tradition, of which this story is emblematic, it is something quite different from what they expect from their mothers.

In normal circumstances, all children love their mothers. And how do things stand when a mother is treated badly or exposed to humiliation? Her children continue to love her, and perhaps attempt to feel compassion for her.

And do children normally love their fathers? Of course they do. But when a father is the victim of an injustice, things become more complicated than in the case of a mother, since the father–child relationship is much more highly conditioned by the other relationships in the surrounding environment. The dyad of mother and child, above all in its earliest phases, is of so exclusive a quality as nearly to stand apart from any other world. The situation with fathers is quite different: our customary image of the father–child relationship sees it from the very start within the context of a group of at least three people. From the very beginning, it's a part of society. The father, in fact, is the person who is expected to teach his children the art of relating to society, just as the mother has already taught them how to relate to their bodies.

If a mother submits to an act of humiliation, the reactions of her child may well be negative. But our literature contains no reports of her having been rejected in the way Freud rejected his father. There's not much chance her child will declare, "You're not a real mother." A father, however, who accepts an offense quite easily risks hearing his child accuse him of not behaving like a father. Children's adherence to this point of view tells us that the comfort they want from a father doesn't exclusively derive from his love and rectitude; they also demand that a father be strong. This is part of their awareness that society's relationships function not only on love, and again not only on rectitude, but also on facts of pure and naked power.

Children want their fathers to be strong and victorious. If the father can be a winner while also a man who is good, just and full of love, so much the better. But often the most important thing is for the father simply to embody the image of a man who knows how to win, and his goodness or not is of secondary importance. Our tradition frequently considers a father whose actions are just but without success in the outside world to be far less preferable than an unjust father whose actions are crowned with victory. Shakespeare, for example, was aware of this paradox: *King Lear* gives us the prototype of the father whose loss of power and prestige results in his rejection.

This father our tradition prefers doesn't, however, run only the risk of adopting impoverished moral standards. The importance attributed to power also goes hand in hand with a limited life of the feelings. This self-limitation becomes the hallmark of his interpersonal relationships, and it establishes a vicious circle in which others can pay him back in the same coin: little Sigmund Freud apparently felt no understanding for his father's weakness.

The destructiveness of the two world wars and then of the war in Vietnam has been associated with paternal aggressiveness, and the perception of such a relationship has led to a steady rise in the number of non-aggressive fathers. But this process of evolution is accompanied by an involution: ever greater numbers of male adolescents now entrust themselves exclusively to the group of their peers and substitute the father with the head of the gang. Though the decline in paternal aggressiveness is an undeniably positive development for children as a whole, many boys distance from a mild-mannered father, seeing him as weak, and direct their admiration to some violent bully who terrorizes the neighborhood, electing him as an adoptive father.

It's possible, of course, for such a moment to be simply a part of a difficult passage to adulthood. Yet, similar situations grow ever more conspicuous. Today's world seems to make it difficult for adolescent males to identify the other shore to which such a passage should lead. These young men follow the pattern of Pinocchio, who quickly tired of his father Geppetto – who was no less dull than honest and respectable – and abandoned him to follow Lucignolo, the arrogant, rebellious schoolmate who was proud of doing only as he liked. This old story from a still rural Italy seems today to remain up to date, which perhaps explains its continuing world fame.[2]

Children clearly expect their fathers to show them a kind of affection which resembles the affection received from their mothers, but they also demand something else. "With me," the child insists, "be good, fair and just. Love me. But with others, be first of all strong, even at the cost of being violent, even at the cost of being unjust."

It might be objected that we've found our point of departure in the patriarchal tradition of the Western world, and in a nineteenth-century episode, whereas the mothers and fathers of today are much more similar to one another, from children's points of view. Current psychological research[3] has studied the dyad of father and child separately from the triad of mother, father and child, and concludes that father and child have their own specific relationship already in the first months of life. Still, however, we intend to avoid the isolation of the father from the family, the society, and the surrounding culture: our basic premise remains that the father's specificity as a parent lies first of all in precisely this complexity of functions; this premise is also rooted in Jungian psychology, which doesn't separate the individual dimension from the collective dimension. The father's authority has yielded to the principles of democracy, and his power has in many ways waned; but our unconscious doesn't eliminate in a few generations what has dominated it for millennia. Despite its loss of fathers, and even if probably now in transition toward a new and different configuration, Western society, at least unconsciously, remains patriarchal.

Much has been said about parents who rear their children in a context of contradictory messages and teachings, thus making them fragile and insecure, and, in the gravest of cases, predisposing them to psychic dissociation: schizophrenia. But children too, through their expectations, have a powerful influence on their parents (different from the influence of parents on children since it isn't primary, but exercised daily and profound in its effects). Expectations and projections contribute to making us become what the other wants us to be. Since small children consider their parents to be good, mature, and absolutely trustworthy, it's usual indeed for them to help their parents to grow more sure of themselves, to explore the satisfactions of generosity, and thus to become more adult.

But in a patriarchal society, this rule holds mainly for the mother. With the father, things are more complicated, since the child's expectations are more contradictory: not as the exception, but as the rule. And not in different moments, but all at once. Within the family, the father must adhere to a code of moral rectitude; but with respect to society, his actions first of all must accord with the laws of power, or, more precisely, with something like the Darwinian laws of evolution where the "good" are equivalent to the "fittest," in the sense of showing the greatest ability to assure survival for themselves and their descendants.

A father, however, is a single individual who cannot and must not split himself in two. So, on finding himself amid forces that promote dissociation, he alternates between two laws and thus grows insecure. Fathers once could hide this insecurity with which their role is largely incompatible, and children had neither the right to evaluate paternal morality and success, nor any great array of tools for doing so. Such tools today are commonplace, to an ever higher degree.

This circumstance must be held in mind, since it constitutes what we have chosen to call *the paradox of the father*. It can briefly be described as follows. The degree to which a mother fulfills her role is generally measured on the basis of how she interacts with her child: the challenge, surely, is great, but clear and identifiable. The father's situation is different: in addition to depending on how he interacts with his child, his success *as a father* also depends on how he interacts with society, and the laws that hold in these two different spheres are not the same.

While personal, psychological and independent of any given period's social conventions, "the paradox of the father" is also public and historical. The core of patriarchal European civilization – which has spread all across the world, owing first to colonization and now to globalization – also houses a second paradox, which is nothing other than the collective face of the first. This civilization finds its creed in Christianity, yet at the very same time its diffusion has taken place in "Darwinian" terms, through the exercise of force: by way of war; by way of the rape and destruction of nature; by way of the subjection and exploitation of weaker or simply more pacific peoples; by way of the systematic flaunting on a planetary scale of the commandments "Thou shalt not kill," "Thou shalt not steal," "Thou shalt not covet thy neighbor's house . . . nor any thing that is thy neighbor's." In this sense, the core of the European culture which has spread the gospel of rationality all across the face of the earth is itself profoundly irrational. Like the individual father, this patriarchy alternates between observance of the laws of love and the laws of power, and remains at quite some distance from their reconciliation.

A young woman who worked with left-wing political groups went to university in the late 1960s and early 1970s. The student protest movement was at its greatest heat. Her father was an industrialist. His whole branch of business was in crisis; and the family firm was in even graver circumstances, since he lacked aggressiveness and the will to combat.

The daughter had a fine mind and a skill in the arts of argumentation, and her talents had been further sharpened by studies in philosophy and participation in political debates. She confronted her father like a gladiator. He, in turn, rather clumsily accepted the challenges with which she drew him into discussions, remaining unaware of doing so out of a need for greater communication with her. His arguments within the discussions were even clumsier. The girl flexed her intellectual muscles and always won. Her satisfaction, however, was always short-lived. Her father was weaker than she was, and had neither the intellectual acumen nor the emotional independence which she herself was in the course of acquiring, and this made her victories bitter.

Her father was extremely fond of her, and he was neither an unscrupulous speculator in business nor a tyrant in his family. So, what made his daughter feel him to be a stranger didn't lie in her ideas. It was a question of a deeper and far more irrational movement of the affects. The man wore the mental garb of a loser, like a shirt of Nessus which couldn't be stripped away. And the creation of suffering and insufferability hadn't yet reached its nadir.

The girl became gradually aware that the family had reached a state of economic distress, and that the problem was largely personal. Her friends too were the daughters of industrialists and all led comfortable lives. Her contempt for her father increased. He grew always more dejected and beaten, and was also physically ill. Examinations revealed a cancer that left him little time to live.

The daughter tried to feel sorry for him, but something inside her rebelled. In addition to riddling his mind, defeat by now had sunk horrible roots into his body. She experienced her father's presence in the house as ever more intolerable, physically intolerable: he provoked an irrational repulsion, invincible, both physical and aesthetic, like a loathsome worm discovered between the sheets of her bed.

The man attempted to force her to talk with him, and he wanted to keep her close by, ordering her to stay at home and forbidding her to go out with her friends. All he managed to do was to cover himself with even greater ridicule. On thinking back to that period, the daughter primarily remembered the thud of the door she slammed behind her, when, abandoning her fretful father, she went out all the same. Then he died, writhing in both body and soul. For a while the daughter felt free.

Later, for a number of years, she underwent analysis in the attempt to find reconciliation with the figure of her father and to work through the sense of guilt he had inevitably bequeathed her. Her feelings for her father, even after his death, continued for quite some time to be charged with a vivid sense of repulsion. In order to overcome it, she had to recount his story and remember his figure countless times. Slowly, now that she no longer felt him to be so revoltingly close to her, nearly experiencing the opposite, or something close to nostalgia, she once again felt pity for him, and finally affection. The work was so slow as never to seem to complete itself. She was able to grasp a number of truths she had already known while her father was still alive, but which formerly had been only rational: she had previously been unable to turn them into heartfelt convictions with an important place in her psyche.

"My father's lack of success in business, like his illness, made him weaker, but not more base; and therefore no less deserving of love. My values never centered on physical prowess and financial success. I'm horrified by this overly competitive society which rewards the ruthless and crushes the weak. I want to be on their side. But it isn't easy when the weak are so terribly close to you, and you feel a person's weakness to threaten you, like a contagious disease. Basically, I am even more horrified by these feelings I have, which are so unfair; but it's hard to overcome the repulsion you feel for people who have been defeated, especially when defeat has gone hand in hand with a loss of self-respect.

"Inside myself, I was screaming at my father: 'Since you've chosen a profession of which you ought to be ashamed, the least you could do is to make money! Don't lie there in bed with that colorless face! Get up and go to your office! Why don't you fight this cancer? You're letting it win just to spite me.'"

A boy grows up in the Italy of the 1940s, in a large family that's also inclusive of grandparents, uncles, aunts and various other relatives. The country's memory of the Second World War and the ensuing civil war between Fascists and anti-fascists was still quite fresh, and another great struggle was in the making, to be fought in the plebiscite that would finally decide if post-war Italy would be a monarchy or a republic. This is a cultivated, upper-middle-class family where varying opinions and points of view must be tolerated and respected, and where voices are never raised. The boy remembers the atmosphere surrounding the political discussions – in which tones were always civil – as charged with flames, always lively and moving and capable of leaving burns.

The boy's father favors the republic. Some of the family agree. Others might favor retaining the king, fearing that a republic might be a first step toward Communism. Only an uncle is a truly fervid royalist. The family does not see a great deal of him, but his visits are sufficiently frequent to lead the boy to a revelation: one of his earliest memories – from kindergarten times or at the start of elementary school – is of having been a passionate royalist.

As a grown man who had entered analysis, he spoke of these royalist sentiments as an act of betrayal of his father.

"But, as a child," observed the analyst, "as small as you were at the time, could you have been responsible for a betrayal?"

"I don't think so. But I already knew enough to be able to reach the right conclusions. Whereas my father spoke very little and was dedicated entirely to his duties, my uncle was an arrogant, superficial ne'er-do-well: his only real interest was in an easy, comfortable life."

"Wouldn't you say that you made these judgments later? What did you and your uncle talk about?"

"I asked him about the war. He hadn't, in fact, seen a lot of action, since he had been assigned to the supply lines. But there was a story I asked for again and again. He had once been caught at a road block, with his truck under fire. My uncle sent for a tank that completely destroyed the barricade and the men firing from behind it: people defending their own country.

"When I remember that story, it makes me dizzy: it's as though today I see that scene again from a great height, as though trying to rise above it. But it thrilled me to hear my uncle recount it; and the child who felt those feelings, after all, was me."

"Did you talk about the war with your father?"

"Never. He knew nothing about it. He was an officer in the reserves, but was never recalled to duty since some of his specializations as an engineer were considered more important, for example in constructing bomb shelters. And clearly he was happy with that. With having avoided the danger, and also with having done something useful rather than something he found repugnant. But I felt he had gone into hiding. And since shelters in fact are hiding places, it even seemed that he had somehow doubly gone into hiding. My father was also older than my uncle, and not as strong, so everything seemed to declare that he hadn't been fit for combat. I'd watch them shave in the morning. My father used an electric razor, my uncle a straight razor. That motorized razor may perhaps have reminded me of the first electrical appliances that I had seen in the hands of the women in the kitchen: something a man should be ashamed of. But it was the referendum – which demanded a vote in favor of the monarchy or a republic – that really summed up the contrast between these two different sorts of men."

"Did you and your father discuss the referendum?"

"He limited himself to essentials. He'd say, 'You see, things in Italy weren't the same as in Germany. It was the king who appointed Mussolini to head the government. So, it's not enough to have rid ourselves of the dictatorship. We have to get rid of the king too.' And then I think he'd also add, as though talking to himself, 'Even a republic runs the risk of an incompetent president, but after a while you dismiss him, without then putting up with some equally incompetent son.'

"The absurd thing is that already then it struck me that he was right, but I refused to give him the satisfaction of agreeing with him."

"Did you talk about these things with your uncle?"

"That's precisely the point. My uncle had no ideas at all. He'd simply bluster, 'A republic?! What's that supposed to mean? Don't you know that the president of the republic is a decrepit old man?' (I even think he showed me a picture in a paper of an old man. But maybe that was later, when the republic had already been established: but my memory sees all the crucial images as belonging to a single moment.) 'The king,' he'd say, 'on the other hand, is young, strong and handsome: just look at him.' (He'd point out a man in a photograph, dressed in a dashing uniform, and surrounded by cavalry officers.) My young and still developing faculties of thought remained paralyzed. Appearances were everything, and reason seemed to count for nothing. I identified the king with my uncle, and the tired old president with my father. I preferred the figure which I saw as stronger and more exciting, the figure charged with the greater sense of certainty, the one that didn't depend on being chosen by anybody else: a king, after all, is born a king.

"This was also the period when my grandparents were reading me *Pinocchio*. Perhaps I was like that puppet son who knows that his father Geppetto is in the right, but who runs away with the wild Lucignolo, since he feels that only Lucignolo can offer him new experiences, and new ways of having fun. Perhaps my uncle, in that overly civilized family, was the only person who gave me an inkling of the existence of a simple and instinctive masculine personality, which is a stage you can't just skip without actually going through it.

"My father too can be criticized. Why didn't he share his thoughts with me? Why didn't he explain that building shelters that offer protection from weapons is better than using weapons? That building shelters is another form of strength. In this sense, I really needed him, and he wasn't there. Because he failed to tell me about how he reasoned, not because he never told war stories."

Do we truly live in an epoch of the absent father? Numerous studies have already sounded the alarm and declared the missing fathers to be a malady that knows no precedents.

But there's an error in rushing to the conclusion that the instability of the modern societies of the Western world can be attributed to the diminished authority of the father, since this diminution may itself be only another of its manifestations. We likewise gravely limit our thoughts if we see the crisis of the father as entirely a phenomenon of recent generations, or only of the twentieth century. We'll see that the underlying image of the father in the Western world was profoundly shaped by Greek myth and Roman law, even if later it was modified by the advent of Christianity, and then by the French and industrial revolutions. The changes which have occurred in the 1970s, 1980s and 1990s are surely important; but they are also crests of froth on the great ground-swell of history.

To concentrate on present times and current situations would amount to paying obeisance to the culture of the mass media: a culture of immediate, bulimic gratification for which momentary appetites are of more importance than any notion of long-range project that unfolds in time. If these are the secret guidelines of many studies, they are finally at odds with themselves: their words bewail the absence of the good father, but they in fact increase the vigor of things that stand at the antipodes of the sobriety, stability and responsibility that the collective imagination – just how objectively makes no difference – attributes to such a father. Peddling the chronicle of current events is like vending fast food: lots of calories, of low quality, for a vast number of consumers. And if this is how things stand – as indeed we fear – the investigation that limits itself to the facts of the world as known today makes itself guilty of the same criminal impatience through which television slowly kills the book: those very books which provide the form in which such investigations are marketed.

The times in which we live have doubtless effected a dizzying acceleration in the rate at which change takes place in collective psychology. Yet we have to remember that changes within the sphere of what we see directly always expose us to the risk of their over-evaluation: looking down from the crest of a wave to its trough, we conclude that their difference in height is the depth of the ocean. Reliable studies[4] inform us that the image of the father most widely shared and generally approved of in the United States has shifted in only a couple of decades from the "head of the family" to the "co-parent" (the father who shares the tasks of the mother). Yet, the real involvement of American fathers with their children has remained substantially unchanged. Their level of involvement is in fact quite low[5] and virtually infinitesimal when compared to that of mothers.

What surveys bring to light often has more to do with the convictions we harbor in the conscious mind than with how we truly behave: they reveal our image of the father, or the ideal in which fathers imagine themselves to believe. Unlike the weighty, tragic archetypes that mill within our depths, such conscious values can change quite rapidly, especially in an age of incessant communication that lives on the sale of newer values. The process of selling itself leads mass communication to promote and accelerate superficial changes. Novelties sell at the fastest speeds, on the cunning model of the fashion industry, which creates the need to purchase its products by revamping them every year. This is no indication of a change in the depths of the human mind. The practice of analysis makes it clear, for example, that public discussion and the flowering of a previously unknown market of pleasures have led the Italian people to change their conscious ideas on sex more in the course of the last generation than in the whole previous century: but unconscious inhibitions have not relaxed to a similar degree, and the overall shape of the field of sexual problems has not significantly changed. Heads have been modernized, while feet remain firmly rooted in millennia of Catholicism.

We know that a discussion of the father holds no room for absolute truths. Historical reality – especially in today's world, with its rapid shortening of the distances between the roles of men and women – presents infinite gradations. There are also mothers who are heads of families, mothers with careers and whose children regard them through complex expectations: mothers, therefore, who are likewise enmeshed in "the paradox of the father," with the additional complication that their children are unlikely to abandon the expectation of also enjoying the rotundity and dedication of a traditional mother.

It is clear, however, that this occurs because such a woman is a modern "unified parent" who has added a paternal figure to her personality. In dealing with the father as a psychological principle and not only as a physical person, we must also lend attention to cases like these. We are interested in this figure's essential features – in the archetype of the father – and not only in its variations, and most certainly not in only a few of them: we are concerned with "the father, of whatever sex."[6] And therefore, we can add, of whatever country and period of time.

Since our interest is psychological, we want to discuss a collective *image* of the father, as found in the unconscious no less than in the culture in which we are immersed. Even when referring to persons who have actually existed, we do so in the light of their particular ability to sum up the features of this far more general image. At various moments in our discourse, this figure will find its incarnation in women no less than in men, and in groups no less than in individuals. Our interest is focused on a psychic principle, and for greater simplicity we'll continue to call it "the father," without further adjectival modification.

Our study of the father will therefore begin with the most distant origins we are able to discover. Numerous highly worthwhile texts have already lent attention to the history of the father, but not to his *psychological evolution* in the course of time. This use of the word "psychological" can be taken to refer, substantially, to the kinds of things with which analysts are properly concerned: the intellectual convictions and social norms that surround the father – which, moreover, are already visible – are of far less interest than images and models that lie at a greater depth. Though often unconscious and forgotten, they still remain powerful and surprisingly present.

These intentions are responsible for the way this book is structured. We won't pursue the history of the father century by century, but concentrate instead on its crucial psychological phases: first, the prehistory of the father; then Greece, Rome, the advent of Christianity, the French Revolution and the Industrial Revolution; and finally the world wars and the "revolution of the family," both of which became revelations of the separation of fathers and children.

We will turn our attention to parts of the past which have left no historical traces, and more to the precepts and myths of antiquity than to religions and conventions which still today remain, at least formally, in vigor. The latter too are of capital importance for reaching an understanding of today's father, but the analyst is mainly interested in the less visible sides of things, those *Acheronta* which Freud borrowed from Virgil. Depth psychology would like to understand why the arms of Ulysses and Aeneas are still to be found beneath the shirts and ties of fathers today.

While aware of being forced to rely on conjectures in a field of great uncertainty, our study of the image of the father will lead us to step through the walls of history. Part I of the book will turn its attention to prehistory, and to the zoological course of development that led to the human father.

The origins of fatherhood will in fact be seen to lie along the suture where nature and culture meet. This assertion holds true since the monogamic patriarchal family, which predominates in all historical societies, is a product of culture and seems not to exist in nature (for example, among the anthropomorphic apes). It also holds true in more obvious terms: unlike the mother, who gives life and nourishment to her offspring in clear and patent ways, the male, in order to perceive his participation in the act of procreation, and thus to transform himself into a father, must first have acquired a certain capacity for reasoning. Finally, and most importantly, it again holds true when we look at the relationship between nature and culture from the inverse point of view. In addition to considering that culture has given us the father, we must also address the probability – or at least the possibility – that the appearance of the father was itself responsible (along, to be sure, with other new developments, such as technological innovations) for the birth of culture: for humanity's definitive exit from its primordial state of existence, and thus from the ranks of the animals. Part I attempts to reconstruct this process.

The father is a construction, an artifice. As such he differs from the mother, who brings into the world of human life a condition which already in animal life was fully affirmed and omnipresent as the principal premise of survival.

The father is a program, perhaps the very first program. He belongs to the world of will and intentionality. (Is the advent of the father perhaps synonymous with the invention of will?) And the father's condition is self-imposed. The father's status as an artificial creature, and, also, his lack of experience – given his "recent" birth – are inevitably the source of a disadvantage, much as apples are plagued by worms, or as roses bear thorns. Despite the appearances imposed by patriarchal culture, the father experiences his condition with far more insecurity than is true of the mother.

Even if we limit our attention to the animals that evolved most recently – the mammals – females and mothers in the sphere of zoology have always been one and the same thing. The females know how to behave like mothers. Male mammals, on the other hand, have almost always been simply males, and nothing more, without at all being fathers. In hundreds of millions of years of zoological history, it is only in the human species – and only in the span of the last few tens or hundreds of thousands of years – that one can descry a condition of fatherhood. Its construction received no assistance from any previous or corresponding instinct.

The male, finally, has assumed the status of the father for reasons which are wholly exterior to the process of animal evolution: the reasons lie only in history (in the broader sense which is also inclusive of pre-historical times) and the life of the psyche. And he embraces his status with greater rigidity, diffidence and aggressiveness, as well as with less spontaneity, than is true of the mother's approach to motherhood. Because if history alone has given it to him, history can also reclaim it. Because it's something that every male, not having received it from nature, must learn in the course of his life; and in the course of his life he also runs the risk of once again forgetting it.[7] This possibility of forgetfulness is precisely what he has to confront.

If the father is more aggressive and rigid than the mother, not only in general, but also in his dealings with his children, this has little to do with personal failings on the part of certain fathers, nor even with degenerative developments on the part of certain epochs – such as the period, for example, of the rise of the bourgeois patriarchy. These qualities are a structural part of his true, original condition. One would call them a part of his nature, if it weren't that the nature of the father lies precisely in stepping beyond the bounds of what we normally think nature to be.

It follows that the father – as Greek mythology was well aware, and also as we read in Homer – was always dressed in a suit of armor, both aggressive and defensive, even while embracing his children: clearly a cold embrace to which it's hardly surprising that his children react with wonder no less than fear. That's simply part of the way things stand.

We thus discover an unconfessable feeling of insecurity, an ambivalence *within* the father. It's the correlative reflection of the external ambivalence – the ambivalent expectations his children harbor – to which we refer as "the paradox of the father."

Part II will discuss the father in classical Greece and Rome. The Greeks, in fact, reacted to the father's fundamental insecurity by inverting the problem's appearance (but only its appearance, and not the profound insecurity). They invented the notion of the father's superiority to the mother, and they made it the basis not only of their myths but also of their first endeavors in scientific observation. For the ancient Greeks, the father alone was responsible for generating a child. The mother's function, even during pregnancy, lay exclusively in its nourishment; these erroneous scientific notions continued, moreover, to find adherents up until the start of modern times. While standing at the origins of Western civilization, the Greeks are also the authors of the society that most elevated the father with respect to the mother.

The Romans took things further: they elevated the father with respect to the child as well. But Roman law also contains a perception which holds validity for the fathers of all times: even in the case of legitimate children, the father must perform a public act through which he affirms his intention to be his child's father. Though formulated for the purpose of drawing a divide between legitimate and illegitimate children, this norm becomes an unconscious metaphor of the condition of every father. To be a father – unlike the case of the mother, as we'll repeatedly insist – it is not enough to generate a child, fatherhood also requires a specific act of will. Fatherhood is always a decision and always implies an adoption, even when the child is the father's legitimate, biological offspring.

All of this reiterates our basic affirmation: fatherhood is a psychological and cultural fact; and biological parenthood isn't enough to ensure its existence. Even if the rite decreed by Roman law has today been set aside, in the sense that a man's paternity with respect to his legitimate children is now taken for granted, this doesn't exempt the father from elaborating the same process: fatherhood must be declared and constructed; rather than revealed by the moment of birth, it has to be discovered step by step, in the course of the relationship between father and child.

A clear synopsis of this point of view is found in a classic film by Charlie Chaplin. At the beginning of *The Kid*, Chaplin walks through dark alleys where trash is unceremoniously thrown from windows above. He encounters a boy he has never seen before, and the child touches something inside him, arousing a feeling as previously unknown as the boy himself. Chaplin looks upward, to see if the boy as well has dropped from the skies like the trash.

The boy had been kidnapped by mistake and then abandoned by two outlaws. But the protagonist, who is to become his adoptive father, doesn't know or care about these previous events. It's as though the identity of the boy's biological parents were of no importance, or, better, as though the boy had begun to exist only at the moment of having been abandoned and then encountered. The bandits, the dismal alleys and the uncivilized rain of trash can perhaps be seen as a telling summation of the state of pre-civilization from which the father and fatherhood originate. What makes a man a father has little to do with the fact or absence of biological generation: fatherhood lies in the encounter with the child – which, in any case, is sudden and unexpected, even in the presence of the previous fact of biological generation, since it's different from the act of generation – and then in the adoption that follows, and finally in the exit from the condition of savagery, in the budding of society – which is different, again, from the pre-social symbiosis of mother and child – that lies in the assumption of responsibility for another being, voluntarily, and not instinctively.

With its presentation of the man and the child who discover one another, and then of the gradual birth of a relationship between them, the film provides a glimpse of the birth of every individual fatherhood, no less than of the history of the whole condition of fatherhood.

The man is a tramp, a vagabond, like the prehistoric hunters who invented the family, even while continuing to be nomads. In his attempt to grasp the boy's origins, he imagines him not to spring from the earth and the world of matter, but as having descended from the skies, from the world of the mind, of ideas and of will. The child immediately avails himself of the adult's protection, but also gives something in return: the boy makes the man see the world through new and different eyes, thus opening his road to a form of intelligence which males in nature do not possess, since in the world of animals – as soon we'll discuss more fully – only the females are capable of learning from their offspring. The subsequent acts of acceptance which the man performs, moment by moment, are symbolic descriptions of precisely the state of mind which is unique to fatherhood.

In terms of the weight of the encounter, it makes no difference if the father is literally adoptive, or in fact biological. Even in the latter case, the father had entrusted the child's gestation entirely to its mother: so the creature he finally sees is totally new to him. Whereas the mother experiences the new-born baby as the very same child she carried in her womb, the father sees his sperm and the child it called to life as two different things. Peter Handke gives the following description of the moment in the maternity ward when he saw his daughter for the very first time: "What they showed him behind that pane of glass wasn't a 'daughter' but only a 'new-born child'".[8]

Our goal is to look at the father from the father's point of view. Until now, this has rarely taken place. In addition to being far more numerous, studies of the mother are more evenly divided in terms of their adherence to the mother's or child's point of view. Studies of the father, on the other hand, again leave much to be desired.

Since our discussion deals with Greece, Rome and Europe, our study can be called Eurocentric; and in terms of the attention it lends to the origins of European civilization, it can even more specifically be said to center on the Mediterranean. These are also the places of my own personal experience, which, in addition to the impossibility of exploring the whole world, makes me find it only natural to follow these lines while attempting to reconstruct the father as we know him today. The expansion of Mediterranean culture throughout the rest of Europe was also the start of the process that later saw Europe itself expand its dominion over the rest of the world. Southern Europe made a fundamental contribution to the invention of the father as we know him throughout the Western world. Part III discusses a number of the ways in which fatherhood was affected by the advent of Christianity, the Protestant reformation, the French and American revolutions, and the two world wars. Here too I have given particular attention to Italian points of view.

Finally, much has been said and written on the problematic father, the destructive father. The father is in fact more frequently pathological, both disturbed and disturbing, than the mother, just as is generally true of men with respect to women. The phenomenon of the anti-paternal father arises much more easily than that of the anti-maternal mother.

To speak of the monstrous mother in itself hones close to monstrosity. Such a subject is in fact exceptional. Discussions of the monstrous father are fairly normal, but to travel this road alone is to run the risk of losing sight of a true understanding of fatherhood.

We don't use pathology as our point of departure. We are primarily interested in normal fathers. We know that such fathers exist – even if the percentage of normal fathers is lower than that of normal mothers – and we know them indeed, when all is said and done, to continue to constitute the majority.

It is easy to respond to the voices that object that there's no real point in talking about things that are normal, functional and in good working order. In the father, in fact, there is nothing that functions without artificiality, without rigidity, without ambivalence and self-laceration. So, the normal father can already be said to experience and inflict a sufficient degree of pathology (in the original, etymological sense of suffering) as to justify any number of studies. Part IV will thus concern itself with the current condition of the father in everyday life.

Given the intimate nexus of contradictions that characterize the father – the father pure and simple, not only the problematic father – and the explosively public contradictions that typify European culture – which in a constant oscillation between philosophical/religious generosity and military/economic plundering has extended the sway of its patriarchy across the world – one might be less surprised by the fact that certain chapters of history have turned out badly, than by the fact that history and civilization have managed to exist at all.

This perception has the force of a revelation. An optimistic revelation. While basically surprising, it seems to confirm the notion that trustworthy fathers, despite their constitutional insecurity, the fathers who are "good-enough," have been and remain quite numerous. For better and for worse, in silence, they have constituted the primary force in the shaping of human history. They have been history's beasts of burden.

NOTES

1 Freud, S. (1900) *The Interpretation of Dreams*. In *Standard Edition*, Vol. IV; Jones, E. (1953–7) *Sigmund Freud. Life and Work*. London; Roazen, P. (1975) *Freud and His Followers*. New York: Knopf, II, 2; Krüll, M. (1992/1979) *Freud und sein Vater. Die Entstehung der Psychoanalyse und Freuds ungelöste Vaterbindung*. Frankfurt: Fischer.
2 Collodi, C. (1981/1883) *Pinocchio*. Turin: Einaudi.
3 Lamb, M. E. (ed.) (1976, 1981, 1997) *The Role of the Father in Child Development*. New York: Wiley; Blos, P. (1985) *Son and Father*.
4 Pleck, J. H. "Paternal involvement: levels, sources and consequences" in Lamb (1997).
5 Ibid. See also: Hite, S. (1994) *The Hite Report on the Family*.
6 Samuels, A. (1993). *The Political Psyche*. London: Routledge; Samuels, A. (1995), "The good-enough father of whatever sex," *Feminism and Psychology*, 5(4): 511–30.
7 Mead, M. (1949) *Male and Female*. New York: William Morrow.
8 Handke, P. (1981) *Kindergeschichte*. Frankfurt: Surhkamp.

Part 1

Prehistory

Chapter 1

The mammals: the animals' retreat from fatherhood

By nature, a creation on the part of culture . . .

A. Gehlen

When and where did fatherhood begin? Or when and where are fathers first to be found?

As we ply our way up the river of time, all hopes of discovering the sources of fatherhood will first have to make their way through a swamp where nature and culture intermingle; and in places such as these, research can only look for questions, rather than furnish answers. What parts of paternal behavior are instinctive, or innately present without any need to be learned and taught? And which of its parts, on the other hand, derive from social inventions, or from bodies of rules with which human beings have chosen to govern themselves? And when, for the very first time, did men begin to act like fathers?

Nature has traditionally been seen as feminine, whereas an equally ancient commonplace sees culture as masculine. Here again, as always, the stereotype is partly an expression of mental sloth, while nonetheless containing a measure of truth.

Fatherhood, like motherhood, has to be seen as a continuous activity. No one moment can determine it. It lies in something more than the simple act of procreation. What makes a man a father has far more to do with assuming an enduring role that accompanies the growth of his child. But there is also a basic difference between fatherhood and motherhood, since motherhood is a clear extension, after the birth of a child, of the condition of the female parent who conceived it and bore it within in her body: the two events flow seamlessly one into the other, in the life of the individual mother no less than in the course of the evolution of the species. With men things stand quite differently. Since time immemorial, the physical act of procreation and the process of being a father have always been separate and different things.

Unlike motherhood, fatherhood cannot be linked to a pattern of physical acts, and it cannot be constructed by extending and perfecting the facts of biology, or by dressing them in socially acceptable forms. Fatherhood implies a radical and permanent departure from the norms of purely animal life. In addition to noting that the father's role in the life of a child begins – in accordance with traditions of education – at a later date than the mother's, it is even more important to stress that the institution of fatherhood appears at an infinitely later date in the course of the history of human life. It implies an initial capacity for reflection, no less than a beginning of civilization. It may indeed be the primary cause – and this is one of the topics we hope to explore – of the advent of civilization.

The expanse of time in which nature preceded civilization is so immense, and the arc of civilization so disproportionately minuscule, as to counsel us to view them in terms of an image, even if doing so is nothing new. Their disparity in span can help us understand why it's still quite common – in spite of the enormous costs, both social and psychological, that the situation implies – for motherhood to be characterized by warm and harmonious modes of behavior, whereas fatherhood generally finds expression through forms of conduct which are less predictable and less spontaneous.

The earth is about four and a half billion years old. If we view this veritable eternity as a single solar year, the mammals make no appearance until the middle of the month of December. A proto-human being first arrives on the scene at nine o'clock of the evening of December thirty-first, *homo sapiens* at about ten minutes before midnight, *sapiens sapiens* (with our own physical characteristics) at hardly three minutes before the end of the year, and Neolithic civilization in the course of the very last minute. Socrates, Christ and everyone else whom we see as belonging to antiquity are all bunched together in the last few seconds.

Much of this span of time is ignorant not only of the human being, but even of the act of procreation. It's only in the spring of this year that we see the beginnings of organic life. Still more time had to run its course before single-cell organisms began to share the earth with simple multi-cell organisms, and then with others that were so complex as no longer to be able to limit reproduction to splitting off a few of their cells, and instead to pursue the road of coupling between differently sexed individuals. Asexual reproduction results in offspring which are always genetically identical to their single parent: so, it doesn't facilitate evolution or adaptation to environmental change. With the coupling of two sexes, on the other hand, every reproductive event gives rise to a new and unique genetic combination. Such forms of life enormously increased their possibilities for self-defense and survival while nonetheless inaugurating problems that reach right down to us. Life, henceforth, was eternally divided into male and female forms.

Ever since this duplication first took place, and little by little as the ladder of evolution rose up toward the human being, the role of the female has been growing more stable and precise than the male's. The well-known proverb *mater semper certa, pater numquam* – the mother is always certain, the father never – speaks of something more than the dilemma of the child who wants to know who his or her parents might be. It also defines the attitudes with which parents resolve the question of how to relate to their offspring. Among the higher animals, the mother is always certain, in the sense that she knows who her offspring are. The father lacks that knowledge.

We know that the course of evolution, in all its vast and hasteless meanders, has proceeded through infinite numbers of variations. But its most recent phases established an irreversible division of sexes which since has exerted its influence not only on biology but also on the process of human society and civilization.

While perfecting life, evolution restricted the role that fathers were to play in it.

Any number of species of fish give the males the task of caring for the fertilized eggs. This counts, however, in the lives of such fish as a simple extension of the act of mating. The female expels her eggs, and having been the first to complete her functions, she can also be the first to depart the scene. The male then performs the subsequent task of spraying them with sperm, so it's only "natural" that he also assume the duty of thenceforth looking after them.

But nature's view of "natural" turned itself upside down as life left the seas and began to inhabit dry land. The new forms of life could no longer rely on water as a medium to which both eggs and sperm could be entrusted, and therefore invented interior fertilization. With this new form of mating, the male is the first to conclude his reproductive activities, and is therefore likely to abandon the scene, whereas the female has other functions that remain to be performed.[1]

This great new advance in physiology has a secret existential rub that was greatly to condition the behavior of the male and to stand in the way of his becoming a father. Internal fertilization displaces all the crucial events into a dark and mysterious recess: the female body encloses both eggs and sperm, removing them from all possibility of the male's control. The ever more lengthy lapse of time with which nature separated the act of mating from the birth of the offspring created a new uncertainty: what has actually happened? The male is deprived of all perception that the new-born creature has anything to do with him.

The parents' drive to transmit their genes to the largest possible number of offspring is surely the most powerful of all the drives that regulate animal behavior. Since his progeny could also have been spawned by another, the male has little reason to remain in the female's vicinity up until the time of its birth. Surely it's wiser, from the male's point of view, to use that lapse of time for the fertilization of other females, thus increasing the possibility of passing along his genes.

When nature alone controls reproduction, the males of every species have purely quantitative functions. Each of them constantly produces millions and millions of sperm cells. In theory, an extremely exiguous number of males would suffice to populate the earth. In practice, however, the dynamic of natural selection has proved to be better served by a greater number of unfaithful males – competitive, seductive and sexually "violent" – since the victors among them are better equipped to transmit their genes to a higher number of descendants. These, in turn – thanks to their inherited genes – will tend again to be seductive, competitive and physically powerful, thus setting up a pattern that more efficiently perpetuates the species.

The female has a qualitative function. The number of descendants she is able to bear is highly limited. The female who lapsed into the behavior displayed by the seductive male – the female who immediately abandoned her young – would be punished by the process of natural selection: rather than increase, her descendants would diminish in number, since their chances for survival would grow more tenuous. Unlike the male, she can't make up for their loss by immediately generating others: the further production of eggs takes time, and gestation too is a long, drawn-out process. And offspring who inherited her characteristics – if they managed to survive, despite her lack of attentions for them – would tend again toward the same behavior, in turn exposing their offspring to danger, in a spiral of ever diminishing returns.

Mothers, in short, simply cannot allow themselves to be anything other than good mothers, whereas males, quite to the contrary, can allow themselves not even to be fathers at all. Zoology makes it clear that the pre-moral laws of survival already guide the females of the animal kingdom toward the greater stability and family morality which continue in human society to set them off from males.

But let's return to our march through the course of evolution.

Whereas reptiles generally abandon their young, assuming no parental functions, most species of birds form stable couples in which the male and the female share the tasks of constructing a nest and nurturing and raising their young. Among many of the ostriches and penguins, the males are even exclusively entrusted with the incubation of the eggs. Certain other aspects of bird behavior are even more surprising, since rather than natural they have to be seen as protocultural. There are species of which the song – a male prerogative – is not an innate ability, it has to be taught by the father.[2] So, in slightly different parts of their range, birds of such species sing in different ways, the song of any particular group of these birds is a "dialect" with a local tonality of its own; it isn't dictated by instinct, and belongs instead to a particular tradition which the throats of the individual fathers interpret and preserve.

While producing creatures that demanded ever more complex processes of gestation and growth, evolution was also to take the step of prolonging the symbiosis of offspring and mother, pulling it into her body in the period previous to birth, and extending it into her metabolism once birth had taken place.

Between 200 and 250 million years ago, mammals appeared. The mother's importance leapt to even higher levels, since she found herself responsible for ever longer periods of her offspring's growth.[3] Her young are wholly dependent on her since she also functions as their only source of nourishment for a lengthy period of time.

The primates, whose infants show no autonomy at all, appeared around 70 million years ago.[4] The dyad of mother and child grew even more special, to the point of forming a complementarity that excluded the rest of the world. The social life of the apes now serves functions which have ceased to be exclusively physiological, it already nurtures an embryo of culture, of which motherhood is the one and only vehicle.[5] In addition to assuring the growth of its young, the lengthy nursing of the great apes serves proto-cultural functions. While carried against their mothers' bodies for an extended period of time, infant apes take the world into their eyes in ways which are not much different from those that hold in human life. When the infant ape becomes autonomous, it's equipped not only with instinct, but already with patterns of learned behavior – such as the use of the limited number of tools it has seen its mother manipulate – which are no less essential to the mode of life on which its existence will depend.[6]

All apes are capable of learning by observation. The young, obviously, more than the adults. And the fact that adult females learn more than males seems to derive from their repeated periods of symbiosis with their young, rather than from any innate superiority.[7] In addition to teaching their offspring, the mothers learn from them. The relationship between the female ape and her young marks the beginning of the first modes of behavior which no longer originate in nature: the first thread from which the cloth of culture will be woven, and a thread which runs both upwards and downwards.

With the males, things stand quite differently. They prove that males, while ascending the ladder of evolution, contribute ever less.[8] The males of the higher apes continue to furnish nothing more than that light and volatile fluid, sperm.

The males of the anthropomorphic apes sit dozily on the topmost rungs of the ladder of animal evolution: nearly as bright as a not too dull human being (their calculated IQs easily rise above 80), but irrevocably absent fathers, and polygamous partners. Male gorillas and chimpanzees, as always among animals with exceptional strength and particularly effective arms of aggression, are attentive and delicate with their little ones. They can even play with them. They defend the territory, and thus, indirectly, the females and the non-adult members of the group. But they do not recognize their offspring. They prepare no lairs to protect them. They do not feed them.[9] The only food they share is the meat of larger prey, for the capture of which they have to act as a group, and which perhaps they have to distribute since it quickly rots and they are unable to eat all of it.[10]

We haven't yet reached psychology. We are following the formation of its biological groundwork. Evolution has carried its course to the near vicinity of the human being. But the father has returned to levels lower than found among fish.

NOTES

1 Wickler, W. and Seibt, U. (1983) *Männlich weiblich. Der gross Unterschied und seine Folgen*. Munich: Piper, see Chapter 8; Dawkins, R. (1976) *The Selfish Gene*. Oxford: Oxford University Press, see Chapter 9.
2 Wickler and Seibt (1983), Chapter 9; Wickler, W. and Seibt, U. (1977) *Das Prinzip Eigennutz*. Munich: Piper, IX, 2; Hediger, H. (1984), in Schultz, H. (ed.), *Vatersein*. Munich: DTV; Dawkins (1976), Chapter 11.
3 Eibl-Eibesfeldt, I. (1987/1967) *Grundrisse der vergleichenden Verhaltensforschung* München: Piper, 18, 7, 2; Eibl-Eibesfeldt (1986) *Die Biologie des menschlichen Verhaltens. Grundrisse der Humanethologie* (1984). Munich: Piper, 4, 7; Fthenakis, W. E. (1985) *Väter*, 2 Bd. Munich: Urban & Schwarzenberg, 3, 3, 1.
4 Dunbar, R. I. M. (1988) *Primate Social Systems*. London and Sydney: Croom Helm, 1 and 9.
5 Wickler and Seibt (1977); Morin, E. (1977) *Le paradigme perdu: la nature humaine*. Paris: Seuil, Chapter 3.
6 Goodhall, J. (1986) *The Chimpanzees of Gombe. Patterns of Behavior*. Cambridge MA and London: Belkanp, Harvard University Press, 19; Vogel, C., Voland, E. and Winter, M. (1979) "Geschlechttypische Verhaltensentwicklung bei nicht Menschlichen Primaten," in Degenhardt, A. and Trautner, H. M. (eds), *Geschlechtstypisches Verhalten*. Munich: Beck.
7 Kawai, M. (1967) "Newly acquired pre-cultural behaviour of the natural troup of Japanese monkeys in Koshima Island," *Primates*, 1: 1–30.
8 Hediger (1984), in Schultz (ed.), *Vatersein*; Fthenakis (1985).
9 Morris, D. (1984) *The Naked Ape* (1967). New York: Bantam Doubleday Dell, Chapter 1; Eibl-Eibesfeldt (1986) 4, 3, 7; Fthenakis (1985), 3, 3, 2.
10 Goodhall (1986), 11; Fisher, H. E. (1982) *The Sex Contract. The Evolution of Human Behavior*. New York: William Morrow, IV.

Chapter 2

The sexuality of the great apes

Culture doesn't rest upon a void; it rests upon the previous, pre-cultural complexity of the society of the primates.

E. Morin, *Le paradigme perdu*

When the human being began to establish itself as a species of its own, detaching itself from the other quadrumanes, the world knew none of the species of apes we know today. It could hardly have been otherwise. How could evolution have been forced to pursue so many by-ways on the road to man, the horse and the rattlesnake while not with the chimpanzee or gorilla? At the time of our beginnings, the apes which now are our closest animal relatives were likewise enclosed in forms quite different from those one sees today. Yet, no one who studies the distant human past can resist the temptation of viewing the great man-apes as a possible point of orientation.

The greatest of the great apes (the pongids: orangutan, chimpanzee, bonobo and gorilla) could easily have grown extinct in the course of the twentieth century, and their disappearance would hardly have ranked as a cause for general dismay. They owe their exiguous survival to our own ferocious curiosity – here in the Western world – about the origins of the human being. As living fossils of pre-human beings, they have received a further lease on life so as better to allow us post-animals to experience the excitement of a mirror in which to view ourselves.

Physically, these large apes quite highly resemble us; but their roles as males and females are far less similar to ours than to those of simpler mammals, which they resemble very little. This implies that such roles have remained fairly stable during the vast stretches of time in which they have evolved to their current forms, which in turn makes it reasonable to assume that the male and female roles of the present-day apes are only slightly different from those of our common ancestors. Everything leads us to believe that great innovations in male and female behavior patterns are a relatively recent and specifically human development. Surely there's a risk of imprecision in using today's great apes as a basis on which to attempt to reconstruct the transition from animal to human sexuality, but the level of risk seems tolerable. Fossils tell us almost nothing about the sexual behavior of animals which are long extinct, or of prehistoric human beings. The apes allow us to take a look at the behavior patterns of living creatures.

All species of apes give birth to equal numbers of males and females. This equilibrium might lead us to imagine that monogamy is natural and universal, or that nature tends to provide a male for every female, a female for every male. Such a fantasy, however, most likely voices an unconscious attempt to confer the status of zoological law (biology) on a law of civilization (the norm of monogamy) which in fact has nothing to do with it, since it first appeared at an immeasurably later date.[1] Among the mammals, only an exiguous three percent are monogamic.[2]

Among humans, the norm is for every monogamic couple to give birth to children. With the great apes, things stand differently. Nearly all females give birth to descendants. But among the males, the privilege of procreation lies exclusively in the hands of the stronger, or, more precisely, in their testicles. The males of the various species of apes are specialized in battling one another, thus assuring the physical strength and viability of each new generation, since it always descends from the winners.

We mustn't however conclude that male competition is the only salient feature of the process of natural selection. Evolution isn't guided exclusively by male characteristics, nor is physical strength always the decisive factor. Even among the apes there are various factors that mitigate and compete with strength. Even the strongest male can't hold together a harem of more than a certain number of females, just as he can't control a territory of more than a certain size. The females too can be quite capable of asserting their preferences for sexual partners, and this fact begins to bring pongid and human societies closer to one another.[3] Competition in bonobo society – the society of the least well-known of the great apes – seems, moreover, to be quite low.[4]

But beyond all need to qualify generalizations, male competition remains the dominant structuring force in the societies of the great apes. In groups that contain various males, its manifestation is constant; and it's also present, though surely less visibly, in harem groups composed of a single male and a number of females. The battles have simply been completed, and all took place before the group's formation. They in fact determined which of a number of males would be the only male with the right to constitute a family.[5] The defeated and humiliated are banished from the group and band together into all-male gangs that patrol the flanks of the harem group while waiting for an aged leader, as happens from time to time, to be dethroned, thus making room for a younger one, and allowing the hopes of the others in line to rise a step or so.[6] But it's also possible that a male's turn will never come: those who live in all-male gangs may lose the battles they would have to win in order to set up a family of their own; those who belong to a mixed group, with a number of both males and females, may be blocked by stronger brothers and never succeed in mating.[7] Natural law has already decreed the male's dispensability as an individual. It makes no difference that he's nearly as intelligent as a human being; he remains as deciduous as a leaf on a tree.

We are sometimes inclined to do the apes an injustice, allowing ourselves to evaluate their lives in terms of emotions that belong to human civilization. We think that if the forces of natural selection allow the survival of extravagant numbers of useless males, then surely they must have a social function and be of some sort of use to the group. But whatever social role the males of the great apes may play must not be over-evaluated. We have already noted that they share their food to an extremely limited extent, and also that they do nearly nothing for the custody of baby apes. The great apes, moreover, no matter if male or female, have great strength and agility, and few natural enemies: this is also to say, since they live in groups, that the females would be perfectly capable of defending themselves even if they had to count on a considerably smaller number of males.

These brief observations yield an important perception – important and in its own way tragic – on the condition of the male among the mammals, even at the levels closest to man. Whereas the existence of the females is justified in terms of their functions as individuals – since each of them, generally, has offspring – and finally expresses an embryo of individual psychology, we have seen that motherhood among the great apes is a question of something more than simply following instinct, the existence of the males is meaningful only in terms of their function as a group. The males are simply the gene pool for the next generation.

Just as most of the spermatozoa in a gush of seminal fluid end up in absolute nothingness, the birth of most of the males is an event with no further consequences. The existence they're to lead is to be simply discarded, and counts as the blindest of alleys on the path of the life of the species. They are nothing but the rungs of a ladder which only the strongest will climb, bit by bit, as they win competitions in the tournament of reproduction. Aside from the victors, all of this boisterous male potency is just as useless as its ocean of sperm.

The females of the primates usually remain in heat for only a brief period of time; and these few days are the only period in which they are sexually available. While in heat, they mate with one male after another, or repeatedly with the same male, and at the end of their period of heat they are highly likely to be pregnant. They won't be ready for copulation again until after weaning their offspring. With such strict rhythms, copulation on the part of the female chimpanzee – the species to which we are closest – can be seen to be restricted to only one percent of her life span.[8] Calculations from other sources are less extreme, but nonetheless show great disproportion between periods of chastity and sexual activity.[9] Only the little-known bonobo apes seem to distance from this model.[10]

With the males things stand differently, all the males of all the great apes are always in search of sexual relationships. So, even as many as a hundred males, at least in theory, might be ready and waiting for every available female. It's therefore easy to speculate that the darkness of the perennial sexual mania in which they find themselves engulfed is the fundamental reason for which the males of the great apes remain outside the range of the flame of proto-civilization which their females lit. The enormous numerical difference between the number of eager males and available females might seem unfair to the males, if we didn't know that nature's laws are never "good" and never "pernicious," since they are always and only functional. Sexual activity is also a question of the activity of the laws of supply and demand, just as in economics. The laws of the market deride the best of intentions, and if they make short work of socialist and Christian ideals, surely they are able to remain indifferent to the humiliation of the male apes.

The correction of the great disparity could only be effected by their transformation into men. And it took place quite successfully.

NOTES

1 Wickler, W. (1969) *Sind wir Sünder? Naturgesetze der Ehe*. Munich and Zurich: Droemer Knaur, III, 2 and 4; Wickler and Seibt (1983), III, 3; Lévi-Strauss, C. (1956) "The family," in Shapiro H. L. (ed.), *Man, Culture and Society*. Oxford: Oxford University Press.
2 Bischof, N. (1985) *Das Rätsel Oedipus. Die biologishchen Wurzeln des Urkonfliktes von Intimität und Autonomie*. Munich: Piper, 17.
3 Fisher (1982), VIII; Goodhall (1986), 15.
4 De Waal, F. and Lanting, F. (1997) *Bonobo. The Forgotten Ape*. Berkeley, Los Angeles and London: University of California Press.
5 Dunbar (1988), Chapter 8.
6 Ibid.; Eibl-Eibesfeldt (1987), 15. 3. 2. 6.
7 Ibid., 18, 7, 1.
8 Fisher (1982), I.
9 Goodhall (1986), Chapter 16; Fossey, D. (1986) *Gorillas in the Mist*. Boston: Houghton Mifflin, Chapter 4; Fisher, H. E. (1992) *Anatomy of Love. The Natural History of Monogamy, Adultery and Divorce*, XXXXX Chapter 6.
10 De Waal and Lanting (1997), Chapter 4.

Chapter 3

The prehistoric horizon of the father

To the rear of the slender period of recorded human history – a few thousand years – and of the limited portion of pre-history of which some trace remains – another ten or twenty thousand years – lie the millions of years that contained the lives of the first human beings. We know nearly nothing about this period, but speculate almost everything.

This era is itself a tiny thing in the vast pageant of life on earth. But still it's the time in which evolution gradually detached us from animal existence and made us human beings. Our desperate attempts to pull prehistory into history, or our colossal effort to thrust ourselves beyond the temporal horizon where our knowledge begins, might well remind us of orphans or adopted children who while growing up are obsessed by the question of their origins.

This hunger for genealogy seems insatiable. What guides us back into time, directing us towards our origins, is more than the need for knowledge. It is also the need for narrative. Every civilization – especially patriarchies – asserts the right to have myths its own and to ground them in cosmogony in a final narrative that addresses the origins of everything, effectively creating the world and the paths it's destined to follow, no less than the final horizon of knowledge, including our knowledge of ourselves. This forge that the psyche alone controls is better than absurdity, and better than feeling ourselves to derive, in times in which God maintains his distance, from exclusively chemical phenomena. So, a great mystery is a subject of conversation and speculation even when knowledge is impossible, not for the purpose of shaping scientific hypotheses, but in order to fill the void with narrative, just as when we were children we wanted to be told a fairy tale, so as better to be able to enter the night.

If a scholarly discipline assumes the functions of the biblical story of Genesis, it necessarily inherits a part of that story's solemnity. Whether or not its conclusions can all be ranked as science is of no real importance. What's important, indeed, is to understand that the scientific truth it may or may not hold is of far less interest than the meaning it gives our lives. Just as Hesiod described the original night from which the gods first issued, we too continue to chronicle the night that lies to the rear of the race of human beings who

since have inherited their place. When we ponder the question of our origins –
whether temporal or metaphysical makes no difference – we learn something
about ourselves.

There's an indeterminate point at which an ape slipped into the river of
evolution and swam beneath its surface for millions and millions of years,
traversing the waters of paleontological unconsciousness, and then emerged
as a man. The course of that event, moreover, had shaped a great deal more
than a new physical constitution. This creature had also experienced the
greatest cultural transformation which the world has ever seen, if we can use
a modern word like "culture" while speaking of the proto-human being.
Culture, however, as we employ the term today, is a question of even the
simplest human tools or modes of behavior that lie outside the sphere of
the instincts to which we find access by birth. That first human being resur-
faced with the first stone tools in his hands, and in the course of his long
immersion had also fashioned the first of the stones with which to build
society. He had constructed not only the biological, but also the social basis
of psychic life.

Our speeds in the achievement of technological progress have greatly
increased in recent years. Yet it almost seems that the tempo of the progress
of civilization has never again been as quick as at the time of our origins.
Humanity entered the Old Stone Age – perhaps some two million years ago –
by virtue of the invention of the stone axe. We didn't learn the use of iron
until only about three thousand years ago – at the start of the last 15 ten-
thousandths of the era of human technology. It was only two centuries ago –
a single ten-thousandth – that we started to use machines as replacements for
muscle power, thus endlessly multiplying our strength. But in terms of the
progress of civilization, it was during the Old Stone Age, or perhaps even earlier, that the human being shattered the order of animal society by inventing
the monogamic family and the father. Today, as we enter the third millennium
AD, our civilization continues to depend on these very same social instruments, or perhaps on what remains of them.

Such a statement on the birth of the family is perhaps a declaration of
belief. If in fact we have very few bones of the bodies of those very first
men, we have nothing of their society and families, previous to the era of
writing, painting and sculpture. The prehistoric graffiti deal with isolated
men and women, or with groups – groups of hunters, for example – and not
with their relationships as couples. The beginnings of family life might be
reconstructed on the basis of studies of the first habitations, or of prehistoric
bodies that throw a light on the evolution of sexuality. But huts don't survive
like stone, and genital apparatuses don't endure like bones. We know how prehistoric men killed mammoths, but not how they embraced their women.
The extraordinary moments of their lives are more clearly understood than
the day-to-day events they experienced, the moments of violence more than
those of love.

Up until very recently, human beings have always behaved as though the family had existed from the beginnings of time, like the myth of creation and the gods. Even the earliest historical documents make no mention of any primordial phase of human society, at the moment when the family was born. Just as with religion and language, when the family comes into view it seems already to be very complex and ancient. And again like religion and language, it must be the fruit of an infinite number of alignments and adaptations which we now have no way of reconstructing.

Only a century ago, it was thought that Neanderthal man, of only some 35,000 to 80,000 years ago, was the missing link between humanity and the apes; today, the Australopithecus, two million years his elder, has been renamed Australanthropos, and is classed as already human. The horizon where our species first comes into view seems always to recede to a greater distance, bit by bit as we approach it.

Even that aspect of individual life to which we refer as the psyche can have made no sudden appearance, complete and fully formed. The transition from the animal mind to the human mind was surely quite gradual, and it counts as the greatest of the alterations that occurred in those millions of years. But, unlike the changes that transformed the body, it has left no traces, if not within the period of its final, almost imperceptible coda: these last few thousand years in which the word has taken written form, and art the substance of solid objects.

At the prehistoric horizon of the human family and the institution of fatherhood, we encounter, ideally, the Australopithecus (Australanthropos). Their beginnings went more or less hand in hand with walking erect, with the permanent acquisition of the use of tools, and with the mouth's transformation from an organ of aggression to an organ of communication. We can take the Australopithecus (Australanthropos) as the point at which a human form of life begins since its process of evolution is concerned with changes which are no longer exclusively corporeal. Though the changes in the jaw and the spinal column are conspicuous biological shifts, they can no longer be fully explained as adaptations to the external, physical environment. It's as though this pre-human being had reached the point of formulating intentions. The gaze is anxious to peer into greater distances; the hand desires to free itself in order to take hold of objects; the mouth aspires to communications which are more than a cry. Such needs were experienced by a subject; and even though the mode of that experience was less than conscious, as psychology employs that term today, it had ceased to be so fully unreflective as to allow us to call it instinctive. These various needs, moreover, present themselves as coordinated, each with all the others, as though rooted in a project; and the system that allowed their coordination was to turn into what we call the psyche.[1]

This obscure and distant epoch also hosted a second basic transformation in which biological and social shifts are a complex and indivisible whole. In addition to being the time in which humanity and the animal grew definitively distinct from one another, this was also the era that saw the formation of the separate identities of men and women.

The transition from animal to human societies was marked by the passage from the irregular mating of the apes to the first forms of the couple. The laws of natural selection were thus inverted by the first of the laws of civilization, and it makes no difference that observing such a law was far from conscious.

The way in which a species mates – no matter if mating is monogamous or polygamous, permanent or temporary – is always inherited and genetically determined.[2] It is only among humans that the form of the family has been freed from the tyranny of genetics. Humans can choose among countless forms of mating – monogamous or polygamous, permanent or enlivened by divorces – just as they have also relieved themselves of environmental limitations, and have thus become the only species which can make its home at no matter what latitude of the earth.

With the advent of the couple, procreation on the part of the male became as universal as it is for the female: the rule, from that point forward, is for all males to generate offspring. In this sense, the birth of human society represents a revolution in the lives and status of males: it marks the beginning of the male's achievement of a function as an individual. And if all of them were now to have offspring, those most encouraged by the laws of natural selection were those that most provided for their offspring: those who not only were men, but also fathers. We already know from zoology that the males most active with their offspring are those of the monogamic species.[3] Here, however, for the very first time, this attitude was determined by something more than instinct.

There came a day when the proto-human beings reached an agreement which was not, as Freud[4] imagined, to attack the patriarch who monopolized the females, but, quite to the contrary, to relinquish attacking each other, so as then to be able to apply a rule to dividing the females amongst them. Anthropology, in fact, informs us that the most elementary rules of the simplest and most ancient societies are concerned with the sharing and division of the women.[5]

This is the point at which male behavior comes to be governed by different norms. The rule is no longer that the male must compete in order to procreate; the male, instead, is to furnish life in the more complete sense of feeding as well as conceiving it. The male must now follow the rule which females have always obeyed. Yet the bodies and instincts of males will not have the time – the virtual eternity that women enjoyed – for a process of biological evolution that could bring them into harmony with their new task. Could nature ask females to nurse their babies without giving them breasts? The male's problem is not too different from that. He has acquired a meaning as an individual, by virtue of acquiring the ability to transmit some part of himself to future generations, but at the price of experiencing a conflict between his psychological disposition and his biological predisposition. And this is perhaps the reason, in spite of his arms and underneath his uniforms, for which he has always been plagued by a sense of insecurity of a kind which his female companion has never experienced.

NOTES

1 Leroi-Gourhan, A. (1964a) *Le geste et la parole. Technique et langage.* Paris: Albin Michel; Leroi-Gourhan, A. (1983) *Le fil du temp. Ethnologie et prehistoire.* Paris: Fayard.
2 Wickler (1969), III, 2.
3 Ibid., III, 4 and IV, 7; ibid., II, 5; Wright, P. C. (1993) "Variations in male female dominance and offspring care in non-human primates," in Miller, B. D. (ed.), *Sex and Gender Hierarchies.* Cambridge: Cambridge University Press; Katz, M. M. and Konner, M. J. (1981) "The role of the father. An anthropological perspective," in Lamb (ed.), *The Role of the Father in Child Development.*
4 Freud, S. (1912–13) *Totem und Tabu. Einige Übereinstimmungen im Seelenleben der Wilden und der Neurotiker,* in *Standard Edition,* Vol. XIII.
5 Lévi-Strauss, C. (1949) *Les structures élémentaires de la parenté.* Paris: PUF; Lévi-Strauss, C. (1983) *Le regard éloigné.* Paris: Plon, Chapter III; Zonabend, F. (1986) "La famiglia. Sguardo etnologico sulla parentela e la famiglia," in Burguière, A. et al. (eds), *Histoire de la famille.* Paris: Armand Colin.

Chapter 4

The paternal revolution

The grand event that prepared the arrival of the human being, and of which *homo sapiens* appears to have been the protagonist, was not "the killing of the father" but the birth of the father.

E. Morin, *Le paradigme perdu*

The pre-men lived in Africa, a few million years ago, in areas of abundant vegetation. To shape a clearer image, we could also call them the ape-men, since many of their characteristics were probably fairly similar to those of the modern man-apes.[1]

Their mating must still have been regulated by the females' periods of heat, just as we find today among the animals. Males and females formed no stable ties. They mainly fed on leaves and fruit, which they were able to collect without any need for lengthy forays, or for working together as an organized group. Their social life probably took the form of the small to medium size bands which are typical of most of the higher apes.

They walked on all four limbs. But they could also stand erect. They had begun to venture beyond the edges of the forest and out into the open savanna, where an upright posture was advantageous. It allowed them to see to a greater distance, and also improved their locomotion, little by little as natural selection led to the evolution of longer lower limbs.

Walking erect held the further advantage of freeing the hands for the gathering of food, and for the ever more frequent use of tools. When employing tools became habitual, and when the ape-men learned the advantage of collecting and preserving useful objects, their hands discovered a new function: carrying things. And their children were the most important things for our distant forebears to be able to carry.

The evolution of an ever more erect posture demanded progressive changes in the species' pelvic bones, which called in turn for ever shorter pregnancies. The offspring, on the other hand, needed ever longer periods of gestation, mainly because of the increasing size of their brains and heads: larger brains were needed for the coordination of ever more complex activities. The result was a kind of premature birth. The infant that waited for long enough to be completely developed before leaving the womb risked causing the death of both itself and its mother. So, infants born prematurely had greater probabilities of survival.

The length of the baby's period of growth, and of dependency on adults, therefore had to increase, so as to allow the conclusion of the phases of development which the period of gestation had left incomplete. (Whereas the cubs of the other mammals are immediately capable, or almost immediately, of standing up and walking, the human baby may need more than a year.) This period, indeed, continued to lengthen, more and more, since later phases of development likewise came to require more time. Humans, today, are the only species in which the process of development seems never to reach its end. Unlike every other animal, the human being continues to be marked by typically infantile characteristics (a large head, hairlessness, and so forth) even after reaching sexual maturity. This phenomenon is known as neoteny and was initially studied from a zoological point of view,[2] and later in terms of the characterization of behavior.[3] Here we are mainly interested in its psychological features: it already harbingers the insatiability and the curiosity, the neurosis and the triumph of the human being. Much more than might be said of any bodily characteristic, these are the qualities that set us apart from the animals.

But let's return to the pre-human infant, who for the very first time was in no way autonomous. Its mother's hands had to be free and efficient so as to be able to carry and care for it. She couldn't rely on the behavior of female apes, who, walking as a rule on all fours, carry their infants on their backs. Nor could she teach it to clutch her pelt, since our ancestors were losing their body hair. When the proto-human being stood up and walked on two legs, the freedom of its hands became less a possibility than a sheer necessity; mothers without that freedom couldn't have assured their children's survival. We shouldn't be surprised that our hands, unlike those of the apes, also have an important erotic function: the human hand was born for precisely the purpose of delicately touching another body. Rhetorical conventions have given us an image of the first human hands as male, intently shaping the first tools; but the hands of such males were a later development than those of the mothers who carried them.

We may also, here, be close to the origins of another human characteristic: the clear separation of the tasks of the sexes. If the mothers' hands were busy with the children, male hands would have to provide for food and defense. It was perhaps for precisely this reason, and perhaps at precisely this time, that the males could begin to call themselves fathers.

Life in the open spaces presented a greater number of dangers, but also of possibilities, thus stimulating the growth of intelligence to an ever greater degree. Having descended from the trees and advanced into the plains, they encountered large and dangerous animals: a new challenge that encouraged cooperative defense, as well as the ability to use objects as arms. These constantly developing talents – in social cooperation and technical know-how – also encouraged the hunting of other beasts, of which the flesh became the basis of a new, high-protein diet. Our ancestors ceased to be vegetarians. Those, in turn, who most mastered these new techniques were the ones most likely to assure the lives of their females and offspring, as well as their own, and thus to pass along their characteristics.

Remains of the skeletons of these pre-humans, from more than two million years ago, have to some extent been preserved. The size of their brain was more ape-like than human, yet still they made use of tools, and there are numerous indications of the achievement of a modicum of social structure. Having taken their destiny into their hands, they had also freed their mouths, which had lost the large, aggressive teeth of the apes.

The new developments in their bodies, their social lives, and the activities through which they procured their nourishment were accompanied by profound alterations in the relationship between males and females, which in turn enlarged the scope and increased the speed of the process of evolution from which it stemmed. As stated before, there's no way of knowing the dates at which such changes took place. Yet nothing should stop us from trying to shape an image of these creatures, who, after all, at just this time, were beginning to specialize in mental images. Let's think back to the very first set of petrified footprints to have reached us: the footprints of two proto-humans who clearly walked erect, accompanied by a third and smaller individual. The footprints continue together, clearly outlined, for a lengthy stretch. They were found in Laetoli, in what now is Tanzania, and date at least from three and a half million years ago. We have no way of knowing if they represent a chance encounter, or if they stem from a true and proper family – father, mother and child – that was on the move together.

The most highly evolved of today's apes seem to stand at the threshold of a division of male from female labor. Hunting, defending the territory, and wars with neighboring groups mainly fall to the males.[4] Since their society is probably similar to that of the pre-human ape-men, and since the division of male and female labor is now a common feature of all human societies, it's a fair assumption that the two sexes continued their specialization while further evolving: the males in hunting, the females in gathering vegetables from sources closer to home, as demanded by the presence of offspring that could not be left behind. (In the most primitive nomad groups that still survive today, this principle still holds.)

All of this led to a form of society with rules and regulations, and which also included the first modes of exchange. Foods too tended to become typically male or female, but the diet of all remained balanced, in spite of these specializations, thanks to the bartering of the different foods that males and females procured. The search for a balanced diet seems independent of social considerations, it belongs already to the instincts. For example, the apes observed by Goodhall were in the habit, while eating meat, of putting leaves into their mouths at the same time. But the division of labor between the sexes transformed this equilibrium on the part of individuals into an element of the equilibrium of the society they were starting to form, it became part of the relationships between individuals and encouraged their communication with one another. So, feeding habits too were a part of the web that wove the family, since the young received vegetable food from their mothers, and meat from their fathers.

Greater mobility, the ever increasing ability to work together as a group, and the availability of the first weapons allowed the males to fell ever larger prey, and to undertake hunting excursions to ever greater distances. Though they inevitably ate more meat than the females[5] – it is interesting to note that men today still eat more meat, and that women are more frequently prone to a vegetarian diet – they would have found it hard to consume it all, meat spoils quickly in the heat of Africa. So, the males – exploiting their recently acquired ability to carry things – began to bring a part of it back to the females and their offspring. It makes little difference that this habit was at first acquired by only a few of them: their proclivity in any case improved their children's diet, and amply increased their children's chances of survival. So the practice was promoted by the natural selection. The fathers who observed it had a greater number of descendants. Those who stuck to the behavior of the male apes, who share none of their food with their young, lowered the chances of their offspring's survival. So their number diminished.

No matter exactly how it came about, a new attitude had appeared. Unlike male pongids, who consume their prey on the spot, the pre-human male was learning to take it home. His contribution to the course of life ceased to be limited to his sperm. He no longer approached the females for nothing more than the very brief act of mating. He became a constant presence, even if intermittently so, as demanded by his hunting expeditions.

The males' inclination to ever more demanding forms of hunting was also to lead them to a new and higher level of psychic complexity. The animal hunts for as long as its prey excites its senses; and as soon as its prey is beyond the range of ears, eyes and nose, the animal grows disinterested. Proto-man, on the other hand, began to follow psychic rather than simply physical spoors: he began to preserve, throughout the long approach, a mental image of the beast he was tracking, even when his senses no longer perceived its presence. This extended span of memory was coupled, moreover, with the increasingly likely possibility that one or some few of a group of ever more numerous and organized hunters might remain in contact with the prey. So, the hunt could last for much longer periods of time, up until the moment of final success, thus rewarding those who were capable of constancy, memory and effective communication with their hunting companions. The group pressed out to ever greater distances.

At this point, however, tracking wasn't the only activity that demanded psychic effort: there was also the question of returning to their starting point; and at the end of such extended expeditions, it surely had ceased to be visible. The development of memory – the ability to lend attention to something no longer in view, remaining faithful to a stored mental image which is unrelated to the current message the eye is sending to the mind – was also of assistance for the second half of the task, the task of returning to the point of departure. Success or failure in learning to do so would determine whether man would take possession of the earth, as ordered by the biblical story of creation, or grow extinct, as happened with the dinosaurs. It was the greatest challenge of all times, and crowned by great success. Psychological reconstruction and the study of biological evolution both tell us that the males' return became habitual, and that it wasn't simply a matter of groups that made a return. Couples and nuclear families began to form.

In the situation of a growing distinction between male and female roles, those who failed to return abandoned their descendants, depriving them of meat and of male defense. The food consumed by all, no less than the safety of the young, who lay exposed to the dangers of the open savanna for ever longer periods of time, required that the males, as a counterbalance to their growing habit of roving to ever greater distances, form ever stronger ties with the places from which they had departed. These largely nomadic creatures had to invent the feeling of belonging to a place. And since a certain degree of nomadism is in any case required by both gathering and hunting, that place of safety and stability had to be something other than a geographic place. It had to be a psychic place. They thus discovered the family as the place to which to return, and they likewise invented the experience of nostalgia: that sense of pain and emptiness when one's children and companion are somewhere else; the desire once again to be with them. Perhaps – we have to say it softly, since we are using a weighty word – they invented love. Surely, of course, this need was less than pure, since it wasn't distinct – as even now it is never distinct – from questions of control and power. But it remains a need, and encompasses ties, which before had been unknown: a creation on the part of the beginnings of a life of the psyche.

Returning to the family was in some sense invented before the family itself; going back home before the invention of a home to go back to. A single gesture on the part of the proto-men – no matter how vast the ages in which it came about, and no matter how unconsciously – simultaneously laid the basis of both psychic and social life. The appearance of the father coincided with the invention of postponement and the ability to formulate projects. It was a construction that took place in time, no less than an act that constructed time.

We do not know how many generations are needed for a new behavior pattern – a variance that doesn't derive from physical evolution – to become a permanent characteristic of a species. Part of the success of analytical psychology derives from its notion of the archetypes, as universal psychic tendencies, but few have offered suggestions on their genesis.[6] With respect to paternal behavior we can only say that it one day appeared, then developed, and then became a constant. It is found in all known human societies, with a single, minuscule exception.[7]

The dawn of psychic space – that very same dawn which had brought the need to explore the savanna in pursuit of ever larger animals, and as well of the excitements of a lust for knowledge and conquest which amounted by now to something more than any simple hunger that had to be stilled – had invented the entirety of the structure of the voyage: departure and return; the thirst not only for discovery, but also for security.

If the new impulse had consisted entirely of curiosity, of the need to explore and to vanquish, it would never have led to the human being. Such a temperament would have forged ahead into one of evolution's blind alleys, the new breed of adventurers would have run aground on extremely high levels of mortality, and their offspring would have perished at even greater rates. There's also something more. They also would have collided with psychic catastrophe: without a vessel in which to contain it, or an adequate counterbalance, a one-sided interest in adventure would have created disorders in temperament and fostered mental instability. Nothing prevents us from imagining that the infinite twists and turns and variations of the process of evolution may also have produced individuals, or groups of individuals, who were wholly and exclusively prone to discovery; but at the very same time we must also imagine their elimination, less by the claws of their natural enemies, than by mental explosion, by confusion, by a paleo-madness that represented the outcome of their unconditioned frenzy for novelty. The bottleneck in the flow of evolution could be overcome only by a psyche that prolonged and effectively imitated the nature on which it was superimposing itself: by a psyche that could choose to contain itself, equipping itself with a mechanism of homeostasis; by a psyche that functioned not only as a river, but which also had a river's banks.

The process of natural selection had formerly worked to the advantage of the female who followed the path of instinct, as expressed through periods of highly visible heat, and attracted the highest possible number of males, thus increasing the probability of a pregnancy. It had likewise rewarded the male who accosted the available females with the greatest possible energy, beating out his rivals, and thus maximizing the probability of being responsible for it.

With the advance of gender specialization – the males becoming hunters, the females gatherers – everything changed. Natural selection now offered the best chances to the females whose menstrual cycles were marked by a less violent period of heat, and by a longer period of sexual availability. This wasn't however a question of any new and different way of increasing the probability of pregnancy (the period of fecundity within the cycle probably remained much the same); it was rather that sexuality was acquiring a whole new function. In addition to serving the vertical function of transmitting life to a new generation, it was beginning as well to serve the horizontal function of shaping the beginnings of the family, of the stable couple relationship. This relationship, entirely unknown among the apes, was a revolutionary novelty, and encouraged by an equally radical redefinition of sexuality. Sexuality became continuous; it became a form of communication; and growing communication in turn promoted still further increases in the frequency and depth of sexual relations. Sexuality became infinitely more complex than any instinctual release of energy.[8] It became a forge for the creation of psychic life.

The female with a constant desire for her companion was now the logical counterpart of the male who was capable of returning, and who counted as a constant presence. Evolution was at this point more involved with the selection not of the physiological, but of the psychological variants that proved most favorable to the life of the species: constancy and fidelity are qualities we'd see today as a part of the definition of character.

The individual sexual relationship also began to last longer. Rapid ejaculation on the part of the male began to be retarded: it's a well-known fact that human sexual relationships generally last for a great deal longer than those of animals. This evolution too was probably guided by the females, who have always given greater importance to their relationship with their mates: to the individual sexual encounter, and to the relationship as a whole. The wife fosters the husband, the mother fosters the father, just as the woman fosters the child. Without the mother there can be no child, and likewise there can be no father. Could the father be said to have been invented by the mother? On realizing the father's revolutionary importance, the mother surely invented an attitude of welcoming that no adult had ever before expressed towards any other: what men still today refer to as "femininity." She then directed the gaze of the child – which previously had rested only on her – to the face of the father as well.

Still other typical features of human sexuality appeared during this phase of transition: features which are always a part of human life, yet thoroughly missing among the apes to which we are most closely related.

First of all, sexual activity during pregnancy had formerly been unknown, but now became normal. The proto-humans thus set themselves apart from all other zoological species; their sexual activity had become virtually continuous, and much of it lay beyond any bounds that might have been assigned it by reproductive needs. Excess sexuality wasn't invented – as moralists might like it to have been – by the corrupt customs of recent times, but by evolution itself, millions of years ago. And its function has always remained the same: to direct sexuality not only toward procreation, but also toward a psychic task, as a forge for the creation of relationships. As though to assure us of her intentions, nature furnishes women with hormones that have birth control functions during the period of breast feeding; sexual relationships can therefore continue, without their being saddled with too many pregnancies. Greater sexuality can be a sign of a more intense interpersonal relationship; and if that's the case today, there is all the more reason for its having been so in these still pre-human times when communication had to take place through bodily gesture much more than by way of the word.

Secondly, orgasm, a characteristic of the males, also appeared in the female. Though the females of a few animal species display some form of sexual enjoyment, nothing compares to the phenomenal intensity and frequency with which nature empowers the human female to engage in sexual intercourse: she's endowed, indeed, with capabilities that only neurosis can eclipse. Orgasm, moreover, is independent of fecundity, and its appearance in the course of evolution must have less to do with increasing the likelihood of pregnancy than with augmenting the frequency and emotional intensity of sexual relationships, and thus the male's and female's sense of reciprocal psychic belonging to each other. We'll return later to the implications for the male of the female's discovery of orgasm. For now we'll only note that the frequently encountered notion of the animality of sexual enjoyment is perfectly nonsensical: exactly the opposite is true. The orgasm of the human male may be animalesque, since it has only slightly changed with respect to what we observe among our animal ancestors; the woman's orgasm, on the other hand, is an evolutionary leap which humans alone have accomplished: the experience of orgasm is precisely the feature that most radically sets her apart from animal sexuality.

Homosexuality too – which is already present among the animals, but overpowered by the process of natural selection since it creates no descendants – probably became a more stable presence in the moment in which relationships began to take precedence over procreation.[9]

We've seen the sexual act undergo a change, unprompted by alterations in the physical body. The function of sexuality ceased to be entirely reproductive. It assumed an importance all its own, as a term of relationship. In its passage from apes to humans, nature had also equipped the latter with much more conspicuous sexual attributes: the sexual organs of the male and the breasts of the female are a great deal larger than among the apes. Seen zoologically, this evolution in sexuality has to be understood as an end in itself, since it involved no benefits in terms of offspring. A larger penis is of no advantage in conceiving them, just as prominent breasts don't increase the ability to feed them. Other evolutionary changes seem even to diminish human fecundity. For example, the disappearance of heat reduces probabilities of pregnancy: in periods of fecundity, the female chimpanzee attracts all the partners she can reach, and all of her sexual relationships thus take place at the moment in which she is able to conceive; the behavior of the human female is entirely different.

In its development of apes into human beings, evolution emphasized changes of which the family and the ties that hold it together were the major beneficiary: it was no longer a question of changes that directly benefited the offspring.

In this new situation, the defense of the offspring was entrusted to the whole of the new society. Infant mortality decreased. Natural selection didn't work to the advantage of human beings by making their children strong: we know, indeed, that infants grew ever more defenseless and dependent as apes turned into men. Natural selection increased the strength of the new family, which in all probability was already monogamic and patricentric, and thus without precedent among the higher mammals.

Sexuality began to be a sphere of psychic no less than of physical communication, and it likewise began to grow private. The disappearance of heat, with its call to all reachable males, was the prehistoric seed from which modesty and reserve would grow. In ape society, female heat had been encouraged by the laws of natural selection, since the females most conspicuously in heat were the ones most likely to be fecundated; but in the far more complex society of the proto-humans, burdened with the difficult task of creating their own particular patterns of organization, there came a moment at which such females found themselves rejected, owing to the excessive level of disorder and rivalry they created among the males. This ancient interdiction left a mark which has never been erased. From prehistory to the birth of Christ, throughout the era of Christianity and into the third millennium, the adulterous, promiscuous or even unconsciously seductive woman arouses the suspicion and excites the reproach of society. Few creatures are as likely to be turned into scapegoats.

The forces of natural selection also led the males toward novel modes of behavior that converged with the prolongation of the females' sexual availability: males who perceived fidelity to a single companion as a way of augmenting their sexual activity gradually prevailed over those who remained promiscuous. As still seen today, monogamy – so long as it is chosen and not compulsory – is generally accompanied by a more relaxed sexuality, less anxious and less discontinuous: the individual comes to possess a sexuality, rather than to be possessed by sexuality. What many see today as a step towards stability in the life of the individual was already a fundamental turning point in the existence of males as a group. It's also clear that one of the most profound of civilization's discontents lies in the fact that this transition never grew complete or fully irreversible. It was a choice made by human beings, based on no revision that nature itself had made of its norms. So, the human male also continued to experience the kind of sexual impulse – frenetic, promiscuous and quantitative – which had previously marked his life as an animal; its visibility, moreover, remains undiminished in the styles of male sexuality which are currently encouraged by consumerism, with barely a veneer of "civilization."

It's clear, by now, that the principle biological transformations took place in the females. The great innovation for the female lay in more frequent sexuality. This shift, moreover, required no modification of the male, nature had already equipped him for continuous sexual activity. So, innovations in the lives of males took place in their behavior, rather than their constitution, and can be called proto-cultural. Once cultural evolution had begun, it worked in tandem with natural evolution, even while outstripping and depriving it of space, since the speeds of cultural evolution were much more rapid.[10] In any case, these two forms of evolution coexisted for a great deal of time in the crucible that was forging the family. This prehistoric era in which natural and cultural evolution were welded together was also the period that first joined together the couple.

Natural selection can usually be said to eliminate less favorable natural variants while encouraging others, equally natural, which are more auspicious. But at this point things had changed and indeed had begun to pursue a course that lies outside the sway of evolution, in the sense that the most favorable variant – the "paternal" male – simply doesn't exist in nature. The existence of the father requires the existence of intentions, and thus, no matter how primitive, of a psyche.

While speaking of the competition between male apes – especially among those that are closest to us – we speculated that it might be an obstacle to mental concentration, and thus an impediment on the route toward civilization. So, now it seems natural to imagine that the invention of monogamy – a way of sharing females, and thereby of liberating males from their constant obsession with mating – likewise marks the point at which males became able to tap the energies with which to develop the rules and tools that civilization requires. From this point of view, the male's return to the same companion was more than the simple observance of the very first rule of civilized social behavior; it also created the psychic conditions for the construction of civilization. And while always returning to the same female, the males began as well to construct that father–child relationship which nature had largely seen fit to overlook.

The males of non-monogamic species of animals abstain from attacking their species' young,[11] but do nothing to further their existence. The cub could be called a non-subject for its male parent. But with the dawn of psychic experience, the cub ceased to be simply a cipher which the male did best to ignore, and instead became a presence. In eras far precedent to any awareness of biological paternity, the father began to perceive his young as the potential being *par excellence*, simply by virtue of bearing witness to its process of growth and learning. The adult who observes the child's growth is no longer only its mother. The cub is the natural vessel that holds the image of tomorrow, of which the nascent psyche began to perceive the existence, in a place beyond the present. The child was thus the most suitable slate on which the psyche could practice its very first sums. Relationships with children helped the male to develop a more complex mind, which in turn became part of the process in which natural selection produced more males who showed paternal attitudes.

Their genetic characteristics thus passed on to following generations with greater frequency than those of the fathers with an old, unstable sexuality. With the development of weapons, such old-style fathers, as they fought among themselves for the females, ever more frequently put an end to their rivals, instead of putting them to flight. As Lorenz[12] has noted, only animals with conspicuous incisors, horns or dangerous claws have mechanisms of inhibition that keep them from killing each other in their ritual competitions with other members of their species; the others, like man, who are not equipped with such natural means of inflicting harm are also free of instinctive restraints on the full expression of their aggressiveness.

In expression of this route of natural selection, the polygamous males reciprocally drowned their genetic traits in pools of each other's blood, and those who survived ran the risk of expulsion from the first communities, which refused to tolerate their excessive violence.

The others, quite to the contrary, were the future masters of the universe, since they knew how to hold at bay the immediate gratification of instinct – the instinct of aggression with respect to their rivals, and the sexual instinct with respect to all females – in favor of a life that unfolded according to plans: a fuller life, but less impulsive. This is part of the basis of the typically paternal qualities. We will discover this attitude again and again, all throughout the history of fatherhood.

In order for the males to reach this stage, their mental activities had had to grow more complex, pressing forward into the future, and attaining the ability to operate at a certain level of abstraction. Even though not explicitly, they had had to shape the intention of nourishing a family and of ceasing to attack their peers. Just as sexuality had been deviated toward new functions, the same was true for aggressiveness. It had ceased to find expression in ceaseless male competition for females, and instead had been channeled into hunting, which was no less a source of a new wealth of nourishment than a laboratory for the perfection of the capacity for cooperation.

Long before its codification by any system of laws, monogamy constituted the arms that were winning the battle of survival.

NOTES

1 Morris (1984); Eibl-Eibesfeldt (1986); (1987); Fisher (1982); (1992); Wickler (1969); Leroi-Gourhan (1964a); Wickler and Seibt (1977); (1983); Masset, C. (1986) "Preistoria della famiglia," in Burguière et al. (eds), *Histoire de la Famille*; Badinter, E. (1986) *L'un est l'autre*. Paris: Odile Jacob.
2 Bolck, L. (1926) *Das Problem der Menschwerdung*. Jena: Gustar Fisher, as quoted in Eibl-Eibesfeldt (1986) and Lorenz (1965).
3 Montagu, A. (1989) *Growing Young*. Westport and London: Bergin & Garvey.
4 Goodhall (1986), Chapters 11 and 17.

5 Cohen, M. N. and Bennet, S. (1993) "Skeletal evidence for sex roles and gender hierarchies in prehistory," in Miller (ed.), *Sex and Gender Hierarchies.*
6 Stevens, A. and Price, J. (1996) *Evolutionary Psychiatry: A New Beginning.* London:
   Routledge; Hogenson, G. B. (1998) "Response to Pietikinen and Stevens," *Journal of
   Analytical Psychology*, 43: 357–72.
7 Hua, C. (1997) *Une société sans père ni mari. Les Na de Chine.* Paris: PUF. The Na
   people consist of a few thousand individuals who live in an isolated region of central
   China. The Na men limit themselves to visiting the women in the night, and never
   cohabit with them.
8 Wickler (1969), II; Fisher (1982); (1992).
9 The bonobo, a species of which the sexuality appears to be intermediate between
   human sexuality and that of the other pongids, is once again different from the
   latter in terms of the frequency of homosexual contacts, de Waal and Lanting
   (1997).
10 Lévi-Strauss (1983), Chapter I; Cavalli-Sforza, L. L. (2001) *Genes People and
   Languages,* Berkeley: University of California Press.
11 Lorenz, K. (1967/1965) *Ueber tierisches und menschliches Verhalten.* Berlin:
   Deutsche Buch Gemeinschaft, Bd. II; Tinbergen, N. (1989/1951) *The Study of
   Instinct.* Oxford: Oxford University Press, Chapter VIII; Eibl-Eibesfeldt, I.
   (1976/1970) *Liebe und Hass.* Munich: Piper, Chapter 2.
12 Lorenz, K. (1984/1963) *Das sogenannte Böse. Zur Naturgeschichte der Aggression.*
   Munich: Piper.

Chapter 5

Lucy grows

We never remain indifferent to the ways in which the sexes compare to one another. Sexual dimorphism has a bearing not only on zoology, but also on psychology.

Sexual dimorphism is the question of the differences between the males and females of the same species, and the most conspicuous difference is usually in size. On learning that in certain species of fish the females are enormously larger than the males, and slightly so even among such mammals as the hyena, we humans may even, perhaps, feel slightly ill at ease. The rule that holds for the great apes, where males are considerably larger, is in any case more reassuring.

Generally speaking, females are smaller than males among polygamous species, as in all situations where males compete for mating privileges. Male sea elephants are four times larger than their females; in the mating season, they engage each other in furious combat, and the winners enjoy the prize of a harem of from 12 to 40 partners.[1]

Dimorphism grows in proportion to the degree of polygamy for fairly self-evident reasons. Victory in the battles between the males goes to the stronger, and thus to the larger, and the victors are almost exclusively responsible for procreation: four percent of the male sea elephants account without complaint for 80 percent of the species' sexual relationships.[2] So, in each generation the genetic characteristics of the stronger males are the ones transmitted to the next. Nothing similar, however, takes place among the females.

The species of apes to which humans are most closely related are decidedly polygamous, and likewise highly dimorphic. The males weigh a great deal more than the females: about 30 percent more among the chimpanzees, from 50 to 100 percent among the orangutans, and even over 100 percent among the gorillas.

An attempt to discover an approximate date for the beginnings of human monogamy can therefore rely on comparisons of the bodies of males and females in the epochs that witnessed the passage from apes to human beings.

The most complete of the small number of Australopithecus (Australanthropos) skeletons which have been found until now is known as Lucy and is famous even among laymen. The era in which she lived – and reached the age of about 20 – dates back to approximately 3.2 million years ago. She walked on two legs, even though her skeletal structure was different from our own, and she stood about a meter tall, at a weight between 25 and 30 kilograms. South-east Africa, where Lucy was found, has also furnished any number of individual bones, both male and female, from much the same epoch. Doubt remains as to whether they all belonged to the same type of proto-human beings, but it has nonetheless been hypothesized that the males reached more or less the weight of a present-day man, and thus were close to twice as large as Lucy and the other females. If this is so, their dimorphism would have been equal to that of the gorillas, who are the tallest of the species which count as our closest relatives. So, up until that time male competition must have been one of the major factors in the process of natural selection; if monogamy had appeared at all, it had only appeared quite recently, or was practiced only sporadically.

In the millions of years that followed – the years which led from Lucy to us – it appears[3] that the bodies of the two sexes underwent several series of changes, in several different epochs (increase in the size of the female, increase in the size of both, decrease in the size of the male, and so forth), but with the overall effect of a reduction of dimorphism. One notes, moreover, that the dimensions of males and females seem most decidedly to have approached one another in the last few hundreds of thousands of years.

Men today weigh more than women by 15–20 percent, implying that we have now been monogamous for quite some time, since our evolution must surely have known a lengthy phase of reduced male competition. Smaller males too must have had children, and the difference between the sizes of males and females was gradually reduced.

Even if such data is highly indirect[4] and to be handled with considerable caution, it can tell us a number of interesting things and has manifold implications.

First of all, it seems confirmed that the appearance of the family, and the beginnings of psychic life which such an event encompasses, may have gone hand in hand with the evolution of the body.

Second, we here find fossil proof for the assumption that the male body has experienced fewer changes than the female body. For males to have experienced a lesser degree of natural selection in turn implies a lessening of male competition. But since the changes in ways of life were radical, this is once again equivalent to saying that the transformations underway in the male, already at this time, were mainly psychological. In a certain sense, the female was by nature more highly evolved, as seen, for example, in the fact that already among the apes her behavior isn't guided entirely by instinct. The male, on the other hand, had evolved to a lesser degree and continued to be subject to impulses of a more contradictory nature, with respect to the couple and to promiscuity. His compensation for his disadvantage took the form of a new type of evolution.

Finally, this period may also have spawned a third great novelty that distinguishes humans from animals: competition for partners no longer took place entirely among the males and began to occur among females as well.[5] The revolution that turned the males into fathers was a difficult process, and surely didn't reach immediate fruition in each and every one of them; still today it's far from having been completed. It can also be imagined that the males' expression of their aggressiveness left them with a rate of mortality far higher than that of the females. For both of these reasons, the females came to find themselves with an insufficient number of monogamic males: demand exceeded supply.

So, even if monogamy presented the males with the problem of a reconciliation of social behavior and instinct, it also opened the road to their most fundamental social and psychological transformation. The excess number of useless males was disappearing, along with their condition of solitude. Suddenly – if the word can be used while discussing a process that required enormous stretches of time – their lives became individually meaningful. Problems of solitude began, however, to plague the other half of the species. If everything went well, the female could now count on a companion's assistance in the feeding and protection of her young. But the female who remained without a partner was highly disadvantaged – already millions of years ago, just as today. Her children were exposed to far greater risks, and their chances of survival were considerably lower.

Dimorphism isn't a question only of physiology, and its relevance isn't confined to prehistoric times. It is also a psychological problem and a part of the lives we live today.

Up until very recently, the male ideal centered primarily on physical strength. It is true that the figure of Ulysses reached great popularity in the Western world at the dawn of classical Greece. But this is also an indication of just how special he was, charged with complexities that make us think of Homer as having shaped a vision that would last for thousands of years: as a prophet no less than a poet. Ulysses was the one great model of the non-ordinary mind. Up until the age of the Enlightenment, at the start of modern times, the most predominant male ideal was marked by a materialistic heroism.

Still today, at a time when the use of intelligence and culture as tools for prevailing among males grows ever more complex, the regressive temptation to look for moorings in the build of the body can be very strong, as is clear to the managers of gyms, no less than to authors of comic strips, who use such simplifications to construct their fortunes. This man has the right to possess that woman since he is stronger than other men, and incomparably stronger than she is.

Basically, this unresolved ambivalence finds its formulation not only in the struggle between Ulysses and Polyphemus, but also in the battle between King Kong and an ordinary man of the modern world. Today, it has less to do with disclosing a social dichotomy than with revealing a conflict within the male: not only between intelligence and strength, but also between the paternal and pre-civilized male personalities. Paleontology, indeed, has shown us that this ancient male personality is muscular and dimorphic precisely by virtue of remaining pre-paternal. In short, there's a measure of truth in the simplification that sees King Kong – the ape-man who continues to rove through the popular imagination and the collective unconscious – as the representative of a male personality with no other interest than sex. In the depths of the male psyche, this prehistoric conflict remains unresolved, and the interior inability to overcome it also has a parallel in the outside world. This ambivalence, indeed, is the source of "the paradox of the father" which demands, at one and the same time, that he function as a model of moral conduct while maintaining the ability to respond to adversity with pure and irresistible strength.

Male specialization in strength, power and aggression, and later in the kinds of intellectual activities that typified Ulysses, brings us back to the sharp distinction, found in every known human society, between male and female activities.[6] Only very recently, and only in wealthy countries, have such distinctions begun to attenuate.

One frequently supposes the origins of gender-based divisions of labor to be related to the biological differences between the sexes,[7] and thus to constitute extensions of a pre-human condition. Yet animals obey such distinctions to a fairly limited degree, whereas humans establish them as absolutes. Carnivores, while hunting in groups, may set up certain male and female roles (among lions, for example, the males normally start and frighten the prey, and the females kill it) but males and females are both equipped to slay their quarry; in human society, on the other hand, weapons are reserved for males. Such a clear and sharp distinction seems rooted in cultural criteria, or to summarize ways in which a culture intends to conceive of itself.

In the latter part of the Old Stone Age – just tens of thousands of years ago, at a time when *homo sapiens* already looked much the same as we do now – gender-based roles seem to have existed, but not to have been very marked.[8] But by the time of the appearance of the historical civilizations, the separation of roles had grown profound: indeed, spiritual activities and the priesthood were frequently reserved for men. It therefore seems quite probable that the most radical gender-based divisions of labor are fairly recent, and perhaps arose as an accompaniment to the passage from prehistoric to historic cultures. Their appearance at a time when the major corporeal differences between males and females had disappeared lessens the importance of any conjecture on their biological origins, whereas their psychic origins grow crucial. Nature had done away with the most conspicuous physical differences between the species' males and females, but the march towards culture found it necessary to invent, repropose and insist upon others, in spheres beyond physiology. What were the reasons for such a development?

We have to return to the psyche's propensity to set up counterweights, as a fundamental part of the way it functions. The psyche thus establishes a condition of natural equilibrium that permits the mind to explore the outside world and likewise to continue its own development, but always with the possibility of returning to a state of rest: of traveling during the day and returning home at night; of treasuring its discoveries but prohibiting its voyages from becoming ends in themselves, and thus from turning into a race towards the void.

We have suggested that the conquest of new spaces, like the pre-humans' growing audacity in hunting, became ever more thoroughly a male activity, and that its development can largely be imagined to have accompanied the beginnings of monogamy, and of the male's assumption of fatherhood. These parallel novelties – on the one hand, inside the family, on the other, in relating to the outside world – seem to imply an active process of transformation which was psychological as well as social. Their exploration of new spaces – on forays which took them to ever greater distances from their places of habitation, likewise imposing ever longer interruptions of habits to which they had grown accustomed – also led the male to the even more novel discovery of the female, or of the female as a creature whose existence extended beyond the act of copulation and the moment in which it took place.

Males also grew familiar, little by little, with their offspring, or with a "family" dimension that no longer reduced to the simple fact of their offspring's physical presence. But just as the exploration of new geographic spaces went hand in hand with the discovery of the fear of getting lost and going astray – an entirely new psychic and existential risk, even larger than the danger of becoming a lion's meal – the discovery of an unexplored private space, of a state of communion and symbiosis with the other, with the female companion, likewise introduced the male to the anguished feeling that his nascent ego might dissolve and lose all distinction from the mysterious *thou* which so recently had entered his life. The male, as a rule, unlike the female who has raised a child, has a highly limited knowledge of symbiosis: it's little more than a faint recall of the period in which he himself was nursed; of a condition, that's to say, in which he was totally cared for, and so weak as to be virtually insignificant. Symbiosis, for the male, is tantamount to the original condition of fusion with another being from whom he had to free himself, victoriously growing up and acquiring an identity of his own.[9]

Such hypotheses clearly lay us open to the risk of attributing the feelings of modern men to beings of whom we know quite little. But the current number of divorces and adolescent rebellions which find their explanation as attempts to reject a condition of symbiosis that threatens individuality makes it natural to assume that even greater vacillations in the sense of personal identity – which, moreover, had just begun to dawn – must surely have been a part of the earliest experiences of being a member of a couple, in terms of something more than simple physical intimacy. We have to imagine attitudes which were charged with painful ambivalence. On the one hand stood the discovery of a whole new dimension of communication: of communication with the partner in ways which grew ever deeper, both increasing the intensity of existence and leading to greater knowledge of self. On the other stood the terror of fusion, which in less than an instant could thoroughly annul precisely that sense of individuality which greater intimacy with the partner had helped to construct. If we place two differently colored drops of water – let's say red and blue – ever closer to one another, we are ever better able to compare them, and thus to perceive their specificity. But there's a threshold we must not cross. To do so would mean the instant, total destruction of all previously established clarity: the two drops merge into one, and an indistinct violet replaces a red and a blue which can no longer be separated from one another.

So the male who now returned to the female – for sex, surely, but not only for sex – and who gradually gave in to the interest her presence aroused, to the expectation of feeding her, and likewise of feeding their young, also had to find ways of counterbalancing his new condition. He had to discover a retreat in which to come to terms with all these novelties. His task was to construct the dimension of the family without fusing with it; he had to learn to perform the psychic work of dialog – that recently discovered place where events were even more unpredictable than while hunting in the open savanna – while maintaining his absolute separateness. He could entrust himself to these novel ties only by deploying an explorer's caution.

This, most probably, is the reason why a number of the very first forms in which culture found expression were male, unconsciously serving the purpose of fencing off the male identity, so as to hold it separate from the female. Still today, the fear of displaying characteristics which are typical of the other sex is far more sharply felt by men than women. Suspicion of effeminacy is to be thoroughly avoided. So, the first forms of culture were probably as well the first expressions of misogyny, and of the neuroses and superstitions that flank it: gender-related divisions of labor seem to be part of the very origins of culture. In our own civilization, this tangle of confusions still persists and misogyny appears to be a structural rather than simply accidental component of it. On looking at Don Juanism and nymphomania – the forms in which sexual attraction is experienced most acutely – we note that the former is far more likely to be charged with contempt for the other sex and with latent homosexuality.

There is still another reason why the birth of the couple created a basis for feelings of diffidence, even while marking the start of an alliance. The first social groupings arose for reasons of mutual convenience, and male competition had to be banned from them. These proto-humans confronted a new and difficult task: the control of their own aggressiveness.

Aggression, in fact, was gradually channeled into hunting, which even augmented the males' need for combat.

Killing became an exclusively male specialization, and there is reason to hypothesize that humans found access to the first forms of consciousness while performing this task with ever greater precision.[10] The males' perfection of their profound relationship with blood was also accompanied by a strange coincidence: evolution saw fit, at much the same time, to make human menstrual blood much more abundant and conspicuous than it is among animals.

A magical need to hold one's distance from that fluid which had to be loved no less than abhorred – spilling the blood of the prey brings life, the spilling of my own brings death – may have encouraged the earliest misogynous superstitions and gender-based divisions of labor. Menstrual blood may also have led the male to perceive the female as somehow similar to the prey of his hunts: wounded, a victim, defeated, charged with a diversity that inspired both terror and respect. Today we see such ambivalent feelings to be complementary parts of a taboo. Then, as female alterity became ever more consciously perceived, giving rise to rites and the classification of tasks as male and female, the males must have started to harbor that notion of alterity as equivalent to inferiority which was later to be canonized by Aristotle and to turn into part of the fabric of the whole of the history of the Western world. This subterfuge allowed them to explain the female characteristics they found most incomprehensible, and as well to surmount the feelings which the perception of alterity inspired, transforming them from feelings of anxiety into feelings of superiority.

We have already noted that the transformation of the quadrumane into a human being was accompanied by the female's acquisition of orgasm. This is a physical phenomenon, but all the same – and much more than in the case of the male – it reveals itself to be in many ways precarious, highly subject to culture conditioning,[11] and always dependent on the psychological situation. In short, this evolutionary innovation is both recent and fragile. Female orgasm doesn't, indeed, seem likely to find its source in the distant roots of our animal past – it is virtually absent among the primates[12] – and instead should be seen to develop from circumstances which were much closer at hand. The symbiosis which the female experienced within the radical innovation of stable couple relationships led her to assimilate this feature of sexuality, taking it over from the male. Such a way of growing closer to the partner could itself be one of the innovations which were generated by the psychic elaboration of their bond.

For a species' males and females to grow radically more similar isn't entirely unprecedented in the process of evolutionary adaptation; but this, surely, is the first occasion on which this sort of development appears to presuppose a psychological dimension, and as such it functions in a circular way with respect to the couple relationship, presenting itself as one of its possible consequences, but also as one of the possible causes of its growing more profound. For the female ape, there is no such thing as orgasm; for the human female, it becomes a possibility, but whether or not it occurs in any given situation depends upon her psychic condition.

The orgasm of the human male is one of the conditions for the fulfillment of his function, just as with animals: without orgasm, he doesn't deliver his sperm, and therefore doesn't reproduce. To become a father, one has to have had the experience of sexual enjoyment. That's not at all true of becoming a mother. Some have asserted that the appearance of the female orgasm was due to the gratification it gives the male.[13] But what does that really mean? The male's physical satisfaction lay already in his own orgasm and wasn't altered by the invention of the female orgasm. Any new or additional degree of male gratification was entirely psychological, and probably connected with the sublimation of aggressiveness. The male was being forced to sacrifice and redirect his aggressive impulses, and at the very same time the growing strength of his bond with the female left him increasingly exposed to interior ambivalence and the terror of losing control; so, the possibility that the female might abandon herself to their physical relationship and die within his arms, the possibility that she might be the person who lost control and orientation, had the valence and value of a sublimated satisfaction of his aggressiveness, in addition to representing an intense symbolic experience that restored him to a sense of dominion. Still today, a characteristic that distinguishes the sexuality of men from that of women, and probably from that of the male animal, is the presence of an element of sadism. It occurs with such frequency and under such widely varying circumstances as to make one think that it isn't an occasional deformation, but a part of the profound psychic structure of male sexuality.

Studies of the prehistory of male supremacy may perhaps have lent too much attention to the physical differences between the sexes[14] – differences which are far less marked among humans than among the apes – and not enough to the appearance of the female orgasm, which puts an end to the simplicity of animal sexuality. From that point forward, human sexuality acquired a psychological plane and ceased to be a question of simply physical release: it became an act of communication and confrontation between two psychic organisms. Whether or not to abandon oneself to the experience of sexuality is in fact the language through which that confrontation, which now persists in time, continually finds expression. The complexity of its psychic dimension, unlike its physical consummation, is never exhausted by any single act and belongs instead to a continuum of which memory too is a part. Rather than by sensations, it is now primarily guided by expectations and mental images. The occasional nature of the sexuality of the apes had now been definitively abandoned.

We return here to a pivotal aspect of the evolution of the two sexes: just as her body began more closely to resemble his in the process that attenuated corporeal dimorphism, the female's sexual behavior likewise tended to grow more similar to the male's. The male, in turn, probably re-established distance by shifting his supremacy to a non-material plane. He felt the fascination of this creature to whom he was ever closer, but who also grew ever more mysterious as he started to perceive her unplumbable specificity. As well, he was ever more terrified by the feeling that this creature might contaminate him, that he might fall victim to this female who gradually acquired humanity while nonetheless remaining a *continuation* of nature; as such she could suck him back into it, engulfing his first stirrings of consciousness; he, on the other hand, in order to make himself human, had to work in *opposition* to nature, taming his natural aggressiveness. All of this invited him to underscore the ways in which he differed from her, and at the very same time – since he couldn't reject their reciprocal attraction for one another, or their mutual dependence on one another – to tie himself to her, accepting their complementarity.

Male, the hunt; and female the gathering of vegetables, which as yet were not cultivated. (Agriculture, along with its technical, social and religious revolutions, was born only a few millennia ago.) Everything leads us to believe that these two basic activities – the pre-humans' principal occupations for millions of years – were separate though interdependent, and perhaps already ritualized, as indeed they remain today among the populations in which similar economies survive.[15]

What might have hindered the male hunters, who in certain seasons or following an abundant catch had time to spare, from taking part in the gathering activities of their females, whose time and mobility were in any case limited by the constant chore of caring for the young? Explanations based in exclusively material circumstances remain insufficient. The missing answer lies in the realm of symbol. The females' way of touching nature, that constant, familiar way of searching about within it – never opposing it, attacking it or gutting it, as the hunter does – was something the male found suspect. The male attempted to set up and follow a law of his own, overwhelming natural fact by way of his own display of power: demanding its blood and truncating life were his route to exultation and as well to the dawn of self-awareness; that other female creature gratuitously spilled out blood from her own body and gave birth to life with no apparent effort. Her way of bending down to the earth was charged with contamination; her continuity with the plants might be admired, but not imitated.

The relationship between the male and the female thus grew more intricate, consisting of both knowledge and separateness. The work of the psyche had to begin: contradiction was present and had to be contained. In every culture, since time immemorial, the male and the female are lovers, but also enemies. Literature reveals this paradox, as well as others: partners want endlessly to explore and discover each other; yet they also feel they have known one another forever. The drastic separation of the sexes and the myth of their original unity are rooted in the same unconscious fantasies. This is a masculine world of symbol. Plato was male, like all the thinking of Greek antiquity, and his *Symposium* contains the most widely known of these traditional fantasies: human beings were originally androgynous; Zeus, the prototype of paternal power and authority, violently split them apart into separate halves. Ever since that time, the two halves have desperately sought each other out, always pining in nostalgia for the one that's missing.

Rather than a simply physical development, the apes' transformation into humans was primarily a transformation of the relationship between the sexes. Curiosity, which set our ancestors apart from the animals, led first of all to the novel and complex experience of the couple. For an overview of the passage "from ape to man," comparing the skeletons of men and gorillas is of far less interest than a comparison of human and gorilla *couples*.

The need for novelty which has brought us so far is more than a need for new knowledge and new objects. An even more meaningful difference between humans and the animals lies in our exogamy, or in the universal rule that we are not to seek our partners within the family from which we come, and instead must find them in other groups.[16] Exogamy puts an end to the animals' practice of mating within the family.

This search for the new and different stimulates the process of eugenics – the redistribution and renewal of genetic characteristics – which led nature to pass from asexual reproduction to the mating of two different genders. But it also accomplishes a great deal more: it carries the need for variety from the strictly biological plane to the plane of mental activity. The typical neoteny of human beings – our continuous lust for growth, our attitude of infantile curiosity – was now to find expression in principles of social organization. This marked the start of the characteristic which most defines us, and the consequences were to grow incalculable. Exploration, discovery, the pursuit of the new: this commandment was the great innovation which the psyche decreed, and the field to which it applied was to extend beyond hunting and the other economic activities. It was also to include the transformation of sexuality into eros. Still today, the most passionate experiences of love take place between persons of different groups, cultures, or races: the Romeos and Juliets. Their construction of bridges that span cultural differences is an extension of the need to complete oneself by conjoining with something different: the need which in nature finds manifestation in the search for the opposite sex.

Compared to endogamy, exogamy offers an infinitely greater range of physical and psychic attractions. Even in primitive societies, marriage with a person from a different tribe is of great advantage, since it opens the door to a different world. In addition to effecting the renewal and recombination of genetic characteristics, it also produces new fantasies, expands intelligence, and doubles the number of available tools and procedures. In today's society, a couple's strength is often directly proportionate to its members' difference in origin. Various studies inform us that one isn't happily inclined to marry a person with whom one grew up at school, or on the grounds of the same kib-butz.[17] And when marriages between people with a common past take place, the probabilities of divorce are higher. All of this is part of the universal attraction we feel for things which are new and complementary, though only up to a certain threshold where difference begins to be perceived as monstrous, and where repulsion becomes the most dominant of a number of ambivalent feelings.[18]

The notion of exogamy as a revolutionary innovation that separates psychology from zoology is fairly unfamiliar. Anthropology and psychoanalysis have spoken primarily of its proscriptive side – proscriptive and limited to the sexual relationship – to which we refer as the incest taboo. Yet, the essence of exogamy is prescriptive, just as prescription is the most important component of all commandments. It elevates the imperative to breed with the other from a carnal norm to a psychic norm. Man can be defined as an animal which has given itself the law of an ever higher level of exogamy, not only in relationships between the sexes, but also with respect to the whole of the sphere of knowledge.

Exogamy is the most commonly shared and basic rule of mating,[19] and so much so that anthropological investigations see it as the universal denominator of human society. But the male and the female obey it in different ways, and this fact is of special interest to our current theme. At a certain turn of the path from the animal to the human being, exogamy appeared and established the rules that regulate relations between the sexes, but it also brought into relief a fundamental difference between them.

Even among animals sexual attraction seems to be influenced by a certain interest in difference and novelty. Curiosity promotes learning. In the sphere of sexuality it also furthers a more extensive sharing of the gene pool, and in this sense is especially important for animal populations of limited size and for species on the verge of extinction.[20] This tendency knows no boundaries other than those that delimit the species itself, after which point it declines, since if carried any further the sexual encounter can only be sterile: the mule – a perfectly viable animal, but with no possibility of offspring – is the exogamic experiment that nature has no further intention of pursuing.[21] Among the animals, the proscriptive side of exogamy – their "incest taboo" – is a lack of interest in sexual relations with individuals with which they've experienced an extended period of physical proximity. Given the length of time for which many mammals suckle their young, and especially among the apes, it is highly unlikely that a son will mate with his mother or even with the sister with which he was raised.[22] Exogamy with respect to the mother already exists among animals, without any need for prohibitions that hold instinct in check. So, in human society, this form of exogamy was simply codified, rather than invented.

The case of the father is quite different. With respect to the animals to which we are closest, we have already remarked that the male is a father only by virtue of the act of conception. He has no subsequent "knowledge" of his relationship with his offspring[23] and can entertain any ordinary kind of relationship with them, including the sexual relationship.

Unlike exogamy with respect to the mother, prohibition of mating with the father is an entirely human law.[24] It has no antecedents in the animal world, and by the time we first see it in human society it is already fully formed. We therefore know nothing of its origins and development. In the civilization of the Western world the commandment of exogamy with respect to the father is thoroughly as drastic as the one with respect to the mother, we simply take note that it is more frequently disobeyed. But this is also indirect proof of its being more recent and precarious. We can imagine this rule to have been anxiously "chosen," thus blocking the path of instinct, rather than gradually to have taken shape as a result of a process through which instinct itself evolved. Here again, the passage from the animal mother to the woman takes place in terms of a continuum; the elevation of the animal "father" to a human condition involves a leap, perhaps so arduous as still to remain incomplete.

The rupture and persistence of natural continuums may indeed be the question that most defines the differences between the evolution of the human male and the human female. Nature "makes no leaps" with the mother. It does, however, in producing the father, who seems to be tantamount to the threshold of culture. This leap, moreover, bears the indelible marks of an act that ran counter to nature: an act for which the father will continue to pay for quite some time. If exogamy with respect to the father isn't found in nature, the natural father is naturally incestuous. So, this highly disturbing observation becomes an invitation to destroy the bridges that connect with nature. Allegiance to civilization may well have been a choice which the male chose to make, turning away from the alternative of animality, incest, and the lack of all intention and foresight. But to what point can the rejection of instinct establish a civilized society without bankrupting the subject on which its life is based?

It is possible that the father and the whole of human civilization arise from precisely such an antinomy: I desire, but prohibit myself from following my desire. And antinomy itself – still unresolved ambivalence – may constitute the model that shapes the whole of the following course of the creation and operation of the human psyche, it begins to move and swell forward at the moment of the solidification of the banks that edge and contain it. It is both the ship and its anchor, constructed simultaneously.

NOTES

1 Wickler and Seibt (1983), Chapter 7.
2 Wickler and Seibt (1977), III, 3.

 3 Silk, J. B. (1993) "Primatological perspectives on gender hierarchies," in Miller (ed.), *Sex and Gender Hierarchies*; American Museum of Natural History (1993) *The First Humans*. San Francisco: Harper, I. 4 and II.
 4 Zihlman, A. L. (1993) "Sex differences and gender hierarchies among primates: an evolutionary perspective," in Miller (ed.) *Sex and Gender Hierarchies.*
 5 Mead (1949), Part III, Chapter II.
 6 Lévi-Strauss (1956); Müller-Karpe, H. (1974) *Geschichte der Steinzeit*. Munich: Oskar Beck, I; Badinter (1986), Part I, Chapter I; Masset (1986).
 7 Eibl-Eibesfeldt (1986), 4. 7.
 8 Müller-Karpe (1974), Chapter IV.
 9 Neumann, E. (1949) *Ursprungsgeschichte des Bewusstseins*. Zurich: Rascher, Part I.
10 Burkert, W. (1972) *Homo Necans*. Berlin: de Gruyter; Giegerich, W. (1994) *Tötungen*. Frankfurt a.M.: Peter Lang.
11 Mead (1949), Part III, Chapter III.
12 Morris (1984), Chapter 3; Fisher (1982), Chapter I; Eibl-Eibesfeldt (1986), 4. 4; Eibl-Eibesfeldt (1987), 18. 7. 2.
13 Fisher (1992), Chapter 1; Eibl-Eibesfeldt (1986), 4. 7.
15 Eibl-Eibesfeldt (1986), 4. 7.
16 Lévi-Strauss (1949); Fox, R. (1967) *Kinship and Marriage. An Anthropological Perspective*. Cambridge: Cambridge University Press, 2; Lo Russo, G. (1995) *Uomini e padri. L'oscura questione maschile*. Roma: Borla.
17 Eibl-Eibesfeldt (1986), 4. 4. 6.
18 Bischof (1985), 3.
19 Lévi-Strauss (1949).
20 Fossey (1986), Chapter I.
21 Wickler and Seibt (1977), Chapter VIII.
22 Goodhall (1986), 16; Eibl-Eibesfeldt (1987), 15. 3. 2. 5; Eibl-Eibesfeldt (1986), 4. 6; Fisher (1982), Chapter 8; Fisher (1992), Chapter 13.
23 Goodhall (1986), Chapter 16, p. 469.
24 Eibl-Eibesfeldt (1987), 15. 3. 2. 5; Eibl-Eibesfeldt (1986), 4. 6.

Myth and the classical age

Chapter 6

Patriarchy and matriarchy

The father, on becoming a father, likewise becomes his own son.

Heraclitus

This is the most beautiful law of all: obey the father.

Aeschylus

The man who has no father must invent one.

Nietzsche

The debate as to whether or not fathers have always been in command has been underway for about a century and a half, and many maintain that the patriarchal forms of society which dominate the history of the Western world were preceded, in prehistoric times, by a matriarchy.

No subject could be less neutral. The notion that the first human society must surely have been a matriarchy has often gone hand in hand with the fervent idealism of some of the authors who propose it. J. J. Bachofen (1861) intended to reach a new understanding of the historical foundations of law; H. L. Morgan (*The League of Iroquois*, 1851; *Systems of Consanguinity*, 1871; *Ancient Society*, 1877) was one of the earliest voices to speak in defense of the rights of indigenous peoples; Frederick Engels (1884) joined forces with Marx for the liberation of the proletariat; E. Neumann (1956) offered a reinterpretation of prehistoric times in the light of analytical psychology; the vast research of M. Gimbutas (1989) is dedicated to the re-evaluation of the feminine matrix of European culture.[1] All of these scholars were motivated by interests which extended beyond their fields of specialization, and all were firmly opposed to the typical aggressiveness of patriarchal culture.

In addition to summoning powerful ideals on the part of the writers who address it, this subject also awakens intense emotions in those who read their works. Discussion as to whether the roots of our society are more highly indebted to the Sumerians or the Accadians doesn't touch any special memories and is highly unlikely to arouse our strongest feelings. But each of us couples our abstract images of patriarchy and matriarchy with actual memories of a real man and a real woman. The memories with which we link them are indeed so deeply rooted and highly charged as usually to lie beyond our ability to call them up in any conscious or volitional way, which is also to say that their influence on our faculties of judgment is all the more pervasive. We are dealing here with a subject that fires the passions even of those who know nothing at all about it: our interest in our parents is emotional rather than intellectual.

The matriarchal hypothesis is not necessarily equivalent to a feminist point of view, and women stand on both fronts. M. Gimbutas and C. Meier-Seethaler[2] speak of an ancient society controlled by its mothers, but Simone de Beauvoir,[3] E. Badinter[4] and various Italian anthropologists like Ida Magli[6] and Giuditta Lo Russo[6] maintain that no such culture ever existed.

What is the source of the fervor with which so many observers insist that human society was originally matriarchal? Any number of objective indications clearly might favor such a conclusion, but beyond all factual considerations there may also be psychological reasons for the intensity with which this thesis is defended. We unconsciously place our own experience and point of view at the center of the world, and therefore think of history and society as a higher or exponential degree of individual experience, extended into space and time. And since even the most powerful man is at first entrusted to the arms of a mother, one is tempted to imagine something similar for civilization as a whole.

And, on the other hand, what fundamental memories guide the thoughts of those who believe that human civilization has always been patriarchal, from the time of its inception? Here the answer is more complex. This too, moreover, is an indication that the psychological considerations that center on the father and the mother – just as with the physical relationships – are far from symmetrical. Those who maintain that the original forms of human society were patriarchal rarely present their arguments with great emotional energy, or with any display of ideological allegiances. It might be said that those who opt for the matriarchy do so with a certain heat, whereas those who opt for the patriarchy do so coldly: with a cold reliance on historical documents, without emotional participation and with no apparent indication of having personally preferred their fathers to their mothers. But it must also be added that precisely this ability for reaching objective conclusions is considered a quality of the father, and part of his task is to teach it to his children, thus preparing them for adult life. Those who lean to the notion that patriarchy corresponds to the first form of human society may perhaps have identified with the father image even while revealing no special emotional attachment to it. The father appears indirectly, by way of the clarity of the mental functions that typify him.

If there's a psychological link between personal experience and a preference for a theory of the primacy of fathers with respect to mothers, or of mothers with respect to fathers, it can't be imagined to hold only for the modern mind, and would surely have been charged with even greater power among the people of primeval times, since their exposure to unconscious and magical influences was considerably greater than our own. The primordial phases of civilization also included the initial phases of human self-representation, or of the ways in which we conceive of ourselves. So isn't it possible for the modes of behavior of prehistoric times (at the beginnings of the human condition) to have been particularly under the sway of primary images (the images concerned with the beginnings of every individual)? The start of every human life, no matter if male or female, takes place in the shadow of an imposing woman who is vastly larger than ourselves: a veritable queen – the mother – whose reign includes total control of the body of her child. So was it only natural, when the first social nuclei began to form, for the mothers, by analogy, to assume the role of the queens of the whole of society?

We have many hypotheses and very few facts about the original nature of human society, and as to whether it took the form of a patriarchy or a matriarchy. We can only say that the most complex and highly developed societies are generally those that center on a myth of paternal authority, and which in the attempt to maintain stability while coming to terms with ever-growing problems of coordination effectively revolve around the father. Yet nothing, unfortunately, allows us simply to reverse this line of reasoning and to say that power in the simplest societies, unlike those of the modern Western world, lay in the hands of the mothers. The most we can show is that fathers in the limited number of still surviving subsistence societies are particularly active in the rearing and custody of children.[7]

Many of the authors who have studied the oldest historical societies[8] and assessed the simplest of the still surviving primitive cultures[9] find no convincing traces of any primeval matriarchy. The study of the Western languages seems to lead to similar conclusions, by way of reconstructions that address historical societies for which there's a dearth of material evidence, no less than prehistoric cultures. The words that indicate kinship, such as "father" and "mother," are the ones which remain most constant as a language changes in the course of time, as well as the ones which are most recognizably related in languages that stem from a common source. In the comparative study of the Indo-European languages, kinship terms not only disclose their common origin but also refer to a common model of the family; and that model presents the family as both patrilocal and patriarchal.[10] If a matriarchy ever existed, it would have to date back to the very remotest of times, and to pre-Indo-European cultures.

And if animal society is our point of departure, then pursuing its gradual development into human forms of culture, we discover, even among the apes to which we are closest, that power is held by the males, even if the females frequently succeed in challenging their authority. So why should the now missing bridge which once connected these two extremes – the bridge between the humans from whom we are now most distant, and the animals to which we remain the closest – have been characterized by a society of mothers?

Hypotheses concerned with a primeval matriarchy turn their attention to epochs which long predate writing. So, they can offer no more than indirect reconstructions of societies of which our actual knowledge is extremely slight. In some of the later periods of the Old Stone Age in Western Europe (the Aurignacian, and above all the Gravettian and Solutrean periods)[11] and then more distinctly in the New Stone Age in the Middle East and the Mediterranean countries,[12] the representations of human figures on walls or as statuettes are mainly of women. Their thighs and breasts and the other parts of the female body which are associated with fertility are often enormous, whereas their heads, hands and feet are minuscule, if not entirely absent. This has led to the theory that the female's power of procreation may have elevated women to positions of enormous importance in these particular eras, and that the figures representing them must be images of goddesses.

The theory presumes the invention of agriculture to have raised the status of women, with whom plants and fecundity had already been associated in the previous era of hunting and gathering societies. The golden age of the mothers (or, perhaps, more realistically, of a "gilanic" society in which men and women were essentially equal) would thus have taken place in the era that witnessed the growth and diffusion of a new economy which was rooted not only in agriculture, but also in any number of novel and radical developments. The great matriarchy would find its site in the era of the passage from the Paleolithic to the Neolithic age: in the era to which Gordon Childe and Hermann Müller-Karpe refer as having fostered the greatest and most thorough revolutions which human history has ever known.

Others tell us that the construction of patriarchal societies could date from the much more recent period, at the dawn of the historical societies, in which the father's role in the act of conception was first discovered.[13] A role, in fact, which still remained unknown to many primitive peoples in the early years of the twentieth century.[14]

But what allows us to conclude that all these prehistoric female figures are representations of deities? Some maintain that anthropomorphic deities probably didn't appear until later.[15] In this case, these figures would be effigies of simple women, remembered and represented in the places in which they lived and died. The large number of female figures and the paucity of representations of men might be due to the different kinds of places in which the two sexes primarily lived. The females resided on a fairly stable basis in the caves, and later in the agricultural settlements, whereas the males were often at a distance and on the move, pursuing the fortunes of the hunt. So, the places in which they performed their tasks and met their deaths were highly variable, and their bodies would only occasionally have received a ritual burial. Perhaps this period of remote antiquity was acquainted already with the phenomenon of "the invisible father," much as we still observe it today. It would partly have been due to the complexity of the tasks which the fathers had to perform. (One modern study that revealed a lack of relationship between fathers and children had to be revised in the light of subsequent investigations that showed family interaction to take place in the evening when the fathers had returned to their homes, when the social workers had likewise returned to their own.[16])

Even though the scholars who propose the existence of a primordial matriarchy have produced a number of interesting arguments – in recent years,[17] no less than in the past – most of the currently available information supports the opposing hypothesis: that patriarchy has been the predominant form of social life since the very beginnings of civilization. The fact that certain epochs left behind a clear majority of female images is far from enough to prove the contrary. Modern minds are little versed in psychological thinking and make up for it by taking things literally, viewing these prehistoric figures statistically: a great quantity of female images makes us imagine that women must have held great power. But the images most frequently found in a given society don't necessarily describe the way it actually functions, or the balance of power on which it is based. Images wholly unaccompanied by information on the context to which they belong suffer, in Eliade's terms, from "semantic opacity."

Prehistoric art is also rife with powerful representations of certain animals; no one, surely, would want to conclude that these animals held command in the societies that depicted them. If an image count were sufficient basis on which to determine the social roles of the figures they represent, and if our current civilization might be imagined to share the fate of Neolithic cultures and to leave behind no written documents, future archaeologists who unearthed our world of images, a few thousand years down the road, might imagine themselves to have rediscovered a matriarchal civilization. Female figures of which the sexual attributes are quite emphatically represented are today preponderant not only in advertising and in glossy periodicals, but also in official images of which the emblematic value could hardly escape the eyes of our future archaeologists: statues of liberty and spirits of the nation; minted coins with Britannia, Marianna, or Helvetia in low relief, like modern renditions of the goddess Athena. Athena herself, moreover, was the figure represented by the greatest number of statues of the greatest temple of the greatest city of ancient Greece, which also bore her name: Athens. But that culture, country, city, and even that goddess were unsurpassed in their commitment to patriarchy.

In a culture that's rooted in myth, rather than history, it is likely for sculptures and paintings to represent the fantasies to which its myths give formulation, and largely to ignore the actual historical persons who govern its social activities. And even if annoying to traditional historians, such limits in the scope of a culture's figurative art are of no real bother if our interests lie in the study of psychological history. Such limits in fact restrict the field to precisely the kinds of things we want to know. We don't make use of archaeological artifacts for the purpose of reaching conclusions on who held the reins and guided the course of history; instead we make use of history itself – not only of rediscovered artifacts, but also of yesterday's myths and today's interpretations – for the purpose of reaching an understanding of the forces that guide the imagination. And if this is our goal, everything allows us to "see through facts into fantasies. History provides an entrance into the imaginal."[18]

If the societies at the origins of Western history were in fact patriarchal, the models of masculinity which must have lived in the minds of those patriarchs would seem to have been accompanied by a far greater number – if not, indeed, an amazing number – of extremely powerful images of women. So, even while voicing suspicions on the notion of the existence of a matriarchy as a sociological reality, we must surely regard this plethora of images as an indication of a potent psychological reality, and as such we have to take it into proper account, in no way underestimating it. It is likely that the early patriarchy – with fathers in control of the family, no less than of the whole society – was able to maintain itself as such only by acknowledging how hard it had been to bring the mothers beneath their control, and by making them as well the object of superstitious attention. Fetishistic regard for the functions of the female body was tantamount to an exorcism of the female powers – the natural, not political powers – from which the patriarchy had only recently freed itself, and on terms which it knew to be fragile and non-definitive. This female world continued to present itself as the principal object of its fears and longings.

We are entirely ignorant of the nature of the chapter of the *history of society* that finds its narration in those remarkably fecund female bodies. But the story they recount is surely central to the *history of the psyche*. They speak of fantasies of pregnancy. They speak of states of mental fixation that revolve around themes of production, procreation and nutrition. One can wonder if these powerful fantasies might not have had something to do – at the time of the long, laborious and strenuous transition from hunting and gathering to agriculture – with the "gestation" of the very idea of tilling the soil, and thus with the impulse to entrust one's fate to the generative powers of immediately surrounding nature. Do we here perhaps descry an attempt to activate nature through a "sympathetic" process of induction that hinges on the constant celebration – constant and superstitious – of female fecundity? When we attempt to reconstruct the premises that led to a new discovery, we must find our point of departure in something other than the technical innovations which it finally produced – which in this case were the practical techniques of agriculture – if only because such innovations were as such beyond the range of all possible thought. Their premises, instead, are to be ferreted out in the light of the epoch's *beliefs*. It makes no difference if the epoch's convictions were false. Columbus wanted to reach the Indies, and his faith in this possibility – faith is precisely the opposite of the rational frame of mind that concentrates on facts – was the vehicle of an unconscious project that opened a road which still knows no end.

Without losing itself in the details of specific archaeological and anthropological questions, psychology should rethink the mystery of the possible existence of a primordial matriarchy from its own point of view, treating that hypothesis as a mental fantasy, and also as a fantasy which is still today alive in minds that while studying the epoch in question adapt it to their own particular emotions, which in some are pro-maternal, and in others pro-paternal. The sculpting of these prehistoric female statuettes in any case required the presence and exploration of a pregnancy fantasy, even if the mind that contained it was the mind of a male. The epoch's thinking was dominated by images of procreation; and this is surely and explicitly a symptom of the way in which the human being, the human condition and the workings of human psychology all desired to reproduce themselves, to find rebirth, to seminate, to procreate. And then to cultivate, and make things grow.

The observation of the bodies of women allowed the highly impressionable minds of those times to grow pregnant by analogy. They began the gestation of the idea of gestation. The fantasy that modeled the corpulent bodies of those prehistoric statuettes was observing and speaking of itself; it was subject and object at the same time. Even if the epoch resists descriptions that call it matriarchal, its psychology was surely matricentric.

The first inevitable step – as a result of the sympathetic relationship between the human being and the surrounding environment, of its observation, and of the projection onto the outside world of the mind's interior landscape of fruits and fructification – was the invention of agriculture. The mind had begun to shape the thought that generation (the "feminine" activity of agriculture) could be an alternative to killing (the "masculine" activity of hunting). The florid and fecund "goddess" figures were no simple emblem of the acquisition of agriculture: it's rather that the birth of agriculture was encouraged, induced and forced to take place by virtue of its analogy to those sacred pregnancies; the birth of the art of agriculture was the symptom and outcome of a growing fecundity of the imagination, which itself was destined to generate, nurture and multiply itself. We have no way of knowing if these fetish statuettes were representations of female deities; but surely we know that they were magical, and capable of the act of creation.

The second step took place with the full flowering of the Neolithic age, which was truly the moment of greatest renewal the world has ever seen, since it started the process of civilization and its aspiration to unlimited growth.[19] Thought crossed the threshold of puberty, and, far from remaining content with the acquisition of agriculture, voted the whole of its future life to the purposes of growth, expansion and ceaseless generation. After entering the Neolithic age, the human being was never again to accept a static existence.

The mind had come to be dominated by a mythic theme of fecundity. Fertility, moreover, lay not only within the images, but also in the act of producing them. The forces of generation had ceased to be perceived as lying entirely and exclusively in nature: their principal place of operation had become the mind. Humanity's achievement of spirituality and a sense of the transcendental – and thus, as well, of the mind's ability for higher, abstract activity – has been said to date from the moment when the human being ceased simply to abandon the dead and began instead to develop rites for their veneration. But the inception of spiritual life must also be descried in the moment in which the human being surrounded *birth* with attitudes and acts of devotion: in the moment in which the human being raised the question not only of what we become after death, but also of what we are before we enter the world, and of the nature of the forces that conduct us into it.

The cult of the dead dates back, in fact, to fairly early times, and is already found among the Neanderthals, who lived in what was still the late Paleolithic age. And in spite of the invention of the cult of the dead, the conditions of human life continued to remain unchanged for many tens of thousands of years. Things stand quite differently with the cult of fertility, and thus of birth and procreation, of origins, generation and growth. The inception of the cult of fertility was coeval with the birth of a general craving for generation that stamped its seal on every area of human activity. This is the era that marked the beginning of everything which counts as human and no longer as simply animal. The Neolithic mind was possessed by the notion of fertility, and thus revealed the fertility which the mind itself had come to possess. The fields had been made to be fecund, and human life was fecund. Since written language was still a thing of the future, this mystery was given the form of the culture's most significant ideogram: the abundant female body. And the hands that shaped it may well have been male.

We do not know when the patriarchal form of society firmly established itself; and we cannot say if agriculture was the discovery of a lineage of mothers. We are not attempting to reconstruct a history of human society, nor indeed of techniques and economic structures; we are interested in a history of human psychology. From this point of view, we imagine that males began to grow aware of their power – and perhaps to assert it – in the moment when they took the step of transforming themselves into fathers, and were more or less conscious of doing so in the moment when they began to intuit their own role in the creation of life. This isn't to refer to any awareness of the role of their sperm in procreation – which is a matter of technical knowledge that wasn't acquired until much later; it's the question, instead, of the male's awareness of his role in sustaining the family and constructing a continuity that extends from one generation to the next. The establishment of such a continuity marks the human being's definitive exit from a mode of existence which is simply entrusted to whatever the day may happen to bring: this was the event that marked our entrance into the world of projects and planning.

Yet the role that fathers began to assume wasn't entirely new. It made them a continuation of the mothers, partly as their collaborators and partly as their rivals. The lives of mothers had always been dedicated to those of their children as well. The primordial male, on the other hand, had always lived for himself alone. It was only by turning himself into a father that the male discovered that life is something that needs to be shared. And his transformation brought the further discovery that the mother was the term of comparison through which he had to view himself. This is still another source of those images of fecund mothers.

Confrontation with diversity – which here is the opposite sex – through reproductions of the image of the other, and through obsessive identification with the other, is a typical object of study for the field of modern psychology; but the phenomenon is nothing new and has always been a part of human life. It is clearly present in tribal societies, where psychic experience is socially visible: a tribe that survives by hunting and killing buffaloes in the spaces of the open prairies surely doesn't kill them off in its psychic life. Quite to the contrary: rather than in any way suppress them, the collective imagination populates its paintings, artifacts, stories, songs and dances with them. Just as the hunter appropriates the strength and vitality of his prey, the fathers attempted to appropriate the mothers' ability to produce life.

If there is any truth in these assertions, the histories of men and women are radically asymmetrical.

One possibility is that society was patriarchal throughout all prehistoric times, inclusive of those which have bequeathed exclusively female images. In this case, the men of those times would have to be seen, even while subjugating women socially, to have continued within the psyche to feel their influence. The only remaining thing to explain would be why the fixation with female images became nearly absolute in certain epochs, rather than simply predominant.

The other possibility is that the eras dominated by female images were truly matriarchal. This would also demonstrate that the matriarchs were much more self-sufficient than men are seen to be by the patriarchal hypothesis, since surely they were not obsessed by any need to exorcise the psychic power of the male. Their images, and perhaps their cults, would celebrate only themselves.

Are we therefore to imagine the male but not the female mind to feel a need for alterity? According to the first hypothesis, men would have dominated women from an institutional point of view, while in turn being psychologically dominated. The second hypothesis leaves men crushed and defeated at both levels. And in both cases, males are seen to have felt the power of the other sex, whereas no such thing would seem to have occurred in the female mind. This archaic lack of male self-sufficiency is something to hold in mind: it counts, to be sure, as an interior defect, but from our point of view it makes the male more fragile than might result from any weakness in his hold on institutional power. When we speak of modern times, we will be dealing with a fragility that isn't much different. We do not know which sex was socially dominant in prehistoric times. But we do know that the psyche was dominated by female forces. As psychological quantities, male forces were relative, whereas female forces were absolutes. The presence of men in human life was perceived to be contingent, the presence of women as necessary.

After immeasurable amounts of time, a trace of the uselessness of the male ape continued to survive. Moreover, almost until the present, the peoples who pay least attention to fatherhood are those who have remained most "primitive."[20] In order to erect the edifice of patriarchal history, it was first of all necessary to create the institution of fatherhood.

We once again see the falsity of the symmetry of father and mother, and how ingenuous it is to promote it. The world of the fathers has no other choice than to include the world of the mothers, independently of whatever the position – as equals, subordinates or superiors – in which it chooses to place them. The world of the mothers, on the other hand – returning in a sense towards our animal origins – has the power, at least abstractly, to repudiate fathers, and to replace them by taking recourse to occasional contact with males. This is the message of the myth of the Amazons, who were said to have preceded historical Greek society: the ancient tribe of warrior women didn't prosper by subjugating men, but by doing without them.

The analysis of the origins of European history always leads to reconstructions which are far less social than imaginal. We know that a society existed, and we know that a family existed, but we cannot define their specific features. We do, however, have a clear idea of the stock of imagery that guided their psychic and symbolic life. In Neolithic times, the dominant figure was the mother figure. The father figure hadn't yet managed to emerge. Our history must always remain aware of these obscure and difficult beginnings.

Let's return to discussing men and women, attempting to put aside the question as to whether the first society was patriarchal or matriarchal. That's a subject we want to address as little as possible. The mothers are not the only victims of Western patriarchal society. In the course of time – even if in different and indirect ways, by de-emphasizing the affects and the psyche and insisting on institutional relationships, by emptying symbols of their meanings and thinking entirely in material terms, by decking its uniforms with medals and stripes – it also invalidates the father.

The patriarchy's triumph may even render the true and proper father invisible. He finds himself with the task of silently constructing the possibility of becoming the kind of personal presence that social conventions and collective codes refuse to allow him to be. A mother can become a matriarch in more harmonious ways, without losing herself in institutions, by as well remaining a mother, without altering her personal relationship with her children. For the father things are more difficult. His identification with the social institutions around him is more thorough; and his construction of a relationship with his children is more precarious, and more dependent on conscious intentions. That doesn't necessarily compromise the depth of this relationship, but it limits his freedom to express it. It imposes that silence which becomes the stone that he has to continue to roll along the course which the patriarchy has historically followed, and it marks that path with still another furrow of melancholy.

NOTES

1 Bachofen, J. J. (1861) *Das Mutterrecht*; Morgan, H. L. (1851) *The League of Iroquis*; (1871) *Ancient Society*; Engels, F. (1884) *Der Ursprung der Familie, des Privateigentums und des Staats*; Neumann, E. (1974) *Die Grosse Mutter*. Olten: Walter; Gimbutas, M. (1989) *The Language of the Goddess*. New York: Harper & Row.
2 Meier-Seethaler, C. (1988) *Ursprünge und Befreiungen. Eine dissidente Kulturtheorie*. Zurich: Arche.
3 De Beauvoir, S. (1976) *Le deuxième sexe*. Paris: Gallimard, Vol. I, Part II, Chapter II.
4 Badinter (1986).
5 Magli, I. (1978) *Matriarcato e potere delle donne*. Milano: Feltrinelli.
6 Lo Russo (1995).
7 Bloom-Feshbach, J. (1981) "Historical perspectives in the father's role," in Lamb (ed.), *The Role of the Father in Child Development*.
8 Burguière et al. (1986), *Storia Universale della Famiglia*. Paris: Colin.
9 Ibid., and especially Evans-Pritchard, E. E. (1965) *The Position of Women in Primitive Societies and Other Essays in Social Anthropology*. London: Faber & Faber.
10 Benveniste, E. (1966) *Problèmes de linguistique générale*, Vol. I. Paris: Gallimard. Benveniste, E. (1969) *Le vocabulaire des institutions indo-européennes*, Vols I and II. Paris: Les Editions de Minuit.
11 Leroi-Gourhan, A. (1964b) *Les religions de la préhistoire. Paleolithique*. Paris: PUF; Eliade, M. (1975) *Histoire des croyances et des idées religieuses*, 4 vols. Paris: Payot, Vol. I, Chapter I, 6; Müller-Karpe (1974), IV, V, VI.
12 Eliade (1975), Vol. I, Chapter II; Badinter (1986), I, 2; Gimbutas (1989).
13 Dupuis, J. (1987) *Au nom du père. Une histoire de la paternité*. Paris: Le Rocher.
14 Malinowski, B. (1927) *The Father in Primitive Psychology*. New York: Norton & Co.
15 Müller-Karpe (1974), VI.
16 Kewlett, B. S. (1991) *Intimate Fathers: The Nature and Context of Aka Pigmy Paternal Infant Care*. Ann Arbor: University of Michigan Press.
17 Gimbutas (1989).

18 Hillman, J. (1972b) *The Myth of Analysis. Three Essays in Archetypal Psychology*. Evanston IL: Northwestern University Press, III, 2, p. 221.
19 Zoja, L. (1995) *Growth and Guilt*. London: Routledge.
20 Hartland, E. S. (1894) *The Legend of Perseus*, 3 vols.; Hartland, E. S. (1909) *Primitive Paternity*, 2 vols.; Malinowski, B. (1929) *The Sexual Life of Savages in North-Western Melanesia*. London: Routledge & Kegan Paul; Lo Russo (1995).

Chapter 7

The historic horizon of the father

The horizon is the limit to which our gaze can uninterruptedly reach, enclosing us beneath a shared celestial vault. India, China and various societies of the past, like those of Egypt and of many other great civilizations, lie beyond the European horizon, and for reasons which are more than geographic: they are not continuous with Western culture. More than any other, and thanks to its tendency for globalization, it is Western civilization which has exported its patriarchy throughout the world.

Greece emerges, as the origin of Western patriarchy, from the prehistoric, a-historic and perhaps mythic world of the Great Mothers. To understand the modern father, we have to look back at ancient Greece for at least two reasons. Ancient Greece is first of all the place in which he finds his roots; and it was also a place in which the father figure experienced a crisis that resembles what we now discover in our own epoch.[1] For the Western world, the historic horizon of the father lies in Greece.

The modern world of Europe and America is also rooted in ancient Rome. Any number of Roman laws and institutions are still today alive within it, many of them centering on the father. But the Romans came after Greece, and made themselves its continuation.

Judeo-Christian monotheism is still another element of the common heritage of a large part of Western civilization. But not of all of it. Even after the advent of Christ, Judaism played a role of its own, and that role was far larger than the size of the Jewish people. Judaism precedes Christianity only from a Christian point of view. Historically, it represents an alternative. The same can be said of Islam. And for a number of centuries, in the Middle Ages, Islam's contribution to Western culture was greater than Christianity's, before Islam then returned toward the East.

Most of us don't descend from the Judeo-Christian tradition in the way we descend from the Greco-Roman tradition. The hyphen in "Greco-Roman" indicates a continuity, whereas the hyphen in "Judeo-Christian" represents a shift or a rupture, or even at times a rejection, as the annals of persecution attest. Christianity acknowledges its Judaic roots, but doesn't regard them as a source of nourishment. It re-read the texts of the older monotheism through its own particular spectacles. It didn't find its affirmation through the assimilation and admiration of Judaism, as Rome did with the culture and religion of the Greeks: the Christians were intransigent converts and did their best to invalidate Judaism.

The historical part of our study will give more space to Greece than to Rome or to Christianity. This isn't, however, to deny the importance of their roles in the construction of Western civilization and in determining its patriarchal form. It's rather that their institutions – juridical in the first case, and religious in the second – are continuous with our own and have continued to vehicle their influence: so they stand implicitly before our eyes when we speak of present-day problems.

A psychological history is more interested in symbols than in concepts. In comparison with Greece, the traditions of Roman law and Christian theology contain more ideas, and fewer images. More reason and fewer myths. From a psychological point of view they have less to do with the unconscious (which guides us, but of which we are unaware) than with the collective consciousness (of which we are aware, but which often counts less than we believe it to do).

With classical Greece, things stand differently, since its continuity with our own culture is far less visible. Greeks today are only a small minority among the peoples of the Western world. Yet, Greek culture has left us with an array of instruments of which our minds – whether Neo-Germanic, Neo-Latin or Neo-Slavic, Catholic, Protestant or Jewish, European, American or whatever else – still make abundant use. These instruments, moreover, go beyond the question of scientific and philosophical concepts, which are used by the conscious mind. It's a question primarily of our culture's mythic images, which are used by the unconscious mind, and from which we inherit the myth of the father.

Greece created ideal types: universal models and aesthetic canons that have never been surpassed or invalidated. They don't reach us in the form of official institutions – such as Roman law or the Church, which we are able to a certain degree to reject – but as inspirations which we have no freedom to deny, since they constitute the deepest stratum of our imaginal world.[2]

Ancient Greece had no religion which was subject to absolute rules and embodied in strong institutions, such as those of Christianity or Judaism. The values that gave the culture its orientation were contained in its myths, which constituted a total world, in perennial ferment and evolution. The area of the Greek myths was never circumscribed by any clear boundary, and they never assumed definitive, canonical forms.

Bernal,[3] an unorthodox scholar, now maintains that the origins of Greece were strongly influenced by forces that came from the south, especially from Egypt and Phoenicia. But the prevalent historical view sees the birth of Greece to coincide with the arrival of the Hellenes. The Hellenes, whom the

Romans later called the Greeks, were a people of patriarchal warriors, of Indo-European origin. But we know almost nothing about them in the period before they settled on the Greek peninsula and the areas adjacent to it. Their history begins with the history of the lands in which they arrived as foreign invaders. They came in waves that continued for centuries to descend from the north. The indigenous peoples who lived in the area before them were subjugated but not exterminated. The roles of males and females, which formerly, among the indigenous peoples, are likely to have been fairly well balanced (Gimbutas and others speak of a "gilanic" or essentially egalitarian society), underwent a shift, in the direction of male domination.

Greek mythology also held a place for incomparable images of powerful goddesses and remarkable women: deities such as Athena, Aphrodite and Demetra; and heroines – both good and evil – like Antigone and Medea. There were even great sages, like Diotima, of whom Socrates, according to Plato's *Symposium*, was the disciple. But calling them "incomparable images" defines them quite precisely. They were nothing more than that. They were objects of veneration rather than models to be emulated, and as such were projections of male fantasies, replete with the attitude of admiring diffidence with which the male mind regarded the female. Thanks to its continuity with the Western world, Greece has left us with a great many documents that allow us to separate its world of images from its real society. Real women, regardless of their age, had more or less the status of minors, rather like their children. The Greeks even say little about their maternal qualities, especially in comparison with the hymns of praise they constantly sang about the father. Demeter, moreover, was the only truly maternal goddess, and was always the subject of a separate, esoteric cult.

Male fear of a previous world of terrifying female power survived in the myth of the Amazons, a people of warrior women who avoided and slaughtered men. They were even said to have laid siege to Athens, and only Hercules, the prototype of masculine strength, had been able to defeat them.

To degrees that varied from one locale to the next, the Hellenes subjugated the indigenous peoples, but at the same time mixed with them. Something similar happened with the gods. In addition to their blood and genetic characteristics, the values, deities and myths of the conquered peoples survived beneath the victors' shining armor.

The gods destined to be dominant likewise descended from above: not from the north but from the skies. Or, at least, from Mount Olympus, which owing to its height was regarded as equal to the sky. The gods who finally established power were also a patriarchal group. They recognized Zeus, at least on formal terms, to be their king, and he was also the father of most of them.

But Zeus didn't hold his post since time immemorial, and at times he had to accept a status as an extension of other gods. In his sanctuary at Dodona, he belonged to a sacred couple of which the other member was Diona, the indigenous nature goddess. The previous world was still quite alive. Zeus simply did his best to control it, at times through diplomacy, at others by force. Just as the other Olympian gods were always unruly and ready to rebel against Zeus' patriarchal authority, the whole panoply of celestial deities was menaced from below by the agitation of the previous terrestrial gods, who had been conquered but never eliminated.

The Olympian gods were the religious figures who guided the victors and the nobles, maintaining the paternal order of their warrior society. The terrestrial gods belonged to the ancient peoples who invisibly lived beside them: the gods of the disinherited, of the social fossils of an epoch in which the father didn't yet hold sway. And owing to its unofficial, semi-clandestine nature, this subculture was also to enrich itself, as time went by, with foreign contributions, primarily from the East.

Our knowledge of the most important of the anti-Olympian gods, Dionysus, dates mainly from later periods. Older studies see his late appearance to result from his having entered Greece from the Orient. It is likely, however, that he was already worshipped in earlier times but wasn't officially mentioned until after he had reached a compromise with the dominant deities. Dionysus was the god of a popular religion, and presided over mystery cults and the theater.[4] He was a non-official alternative to the father who sat on Olympus, and his masculinity was ambiguous. At times he was even bisexual. Originally, on the island Crete, which abounds with images of the Great Mother, he was probably a divine child who had only a mother. It was only later, with the affirmation of the Hellenes during the second millennium BC, that he became a part of a triad of father, mother and son, and properly became Dio-nysos: both the son of Zeus (Dio) and the divine child.[5]

The forms of the gods and the shape of the whole mythology were officially compiled and established in about the eighth century by Hesiod and Homer (Herodotus II, 53, 1), who in every sense were among the first of the poets of antiquity.

Hesiod was fully aware of the values of his time and flanked himself on the side of the new order. He was radically distrustful of women. But he also told the tale of the silent face of the world. In *Works and Days* he spoke of the poor, of the fields and of daily labor. In the *Theogony* he recounted the birth of the gods and the victory of the celestial deities; but he also spoke of the considerable price of their victory, which the surviving terrestrial gods were always ready and anxious to make them pay.

Homer, radiant and noble, speaks only of the celestial gods and of the society of the nobility. He had no interest in anything base or terrestrial, no matter if a question of the anonymous and uncultivated masses, or of the old deities. Unlike Hesiod, Homer left the ancient world of the generous mother to drown in silence. His voice is perhaps the most powerful which the world has ever known – an ironic fate for an author whose very existence has been doubted – and the imprint he left on our unconscious mind was decidedly and decisively paternal.

NOTES

1 Gadamer, H.-G. (1976) "Das Vaterbild im griechischen Denken," in Tellenbach, H. (ed.), *Das Vaterbild in Mythos und Geschichte.* Stuttgart: Kohlhammer.
2 For the psychological perspective, see Hillman, J. (1972a) *An Essay on Pan.* New York and Zurich: Spring. For the figurative arts, see Georgoudi, S. and Vernant, J.-P. (1996) *Mythes grecs au figuré.* Paris: Gallinard.
3 Bernal, M. (1987) *Black Athena.* London: Free Association Books.
4 Kerényi, K. (1976) *Dionysos.* A. Langen & G. Müller Verlag; Lekatsas, P. (1971) *Dionysos.* Athens: Idryma Moraiti; Eliade (1975), pp. 122–5; Dodds, E. R. (1951) *The Greeks and the Irrational.* Berkeley: University of California Press; Burkert (1987); Detienne, (1986).
5 Lekatsas (1971), p. 50.

Chapter 8

The mythic origins of the father

The Greeks' radical pessimism viewed everything as limited and saw nothing as eternal or omnipotent. Though it's true that the gods were not destined to die, they had had a beginning, and in order to affirm themselves they had had to do battle and had risked defeat. Their power was limited. They found themselves obstructed by the injurious rivalry of the other gods and were subject to the will of destiny, which they had to obey, just like human beings.

Judeo-Christian monotheism declares God to have existed forever, and the Book of Genesis begins with a description of the birth of man and the world in which men live. Hesiod's *Theogony*, on the other hand, the first compilation of Greek mythology, recounts the genesis of the deities.

In the beginning was Chaos: not only disorder, as we understand the word today, but openness and possibility (the verb *kaino* means for something to throw itself open). Then came Gaea, the Earth (106–7), who generated Uranus, the sky, who resembled her (126–7). As an extension of herself, not through coupling. The earth was female and the seat of the chthonic deities, and the center of worship and ritual for the ancient Mediterranean peoples. The sky was male and the seat of the Olympian gods, who received the devotion of the new patriarchal civilization. The myth informs us as to who came first and who came second, by splitting off from the first.

Gaea and Uranus then gave birth to the race of the Cyclops, who created thunder and lightning, the powers that reside in the sky.

Conflict, now, grew open and chaotic: between the Sky and the Earth, the male and the female. The original couple gave birth to other children. But their father despised them, and to rid himself of their presence he stuffed them back into their mother's belly. This is the most archaic of all these archaic tales and seems, by way of images, to preserve a memory of the kind of male who preceded the invention of monogamy and the family, a man who was virtually an animal. His offspring had nothing to do with him, and he gave them back to the body of their mother.

Gaea was pained and offended. She made the sickle and instructed her sons to punish their father. The sons drew back in fear. Only Cronus was ready to do the job. Full of desire, the father-sky came forward and everywhere lay down on top of the body of the mother-earth, and Cronus used the sickle to cut off his genitals, then throwing them far behind him. But the drops of blood again made Gaea pregnant and the Erinyes were born, the goddesses of the first form of justice, which rests on blood and revenge (185).

Here we might find an allegory of the process through which the family was formed. The primordial male, who generated children but did not raise them, found himself castrated, or sterile: discarded by the course of evolution because of his antagonism to the female who wanted to multiply life, and as well to the very survival of his offspring. The language of the myth is quite concise and goes directly to the point: the animalesque father is shown in a duel not with the provident father, but with a son who desires to live.

The sky and the earth thus lost their primordial unity and were violently separated, as is often the case in the myths of origin of many cultures. Uranus was eliminated, but without erasing the father's archaic propensity to impose himself upon his sons, and to compete with them for authority.

Cronus was next in line. He coupled with Rea and fathered many offspring. But having learned from the story of Gaea and Uranus that a son might strip him of command, he devoured them all in the moment in which they came to birth. All of them, until coming to Zeus. Gaea, here, was once again to determine the course of things.

The divine child, destined to reign throughout the heavens, was about to be born and his Herod awaited him with open jaws. In order to be able to survive, and to bear the enormous weight of their new responsibilities, the skies and their new-born aerial gods needed the support of the earth. The great original mother did not refuse to come to their aid. Gaea duped Cronus by making him swallow a rock bound in swaddling clothes and meanwhile spirited Zeus into hiding in the ample spaces of Crete, where she intended to nourish and educate him. She hid him in an inaccessible cave, in a region of forests and mountains. And that was the place – in the bowels of mother earth, entrusted to the primordial goddess of the earth, on the island that was dear to the great goddesses and the divine child Dionysus, at the center of that eastern part of the Mediterranean where the cult of the mothers perhaps had held sway – where the new god was raised, and the new order stipulated. The terms on which it came into existence foresaw that absolute authority would belong to the young celestial father, but at the behest of the ancient mother earth. Just as we're told by the reconstructions of the prehistoric civilizations, the two powers were linked together on a basis of alliance and compromise.

Having once grown strong, Zeus proceeded to mete out justice: this, in fact, was the first occasion on which justice amounted to anything more than an act of personal vengeance, or of demanding and taking something for oneself. It became a question of giving satisfaction to the Erinyes, who constituted an external principle of justice (472). Zeus rendered justice to the old god Uranus and established from that time forward a principle of equity. It's of no importance that equity, here, is harsh and primordial. The new king has in any case formulated an intention. Something new has been achieved with respect to the mindless ferocity at the start of the *Theogony*, no less than with respect to the parallel myths in Asia. This too was to become a characteristic of the father's rule: the observance of a program.

So, Zeus liberated his father's brothers. In recognition, they gave him possession of the thunder and lighting which Gaea held in custody beneath the earth. Once again, the tale shifts power into the skies. Once again, the transferal takes place with the approval of the precedent power of the earth.

Still, however, the hegemony of the Olympian gods had not yet been definitively established and the same was true of the rule of Zeus among them. A mortal battle was to follow between the lords of Olympus and the Titans, and their victory was due to the aid of the monsters with a hundred hands, whom Uranus had imprisoned, and who allied themselves with Zeus. Gaea spoke at the end of the battle and convinced the gods to recognize Zeus as the supreme authority.

Hesiod, who probably counts as a more realistic representative of his times than might be said of the aristocratic Homer, weaves a large number of themes into his tale: the antagonism between the sky and the earth, no less than between the father and the mother, and also between the gods and men, between men and women, and between different orders of superhumans, the Titans and the true and proper gods. These images reveal the extent to which the affirmation of the father's authority was a slow and uncertain process.

Hesiod dedicates a long divagation to the most famous of the Titans, Prometheus. He hoodwinked Zeus out of love for the race of men and gave them the gift of fire. Up until that time, the race of human beings had been exclusively a race of men, of males. And as punishment, according to Hesiod, Zeus in turn gave them the gift of women (*Theogony*, 570–612; *Works and Days*, 59 ff.). Women, for Hesiod, were a true disaster. Like the drones among the bees, they exploit but do not produce. Hesiod seems indifferent to the fact that drones are males, and that females are the only productive bees. The man who marries is destined to suffer for the whole of his life. The man who does not marry will likewise suffer, for the lack of sons. The values of archaic Greece are clear. In the face of life's fugacity, having a descendency is the only good: a descendency, clearly enough, where the principle of continuity passes through the father and his male sons. Whereas Zeus, as the highest form of masculinity, was a model in which the male, even if from a very great distance, might find inspiration, all the images concerned with real women were surrounded by absolute pessimism. Hesiod declares that women constitute a *génos* (*Theogony*, 591), or a race of their own, and are constitutionally incapable of giving. Real women and the image of Gaea, the Great Mother Goddess, could hardly have been seen as more radically irreconcilable. Pandora too, the prototypical female whose story is told in *Works and Days* (70 ff.), is an image of recklessness and morbid curiosity, and primarily of avidity: her qualities are a total denial of everything maternal.

Hesiod seems to insist that ideal forms of the feminine can only be found in the realm of the gods, whereas the human woman is irredeemable. So, who assumes the task of the nurture and generation of children? It nearly seems that such merits can be found only in a primordial mother and that the poet sees nothing similar among the real women who surround him. Every particular of this disquieting story of the birth of the gods contributes to the shaping of a highly complex image: at first there was only a divine mother who autonomously chose to create a father who sat beside her as her equal; next, there came a transition to a divine father who established himself as hierarchically superior to the other gods and all the goddesses; and beneath this father we discover the race of human men, whose superiority to the race of woman is even more unquestionable. The tortuous tale conducts us toward a father who counts as everything, while winding as well through episodes that prove the woman to be almost nothing, and, therefore, not even a mother.

As the *Theogony* approaches it close, Gaea makes a disquieting about-face that seems to aim to draw everything back into a former state, within her own archaic reign (820 ff.), thus showing us just how dangerous the Great Mother can be. In the throes of desire, she coupled with Tartarus, the personification of the sad, subterranean realm of the dead: a dark, symbolic denial of the luminous form of life that seemed to be about to flower. This monstrous act of love gave birth to Typhoeus, a tremendous god whose shoulders were sur-mounted by a hundred flaming heads of dragons and serpents – clear emblems of the chthonic order that did not want to succumb – and who found his mode of expression in the cries of a countless number of animals. The world, in fact, was on the verge of reverting to animality since Typhoeus was about to subdue it. But Zeus was able to react with his celestial lightning bolts and struck him down. He writhed in defeat on the ground and was then confined to the nether world, from which he still emits the winds of tem-pests, the typhoons which represent the ruin from which human beings will never have repair.

Zeus then coupled with Metis, whose name means wise and prudent intel-ligence. Gaea and Uranus predicted that she would bear him a child of great distinction who would even be able to take his place. So, as Metis was about to give birth, Zeus swallowed her: a truculent, two-sided act of cunning. On the one hand, he stifled the danger her child might represent; on the other, the goddess of prudence henceforth resided within him and would forever be able to counsel him on the wisest courses of action (900). The myth thus marks the achievement of an independence – by way of an action which itself is charged with violence – from the perilous modes of behavior of the primordial gods. But more, as well, was to come. The divine daughter whom Metis bore in her womb was destined to become the goddess who governs intelligence, wisdom and the powers that make warriors invincible, the goddess Athena. She was still, however, entrapped within the body of her father Zeus, and he had to give birth to her. This came about on the day when she sprang, fully armed, from his head.

With a single stroke, the new king of the gods had established his own pre-eminence, had interiorized the qualities most lacking in the violent, primordial male, had created the sole parent – a father who gives birth without a mother – and had also procured an invincible ally who could also function as an alibi. The goddess Athena was in fact to show all the qualities of a daughter who descended from her father alone: her allegiances were only with males and she offered her protection only to victorious men. She descended into battle at the side of Achilles when the only remaining thing he had to do was to slaughter Hector, who by then had been condemned by the scales of Zeus. She benevolently took her place on the beams of Ulysses' house to make sure that his bow would massacre Penelope's suitors at a time when already they had been disarmed and were kept under lock and key. Athena was endowed with qualities which are traditionally considered mas-culine: "My heart . . . lies entirely with men. I belong to my father alone" (Aeschylus, *Eumenides*, 736–8). She was also represented as a calculating woman of great fascination, and as a kind of spiritual lover of the protago-nists of the *Iliad* and the *Odyssey*.

The *Theogony* seems inexorable as it continues to list still other acts on the part of Zeus which amount to a thorough review, in symbols, of his colo-nization of the continent of womanhood. He married Temis, who bore the Hours, goddesses of the seasons; and Eunomia, good law; Dike, justice; and Irene, peace; then she bore the Moire, goddesses of fate, both good and bad: all of which are qualities that still today are symbolized by female figures. Subservient, as daughters, to the by now single god and father. Later again Zeus was to marry Demeter, the goddess of the fruits of the fields, the benign and indispensable mother; and Mnemosine, memory, who gave birth to the muses, who have ever since been known as the protectors of the arts. The work had been completed. Through of acts of war, cunning, seduction and procreation, the new male power had extended its authority over all the prin-ciple qualities of life, including those that find their emblem in female deities.

Chapter 9

Hector

Among all the personalities who populate the world of heroic epic, there is only one pure hero, once and for all: Hector, son of Priam, the King of Troy, and the city's last defense against the genocidal tide which the Greeks have set in motion. Hector is both patriot and father, patriot and *pater*: two words that ring with a similar sound, and nearly – as will soon grow clear – with the same meaning.

Achilles and his feats are the dominant force in the *Iliad*; but his dominance is also a question of his homicidal fury, which is boundless, egoistic and undiscriminating. His courage and strength are unsurpassed, but are also tainted by arrogance. His heroic splendor is riddled with a sickness of which he's not to be healed until the end of his tale, thanks to the medicine of pain.

The *Odyssey* is the story of Ulysses' adventures. But his adventures are charged with cunning and his goal is his own advantage. The gift *of* himself – which the hero should consign without reserve – conceals his delivery of a gift *to* himself, of which he was in fact the inventor. Here the hero is tainted by utilitarianism and he harbingers the laws of the free market. His criteria lie in something other than a dedication to the absolute: he casts a glance in the direction of the modern world. He too, albeit in a novel and conscious way, has been infected by egoism.

Hector is different. He again, to be sure, is no stranger to temptation, but not to the temptations of ire, like those which enslave Achilles, nor to those of novelty, which seduce Ulysses. He is tempted by the warmth and reason-ability of women. The enticements to which he's exposed are in no way scandalous, and indeed are proffered in a spirit that considers the needs of all. They run counter, however, to the world of his duties. Hector listens to the voices of affection and to proposals that counsel compromise. He under-stands their motivations and acknowledges their reasonability. And he rejects them for reasons which are free of moral prejudice.

Hector, as we find him in the *Iliad*, is guided by magical forces, but he is not an irrational figure. His words are simple, and have the power both to reach us and to touch us. One of the qualities of the ancient hero isn't to be found in Hector: he has no *hybris*, or none of the cataclysmic arrogance that deranges the soul of Achilles, of Agamemnon, and even of Ulysses when he gives free reign to his rage against the already blinded and tortured Cyclops.

Whereas the *Odyssey* tells a tale of voyages, campsites, meals and families, the *Iliad* is remembered as a poem of war. But the armor of the warrior suddenly cracks in the sixth canto, and inside it we discover the interior life that's lived within the walls of Troy, the heart and pulse of the city. We look on as Hector wanders through places marked by the presence of women.

Hector will nonetheless say no to these women, forever returning to the precincts of his manly duties: he abandons all notion of reconciling their private embrace with his public, military obligations. His no, moreover, has a quality which the women find comprehensible, since it is free from *hybris*. And it is free from *hybris* since it's spoken by the father, rather than by the male. He's a father, however, who most goes astray when it comes to relating to his son.

Helenus, the most respected of the soothsayers, has spoken with Hector: the Greeks' formidable advance is due to the aid of the goddess Athena and the only possible remedy lies with the women of Troy, who should place their most beautiful gifts on her altar, as an act of supplication. Hector has just been engaged in rousing his soldiers to the counter-attack: he retraces his paces and goes back into the city. His reversal of direction is not only physical: it is first of all psychological. He turns from the masculine world to the feminine world, to the walls of the home and to the temple where the reigning god is also a woman. Hector knows how to converse with women, and epic poetry will never again show a similar sequence of encounters between a warrior and the female forces in his life.

Hector is met by the whole crowd of the women of Troy (VI, 237–41). Each of them has a husband, a son, a father, a brother: each of them wants news of how their men fared in the battle. Hector, however, is able to put duty before desire, and can do so without sententiousness. This, he says, is no time for news of individual fates, which constantly shift and waver in the winds of destiny. It is time, instead, to pray to the gods concerning the fate of the whole of Troy, since this is a question that concerns them all.

Hector proceeds to the royal palace to see his mother, Hecuba. He meets her in the rooms of his sisters, where the queen has gone to see Laodice, the most beautiful of her daughters. Hecuba takes him by the hand: "My son, why have you come? You return from the battle where so much pain is caused by the hateful Acheans. . . . Here, take wine and offer it to Zeus and the gods. And drink of it yourself, to take comfort. Wine gives strength to the tired man, and you are exhausted by ceaselessly combating for your people."

"Offer me no wine, venerable mother, so that I lose no strength and not forget courage. Nor do I want to pray to Zeus with unclean hands, still dirty with dust and blood. . . . But I ask you to go with the Trojan women to the temple of Athena, bringing her in gift the riches of your cloaks. . . ." (VI,

237–311). Hecuba follows his counsel, gathers together the women, and leads them to the altar of the goddess, where they give her the most beautiful offerings. But Athena rejects them.

The dangers which women represent close in from both sides. First, the queen mother displays her affection and authority for the purpose of enticing her son into precisely the course of action of which he is most afraid: to exit from the battle; to lapse into egoism; to abdicate will and drown it in wine. Then we confront Athena – the goddess whose femininity is armed, intellective and in no way maternal – as she makes a display of inflexibility that stands in perfect, complementary opposition to Hecuba's supplications; her coldness closes the interlude which began with the mother's excessive warmth. Hector, meanwhile, continues along his course.

We next see him in the rooms at the summit of the fortress, in the quarters of the person who stands at the origin of all the woes of which Homer tells the story: his brother Paris, whose abduction of Helen had aroused the vengeance of the Greeks and their march towards Troy. We witness another encounter with an ambiguous voice, and also with a female voice. Shortly before, the ambiguous voice had issued from the throat of a goddess with the character of a warrior; here it comes from a warrior with the character of a woman. And in contrast to the previous female voice of the disarming mother, we listen here to the voice of the seductive temptress. Far from the field of battle, and more concerned with his handsome appearance than his valor, Paris is polishing his armor. Hector's accusation is sharper and more wounding than an enemy sword: confused, the preening warrior makes ready immediately to return to battle and admits his incorrect behavior; he was at home with Helen to give vent to his own personal pains.

Now it's the woman of incomparable beauty who turns to Hector, addressing him with words as sweet as honey: "My brother in law who is dear to me, who am a hateful bitch; to me who on the day of my birth would have done better to die among the tempestuous winds and drown among the waves. . . . But since the gods desired differently, I would at least have desired to be the bride of a stronger man than this. . . . You, however, come closer, sit beside me: you have much pain in your heart, caused by me and by Paris. The only comfort is to know that our pains will one day be sung."

"Helen, if truly I am dear to you, do not ask me to sit down. You cannot convince me since my heart is impatient to return to the place where the Trojans expect me to be. Rather, persuade this man to make haste. I have to go home to salute my bride and son: I do not know if I will return tomorrow or fall beneath the arms of the Acheans" (VI, 321–68).

Hector continues along his path and returns to his home. He searches for his wife Andromache. The house is empty. He questions the maids. His wife has gone off with the nurse and the young Astyanax. But not to the other women, or to the temple of Athena. She had run off in tears, seemingly mad, to the tower that surveys the battlefield, to see if her husband too had been slain by the advancing Greeks. So Hector must once again revise his course. Without pausing to catch his breath, he retraces his way along the roads that lead from the center of the city to its gates. Here he finds his family. He looks at his son and, in silence, smiles.

But Andromache greets him in tears, and, taking him by the hand, says: "Unhappy man, precisely your valor shall kill you. You have no pity for this child still in his swaddling clothes, nor for me, who soon will be a widow, when the Acheans, all together, will assault you. But without you, it is better that I too die. There can be no further sweetness, if you die. If you die, I shall have only pain. I no longer have a father, no longer a mother. My father . . . and all my brothers, slaughtered by Achilles. . . . My mother by Artemis. . . . Hector, you for me are husband and also father, mother and brother. Do not make the orphaned child, me, a widow." Then she delivers her final argument, which attempts to make use of masculine language: prudence has nothing to do with cowardice, and indeed coincides with the best military strategy. "Stay here with us on the tower, call together the army beneath the wild fig tree: there the walls are weakest, there one must stand to defend them, without descending boldly into the field" (VI, 369–439).

The hero, however, isn't to be guided by the dictates of strategy, but only by the code of honor, which demands that he openly face the enemy. And no voice in the world can explain this need to pursue a tragic destiny to a wife and a son who want to remain alive. Now, in his confrontation with the female voice, he no longer can avoid the experience of pain. The hint of a subtle need for power which lay behind the words of both Helen and his mother has now disappeared. And now that the hiddenly adversarial quality of the woman's voice has disappeared, Hector hears only its sincerity and melancholy, which he is fully able to recognize, since in fact they are also his own. Conflict has vanished and a sense of common identity remains.

The *Iliad* marks the beginning of Western epic poetry, and indeed of Western literature. But it is also the work, within the epic tradition, in which the theme of love seems nearly to reach both its apex and conclusion. Why is Hector's dialog with Andromache so highly charged with melancholy and presentiments of death? Why will its tenderness remain unsurpassed? Literature will present us with other great passions, but never again with a similar harmony of feelings. Homer established the canon not only of epic poetry, but also of unbending, unquestionable love. He sang such a story for the first time, and bequeathed it to us for all times.

"I know. I know all this. But I would have too much shame before the men and women of Troy if I were not in battle. I have always learned to be strong. . . . At the bottom of my heart, I also know that Troy will disappear, and with it Priam and all our people. But I do not think of their pain, of that of my father, my mother or my brothers. I think of you . . . of your cries when the Acheans will carry you away. On that day, I will already lie in the embrace of the earth" (VI, 440–65).

Having spoken these words, Hector extends his arms to his son. But the boy seeks refuge and, emitting a cry, clings to the bosom of his nurse: the child has been frightened by his father's armor and helmet, which is topped by a formidable horsehair crest.

The figure of the father, as we see it in Hector, is curiously one-directional. Like Abraham, as he raises his knife towards Isaac, his gaze is charged with respect for the heights, but slow in its vision of what lies below. His respect for the heavenly father is exemplary, but he is somewhat clumsy in his own role as a father. On returning from the heat of battle, Hector gave proof of his devotion to Zeus, the father of men and the gods, by rejecting his mother's invitation (VI, 266–8) to drink a draft of wine in honor of the god, on the grounds of still being grimy with the battle's dust and blood. Yet this awareness of the nature of his relationship to his heavenly father finds no counterpart in the way he relates to his earthly son, or, thus, in any clear image of himself as father. He is aware of being encrusted with dust and blood, yet forgets the crust of defensive armor that encases his body. Rather than offering protection from the enemy, his armor now stands between himself and his son.

As in all situations of complementarity, the knowledge of what a father is is no sufficient basis on which to *be* a father. A father must also know his son, and appreciate the nature of the father–son relationship. This man who knows no arrogance unexpectedly shows himself to be incapable of reaching down to a child. We could say that he is no longer in touch with the child who lives within him. He has grown too familiar with adult warriors, and thus has become estranged from it.

At this point, the father and mother exchange a smile. Hector removes his helmet and places it on the ground, and can then embrace his son. Reawakened by this little incident, the hero now grows aware of the danger of sealing himself up in a melancholy in which everything has already happened. Shaping good wishes for the future, he lifts his son above him, both with his arms and in his thoughts. This gesture, for all times to come, will be the hallmark of the father.[1]

Hector prays for the boy, challenging the laws of epic for the sake of his child:

"Zeus and ye other gods, make this child of mine strong. And one day, on seeing him return from battle, may one of you say, 'He is far stronger than his father'" (VI, 440–79).

These words are revolutionary. Hector's prayer runs counter to the immobile omnipotence of myth, turning the child into a son, and the son into a hope for something better than anything offered by the mythic past. As a way of conferring power to a past that had the function of an unattainable model, epic convention had always insisted that men grow weaker with the passage of the generations (*Iliad*, I, 271; V, 303; XII, 383 and 449: Hector himself was said to have thrown a stone "which two strong men of our own times would barely be able to lift," XX, 287; *Odyssey*, II, 276–7). But here we see Hector as he prays to the gods for precisely the opposite: that his son become stronger than he is. It is difficult today to imagine an equally generous father. Today's most frequently encountered interpretations see the father–son relationship to be constantly riddled with elements of envy and homicidal jealousy. And the modern mind, in the very same moment in which it invented such suspicions (Ricoeur), also attempted to deny that the axiom exclusively applies to a recent condition, and sought out its origins precisely in Greek myth. Freud sees the homicidal rivalry between father and son to go back to the Greek King Oedipus. And aside from any such theorization, distrust and conflict between the generations has now become proverbial: it's the modern father who's no longer permitted to allow himself to be seen without his armor.

Astyanax' achievement, from the complementary point of view, was something the Greeks found nearly unthinkable: he made his father hope in the future, and for an instant he succeeded in linking his father and his mother, united by a single sentiment. Two beings so different as to find it difficult to talk with one another are drawn together by a son who does not speak. The scene suspends the austerity of epic and breathes the anachronistic air of an intimate and almost Christian feeling.

What did Hector reject in his various encounters with the women of Troy? Was he rejecting the women themselves, or a feeling of his own which he saw to be fallacious and feminine? Was he capable of defeating his fear of the enemy, but afraid of the power of his own emotions? What's the meaning of such excessive self-defense on the part of a warrior who was also known for his uncontainable audacity?

And why does this figure whose place in time is so far away from our own – this figure at the center of an utterly simple story – succeed in touching our emotions more than might be said of any other hero, of his own or any other epoch? His words seem immensely immediate, like the voice of a friend, or a sound we have always known, or which reached our ears no longer ago than yesterday.

Hector's status as mythic hero stems entirely from Homer's poem.[2] Unlike other Greek heroes, there is no large body of tales in which he makes an appearance. Here again, we can call him an anomalous hero, entirely free of arrogance. Subsequent epochs, however, were all to make him their own.

Hector is a warrior and the father of a family. Other epic heroes too have children: but their condition as fathers and their condition as warriors remain unrelated to one another. In the depths of the age of epic, Hector's generosity as a father is an anomaly which is scandalously outside of its time; it is also the first of the reasons for which we feel so close to him.

Hector descends into open battle, even in spite of the possibility of confronting the enemy from behind the protection of the city's walls. He puts no stock in any such material advantage, since he sees it as moral defeat. He takes his place in the first rank of the Trojan troops, in order to set an example (VI, 445; XXII, 459). His quality as a father who knows no *hybris* indirectly reappears in his need to teach without commanding. Hector sees the sword as an instrument of duty, rather than of glory. It is only at the end of his life, when he strikes down Patroclus before being killed in turn (XVI, finale), that his tone comes across as exultant. Here, however, we're dealing with a narrative necessity, since epic sees the chariot of destiny to be guided by meaning, not by chance. So, if Hector is soon to be slain by Achilles, that has to take place for a reason: there must at least have been some single time at which Hector, the human and imperfect hero, committed the sin of pride. But do we witness the exultation of a proud man, or simply of a desperate man who hears that chariot run at a gallop, and who knows the next of the deaths it carries to be his own?

Hector alone knows the reasons for his actions, and, once again, is radically anachronistic in fighting for the purpose of defending his family and his city – the subjects of which his era regarded as a kind of extended family – from the enemy's mortal assault (VI, 262 and 403; XI, 243; XV, 496; XXIV, 215, 500 and 730: in the words not only of Hector, but also of his father, his mother, his wife and the poet's external voice). Hector already holds the status of a father from civic no less than from affective points of view. He is two quite modern things at the same time: a father of a family, and a father of his country. He knows it isn't sufficient to have one day given life to a child: that gift must be repeated every day, at a different level. He must daily expose himself to death, in order to hold his children and subjects at a distance from the hands of the murderous Greeks. The epic poems and the tragedies have recorded the image of the genocide which in fact would soon occur: the Greeks were to shatter the heads of the babies against the ground (*Iliad* XXII, 64 and XXIV, 735; Euripides, *The Trojan Women*, 721–23). The people of Troy, moreover, were aware of the bond between Hector and future generations, and expressed it through the name they chose for his son: Astyanax, the "defender of the city" (*Iliad*, VI, 403; XXII, 507). The protective wall that encircles Troy consists of something more than Hector alone; it consists as well of the son he sees beside him.

A modern mind might think of Hector's motivations as entirely normal. But when seen in the light of the norms of Mycenaean society – where fathers related to their children in terms of archaic rights, rather than in terms of duties – Hector's attitude is radically ahead of its times: it's as though one of the characters in the *Iliad* were to switch on an electric light. These were times in which one fought for fame, honor and gold; and here we have a man with the sentimental impudence to go into battle for his children.

Achilles and Ulysses shed indecorous tears for themselves if suddenly confronted with emotions they usually manage to repress (*Iliad*, I, 357; XVIII, 35; XXIV, 511; *Odyssey*, VIII, 86 and 522; XVI, 215 ff.). Hector possesses a level of congruity which is new for an ancient hero: he has the courage not only to face up to battle, but can also face up to memories and feelings. In the sixth canto, he recites the list of his sufferings and listens to his wife's account of her own, with melancholy, but no tears. His dignity commands our respect and helps us to identify with him, in spite of his being an ancient hero so apparently different from ourselves. Hector, in fact, unlike these other warriors, knows no ire. Ire might even be an emotion he would like to feel, and he would surely be happy to exchange it for his melancholy. But he knows that one's temperament is something from which there is no escape, just as with the destiny that determined it.

Whereas Ulysses fascinates, and Achilles fires us with excitement, Hector arouses a mild sensation of warmth, like the indefinable relaxation we feel in the pit of the stomach when someone we love comes home again. In comparison with these other heroes, he represents something truer; and its truth makes him closer to us.

But the sense of nostalgia with which Hector is surrounded is the mark of his survival as a part of our psychology, not as a part of our social reality. What makes his story seem so real and so germane lies not in his life as a continuing presence, but in the fact of his death and absence. His story is also a tale of the intrinsic instability of the father's existence, in no matter what epoch. This leads us to still another reason why Hector's story remains so touching. In addition to containing an archaic description of the responsible and provident father, it also has the quality of a prophecy that foresees one of history's most irremediable events, pre-announcing the infirmity and death of the institution of the father (VI, 447–65). Hector is the image of the father we would like to have, while knowing that image to have met its death in its struggle with more violent forms of masculinity.

The Hector who grasps his spear and descends into battle against the Greeks moves through the landscape of our most powerful experiences of nostalgia. The gesture he performs as a father is no less simple than heroic, he's like the hunter or farmer who goes out into the fields before the house and visibly brings back the life they contain to his family. We are no longer aware of the living reality of such an image, since our distance from nature today makes the tasks of the father ever less visible to his children.

Even Hector's generosity is the tool of a destiny that moves toward death. At the end of a fair and honest duel, he gives his sword to Ajax (*Iliad*, VII, 303). But when Ajax collapses into desperation, this is the sword, as Sophocles tells us, with which he kills himself (*Ajax*, 661, 817, 1026).

Hector's family surely owes its fame to something more than having been described by Homer. Why, among other tens of thousands, are the verses which recount their story so important? In the context of the poem's heroic climate, this family portrait is a further anomaly in the already anomalous sixth canto of the *Iliad*. It might be nearly a Judeo-Christian episode that found its way into the wrong country in the wrong century. In a certain sense, it presents us with a sacred family in which the father is a real and solid presence: not metaphysical, nor represented by the proxy of a humble foster father like Joseph. In another sense, it anticipates the compact nuclear family which wasn't to appear for millennia, describing it in times when the basic social organism was still the much more complex group of the tribe. But even if Hector's encounter with Andromache and Astyanax is a harbinger of the restricted, patriarchal family, it also announces the infirmity by which that family was to become afflicted.

The traditional role of the father of such a family lay in every day leaving the repair of the home and, armed for battle – whether materially or symbolically makes no difference – confronting the world. In addition to mastering the arts of aggression, as represented by offensive arms, the father had to be equipped for defense as well, or suitably encased in armor, shield and helmet. As these defenses have rusted and stiffened, the movements of the father have grown mechanical, and he finds himself the victim of an age-old malady.

Every epoch has made the attempt to imbue its fathers with these two attitudes of the warrior. Aggressiveness finds expression not only in readiness for combat, but also in a firm tone of voice and the ability to make quick decisions. The defensive posture comes to the fore in the father's resistance not only to enemies, but also to the feelings and requests of the other members of his family, or even, within his own personality, to concessions which the anima requests from reason. Since gentleness can undermine order and planning, it has to be held in check by attitudes and modes of behavior which are cold, hard and compact, comparable to the surface of a suit of armor.

We have seen that the father is a tenuous, recent crest on the long groundswell of human evolution. Not even the male's specialization in aggression is an always invariable and firmly established given, and it's not to be found in all sub-human species. In those in which males compete for mating privileges, their battles are largely ritualized, and the damage they inflict upon one another is highly limited. Among predatory species that live by hunting, prey is brought down and killed by males and females alike. The male monopoly of hunting and war is not inherited from nature: it is a human invention. So, the father's specialization in aggression is cultural to an even greater degree.

Fathers, who in turn are the sons of history and culture, were one day to stipulate their very first pact with their women and offspring, accepting a responsibility for their lives. But the lack of an instinctual basis for any such commitment meant that it subsequently had to be taught, and also constantly insisted upon in the process of self-education that belongs to the psychic life of the individual. The threat to its observance and continued existence comes not only from the outside world and from possible reversals on the part of civilization, but as well from those forces in the soul of each father which tempt him to regress to a non-providential attitude.

As an exorcism of the possibility of the father's return to irresponsible individualism, the ancients afforded him ever greater honors, raising him virtually to the level of the gods; and the instability of the condition of fatherhood was concealed by closing him up in an armature of authority and bellicosity so he slowly acquired the monopoly of authority and war. The rigidification of this apparatus which was called into play at the dawn of history therefore holds no statement on the *nature* of the father, and instead reveals the opposite: a terror of regressing to nature, and of returning to insignificance. If the mother loses the authority which culture has conferred to her, she continues to be a mother. If the father loses that authority, he also loses the certainty of continuing to exist as such.

The fact that the qualities of the father are summarized by arms and suits of armor is of central importance. Unlike a horn, a tusk or a claw, such things can never be a product of natural growth. Every son who becomes a father has to procure these arms on his own. And it's not that a suit of armor can make itself over, in the course of time, into a substitute for the skin: it has the nature of a garment and as such can be taken off, and one once again buckles it on only in the moment of preparing for battle: in addition to being unnatural, sleep, repose or making love in a suit of armor would constitute intolerable torture.

The suit of armor is a complex metaphor of the institution of fatherhood. Like all the constructions of civilization which present themselves as recent and fragile, and which every society and every family must reinvent, the father's authority remains a colossus with feet of clay. Even the most arrogant father feels the presence of this truth in some dark corner of the unconscious. And independently of whether or not his education was based on military values, his response to the perception of the fragility of his status always brings the temptation to surround himself with armored defenses.

The defenses erected by the father of a family do not stand exclusively between himself and the outside world, between himself and the other fathers. He also defends himself from his family: from sons and daughters who threaten to become adults, and from a mate with competitive attitudes. Their condition, moreover, is rooted in instinct – in natural drives toward growth and self-affirmation – and they are able to maintain and develop it without the aid of any sort of cultural construct, such as authority. The father's condition, on the other hand, is based on the total repression of all the facets of his personality which are alien to the assertion of authority. But self-surveillance is far from equivalent to true self-knowledge; and repression is incapable of fulfilling its tasks for more than a certain period of time. So, the father's attempt to prune his personality of everything that diminishes his authority, or which simply counts as sentimental, is forced to grow ever more radical. In other words, the truly "solid" father, psychologically as well as socially, has need of a suit of armor not only in his relations with other fathers and in dealing with the members of his family, but also with respect to himself. Civilization, in the course of time, has therefore learned to equip him with something we can all too easily call an internal suit of armor.

The father who is always "true to himself" doesn't alter his behavior according to circumstances. The varying of stances and attitudes complicates the task of preserving the personality. This is true for everyone, but especially for the father, since solidity is supposed to be one of his constituent features. An attitude at which one daily trains oneself can't suddenly be put aside. One doesn't step out of one's suit of armor: one wears it even in the absence of any threat of aggression, and even in the company of one's wife and children. An individual who is always dressed in a suit of armor grows accustomed to a limited range of rigid movements.

The father–child relationship always bears the marks of an invention, and of an act of paternal will. The behavior of a father who lives up to his chosen role is not "instinctive." The child, however, of no matter which sex, has no predisposition to accept or acknowledge the terms of any such deformation of the father's natural personality. Whereas the child can prolong its pre-birth symbiosis with its mother, it has no tools through which to establish communication with its father's socially constructed behavior. The father's very *intent* to assume responsibility for his child is an impediment to immediate communication. A father and a child must first of all study one another, before beginning to know one another. This is what brings a smile to our lips when we see the ingenuous Hector forget to remove his helmet before attempting to embrace his son.

So, Hector is an ancient metaphor of the traditional father, but also of that father's irreparable distance from the world of the mother and the child. Whereas the mother and the nurse experience no problems in relating to young Astyanax, the very different image of Hector frightens the boy. Before attempting to embrace the child, Hector should have removed his armor. The reason for his forgetting to do so lies in his having grown unconscious of wearing the clothes of a warrior.

Like Christ, but many centuries before him, Hector is alone at the hour of his death. Achilles has returned into battle to revenge his friend Patroclus, whom Hector, in accordance with the laws of combat, had challenged and killed. Just as he had previously fought for his personal glory, Achilles now does battle to satisfy a personal thirst for revenge. Overwhelmed by his furious charge, the Trojan ranks retreat in disorder and take refuge within the walls. Only Hector remains on the plain, refusing to close himself up behind the city's gates. He feels indebted to the Trojans, since they entered battle at his behest, on the basis of his conviction that Achilles would not return into the field. He also knows that he is the person Achilles seeks, and that his duty is to accept Achilles' challenge (*Iliad*, XXII, 1–91).

His parents plead with him, calling out that he should now take refuge within the city's powerful walls. Confronted with the instinctive male – with regression to the state of the wild beast – the fragile, solitary father is advised to seek the safety of an impregnable womb. But Hector refuses. That would not be his place. One doesn't defend oneself from regression by means of another regression.

Hector also knows that he isn't as strong as Achilles. He is tempted to seek a compromise. The voices of the women, who counseled him to seek a route towards peace, apparently corresponded to something that lies within him. He struggles at length against his heart (*thumos*)[3] which suggests a pact with the enemy. He rejects its arguments, not because his sense of pride excludes them, but out of the knowledge that the feelings which move in his heart could never touch Achilles (XXII, 96–130).

Achilles stands before him. At this point, revealing the complexity that makes him different from figures who are always and only glorious, Hector is gripped by fear. The will of the father and defender of all gives way to a primordial impulse of self-preservation.

Pursued by his rival, Hector circles three times around the city of Troy, around the walls of the refuge he had believed himself able to do without. If the city's protective embrace is an emblem of the mother, the area beyond its walls is a place where even the strongest of fathers finds himself alone and abandoned.

As Hector and Achilles circle the city for the fourth time, Zeus weighs their fates with his golden scales; and Hector's fate sinks towards the realm of the dead. The gods abandon him (XXII, 136–213). Indeed, Athena descends to the battlefield with a final ruse, having taken on the form of Hector's brother, Deiphobus (a name, significantly enough, which translates as "fear of the gods"). Reassured by what he takes to be a friendly presence, Hector resolves to accept the fight. And, as the sense of duty reawakens within him, he proposes a final pact to Achilles, before passing to the use of arms. Hector promises that he won't abandon the body of Achilles to the vultures and dogs, if in fact he succeeds in slaying him, and instead will return it to the Greeks. He asks Achilles for a similar promise.

But Achilles is a man of ire, and not of civil agreements. His words are charged with images of animals that tear their victims apart: but rather than a horror to be avoided, they represent the controlling logic of the conduct of the pre-paternal male. He declares that there can be no alliance between the man and the lion, nor any pact between the wolf and the lamb (XXII, 261–2), and then immediately hurls his spear, with intent to kill. He misses. Now it is Hector's turn, but his spear can't pierce his enemy's shield: just like the ruse into which Achilles has fallen, that shield is the work of a god. Hector now turns to Deiphobus to ask for a second spear, but finds himself alone, whereas Achilles is comforted by Athena, who returns his spear into his hands.

"Ah, now I understand that the gods summon me to death. . . . The time is over in which I was dear to Zeus and to Apollo. . . . But if death must be, let it be death with glory" (XXII, 297–305). Hector prepares to leave an honorable memory of the death he's about to die. Sword in hand, he plunges like an eagle towards his enemy, but in mid-course is stopped by Achilles' spear. Then, while writhing in the dust for the few remaining moments of his life, Hector again begs the victor to accept the ransom which his father Priam will offer for his body. But Achilles, in turn, repeats that he wants to see Hector's body torn apart by dogs and birds (XXII, 273–354).

From the summit of the walls of Troy, Hector's family wails and cries as they watch Achilles complete the rite of reducing Hector to a slaughtered animal. He pierces his heels, passes a cord through the hole, and lashes the body to his chariot, just as a hunter would do with his prey. Andromache cries out a prophecy on the future of Astyanax: "Never again, Hector, will you be life for him, nor he for you." The fatherless child becomes a beggar, is subject to all indignities and is chased away from the banquets: "Off with you, your father is not seated among us" (XXII, 485–98). The cruel conventions of antiquity asserted that *the child without a father had neither identity nor honor*. Since society was a society of fathers, a child without a father could have no place in society, and no respect from society: he could only be an outcast.

Everything that might have been feared has come about. The two types of males who most represent our origins have confronted one another. The male who chose the path of the father has been crushed by the other, whose behavior is determined by instinct. This is the danger that Homer, while recording our ancient myths, most wanted to relate. The entire Trojan War can indeed be seen to symbolize the precarious state of the father and the danger of regressing to an animal condition: the long struggle in which numberless men do battle for a woman, Helen, is a mass return to the primeval condition in which males fought for possession of females.

Achilles is a warrior hero, outside of the dimension of fatherhood. Though ancient tradition does, it's true, record that he had a son, there is no description of any relationship between them. The son, Neottolemus, was no less ferocious than his father (see Chapter 12, Aeneas), and was the man who murdered the young Astyanax: the generation of the sons repeats the horror that united their fathers. When the Trojan women are divided among the victors, he is also the warrior to whom Andromache is given as a slave.

Hector, a still fragile figure of the father, was taken in by Athena, a calculating goddess whose features are in no way maternal, and died at the hands of Achilles, the violent male. He was subsequently stripped of his armor, having all too naively relied on the defense he thought it to offer, and then abandoned to the mouths of dogs and the beaks of vultures. The animals that tear Hector's body apart are a metaphor of the possible regression from responsibility to instinct, and thus of the dissolution of the project of fatherhood.

*

While gradually compiling the traditional tales on the Trojan War, Homer assigned a central position to a legend that hinges on a great deal more than military events: this final chapter of his story is a series of emblems that describe the risk that anthropology can also reverse its course, and move back again toward zoology.

But Homer also understood that history can never be a path that reaches a definitive conclusion, and he therefore mollified his negative prophecy by presenting an act of divine intervention, and two changes of mind on the part of human beings. Divine intervention by the gods was finally to preserve the body of Hector from the rage of Achilles: Zeus himself decreed that Priam would bear gifts to Achilles, to ransom the body of his son; and that Achilles would listen to his plea (XXIV, 22–119). The first of the human changes of mind is on the part of King Priam, who accepts the notion of humbling himself before the enemy, and of kissing the hand that snuffed out the life of Achilles, and of others of his sons. Then Achilles revises his attitude. Priam asks him to respect his pain as an aged father, and begs him to remember that his own father, likewise aged, awaits his return (XXIV, 485–517). Achilles is moved.

The *Iliad* thus concludes with a problematic nexus of symbols. Hector is dead, crushed by a much more primitive figure. But what Hector symbolized remains alive: the father. Reversing the order of the generations, the hour of Priam's death arrives at the end of the poem. Priam, the earthly father – in accord with the suggestion of Zeus, the divine father – pays homage to Achilles' invincible barbarity. Indeed, there can be no enduring advance along the path of what we see as civilization without an awareness of the intransigent persistence of instinct: of the natural necessities that repropose it, and of the needs of civilization which impose a compromise with it. When this compromise has been established, the beast can be tamed by civil feelings. Achilles respectfully thinks back to his own father, and reconsiders the position of Priam, an enemy father and the father of an enemy. The achievement unavailable to Hector is reached by Hector's father. Priam is physically weak, but not morally. He can clasp a savage hand without being contaminated by it. Wisdom is stronger than heroism.

Hector is dead; the life of Astyanax, his son, will be brief. So, if the myth related by the *Iliad* is to speak to us of the destiny of the father, how can it move against the flow of time and entrust its fulfillment to the father of the father, to Priam, whose life is likewise soon to end?

The emblems delivered by the end of the story resist interpretation. But still we know that the father's task lies precisely in opposition to time: his task is to establish a principle of responsibility that remains impervious to time. To create continuity and memory; to thwart the return to zero which every generation would otherwise have to face.

NOTES

1 It seems that fathers still today lift up small children in ways which differ from those of mothers. An American psychological study, based on a vast selection of the population, lists the typical fatherly gestures: tossing the child into the air; holding the child against his chest, but with the child facing forward; and *lifting him up on extended arms, while looking him in the eyes*. In modern times and the world's most modern country, a modern discipline tells us precisely what Homer already told us. Homer too is modern, since Homer belongs to all times, but there is also a paternal archetype which belongs to all times. See also Popenoe, D. (1996) *Life Without Father*. New York: The Free Press, Chapter 5; Shapiro, J. L. (1994) "Letting dads be dads," *Parents*, 69: 168.
2 De Romilly, J. (1997) *Hector*. Paris: Fallois, I.
3 See, for example, Zoja (1995), II, 4.

Chapter 10

Ulysses

If any mythic hero has become a model for real human beings, issuing from a minor Greek island as a prototype for the men of the Western world, both ancient and modern, that hero is surely Ulysses.

Ulysses has been said, with the exception of Christ, to be the most frequently mentioned and best-known figure of Western tradition. Christ, however, has the world's most powerful religion behind him. Ulysses stands alone. Christ is real and historical, and was perhaps responsible for the greatest revolution which has ever taken place. Ulysses is without historical significance, since he belongs to legend. He bequeathed no new departures. He embodied no force of spiritual renewal and was simply the king of a tiny island. All of this, however, has still said nothing about him. What makes him as important as in fact he is, in spite of historical negligibility, lies in his having transmitted a psychological heritage.

Ulysses is heroic only in particular circumstances: at all other times he is unimpeachably human, and therefore imperfect, ambivalent and even unjust.

Ulysses is commonly seen as the prototype of cunning. But that's a limited point of view. Ulysses is trustworthy and remains courageous in spite of his subterfuges. He counts as a novel psychological figure precisely by virtue of the complexities and contradictions that lie within him: this is what makes him resemble us. He is a figure with whom we identify, with no repudiation of our own shortcomings; they hold a place in a panorama of adventure that effectively redeems them. As the model of the modes of deception to which all of us frequently return, he is finally the only honest model, and this honesty redeems both him and ourselves.

Unlike the traditional hero or benefactor, Ulysses is far less interested in noble actions as such than in the advantages they bring: immediately useful knowledge, and victory in the long run. These things have a price, and he is ready to pay it.

And just as Ulysses' actions are not always and only heroic – always and only sustained by a single, limpid impulse – but also ambiguous, and subject to the harshness of the consequences of self-contradictory behavior, his desires and his will are likewise charged with ambivalence and less than fully clear. Christ vacillates in his moment of greatest suffering, in pain and solitude. Ulysses vacillates systematically. In moments of doubt or fear, or simply when decision seems impossible, his thoughts bound back and forth *kata phrena kai kata thumon*, or between two opposing banks of the soul, which today we are barely able to translate: between the mind and the heart (*Odyssey*, V, 365 and 424; VI, 118; X, 151 for example).

One might ask if this is another of the many standard phrases that Homer employs. The answer is no. Only Ulysses is described in these terms. We thus discover the prehistoric rudiments of interior dialog. The two opposing banks of the soul – with thought and action moving back and forth between them, or as active rather than static forces – become visible features of the anatomy of the psyche, or of the mythic map of interior space. Ulysses' voyage is an endless meander of starts and stops and reversals, and the course of his reflections is likewise marked by an infinite number of shifts and deviations within his soul. When he finally reaches home, we realize that in the course of his serpentine travels his modes of reflection have changed. It is no longer a question of vagrant idea, but rather of directed thought; and we clearly grasp the ways in which it differs from the workings of the minds of the archaic heroes in whom thought was equivalent to will: massive, decided and finally far too simple, and nothing more than a mental restatement of instinct.

Ulysses, unlike the archaic hero, can control his will, since it is guided by thought and no longer by impulse. This introduces two wholly new modes of behavior, both of which are deferrals. He can wait for the propitious external moment, when it isn't yet at hand; he can also maintain patience while waiting for two alternatives to find an interior synthesis.

Memory, for Ulysses, is no sealed, archival repository, but a fluid act of advancing creativity. It doesn't register things which are dead and gone. It nourishes things which have been suspended: things that remain to be completed, and to which it is essential to return. Ulysses was endowed with the first true memory in the history of the human race, and its power lay in its ability, in a single stroke, to couple absolute courage – which in earlier epic was far too easily called into play – with the invention of fidelity to the self and to the self's particular moorings. Before, we find Achilles, with his blindly self-destructive temerity that took no account of circumstances; here, with Ulysses, we see a complex internal calculus which in addition to evaluating acts as such proceeds as well to gauging their costs and timeliness. The primordial hero takes up arms against his adversaries and arouses our abstract admiration. Ulysses struggles, on the other hand, to effect the transformation of the primordial hero – aware of the advancing age of the primordial hero within him – and to make him over into the new historical man. This task is something with which we truly identify, since in fact it is also our own.

The archaic hero behaves as though he were always in battle, the noise of which is the only sound he knew: he battles proudly and bellows out his name to his adversary. His fame must be constantly reaffirmed, since his very existence is precarious and depends on public acclaim. Ulysses too is acutely aware of the fragility of identity, but inverts its implications and turns it to his own advantage. On finding himself in novel situations that contain some possible danger, he invents and assumes a new identity, concealing himself behind a name which has none of the notoriety of his own. He considers the future and avoids useless risks. The archaic hero always stands up tall; like the males of certain animals, they puff themselves up before the duel, in order to be visually imposing. Their flashing shields and great crested helmets are intended to intimidate the adversary. Ulysses is more like the modern soldier who wears mimetic clothes: rather than larger, he makes himself smaller. So, when he tells the Cyclops that his name is "Nemo," or "no one" (IX, 366), he isn't making use of just another stratagem that happens to come to mind: he pushes an accustomed strategic procedure to its final extreme.

Ulysses holds his character in his hands not when he flourishes his sword, but when he grasps a companion's throat to cut off the flow of words. This takes place with Anticlos, a Greek soldier who's about to reveal himself at the moment of greatest danger, the moment that decides Troy's fate. The Greeks had pretended to abandon the siege, leaving only the enormous wooden horse on the beach. Beneath the eyes of the Trojans, Helen circles that "hollow ruse" and one by one calls out the names of the Greeks hidden in its bowels, imitating the voices of their wives. In an instant – like dogs that immediately respond if we pretend to bark at them, since their reactions are guided by instinct – the Greeks forget their identity as warriors. They find themselves in a familiar atmosphere and would like to call out, replying to the woman's voice. Ulysses imposes silence: he orders them to forget their identities and uses his hands to smother the voice of Anticlos, who isn't able to control himself (IV, 271 ff.). Having returned to his home in beggar's clothes intended to fool his rivals, he again does the same when he grasps the throat of the old wet-nurse who has recognized him, and who might betray him with a cry of joy (XIX, 467–90).

Only Ulysses controls himself and is able to control his companions. He too desires the presence of his family above all other things, but he knows immediate gratification to be the tempest that can definitively separate a father from his children. Returning to his family can have nothing to do with the satisfaction of an impulse, and hinges instead on accepting privation and adhering to a project.

Ulysses' task is to control, remember and subdue the archaic hero who still lives within him. Thoughts that suddenly flash through his mind are no different from courses of action that require whole years: they are all in the service of a single goal. Ulysses is at times a tamer, at times a teacher, at times a father to himself. He is both the child and the adult hand that guides him.

There are moments when we see him as a callous warrior. There are others when he's quite the opposite and shows a feminine sensibility. Hardened by the war around him, Ulysses has nearly forgotten his personal sufferings.

When prompted unexpectedly to review them, on hearing the voice of a minstrel who recites his adventures, he is overwhelmed by sorrow and bursts into tears. Roles are suddenly and completely reversed: he cries "like a woman who bewails the death of her husband" (VIII, 523 ff.).

Ulysses is a child and an adult, a man and a woman. His story is proof of the appearance of the complex human being who can organize the resources of the personality by calling them each into play at the proper time. Such forms of interior economy are also the necessary premise for complex economies in the outside world. The personality now has the quality of an educational and social system in miniature: it no longer consists, as with previous heroes, of a series of caprices like so many beads on the thread of the span of a life.

Ulysses' behavior on returning disguised as a beggar to his home will surely not be one-dimensional or entirely controlled by cold calculations. His daring heart would like immediate action.

"His heart barked within him, like a bitch." But he reprimanded and tamed it. And "pressing his breast, he said: 'Bear up, my heart. You suffered a more atrocious evil when the furious Cyclops devoured your companions: you bore it until thought could free you from his cave'" (XX, 13–21). This process of self-education marks the moment when interior dialog and self-confrontation began to make themselves the basis of poetry,[1] of modern introspective narrative and of psychology.

Ulysses also embodies the mind that can discipline and educate the body. But he voices no ingenuous or anorexic attitudes that consider the body to be something that might be done without. The body too needs continuity, just like thought. Achilles, impatient for revenge, wanted in the *Iliad* to launch the attack before the daily meal. His mental horizon encompassed no projects, and didn't even reach until dusk: what warrior could fight throughout the day on an empty stomach. The reply was delivered by Ulysses, whose long, cautious argumentation finally prevailed (*Iliad*, XIX, 155–304): those who think also of food, think more earnestly of victory. The foresightful adult had tamed the impulsive child. In the *Odyssey* Ulysses often remarks that the stomach is a dog that barks no less than the heart (VII, 216; XIV, 343; XVII, 286 and 473; XVIII, 53). It growls without pause, and one has to bend down to listen to it. Every dog must be given its daily bowl of food. Ulysses – an adult and a child, a man and a woman – is also both human and animal.

Ulysses' strength lies fundamentally in a very simple ability. He is always aware of the alternative: the other possibility, which isn't, moreover, exclusively a question of the new and excitedly discovered ploy, but also of continued allegiance to established, fundamental realities which only a fool would ignore. It is often said that Ulysses is the symbol of the need for discovery, and that his lust for innovation makes him the prototype of Western man, both past and present. But his need for continuity is even more prophetic: the need to link the old to the new; the need for forms of renewal that don't demolish the past. Audacity was already rampant, but without being grounded in project, and was therefore condemned to snuff itself out in the wind of its very own impetus.

This new course, more toward construction than innovation, takes shape in Ulysses' interior oscillations, which, in addition to containing hesitation, also disclose choices. Whereas Achilles charges forward with a roar, Ulysses silently draws distinctions. Even when circumstances are so adverse as to cut off all alternatives, Ulysses seems to insist on his right to examine the final extremes of choice. He continues to be active even in despair. He asks himself if it's better to bow to circumstance or to reject passivity by inventing still another new move: suicide (X, 50 and 496).

Ulysses proceeds and decides, he invents the faculty of choice. His course is fallible, but finally victorious; the hero is no longer immobile, and is no longer doomed to the infallibility that results from the absence of choice. With Ulysses, there is no definitive acquisition of authority and the will to action. Ulysses' return to his home is rife with reversals and indecisions since his goal is part of a process. The recovery of his domestic dimension as a father must also result from the continuity of his life as an adventurer. He constantly oscillates; his road towards home is neither clear nor direct, and at every juncture we see him with ambivalent attitudes that have to be resolved; he reaffirms and remakes his decision again and again. The adventure and the return coalesce into a single thing: the voyage.

Ulysses' purpose in life, as the poet, at the very beginning, reports the gods to say, is "to die, in order to see the smoke that leaps up from the earth of his homeland" (I, 57–9). Or, in the words he himself employs, to die "after again having seen what is mine, and the servants, and the tall palace" (VII, 224–5). He sees no greater value than an harmonious family (VI, 182–5). And yet his life, as Tiresias prophesied, will remain an adventure, without reprieve, up until his death. Ithaca doesn't restore him to his house and lands; it teaches him how to conduct his voyage.[2]

Even when his novel ambivalence doesn't immediately take on the appearance of a psychological function – of a movement in the protagonist's interior – one easily discovers its presence in the ways Ulysses compares to his companions. We're confronted with a series of symbolic oppositions that make the tale of the *Odyssey* extremely immediate.

Ulysses is underway for twenty years: the years of the war, and then of his wanderings, in which he's constantly thrown off course by obstacles, by his own curiosity, by love affairs that make one wonder if they aren't by now the center of his life. But throughout this quasi-eternity – more than half the average life span of a person of the time – he holds firm within himself to a single, primary purpose: returning to his home is more important than anything else, and it's something he has to consider while pondering any action he might undertake. This is Ulysses' code, but he travels in the company of headstrong men whose mental horizons are far more narrow. Hunger, weariness and avidity for riches furnish them with reasons for neglecting his program and delaying its realization.

The salient features of Ulysses' companions are summed up in Elpenor (X, 522 ff.). Young, not particularly audacious in war, nor clear in thought, he travels with Ulysses to the island of the sorceress Circe; and here, in a drunken stupor, he falls asleep on the roof. When it is time to depart, Elpenor, as is typical of many adolescents, has an incomplete reawakening. Still dazed, he stumbles while his foot searches for the ladder, falls to the ground, and dies of a broken neck.

These very few lines give a cogent description of the interior adversary. He's short on experience and shows little combativeness. He's given to drunkenness and doesn't have his feet on the ground (his choice of the roof as a resting place). He finds it hard to reject seductions (he meets his end in the house of Circe). He foolishly imagines that repose can be followed by an immediate return to duty (he falls into empty space, as opposed to descending the ladder).

Self-discipline, for Ulysses, is a process that never reaches a definitive conclusion. So, there are also times when roles are reversed: times when his companions show greater wisdom and beg him not to forget the beauties of their homeland (X, 472); they are anxious to depart and return to it (IX, 224–30).

They are also the voice that faithfully holds to the project of the homeward voyage when Ulysses enters the monstrous grotto of the Cyclops. Ulysses himself, on the other hand, is in the grips of the desire to explore it, possessed by adolescent curiosity. His fault lies less in his lack of discretion than in allowing his impulse immediate satisfaction.

When the Greeks enter the cave, the myth once again reverses the poles of the tension of the situation. There is no further opposition between Ulysses and his companions. The confrontation between foresight and irresponsibility continues, but the latter is embodied by the new adversary. Polyphemus appears on the scene as a crude and primitive force that knows neither society nor family; he sleeps on the ground in the midst of his sheep and shares their animal existence. Cyclops has the body of a giant but his soul is imprisoned in an unresolved paternal problem which clearly has prevented him from entering adulthood. The male who is incapable of becoming a father impedes the succession of the generations and in turn remains his father's hostage. Polyphemus lives a hand to mouth existence, wholly engrossed in the satisfaction of his basic, daily needs. Just as no father lives within him, he's entirely cut off from his biological father Poseidon, the god of the sea. Polyphemus captures the Greeks and then passes two days in drunkenness – the constant enemy of the father figure – while proceeding to devour his prisoners.

The conclusion of the story makes two appeals to the father figure, nearly as though the father were the guiding star to which the man abused by destiny has to turn. After blinding Polyphemus and fleeing from his cave, Ulysses returns to his ship. But while trapped in the cave and combating the Cyclops, he has also been tainted by the Cyclops' mind: an equally primitive force has been unleashed within him. He suddenly gives in to an impulsive need for the kind of heroic action that lives for and in the moment. His companions encircle him and hold him back. They appeal to his reason and call him a madman, and admonish him not to provoke the monster. Just as prudence had formerly been supplanted by curiosity, it now gives way to pride: Ulysses proclaims, "Cyclops, if someone shall one day ask about the gaping wound in your eye, reply that it was torn out by Ulysses, son of Laertes. . . ."

The return to Ithaca demands discipline, and lapses such as these will be punished. This is a point on which the *Odyssey* is very clear: moments of impulsive behavior will bring years of affliction on the road towards home: "An ancient prophecy is here fulfilled!" cries Polyphemus, to whom a soothsayer had predicted that a man named Ulysses would blind him. But could a creature who lives for the moment have concerned himself with prophecies, which are only fulfilled in times to come? Cyclops confesses his impotence, and appeals to the only power he recognizes. Just as a child wails out for a gift, the giant begs his father to give him revenge: "Hark, father Poseidon, who girdles the earth. If truly I am yours, give me justice, and punish Ulysses with the greatest of ills" (IX, 500–35).

The poet of the *Odyssey* apparently intended the opposition of these two personages to represent the confrontation between the two male personalities that lived constantly side by side in the protagonist's soul: between immediate needs, juvenile and pre-paternal, and fidelity to the future; between the desire for adventure and the commitment to return to the family. At times these contrasting points of view are found within the subject; at others they are represented by different subjects. At times Ulysses commits himself to the gradual fulfillment of a project; at others he consigns himself to audacity.

Destiny itself seems to model its rules on this alternation. Ulysses was the master of duplicity; and destiny – which for the Greeks was the maximum authority, to which even the gods were obliged to submit – gave him a dual or twofold fate.

Victory, in the *Odyssey*, falls to patience, to the program which is faithfully carried out in the course of time; but allegiance to the programmed goal never ceases to alternate with the flaring excitement of episodes of daring. While embarking on the route of adventure, Ulysses firmly turns his heart to the homeward voyage; while returning towards his home, adventure reappears along his way.

The divine Circe admonishes Ulysses that he has to descend to the realm of the dead to obtain a prophecy on his return to his home from the seer Tiresias. But with whom does he make his first encounter? With Elpenor

(XI, 51 ff.). His shade hovers in a space before the underworld and cannot enter it and find peace since his body remains to be buried. "I beg you," he says to Ulysses, "in the name of your family, which is what you hold most dear. Return again to Circe, to give me a funeral rite and plant an oar upon my grave, in order that I be remembered as the sailor I was."

Ulysses' promise brings a cycle to a close, and the symbols of the story again assume an order which works to the advantage of the homeward voyage. The symbol of the lack of foresight will be laid to rest: a single action permits Ulysses both to eliminate him and to make peace with him. Elpenor will cease to symbolize the enemy of the firmness which the return requires: he represents the first of its first stages, in which it still bears the mark of ingenuousness.

Ulysses can finally question Tiresias. And Tiresias tells him (XI, 100–37) that his return to Ithaca will only be possible at the cost of enormous agonies. As soon as he has managed to reestablish justice in his palace, he is to set out on foot with an oar on his shoulder and to walk inland, ever further from the sea. His voyage will be over and he will finally be able to return to his family when he encounters a people who have never seen an oar. He will grow very old and death will meet him gently.

After his visit to Hades has accomplished its purpose, Ulysses might return among the living. But Homer keeps him a little while longer among the dead, allowing him to meet other shades. He thus comes to speak with Agamemnon. What news from the land of the living does the king of the kings of Greece desire? He wants news of his son Orestes. Later Ulysses encounters Achilles, who asks for news of his father Peleus and his son Neottolemus. The heroes don't grow calm until after receiving this information, and it is only at this point that the voyage to Hades has truly reached its end. The poet has told us that the link between the living and the dead is the link between fathers and children. Fathers can always be depended upon, since even after death they continue to hold us in mind.

Ulysses' voyage is a recapitulation of the birth throes of the male's responsibility to the family and also of the faculty of choice, re-elaborating the sufferings and contradictions that surrounded the appearance of the father figure and the father's code of fidelity. The story's dramatic intensity precludes all comedy.

While endeavoring to convince the divine Calypso to allow him to depart, Ulysses doesn't conceal himself from the various lights she throws upon him. "Ah great goddess, don't be angry with me, please. All you say is true, how well I know. Look at my wise Penelope. She falls far short of you, your beauty, stature. She is mortal after all and you, you never age or die . . . Nevertheless I long – I pine, all my days – to travel home and see the dawn of my return" (V, 215–20). What answer shall we offer to modern, materialistic minds that grow impatient with the epic poems since they show no credible passage of time? Some remind us, for example, that at twenty years' distance from her husband's departure, Penelope, in the reality of the life of the times, was at least middle-aged. We'll reply that the *Odyssey* is more complex than their literal thinking imagines it to be, and that the poem comes to terms with all the salient facts: the suitors court this middle-aged queen for reasons of political expedience, and Ulysses knows that he will lie with a woman whose body is already creased and wrinkled. But while expressing his respect for Calypso, he also lets the truth slip out: if I don't return to the place where I belong, what use will I have for your eternally resilient skin? I want to go home to my wife.

What could he find attractive in the gift of immortality that Calypso offered? Rather than a gift that strengthens, this was a seduction that weakens. It was tantamount to stepping out of time: to a disengagement from the system of the family (*oikos*, which lies at the root of *oikonomia*, the government of that system, or economy); to forever postponing his confrontation with Penelope's suitors. Ulysses rejects the goddesses, but primarily he rejected the most fickle and archaic male fantasies.

Even when recounting the trials of his voyage to the king of the Phaeacians, the hero confesses what Circe and Calypso meant to him. No, he makes no mention of the illegitimate sons he left behind with them – as we learn from Hesiod, who played the role of the census bureau for the world of myth (*Theogony*, 1010–18) – but he nonetheless begins the list of his misadventures with precisely these traps of seduction. And he has good reason. The terrible Cyclops was able to hold him prisoner for only two nights, whereas he remained on Circe's island for about a year, and lived a full seven years with Calypso. "Calypso the lustrous goddess tried to hold me back, deep in her arching caverns, craving me for a husband. So did Circe, holding me just as warmly in her halls, the bewitching queen of Aeaea keen to have me too. But they never won the heart inside me, never. So nothing is as sweet as a man's own country, his own parents, even though he's settled down in some luxurious house, off in a foreign land, and far from those who bore him" (*Odyssey*, IX, 29–37).

These words, however, make no mention of his wife, Penelope. He speaks of his homeland, but not of her. Ulysses' rejection of the other women had less to do with Penelope as a person than with an impersonal or abstract longing for the return: *nostos* (IX, 37), the word from which we derive "nostalgia," the pain of the return. But the words of this passage of the *Odyssey* also tell us something of even greater importance.

Penelope, of course, is at the center of the order and the homeland which Ulysses constantly invokes and to which he desires to return. But that order is a paternal order. We use the word "fatherland" – *patria* – without really remembering what it means. The Greek *pater* means father (from the root *pa–*, which means to possess, nourish, or command). *Patra* or *patris gaia* doesn't mean "my land," but "the land of my fathers." My fatherland doesn't belong to me, but to my fathers. I myself, in turn, am a part of my fatherland only insofar as I am truly a member of the class of fathers. That particular land and my physical person are united by a metaphysical link: the idea of the father. So, Ulysses doesn't voyage toward the place of his wife, but to the place of the father. To his fatherland: to the place where his fathers have always lived and where he himself will always be remembered as a father. The whole of the *Odyssey* is permeated with this warning and appeal: woe to those who forget the land of the fathers!

When Ulysses, tossed about by the waves for two whole days, is about to drown and manages instead to reach the shore, the poet employs a simile with a double meaning that would not have escaped the Greeks: the sight of land for the shipwrecked sailor is like the sight, for a son, of the father who has recovered from a grave illness (V, 394 ff.). The father is strength and tenderness, society and the earth, discipline and nourishment: the father is father and mother at the same time. So the shore the voyager hopes to reach is not the "mother country," as modern parlance would have it, but a part of the all-containing father.

What place does Telemachus, Ulysses' son, hold in this order of things? The answer is clear from the very beginning, where the *Odyssey* presents its values nearly as though outlining a program. Telemachus is described as a mental container that has no content: he can shape no image of the father whose protection he desires (I, 115–16). In addition to being absent from his daily life, Ulysses is also a missing factor in his mind. Telemachus lives in a state of suspension and waiting: not so much for a real person – of whom he has no memory, and who departed when he was still in swaddling clothes – but for an *image* of the father, a noble image he might admire (I, 240; III, 83; IV, 317). His royal lineage – indirectly, as an expression of the institution of fatherhood – is the only thing that offers the external protection he needs; and he needs such protection since within himself he is still a maladjusted boy and possibly faces the future of a social outcast. Ulysses, on departure, had left his son with all the material accoutrements a prince might desire: a palace, wealth, an unswerving mother, numerous friends and allies, a legitimate right to the throne. But from the psychological point of view, Telemachus remained an orphan.

There is only one way to spur his development: the goddess Athena continually assumes the form of male figures who guide and counsel him. The poem's opening cantos – which may have been added at a later date – form the so-called *Telemachia* and recount Telemachus' voyage away from Penelope and in search of Ulysses. But more than anything else we witness his symbolic journey from childhood to manhood. The son's maturation and initiation proceed with the same oscillations that typify the travels of his father: while searching for his father in the external world, Telemachus confronts his father's image in the interior world (Zoja, 1997). The thousands of verses of the *Telemachia* (*Odyssey*, I, II, III, IV) teach the lost son to celebrate the rite of the lost father. So, even though it stands at the beginning of the poem, it is logical to imagine that the *Telemachia* was added when the rest of the work had already been completed: the father, in fact, comes first, and then is followed by the son.

Telemachus remarks, "If men could have all they want, free for the taking, I'd take first my father's journey home" (XVI, 148–9). And this is the point at which Ulysses, disguised as a beggar, throws off his rags and reveals himself to Telemachus alone. Homer might be imagined to have peered ahead into our own times and to offer us a warning. He tells us that the father's disappearance is never complete or irreversible; but he also tells us that one isn't to expect to rediscover him in the boisterous versions of masculinity; those are the suitors, the eternal non-adults. It's in the company of men who are humble and patient, and who thus have survived the tempests and the wars, that we may well stand before him.

Ulysses' wife, son, friends, servants and even his dog await his reappearance; they are all defined by the places they hold in the order that depends upon the father. One is easily reminded of recent behavioral studies in which Lorenz concludes that the dog's obedience to his human masters is in fact an extension of its natural, instinctive obedience to the male at the head of the pack. The *Odyssey* describes a similar situation. The members of Ulysses' family as well as all the beasts that belong to him participate in precisely such a kind of primordial order, and while awaiting the return of the father and head of the pack they mill about in a state of immobility. Argus is Ulysses' dog: a still surviving remnant of an archaic form of fidelity. The dog's life has been held in suspension. He was barely more than a puppy at the time of Ulysses' departure; when Ulysses returns, he is an old, haggard animal that sleeps out the day on the manure heap. On hearing his master's voice – the voice of the animal's human father – as it suddenly pierces through twenty years of silence, he momentarily returns to life, lifting his ears and tail, and then dies from overwhelming emotion (XVII, 290–327).

The moment approaches in which father and son will take up arms against their enemies, and Telemachus' discovery of maturity will be put to the test. We should also be careful to understand that what's at stake is more than a question of a useful and effective alliance between them. What's essential is their reestablished dignity: the return of the dignity of the father, who had had to pretend to be a beggar; and the discovery of the dignity of the son, who until then had been imprisoned in the soul of a child. Ulysses doesn't place his hopes in seeing how a son can rise to his father's defense in the outside world; he wants as a father to become an operative principle in the unconscious mind of his son. Their alliance is interior. For Telemachus too, coming to the aid of his father in the outside world is of less importance than giving himself an interior father. Ulysses commands: "If they abuse me in the palace, steel yourself, no matter what outrage I must suffer. Even if they drag me through our house by the heels . . . you just look on, endure it" (XVI, 274–7). And this is what takes place. By making no gesture in defense of his father, Telemachus allows him to conceal his presence up until the final moment and to take his enemies by surprise. Precisely the opposite of the archaic warrior, the father finds his strength in invisibility.

Telemachus too takes part in the final contest with Ulysses' bow, competing for what he calls "my father's splendid prizes" (XXI, 134). If one of the suitors wins, he will come into possession of everything that formerly belonged to Ulysses: his wealth, his position as king, Penelope as wife. Telemachus tries three times to draw the bow; the fourth time, he is about to succeed. From a distance, his father signals "no" (XXI, 129). The communication of the paternal "no" takes place without words, nearly without movement. It is also a "no" to superfluous gesture.

Telemachus' immediate victory in the contest would have saved his mother and the palace from the suitors, but it would also have saved the suitors from the death they deserve. In symbolic terms, the victory of the son would conclude the confrontation too rapidly and allow the interior adversary to survive intact.

The swarm of suitors who press all the way forward to the queen's bed and the king's throne are the superfluous throng that immediately fills every vacuum of social power. But in psychological terms, they represent the interior adversary: the disintegration of responsibility in the absence of solidly grounded will – the "legitimate king" of the interior hierarchy – and thus the destruction of civilization's accumulated achievements. Ulysses' palace is a recent, fragile construct and has to be regenerated through continuing to construct it. The suitors are the absence of project which inevitably will undermine it if such acts of regeneration do not take place. What Ulysses most fervently despises is not their arrogance – a trait he himself could not entirely disclaim – but their goalless, unplanned actions: the superfluous act (*anenysto epi ergo*, XVI, 111).

The suitors deride the aged beggar, whose rags disguise Ulysses: patience and humility conceal his strength. The young princes hide their indecision by spurring each other on and their attitude grows ever more distant from the restrained wisdom the old man represents. Athena, who desires their destruction, even further shortens their mental horizon and drowns their souls in idiocy: they are shaken by a devastating peal of laughter while their eyes shed tears (XX, 345 ff.). They mechanically continue to sink their teeth into bloody meat. They are only the bark of the dog: they are nothing but stomachs.

Perhaps these men could behave with more courage and generosity. At times they are not too far from doing so, just as there are times when Ulysses' gravity nearly makes them seem cheerful and entertaining. But there is never any change in what they represent, and civilization cannot readmit it, if not at the cost of its own destruction: the hilarity in which the immature conceal their fear; the day lived out with no other purpose than finding one's way to nightfall; the obstinate attempt to take possession of the woman and the house, the queen and the palace, with never a thought for the organization of a family and economic system. This is once again the frame of mind of the careless, maladjusted youth. The society they represent – and not the society of the women, as Hesiod insisted – was a society of drones and the Greeks could not permit it: they couldn't, at least this once, defend the notion of male supremacy, since instead they had to reconfirm their allegiance to the principle of the father.

At the time when the *Odyssey* was written, drawing on the various "myths of the return" which were then widespread, such dangers were certainly feared, and considered far from distant. The risk that the recently established order of the father might be overwhelmed by a return to the horde and to promiscuity (the fantasy of a regression to prehistoric conditions was very dear to the ancients) is clearly if indirectly expressed by the numbers involved in Ulysses' plight. He stands alone against 108 suitors (XVI, 247 ff.). Prudence and self-control are the only qualities that can substantiate his will – a faculty which the horde does not possess – and compensate for the disproportion.

Other versions of the myth offer more explicit descriptions of the dangers of degeneration which the suitors represent, and it's hard to imagine that Homer was unacquainted with such stories; it's rather that he chose to discard them, finding them incompatible with his elevated image of the family. Some related that Penelope, while Ulysses was in distant lands, lapsed back with the suitors into a state of primordial promiscuity that resulted in the conception of Pan (Roscher, 1884–1937, III, 2), the animalesque god of instincts that demand immediate satisfaction. Homer's official myth of paternal discipline stands against the backdrop of a hidden myth of anarchy. In the most extreme versions, Penelope gave birth to Pan as a result of having lain with all the suitors. Pan, who consists entirely of instinct, would thus be the son of all, and Pan, in Greek, in fact means "all." But if Pan was conceived by all, he would best be described as having no father.

The contest with the bow (XXI and XXII) is the final recapitulation of the confrontation between the foolishness of the suitors and paternal discipline. As Ulysses, in disguise, observes them, the suitors attempt to bend his weapon, which has remained unused and stored away for twenty years. Starting with the strongest, the always impatient suitors try to perform the task, with the aid of all possible expedients. They oil the bow with fat and heat it beside the hearth; but the bow shares its owner's qualities and will not bend. One by one, the suitors grow discouraged, and we nearly begin to respect them as they little by little grow serious and step aside: "Shame upon me, who fail where Ulysses succeeded!"

But the most boisterous of the suitors, Antinous, discovers a solution: not for bending the bow, but for relaxing the mind: "Today is the feast of Apollo, god of archers; only he can flex them, and we shall not offend him. Let's put off the contest until tomorrow, today we'll drink to the god" (XXI, 140–87 and 245–72). His words are met with applause and the wine flows. What could be better than to put off a task? These men are human butterflies who flit from day to day, never taking wing toward adulthood, but indulging in psychic fluctuations that know no point of origin, just as they aim to reach no goal.

Then comes the turn of Ulysses, who pursues the opposite course. He patiently studies the weapon (paternal authority) to see if the years (the years of the father's absence) or the wood worms (the proliferating forces of anti-paternal dissolution, the suitors) have in any way harmed it. Having finished his inspection, he bends the bow, and effortlessly pulls its cord into place, "as a minstrel strings his lyre" (XXI, 406 ff.).

This reference to music is not accidental; it reflects the poet's desire to present Ulysses as a combination of power and gentleness: these, according to Greek tradition, were the father's defining qualities. The moment that sees them rejoined by intelligence – or protected by Apollo, to whom the bow and the lyre were sacred – is the moment in which Ulysses has truly returned and once again taken possession of what belongs to him.

He wins the contest in an instant. And in the next few moments he rearms his bow, throws off his disguise and begins the slaughter. It was only very briefly that Ulysses' hands assumed a gentle touch, and surely to no extent that could interfere with the father's code of virility. The moment has come for rigor and inflexibility. Ulysses does not halt until all his adversaries, one by one, have been killed. He refuses the offer of those who declare their defeat and bid compensation for the damage they have done (XXII, 45 ff.). He even deals a painful death to those of his servants – again without heed to his own interests – who had collaborated with the usurpers. Their guilt lies less in having served the enemy than in not having believed in Ulysses' return. The servants who abandoned this commitment to the future in favor of some immediate advantage had made themselves no different from their new and faithless masters.

The poem's themes are powerfully recapitulated in the final scene at the palace. Ulysses has reestablished order and has once again furnished his subjects with a society in which to live. He has directed his son into adult life. He has skewered the horde of suitors on spears, swords and arrows. Unlike Achilles, who bellows his triumph while standing over Hector's body, Ulysses orders a quiet victory celebration (XXII, 411 ff.), free from all arrogance (*hybris*). We see that his disguise as a humble old man was symbolic, rather than in any way accidental. It's precisely because of his modest air that everyone recognizes him. Penelope, however, after his absence for twenty years, continues to harbor a doubt that the man before her is truly Ulysses (XXIII, 97–110; 182–257). And she chooses to dispatch it not through the instruments of love, but by way of a small ruse. Ulysses, fully engrossed in his rediscovered authority, immediately falls into it.

Telemachus upbraids her: "Obstinate mother, mother of stone!"

Penelope asks for time: "My heart is petrified by sorrow. Let the secret signs return between your father and myself."

Ulysses cries: "The gods who made your heart made it hard, if after so many years you do not throw yourself between these arms." And then, turning to the aged nurse, "Prepare a distant bed for me, I will sleep alone."

"And be it so," Penelope continues, "Carry Ulysses' bed to this place, out of our room."

"What do you say, woman? Who has moved my bed. Who, if not a god, could do so. Among men, no one. My bed was not carried to my room, but my room to my bed. The whole room was constructed around it. A great olive stood in the courtyard, and I carved it into it directly, with my own hands, without cutting it from its roots."

This, finally, is the point at which Penelope's knees and heart grow weak and buckle. She has seen the sign she needs, and weeps: "May the gods and not I envy our happiness. I have only put you to the test. Your bed stands ready as it always has."

Throughout the whole of Ulysses' absence, his bed had always remained in the very same place. It could never have been removed to any other place; it had roots.

Ulysses strength is his simple presence, rather than his cunning or his heroism; his only defeat is his absence.

Just as the empty palace had waited for Ulysses' return and only then had filled the void within it, the enemies Ulysses most truly had had to combat were not the monsters or the giants, but the absence of will and memory: forgetfulness. The beds of Circe and Calypso (the beds, rather than simply the love they offered, as symbols of passivity). The deadly, seductive song of the Sirens, calling sailors to shipwreck on the shoals. (Ulysses plugged the ears of his companions with wax, but not his own, and had himself tied to the mast of his ship, in order to be able to hear them, to know the full force of his adversary, to overcome the pain which the adversary inflicts (XII, 165–200).) The excessive wine his companions drank in the land of the Cicones, exposing themselves, like Elpenor, to ambush and death (IX, 45). The lotus flowers which made him forget his journey home (IX, 97). The potions prepared by his paramours, draughts of forgetfulness which can hardly be distinguished from the women themselves (IV, 220; X, 236). The greatest of the dangers he faced were the softest, since they were far more mortal than his enemies' metal arms, or a stony Cyclops. If these were the truest adversaries, everything that combats them constitutes the truest courage. But the forces that combat these adversaries speak as well of the fear and superstitious diffidence with which the newly born world of the fathers regarded the eternally extant world of the mothers.

At the time the story of Ulysses assumed the form in which we know it today, the father must already have sunk his roots into the center of archaic Greek civilization. This is why the traditional version of the tale – which unconsciously desired to record and corroborate the paternal order – didn't place its final accent on the punishment of the malefactors or on the king's return to the throne. Instead, it stresses the moment of recognition that hinges on the bed: a man-made object which is no less intimate than public becomes a symbol of the coupling of nature and the family, having been shaped from a growing plant, without cutting its roots. The room that contains the marriage bed – the first of the stones for the construction of civilization – doesn't stand in opposition to the olive tree; indeed, it adapts itself to the tree, which in turn bends down to protect it. Civilization, unlike nature, is endowed with no life of its own. This bed, however, is rooted in nature and keeps civilization alive even while Ulysses is far away.

If there is such a thing as collective memory – and if it's true that collective memory grows ever less conscious with increasing antiquity, yet no less influential – it is only natural for the story of Ulysses to be the best-known legend of the Western world. Though the armed exploits and amorous feats of a Mycenaean nobleman of more than 3,000 years ago are surely by now irrelevant, they contain a recapitulation of another event which is infinitely more remote, and of capital importance: the invention of the father.

The reconstruction of this invention – difficult, imperfect and egocentric, but essential to the development of civilized life – has shown it to lie at the horizon of prehistoric times, in the period in which the human being ceased to belong to zoology and entered into anthropology. It's impossible to say if the appearance of the father was the cause or the result of that shift, which was infinitely more important than the fall of Rome or the discovery of America. Though it may not be the cause for the existence of civilization, it remains the sign that presided over its birth.

Before being passed along to us, this primordial epos first had to filter into narrative and find formulation in words, which is to speak of a process that lasted for ages. And in order for the narrative to fulfill its highest purposes, it had to assume a solemn form and as well to be recorded in writing. Its growth in solemnity was in fact to result from the development of the songs of the Greek minstrels, the most ancient poets of the Western world. Spurred by their perception of the kinds of events with which their listeners grew ever more prone to identify, the minstrels began to concentrate on particular parts of the traditional tales of heroism. Songs in praise of simple adventures were supplanted by those that recounted the fidelity of a number of heroes who returned to their homes, who established justice, who brought warmth into the lives of their spouses and meaning into those of their children. Passing from mouth to mouth, this cycle of songs became a saga, until finally making the acquaintance of the greatest of antiquity's poets – conventionally known as Homer – and then of the first of the Greeks who mastered the art of writing.

This song has never since left our minds because Western literature was born with Homer and produced its masterpieces at its very beginnings; but also by virtue of recounting a narrative of will and fidelity that lay already, or largely so, in the hearts of all and which corresponded to the solar side of the institution of the father.

The *Odyssey* preserves the memory of the affirmation of the father. It seems nearly, indeed, to present the father as the one true deity, since all possible events, as we have already seen, take place beneath his sign: the shipwrecked sailor's return to land, the reunion of master and servant, even the reunion of the living and the dead. Everything is good if it reunites fathers and children. In addition to exploring the theme of the establishment of the father, the *Odyssey* also preserves a literary fossil of one of the gifts that the advent of the father may have made to civilization: the invention of the process of decision. In making decisions, the ego ceases to be identical with impulse and instead becomes a psychic organism that produces autonomous stances which are independent of instinct. This prehistoric event couldn't be recorded until after the birth of literature. But the narrative instruments required for recording it were already available, since they too derive from the process and share its characteristics: ordered rhythm, and words and purposes that rise above the buzz of daily life.

The tale of Ulysses is a recapitulation of the self-domestication of the male. With a daring, uncertainty and low cunning that resembled those of Ulysses himself, the male pursued a project – again like Ulysses' – which was based on the quandaries born of doubt more than on certainties acquired through courage. When the male, stranded in distant places, stumbles into the realization of having a locus to which to return, and a family nucleus into which to sink his roots, he generates the image of Ulysses. The father cannot truly be seen as the figure that institutes, constructs, finances and governs the *oikos*, the home. The father is the figure who abandons the home and goes off into combat, and who then combats to return to it.

NOTES

1 See for example, Baudelaire: "Sois sage, ô ma Douleur, et tiens-toi plus tranquille" ("Be wise, oh my pain, and hold to greater calm"), "Recueillement," *Nouvelles Fleurs du Mal*, XIII.
2 Thousands of years later, this was to be confirmed by Constantinos Kavafis, a Greek poet who speaks to the modern age. Kavafis, 32.

Chapter 11

The myth of the father as the sole progenitor

The beginnings of life are no simple act of construction or assembly in which already extant things are realigned and take new forms. Life begins with an act of creation that results in something totally new and previously non-existent. The creation of life is a prodigy, and the work of something divine. But according to the Greeks, this divine power, here on earth, belonged only to the father and not to the mother. Here on earth, the male alone was the true parent, the true *genere*, since only the male was capable of the act of generation. And since the male created, he resembled the gods and became an object of veneration, and was to preserve that status for a considerable period of time.

History was subordinate to a myth of the creation of the gods that made Zeus the greatest among them. Physiology was subordinate to a myth of paternal creation that made the father the dominant social force.

The Greeks were the first to understand that there is something that might be called "nature," governed by laws of its own, and in no way subject to the irrationality of the always contentious gods: the observation of the constancy of nature and of the fickleness of the gods accompanied one another. And they led at a still very early date to the invention of science and philosophy, which supplanted religion. In the face of the self-consistency of science and philosophy, the gods flailed about like madmen, and were indeed to encounter the fate of the mad, who initially surprise us, and then annoy us, and who finally are put away. And setting aside the gods was easy, since the true religion found its center not in them, but in the compendium of Greek mythology.

So, animal and vegetable life were regulated by natural laws. Yet, it was also clear to the Greeks that their civilization, which was far more advanced than those of neighboring peoples, wasn't the fruit of nature, but a completion of nature and an attempt to control it (Zoja, 1997).

They also observed that this civilization was a growth that sprang from the vigorous trunk of the father: the special condition of the whole wood – of Greek society – was associated with the special position of the father, the tree that held dominion in those woods. Paternal pride was at its highest point.

The male's function in procreation and the invention of the father's social role were both quite recent, and they dominated the culture's psyche.

The memory of archaic Greece (around the eighth, seventh and sixth centuries BC) could reach no further back than Hesiod and Homer. Beyond them lay a civilization which had left no written records: its alphabet appeared on various plaques but had been forgotten. Aside from a small number of incidents that had entered oral tradition – the abduction of Helen, the Trojan horse – all memory of the highly civilized millennium precedent to Homer and Hesiod had disappeared. Homer and Hesiod had woven the arras that furnished the backdrop at the end of time, and in doing so they had woven together the strands of history and legend. So, it's clear that the Greek had no awareness of the immense expanses of the Neolithic and Paleolithic eras, of which our own limited knowledge is in fact quite recent.

But we can also think of memory as something other than conscious recall, seeing it instead as a stratification of experiences that wind through the generations, or as a phylogenetic record that can be indirectly interpreted by way of the images it has left behind it. From this point of view, the Greek patriarchy can truly be seen as a continuation and culmination of the paternal revolution which had first begun in prehistoric times. They share a myth of the father and everything rests upon it, even if the myth itself isn't explicitly formulated. In terms of the discussion in the preceding pages – where we spoke of the transmission of tales for no conscious purpose, and with all the fluidity of oral culture – Homer's account of the epic return of Ulysses could constitute a recapitulation of the invention of monogamy; and the lyrical salute at the end of Hector's life could sum up the precarious position that innately hounds the father, interwoven with the male's pride at having been able to invent him.

At the time when the Greeks entrusted Homer with their most fundamental tales, they were fully engaged in the daunting task of creating a civilization. They were contriving their exit from an age of obscurity, and indeed from the last of the ages in which a whole civilization had collapsed along with its palaces, returning human life to the caves of an existence that knew no writing, and to a level of almost animal poverty (the so-called Hellenic dark centuries, or Hellenic middle ages). With neither provident gods nor the guide of prophets, and with a *Weltanschauung* in which the best fate was never to have been born at all – or, once having been born, to die at the earliest possible age – they felt themselves to be caught in the claws of destiny; and at their backs they felt the breath of monsters: the lions described by Homer were not the allegories which they are for us, but beasts which only shortly before had ceased to roam the woods of Greece and to fill the Greeks with terror. Life was tragic and precarious, and the slightest event might have been sufficient to pluck it from the luminous reign of Zeus and to plunge it again into the darkness of the reign of Gaea.

The Greeks were faced with a clear alternative between advance and regression, and the depth of their conviction that indeed they had nothing to lose and could only rely upon themselves was the driving force behind their decision to march full speed toward civilization. In the space of a very few centuries, they invented both science and philosophy: knowledge was of far more assistance than any of their egoistic gods, who were always jealous of human happiness (Herodotus, III, 39–43; VI, 8–10). After the Greeks, the speeds of human development could only wane.[1]

The figures of Gaea and the terrible Amazons, who knew how to dispense with males, make it clear that the Greeks were finally to fuse their recent *memory* of the loss of civilization with the *legendary images* of a society of great mothers. We note in the images of the Neolithic age that the figure of the male, when not entirely missing, was often no more than the figure of a child at the side of a grandiose mother. Today it seems inconceivable for males to have found themselves in such a condition of loss and castration. But the new, fragile Homeric warrior may easily have experienced it as a terrifying psychic reality, and nearly as a physical presence at no great distance away from him. Heedless of its absence from the threats of his actual historical circumstances, he fought with all his strength not to lapse back into it: the imagination can be a source of greater fear than any material enemy. Greece, moreover, had only recently managed to exit from a number of very real centuries of obscurity, and the archaic Greeks were able to confuse them – owing to the narrowness of their historical horizon – with the legendary epoch of the Great Mothers. They had no way of knowing that this past was far less remote than Neolithic times. Everything precedent to Homer was an amorphous expanse of time where no particular moment could be distinguished from any other.

To fortify itself against all risks of regression, no matter if real or imaginary, patriarchal society sang its own praises with ever greater insistence: it elevated its pride in its own civilization by elevating the father as well, finally to the point of extremism.

The Greeks thus managed their definitive release from lapses into obscurity. Post-Homeric times would never again experience a period in which civilization was forgotten. But the costs of this effort were tremendous, and part of the price to be paid lay in an ever more painful disparity between fathers and mothers. In post-Homeric times, an already sharp discrepancy continued to grow even further.

The Greeks invented democracy at a surprisingly early date, far before any other culture, but the creature they brought into the world was in fact premature and only partially formed. Slavery continued to thrive, as in every other ancient civilization, and the society's mothers were excluded from all rights, not very different from slaves. The appearance of rational knowledge was extremely precocious, but these newly born fathers were hounded by an insecurity that filled them with the need to see themselves as the axis of the world, and thus to author a science and a philosophy, initially intertwined, which explained fecundation and generation by denying and reversing the archaic veneration for the belly of the mother. The limitless respect of former ages for the female's reproductive capacity was expunged with a near-sighted fanaticism – similar to the racism found in every age – and replaced by a faith in the generative omnipotence of the male. The mother's womb was reduced to nothing more than a warm stable or a field to be plowed: the child's true parent – indeed the only parent – became the father. Heracleitus, in ancient times, and Jung (1921), in the modern age, would both refer to what took place as an example of *enantiodromia*: the reversal of something into its opposite. When things suddenly collapse into their contraries, like mirrors that throw their images each into the other, we stand in the presence of extremes that reciprocally deny each other on the basis of a much more profound recognition of their extreme similarity, and thus of their ability to supplant one another.

Just as ancient wars concluded by scattering salt on the ruins of a burned and defeated city, to prevent the earth from ever again giving birth to its palaces, the victory of the father completed itself by pouring salt on the genitals of the mother, so that nothing further might arise from them.

Let's listen to the most authoritative voices of Greek antiquity, stating with that of Aeschylus, as recorded in the trilogy of the *Oresteiad: Agamemnon, Coephores* and *Eumenides*.

In the first work, Orestes faces the duty of rendering justice to his father Agamemnon, whom his mother Clytemnestra and her lover Egistus had assassinated. His duty is to kill her. Orestes must make a choice. He cannot serve two masters; and his heroism lies in choosing to stand on his father's side.

The second drama, *Coephores*, opens with the plaint of Orestes and his sister Electra at the tomb of Agamemnon. If we listen carefully to their invocations, what we hear seems less the lament of two children at their father's tomb than nearly the prayer of a believer at the altar of his one true god:

ORESTES: To you, my father, I say, come to the aid of the son who loves you.
ELECTRA: I too, my father, am bathed with tears and invoke you.
CHORUS: We all speak with a single voice, with a single cry.
ORESTES, ELECTRA, CHORUS: Come into the light, oh father, and heed our prayers . . . (456–60)
. . .
ELECTRA: Give ear to this cry, oh father: turn your gaze to your children, who crouch beside your tomb; show pity on the sons of your daughter, and on the sons of your son.
ORESTES: Assure that the seed of the Pelopides will not go lost or fail. Thus, even in death you shall live.

ELECTRA: Let children save the name and the honor of the father who has passed away! Just as corks hold high the net, protecting the cloth from the mouths of the bottom of the sea.

ORESTES: Give ear! This plaint is directed to you. (500–8).

Strengthened by this dialog with the spirit of his father, Orestes makes the decision to kill his mother.

In the drama that closes the cycle, *Eumenides*, he is therefore subject to judgment as a matricide. He is persecuted by the Erinyes, also known as the Furies, who are divinities of vengeance and remorse, but also ferocious survivals of the ancient, maternal principle, in rebellion against the new paternal order. Orestes has spilled his mother's blood out of respect for the blood in his own veins, which, from the Greek point of view, linked him only to his father, since it only derived from his father. He is absolved, and the Erinyes are defeated and disarmed. Their fury, henceforth, will be confined within the bounds of the new institutions. The mother is sacrificed to the father, and not only in the life of Orestes, but also in the whole of Greek society, and thus, as well, at the roots of Western civilization.

Apollo – a more recent deity, both masculine and solar, apparently alien to all contorted and irrational forces, a protector of the arts and of civilization – also takes part in Orestes' trial and uses the occasion to proclaim this clamorous victory:

> She who is called the mother does not generate the child, but is the nurse of the just-planted embryo. It is the fecundator who generates, whereas she, except that a god impede it, brings the seed into safety, as a host with respect to a guest. I will give you proof of this. There can be a father even in the absence of a mother. The witness stands before you: the daughter of Olympian Zeus, who knew no generation in the dark of a mother's womb . . . (658 ff.)

These words refer to Athena, who likewise takes part in the trial, and who then remarks: "I come only from the father. So I can take no interest in the fate of a murderous bride," referring to Clytemnestra. "My only interest is in the groom, the custodian of the family" (739–40). She then proceeds to tame the demonic Erinyes with the aid of the goddess Peito (which means "persuasion"). They are no longer to be inconstant and unpredictable, and will accept the honor of a single, stable seat in Athens, converting themselves as well into benevolent forces, becoming the Eu-menides. The male principle continues to be victorious, at times through force, at times by way of compromise.

No god of the Greek Olympus ever enjoyed invocations such as those which Orestes and Electra directed to Agamemnon. Only the father is both strong and good. Only the father can provide protection, as both a physical and metaphysical force.

Even Zeus, when he is just and authoritative, seems to be an Olympic extension of the father: it's not at all that the father counts as a terrestrial extension of the god. While speaking of Zeus at the beginning of *Prometheus Bound*, Aeschylus declares: "It is grave to disobey the father" (17). So, the gravity of Prometheus' disobedience to Zeus doesn't lie in the commission of a sin with respect to a god, but in *disobedience to the father*. Disobeying the father is a weightier sin than disobeying a god: the gods are indifferent to human beings, and their right to demand and expect submission is at best no more than intermittent. The father, on the other hand, always and invariably has that right.

Slightly further on we hear: "Those whose power is recent are always hard" (35). Aeschylus is referring to Zeus' position as foremost among the gods, which Hesiod describes as the result of a recent revolution, but we also see this phrase to contain a more symbolic and more important message: the father has only recently established his position in society and has no other choice than to be authoritarian. The fathers – like Zeus, who is the mythic projection of their affirmation – are always aware of just how recently they have attained their power, of the battle through which they did so, and therefore of having to be rigid in defending it: here, then, is Hector's psychic armor, in which fathers continue to remain enclosed until the present day.

At this point, however, we have to be careful to avoid a misunderstanding. The principle that so powerfully asserted itself in Greek society wasn't primarily a question of the dominance within the couple of the male with respect to the female. It was first of all a question of asserting the primacy and defining the nature of consanguinity, or of the blood relationship that makes another person a part of myself, on the basis of a shared genetic imprint. The Greeks found consanguinity – and it's here that we see the full extent of their male chauvinism – only along the line of the father–child relationship, and never with reference to the mother.

Sophocles voiced it quite succinctly, speaking through Antigone. This heroine wasn't a woman who venerated the male as such. She tells us, indeed, that she would never sacrifice herself for a husband. But she offers her life in order to give her brother an honorable burial. Her duty to her brother is absolute, since, by way of their father, she shares his blood (*Antigone*, 904–12).

A few years later, even clearer words were spoken by Euripides' Orestes. Agamemnon's son explains to his maternal grandfather, Clytemnestra's father, why he had no other choice than to kill her: "It was my father who *generated me*, your daughter did no more than *give birth to me*. She resembled only the plowed field that gathers the seed that others scatter. In the lack of the father, there are no children" (*Orestes*, 551 ff.).

At a somewhat later date, we encounter a more secular train of thought. The new route to truth was to be found in science and philosophy. Yet science and philosophy were to reaffirm *the paternal myth, apparently couched in rational argumentation.*

Let's listen to Aristotle.

As on other occasions, the master of 2,000 years of Western thought had no hesitation about furnishing the garb of natural science to an image that Euripides had created for the theater. The female produces no seed: the seed comes only from the father (*De generatione animalium*, 727 a–b). The maternal contribution to procreation is entirely complementary, as explained in various passages which are also accompanied by examples (*De generatione animalium*, 728 a–b, 729 a–b, 730 a–b, 741 a–b, 766 b; *Metaphysica*, 1032 a, 1033 a–b).

The seed, and therefore the father, holds the characteristics that come to light in its offspring. The mother nourishes the offspring, and furnishes the material – visible in her menstrual blood – with which its pre-existent form is to be clothed. Could these two things be seen to lie on the same plane? Aristotle is very clear: the male and the female contribute to the birth of a child on the very same terms on which a carpenter and a block of wood take part in the construction of a piece of furniture. The father's contribution is active; the female is passive. The product of the act of generation takes on the characteristics of the element that determines its form; the contribution of matter is indeterminate and non-determining. The product of the act of generation is the child of its father because it develops according to the genetic pattern contained in the father's seed; it is not the child of the mother because simple raw material bears no genetic characteristics. Phrases like "the brick house" or "the wood or marble statue" give no indication of the author of the product, unlike the phrase "Socrates' discourse." The substance of which they are made – such as wood, or marble – can be quite identical even in objects which are highly different from one another. Wood, bricks, marble and menstrual blood possess no power of generation; generation belongs to Socrates, to the sculptor, the carpenter and to sperm. The mother is incapable of generation; generation belongs to the father.

The conclusion: "There is a similarity, even in form, between a boy (before the age of puberty) and a woman; a woman resembles a sterile man. One of her characteristics is indeed to be found in an impotence" (*De generatione animalium*, 728 a).

The myth which attributed generation exclusively to the father reached its height with Greek civilization but was nonetheless widespread in numerous areas of the ancient world, from India ("the woman is the field, the man the seed," "It is said of the seed and the womb that the first is of greater importance, since it is the seed that determines the character of its progeny," *The Laws of Manu*, IX, 33 and 35) to Egypt ("the Egyptians . . . adhere to the notion that only the father procreates, whereas the mother simply nourishes the fetus and gives it a place in which to live, and they refer to the plant with fruit as 'father' and to the plant without it as 'mother,'" Diodorus of Sicily, I, 80, 3–4). Still today, in the twenty-first century, the notion of exclusively paternal generation is found in simpler societies ("We have been able to reach a clear understanding of the indigenous theory of conception. . . . Only the male plays a positive role, whereas the female is reduced to the status of a simple receptacle"[2]). But the truly surprising thing is the tenacity with which this bias persisted in the Western world, in spite of the advance of science. Supported by the authority of Aristotle, the myth of exclusively paternal generation was widespread in Europe throughout the Middle Ages, and in part survived until the beginning of the Age of Enlightenment.[3]

It is fairly easy to follow the arguments which were pressed into service for the rationalization of this deeply-seated prejudice. It is far more difficult to grasp the quality of the profound conviction that lived within the Greeks: for the Greeks this was no simple question of a line of reasoning, independent of the feelings. It was, quite to the contrary, a primary affective experience. As we see in the story of Orestes, it connected the child to the father and disconnected the child from the mother. And in broader terms, the myth provided an apparently objective base for holding the male at a distance from the sentiment of heterosexual love. To modern minds, this is the form of love that seems most natural; but "nature" is a word that refers to the instincts, whereas love is a combination of instinct and culture. The experience of love must conform to the theological and philosophical presuppositions of the persons involved in the experience. The Greek idea of female love, and thus the capacity for heterosexual love, was mutilated by the contrary thrust of Greek theology and philosophy, which as time went by were also able to disguise themselves as natural science. The ancient Greeks married in order to have children; but, generally, they had little in common with their wives. This affective distance between men and women was projected into notions of physiology, and served in turn as confirmation, no matter how spurious, of the theory that consanguinity was exclusively shared along paternal lines.

The denial of the creative capacity of women and the reinforcement of the line of the fathers combined and found resolution in an under-evaluation of horizontal relationships. Horizontal links between partners were of less importance than vertical links between successive generations. It's in much the same way that heterosexual relationships were of less significance than homosexual relationships: male pedophilia was the most widespread of the sexual passions, as well as the most sincere.

Let's look at a very clear example. The Greek city-states initially based their economies on the cultivation of the lands around them, but often went into crisis as a result of their own success. They promoted the growth of a population which continued to concentrate in the nucleus of the city itself, thus finally placing a strain on available food resources. The Greeks, moreover, were opposed to the notion of increasing the size of their city-states, since they did not trust expansion.[4] But they were great sailors and the shores washed by the Mediterranean held vast tracts of still unpopulated land. So for at least two centuries (from the seventh to the sixth century BC) it was natural to eliminate excess population by founding new cities, through expeditions of colonists. The colonies were new and independent states, in spite of remaining connected to their mother countries by way of their initial bonds of consanguinity. It is highly significant that most of these expeditions were composed entirely of men.[5]

Certainly, the voyages demanded expert sailors, and then explorers and warriors who could take possession of new and hostile territories, and finally constructors who would be able to proceed to the establishment of settlements. But how were the colonists to reproduce, if they took along no women? Women, it seems, were to be supplied by the lands the colonists conquered, notwithstanding our knowledge that the traditional cults of consanguinity and fidelity to origins were of even more impelling importance to the Greek colonists, who found themselves faced with radically new and different situations. But males were entirely self-sufficient for the preservation of the blood that linked them to the countries they came from. Women were entirely interchangeable, since there was no such thing as consanguinity in the relationship of mother and child. Since the mother was restricted, even while pregnant, to nourishing the father's offspring, it made no difference if she was a Greek or a barbarian, just as it makes no difference if a child is fed on cow's rather than goat's milk. The only function of the womb was to nourish the child that the father, the true progenitor, placed within it.

How could such high minds commit so low an error? Hillman (1972b) has spoken of an "Apollonian fantasy" that constituted the upper part of an archetypal idea that the flowering of Greek civilization dangerously split in two in its effort to rise above everything terrestrial, material and excessively heavy. This is also the error of "the agricultural analogy."[6] It's implicit in the declaration that Euripides placed in the mouth of Orestes. By stretching this analogy, the Greeks imagined to have furnished a demonstration of something of which they were already convinced.

The answer lies in the phase of immense creativity that Greek culture was experiencing. The men mistrusted the women's apparent lack of haste to contribute to it. The fact that the women's actions are marked by a greater continuity with instinct allowed the men to conclude that women were incapable of clear mental choices which can then be put into practice under the guide of sober discipline. Women were subject to the humors, and were talkative and lacked austerity, just as was true of the barbarians, who were likewise thought to be irreparably different (Aeschylus, *Agamemnon*, 918–20).

Women seemed to indulge in the satisfaction of immediate needs, whereas men create – and thus become symbolic fathers – precisely by virtue of the limitation of outward satisfactions, so as better to further interior developments. The result, for the males, was to feel themselves confronted with an insurmountable difference, both constitutional and physiological, rather as though men and women belonged to two different races. This is what Hesiod had in mind when he spoke of women as a *genos*: it is true that this is the term from which we derive the word "gender," but Hesiod used it to indicate a difference in the fundamental nature of men and women, far beyond any question of sexual or "gender" differentiation.

We know today that sexual differences between men and women, as well as a host of others that once were thought to be absolute and genetic, should in fact be seen as relative, shifting and cultural.[7] But one of the most persistent traits of Western minds lies in the tendency to shore up acquired advantages, attempting to make them permanent and irreversible, owing precisely to the realization of their being precarious.

The fathers of the ancient world achieved their status by creating culture. And, inverting the order of things, the culture they created was seen as proof that nature itself had already decreed their superiority. Thousands of years before Western man began to formulate theories that licensed subjugation of less fortunate peoples, the Greeks had already grown convinced of a "manifest destiny" that authorized the subjugation not only of barbarians, but also of their own women.

The Greeks had begun to perceive the existence of natural laws, and to see them as much more reliable than those of the gods. The route to their discovery was direct observation, and the study of the exuberant world of plants, in constant proliferation, most certainly captured the Greek imagination. What could be more instinctive than to associate the seed of the plant with the semen of the male? So the father furnishes the seed, like the flowering plant. But with what can the body of the mother be compared? With the earth, which hosts and nurtures first the seed, and then, in perfect continuity, the plant. Isn't that the same as, first, pregnancy, and then nursing? This function of the mother as a simple wet-nurse seemed to the Greeks, moreover, not only to be arguable from agriculture, but directly observable in women. Things only had to be seen in reverse, starting from nursing, and regarding generation in the light of it. Since the mother's attitude to her swollen belly seemed continuous with her attitude to the new-born infant, why shouldn't it be inferred that the first phase of the relationship, between the mother and the child within her womb, was likewise substantially nutritive?

From modern points of view, these reputedly naturalistic observations were only a reformulation into concepts of an archetypal fantasy, which is to speak of an autonomous, unconscious idea. These agricultural images amount to a reproduction of the myth of the father as creator and of the woman as a separate and inferior species, which in turn was the inevitable consequence of the enantiodromia that had reversed the prehistoric veneration for the generative powers of the female into its polar opposite. (Hillman reminds us that "The true origin is always the archetypal fantasy itself, not the objective scene where the fantasy is 'observed' as 'fact.'"[8]) In terms of real observation, the simple difference of male or female gender should be perceived as remaining internal to any given species of animals or plants. But the

Greeks too greatly feared the natural power of motherhood, and couldn't permit it to hold a place that lay too close to the center of their lives. Their argument was based on the premise of an irreducible difference, since it was based on the fear that female qualities might have been able, if men and women were of the same nature, to manifest themselves in the male as well, thus canceling out his specificity, which was then in the midst of a powerful phase of development. They were fully convinced that the female qualities sucked things backwards: the adult toward the womb, the spirit toward the earth, and history toward prehistory. So, the question was subject to no real observation, and only permitted a foregone conclusion: in Popper's terms, it wasn't falsifiable.

It wasn't a matter of a specific conviction that exclusively referred to the function of the genital organs; it was a question of a comprehensive system of values in which the whole of the mind was immersed, unable to see beyond it. Just as the philosophers of the Middle Ages could shape no thoughts that didn't reside in the Christian faith, Aristotle too could create no knowledge that lay outside his culture's *faith* in the superiority of the father. Genetics – to which he dedicated a large part of his writings (some 37 percent according to Hillman[9]) – is implicitly a part of the philosophy of creation, and the ability for creation belonged to the male.

The authority of the notion of exclusively male generation was largely to derive from Aristotle's authority. It survived for millennia and was transplanted by Thomas Aquinas into the thought of the Middle Ages. Only in 1660 did Nicolaus Steno describe the nature of the ovaries. And the explanation of the mechanism of human fecundation didn't arrive until the nineteenth century.

A prejudice in favor of male superiority thus found its formulation in Greece, and then was to run throughout the course of Western culture, finally to the point of making its way into psychoanalysis.

In Aristotle, no less than in the whole of the mentality of his epoch, the importance of the male and of generation were fundamental themes. Their unification can be seen as the source of a constant fantasy on the male's creative capacities: an obsession not so much with the male, as with the father. It found its manifestation as a faith in the male capacity not only to generate children, but also to father ideas, art and society. Or, in short, to generate culture, which, indeed, at that time, was coming to flower at speeds which had never been seen before; and surely there was no other choice than to see it as something which only the fathers could generate, since the mothers, closed off by a vicious circle, weren't even permitted to bear witness to it.

And isn't this extravagant cult of paternal generation – this Zeus, the representative of the father, who gave birth to Athena, emblem of intelligence, from his head – a male rendition of the spectacular preoccupation with pregnant mothers, of the frenzied interest in female fecundity, which had characterized the Neolithic age and a part of the early Paleolithic? The image of fertility, originally perceived in exclusively maternal terms, was as though absorbed by Hesiod's *Theogony*, then to reissue in equally one-sided but now paternal terms. The extremity of the image remains the same, but a process of enantiodromia had shifted its emphasis from one gender to the other. In pre-historic times, culture still presented itself as a continuation of nature, and its images therefore took the form of extensions of the aspect of generation which presents itself as most visible: the maternal aspect. Culture in Greece, on the other hand, had already found its affirmation as a product of autonomous mental activity and therefore unconsciously opted to describe itself with an image in which only the mind is capable of generation: with the image of the father who gives birth by way of his head.

In both cases, the underlying unconscious perception is of finding oneself at the beginning of complex movements that are destined to produce some-thing new: generation is a question of bringing about the existence of something which formerly was not there. Both the Neolithic age and ancient Greece were overwhelmingly new developments: but with the difference that the Greeks perceived their civilization to be charged with a quality of hero-ism, and as such to be indebted to an almost military need for self-discipline. This shift demanded a repression of the female qualities, and therefore of the images that accompany them.

We here reach a point on which we have to be very clear. Like all myths, the myth of the creative father knows only one moment of true glory, even if that glory lives on in narrative and continues to be sung for quite some time.

The figure of the ancient Greek father was both full and complete: insti-tutional, but also human. Though he was frequently away from his family and entrusted his children's education, at least until they reached a certain age, to his wife or a tutor, the family could not conceive of itself without him. All family affects were concerned with him, and met in him, like the spokes of a wheel at its hub.

From Homer to the tragedies, Greek narrative hinged on the image of a father who was strong and good,[10] or on feelings of nostalgia aroused by his absence. The central feeling in the life of the individual, and the ground on which social life was erected, did not lie in the relationship between man and woman, or man and man, nor, least of all, in the relationship between man and god (which at best was charged with fear). It lay in the love between father and child. Plato's *Republic* sees even the highly political evil of tyranny to derive from a regression to pre-civilized forms of the personality, for which our own term would be "pre-paternal." And this regression, in turn, was seen to derive from the evil which the Greeks most greatly feared: the son who opposes his father, instead of learning from him.[11]

The feelings and attitudes that typified the father – restraint, reserve, a singular delicacy – played a central, even if often unrecognized role in the period's aesthetic, both literary and artistic. Restraint in the use of emphasis assured the balance, preserved the dignity and offered access to the depth of its works, which is also to say that the works themselves indirectly bear the sign of the father. Maternal love, romantic love and the loving adoration of the gods weren't required to observe the strict taboos of such a high level of decorum, and their treatment in narrative could more easily slip into tones of exaggeration, and thus lose profundity. The reserve and self-restraint of the fathers of ancient Greece moved at such great depths as to be able to survive throughout all subsequent epochs, though also at the cost of losing their recognizability. We encounter them again in the modern age, but discover their condition to be palsied and ill.

The total ideal of the father, or the moment in which the real father coincided with the myth, already began to go awry in the austerity of the world presented by the tragedies (fifth century). In Euripides' *Alcestis* the relationship between father and son is marred by bickering and lapses of mutual understanding, whereas only a few decades earlier it was always imbued with an air of religious devotion.

And something portentous surely took place in the brief span of time – barely more than a century – in which the comedies supplanted the tragedies.[12] Aristophanes' comedies often center quite precisely on a paltry relationship between child and father: the conflict of the spendthrift son with the stingy, diffident father. Greek society, as a harbinger of the whole of the Western society on which it left its imprint, rapidly grew ever more secular: it ceased to soar toward the heights of myth and turned its attention to a cult of facts and figures.

The structure of society continued to be patriarchal. But the father as a person found it ever more difficult to show a resemblance to the ego's ideal. The figure of the father had at once been heroic and beautiful: he had furnished the model for the aesthetic ideal. The subsequent course of the patriarchy would find it sufficient for the father to be strong: he could even, indeed, be replaced by institutions, since little by little the father himself became ever less an object of real human affections and ever more synonymous with institutional duties.

When the fusion of Greece and Rome took place, the new strength of the Roman father grew intertwined with the far more ancient strength of the Greek. But this seldom produced an aesthetic ideal in any way comparable to the father of the *Odyssey*, who was always both strong and good.

When Hellenized Rome converted to Christianity, it inherited the veneration for an absolute God the Father which derived from and had formed the basis of Judaism. And the most important fact, for us, in the argument we're attempting to develop, is that this figure of God the Father was so overwhelming as to cause the skies to absorb the part of the myth of the father with which we're primarily concerned: the generative aspect of the father. As Hillman[13] notes, we still today accept the Hebrew/Christian axiom that "first came Adam, and then Eve": this disparity establishes the superiority of the man with respect to the woman, rather than of the father with respect to the mother. It's concerned with the rights of primogeniture, and not with any difference in men's and women's capacities of generation. The Bible asserts that God is the force of generation. Christianity, especially as Catholicism, was then to do away with the reassuring stasis of Jehovah and to introduce the dynamism of the Oedipal triangle. The sacred family seems to reopen a door onto primordial chthonic and female values.

But are we witnessing the resurgence of a psychological truth, or the assertion of a Christian prejudice? The former possibility leaves the Jews behind it, as though they were Christians who failed to take a final step in their process of evolution. But there's also a point of view – in terms of the question of generation – that can look upon Christ as an incomplete Jew (and at Christianity, after him, as an incomplete form of Judaism) since he has been amputated of the dimension of paternity, which is the central structure of Judaism, no less than of all the monotheistic religions, inclusive of Christianity.

NOTES

1 Dodds (1951); Toynbee, A. (1959) *Hellenism. The History of Civilization*. London: Oxford University Press.
2 Lévi-Strauss C. (1948) "La vie familiale et sociale des Indiens Nambikwara," in *Journal de la Société des américanistes,* XXXVII.
3 Hillman (1972b), Part III; Darmon, P. (1979) *Le mythe de la procréation à l'âge baroque*. Paris: Seuil; Pinto-Correia, C. (1997) *The Ovary of Eve. Egg and Sperm and Preformation*. Chicago and London: University of Chicago Press; Delaisi de Perceval, G. (1981) *La part du père*. Paris: Seuil, Chapter I.
4 See Zoja (1995).
5 Mossé, C. (1983) *La femme dans la Grèce antique*. Paris: Albin Michel, I, Chapter 2a.
6 See Zoja (1989) "Il mito di una madre gelosa," in Galliano, T. G. (ed.), *Le Grandi Madri*, Milan: Feltrinelli.
7 Lévi-Strauss, C. (1973) "Race et Histoire," in *Antropologie structurale deux*. Paris: Plon.
8 Hillman (1972b), III, p. 243.
9 Ibid.
10 Lemke, W. (1978) "Das Vaterbild in der Dichtung Griechenlands," in Tellenbach (ed.), *Das Vaterbild im Abendland*.
11 *Republic*, 572. See also the comment in Jäger, W. (1944) *Paideia. Die Formung des griechischen Menschen*. Berlin and Leipzig: de Gruyter, Book III, X.
12 Gadamer (1976).
13 Hillman (1972b).

Chapter 12

Aeneas

Along with the *Iliad* and the *Odyssey*, the *Aeneid* forms the epic base of the Western world: of Europe, and even more of America, since the *Aeneid* is a tale of emigrants who encounter, battle and finally coalesce with other, native peoples.

Virgil, however, belonged to a world quite different from Homer's. He could draw a clear distinction between mythic fabulation and historic fact, and he understood the enormity of the task of giving unity to a poem that included such highly different ingredients.

Virgil lived inside of history, and he knew that history gives every individual a different condition in which to live. No one stands at its center. Yet Virgil was aware of standing at one of its summits. Rome was the greatest of all countries, and had reached its apex of power. Augustus was the head of the state and the most potent leader Rome had ever known. And Augustus had let it be known that he wanted to foster the composition of an epic poem that exalted his personal greatness, no less than the greatness of his city's history. Poets abounded, but all looked askance at the dizzying prospect of having to please such a patron. Their hands trembled, and their trembling voices declined.

At the time of beginning the *Aeneid*, Virgil was already a public figure and had given ample proof of his abilities. He had put off the task for quite some time, since he wanted to be certain of the bounds in which he had to work, and of how much space remained for the creation of a poem with a life of its own.

He knew first of all that he had to reconnect with Greek mythology and Homeric epic. Rome's truest greatness had begun when it had vanquished Greece on the battlefield, and in turn been conquered by Greek culture. In art, literature and all other forms of creative expression, the Romans found their sustenance in Greek tradition, starting necessarily with the *Iliad* and the *Odyssey*.

The other premise for the poem was proper regard for history, and full respect of Augustus' expectations: the origins of the city and its institutions had to shine with the noblest light.

Virgil also decided on a third condition of his own: the avoidance of undue emphasis, of all partiality or falsification, and of all adulation. His own good taste and high sensibility forbade such things, and Augustus was too intelligent not to understand that Virgil's rigor was also in his own best interests. This extraordinary combination – rare at any time, and especially so some 2000 years ago – resulted in the masterpiece we know today.

Virgil's commitment to sober language was tantamount to singing the origins of Rome in the style of Greece and thus harmonized the first two conditions for the writing of his poem: the values of the Greeks lay in self-control, the struggle against *hybris*, and human humility with respect to the gods.

Virgil likewise understood that his poem's achievement of unity and self-consistency depended not only on respecting these dictates of style, but as well on finding its protagonist in a hero who personified them. His *Aeneid* is the epic poem of Aeneas.

The fact that Aeneas is a Trojan in no way contrasted with the canons of Greek epic which Virgil intended to continue. Homer had always placed the Greeks and their enemies on the same plane, allowing us indeed to imagine that the Trojan Hector was the personage he loved the most. Human beings, in any case, are nothing more than ingenuous instruments in the hands of the gods and destiny. If songs are to be sung of ancient heroes, it is not because some were good and others evil, but because all of them show us lives which were lived with grandeur and glory.

Virgil's period knew many legends that described the arduous return of the Greek princes after the Trojan War; and some of them recounted that the surviving Trojans had fled westward, where Aeneas, the son of a goddess and a Trojan prince, was said to have founded various cities in Italy, including Rome. Virgil discarded this version of the story, since it was too direct: not only because it was quite well known that the fall of Troy and the origins of Rome lay numerous centuries apart from one another, but also because of his preference for the allusive language of poetry, as opposed to the crude and explicit figures of propaganda.

The *Aeneid* was to speak of Rome only indirectly. But from time to time the gods and the hero's father, Anchises, were to exhort Aeneas to make his home in Italy and prepare a great future reign. His son Ascanius was to found the city of Alba, which was later to be known as the point of departure for the founding of Rome. We watch a developing process as it slowly weaves through time and geography. Ascanius' second name, Iulus, descended through the centuries along this line: he was the father of the Julian people, to whom Augustus belonged.

Virgil had found a way of bringing together and satisfying a number of different needs. On the one hand, he respected real chronology, giving the poem a seat in history; on the other, he inserted the origins of Rome into the cycle of Greek epic. He thereby linked it to a divine genealogy, since Aeneas was the son of a major goddess, and also to the will of the gods as a group, who all agreed and insisted that Aeneas was to found a great lineage in Italy. He also alluded to Augustus as the noble and natural father of Rome. Finally, the glorification not only of Aeneas but also of Anchises and Ascanius presented the succession of fathers as the fundamental principle of Roman genealogy, and as the source of the strength of Roman society. This principle of continuity is also our own.

Virgil's ambition to follow in Homer's footsteps forced him to respect a number of milestones that already marked the trail. The *Homeric Hymns* are one of the few authentic texts that survive from archaic Greece (the extent to which they are properly attributed to Homer is here of no interest) and one of them recounts the birth of Aeneas. At the very roots of the story of the founding of Rome, this myth was of capital importance, since it determines the quality of the hero's personality and the nature of the society he was destined to found. The roles played in his birth by father and mother were absolutely singular: Aeneas' legacy to Roman society was an abandon into the arms of the first, and a diffidence toward the latter.

The *Homeric Hymn to Aphrodite*, the goddess of love whom the Romans called Venus, recounts her extraordinary power. Aphrodite could arouse the passion of love, which the will can in no way control, whenever she chose to do so. She was able at any moment to throw it into the heart of a mortal or a god, thus making her victim a slave to desire. Only three goddesses lay beyond her power: Athena, the patron of war; Artemis, to whom the hunt was sacred; and Hestia, voted to the home and virginity. The array of these four forms of uncontrollable femininity must have filled the fathers of archaic times with a superstitious terror. Aphrodite and Hestia because they were too feminine, too different from the male; Athena and Artemis because they were too strong, and experts in the use of arms, in competition with the male. These goddesses were the screen onto which these ancient fathers projected the fear that the woman in the social order and the female part of their own souls might escape their control. The myth had to be completed by asserting final and eternal dominion over these forces of absolute female autonomy (8–52).

Aphrodite had total power over even the king of the gods. At any moment at all, she could make Zeus fall in love not only with another divinity, but also with a mortal being; and this, for the ancient gods, was the most profound of all humiliations.

Zeus found revenge by condemning Aphrodite to fall in love with a simple mortal man: mortal but noble, and as beautiful as a god.

Anchises was playing the lyre on Mount Ida, not far from Troy. Aphrodite approached him seductively, and stunningly beautiful. The noble Trojan was immediately overwhelmed by love, but was afraid she might be a goddess and asked her to show pity on him. He knew quite well, according to the morals of his times,[1] that to hope for too much happiness was to prepare the way for ruin. The goddess replied with a lie, declaring herself a mortal who was fore-ordained to be his wife and to give him splendid sons. Destiny and her parents had given their consent and would bear them abundant gifts. Anchises had no greater desire than to be taken in. He immediately made love with her, passionately, and then fell asleep.

At this point, the will of Zeus had been fulfilled. Aphrodite discarded her disguise and brusquely shook the man awake (177 ff.). "Son of Dardanus, why do you sleep? Turn your eyes upon me, and say if I am the same as before!" Anchises immediately understood, was seized with terror for having dared so much, and begged the goddess to have pity on him. Aphrodite, at least on this score, was able to set his mind at ease: he was dear to the gods. She also added more.

Their love would result in the birth of a son whose name would be Aineias – from *ainos*, which means tremendous – since for her it had been terrible to love a simple mortal (198–9). The child would be raised by the nymphs of Mount Ida. When he reached the age of five, they would bring him to his father, who would take him with him to Troy. The boy would be as beautiful as a god. But Anchises would always have to say that the boy was the son of a nymph. No one was to know that his mother was the great goddess. All were to believe that she was a spirit of the woods, a magical but minor and impersonal spirit. If he were ever to reveal the truth, Zeus would strike him with a thunderbolt.

We have to remember these details, since they tell us something important about the hero and his mother. The mother is a liar. And denies her own identity as a mother. She's a mother who never gave him a caress, and who paid no attention to his needs as an infant. Should we really be surprised that in his adult years the glorious Aeneas always shows an underlying melancholy?

This is as far as the ancient Homeric story goes, and this is where Virgil takes it up, transforming the Greek Zeus into the Latin Jove or Jupiter; Aphrodite into Venus; Hera into Juno, and so forth. We too, as we accompany him, will use these names. There were other tales as well. It was also said, as might have been foreseen, that Anchises, in the carelessness of wine, had one day let the truth slip out concerning the origins of Aeneas. The bolt of lightning hurled by Jove had paralyzed his legs: and this is the condition in which we find him in the *Aeneid*.

At the beginning of the *Odyssey*, Ulysses is already close to his goal and then tells most of his story as a flashback. The *Aeneid* again makes use of this narrative technique.

Book I of the *Aeneid* opens with Aeneas already in sight of the shores of Italy. Juno, the wife of Jove, has not failed to notice. This was something she could not tolerate, and the readers of antiquity were well aware that her reasons were entirely self-serving. On the one hand, Juno was already partial to Carthage, which was to be Rome's great rival. On the other, she despised

Aeneas, just as she despised all Trojans. Ganymede, who had been her husband's lover, had come from Troy, as had Paris, who as a judge of the beauty of the goddesses had preferred Venus to herself. On the strength of a series of equally egoistic arguments – normal in Greco-Roman polytheism, where the gods were not expected to be moral, but only to insist that their power be respected – Juno is able to convince the god of the winds, Aeolus, to help her: a beautiful nymph will be his reward if he blows the Trojans back to the shores of Africa. Persuaded by the wiles of the goddess, Aeolus raises a tempest.

But at this point, Venus had reason to feel crossed and angry. She speaks to Jove, reminding him of his promise: Aeneas is to reach the shores of Italy and to found a great lineage.

In Jove's reply, the poet deftly knots the myth to his saga's political program (I, 257–96).

The promises have remained unaltered. Indeed, the glorious destiny of her son can now be revealed more precisely to Venus. Aeneas will reach Italy, and after three years of combat will be king. His son Ascanius – Ilus, for as long as he had lived in Ilium (Troy), and now Iulus – will in 30 years' time found the city of Alba, which after 300 years will give birth to the city of Rome. And the gods will give that city no limits of power or duration. Juno too will change her attitude and support it; and Julius, descendant of Iulus, will stand at its head.

The reader knows by now that Aeneas enjoys divine protection, since the poet constantly describes him as "pious," which here means "respectful of the gods." Modern readers will note that his piety, unquestionably courageous and generous, derives not only from free choice, but also from interior constrictions. His constant obeisance to the exterior gods is equivalent to an attempt to lighten the weight of an overly severe authority that resides within him. This never-satisfied perfectionism is not unrelated to his deeply-seated melancholy. In the final analysis, Virgil gives us precisely the personage he wanted to give us: a man who grew up at the side of his father and whose infancy was marked by the lack of true affection on the part of his mother, who now grows concerned with her famous son only as a way of extending her own self-interest.

The Trojans, meanwhile, have disembarked in a cove not far from Carthage, where Dido is the reigning queen. Venus descends to the earth for the purpose of reassuring Aeneas. Yet the solicitous mother now deploys with her son the same ruse with which she once entrapped his father Anchises. Aeneas does not recognize her, yet nonetheless believes her to be a goddess and treats her with humble respect. Venus provides him with information about the lands he has reached, but conceals her own identity, calling herself a huntress. It's only at the moment of her disappearance that Aeneas realizes with whom he has spoken. He bewails the affection which, again, has been denied to him. "Why must you deceive your son with cruel disguises? Why are we not to take each others' hands, and to speak true words to one another?" (I, 407–9). We have to reflect on this cruelty, since nothing apparently justifies it, if not divine caprice. And the poet must want it to tell us something.

Aeneas advances into the unfamiliar land. Dido, the queen, learns of his arrival and is happy to meet him, since the legend of the hero has preceded him.

Let's look quite carefully at the following scene. Aeneas immediately sends a messenger to call for Ascanius, since "fatherly love never leaves the mind at rest." This phrase (I, 643) contains the whole of Virgil's concept of the Roman father, and of all the social institutions and historical events that derived from it. Paradoxically enough, this love is a question of the *mind*, rather than the heart or the feelings: it is a question of thought, evaluation and will. It is also a question of *incessant* mental activity, around the issues of stability, responsibility and security.

The queen approves, and Ascanius can come to her court without risk: he is to bring the ornaments worn by Helen and to present them to Dido as a gift. The meeting between the boy and the queen will establish a more feminine atmosphere, less warlike.

Venus surveys the scene from the skies. She fears that Juno intends for Dido to make Aeneas her prisoner. Motivated by rivalry, by a self-seeking affection for her son, and by her role as the goddess of love, she seeds a passion for Aeneas into the heart of the queen of Carthage. She makes use of a stratagem, of which Book IV will show us the aberrant fruits.

Aeneas has asked Ascanius to present himself to Dido, who receives him with embraces and a great show of affection. But the real Ascanius has been momentarily spirited away by Venus, and his guise, at her bidding, has been assumed by Cupid, the god who makes people fall in love. Given the strong resemblance between Ascanius and Aeneas, Venus' ruse prepares the transformation of Dido's maternal affection for the boy into a sexual passion for his father.

Juno and Venus are enemies, but combine efforts for the purpose of throwing Aeneas into the perils of Carthage, and into Dido's delicate heart. They attempt to distract him from his duty. Their actions are in no way epic, divine or maternal: a founding father deprived of his duty, like a hero deprived of his destiny, is as useless as a bow with no arrow.

Both of the goddesses are motivated by their own immediate interests, and unconcerned with the epoch-making tasks decreed by destiny. The *Aeneid* is a patriarchal poem and seems to remind us that only the fathers – Jove in the skies, Anchises on earth – assume responsibility for long-sighted tasks. Fathers are acquainted with duties and ideals, mothers know only desires.

But our own point of view is psychological and cannot see Venus as an autonomous force, separate from Aeneas. Quite to the contrary, she represents his seductive side: tortuous, indirect and uncontrolled, as a result of being wholly unconscious; and split off from his will, which is overly linear, masculine and predictable, and obsessed by the performance of duty. By ordering Ascanius, the fulcrum of the ploy, to appear at Dido's court with the jewels of Helen, the prototype of seduction, Aeneas reveals unconscious intentions which perfectly accord with his mother Venus. While formally declaring the superiority of paternal love, the poem secretly reveals its shadow side: an unconscious tendency for the manipulation of the feelings.

Dido at this point receives Aeneas with visible expressions of regard and secret feelings, and then asks him to relate the events since the day of his flight from Troy, thus allowing Virgil a long Homeric flashback – for all of Book II and Book III – that narrates the first seven years of the Trojans' voyage.

Book II recounts the fall of Troy.

Aeneas remarks that returning to those events means a return to shedding tears. But he's ready to tell the story.

The Trojan War had reached its tenth year, and the Greeks pretended to abandon the city in discouragement. They had moved their ships far enough away to make it appear that they had departed, and they had left an immense wooden horse on the beach, with their best soldiers hidden in its belly.

Faced with the horse, many Trojans behaved like curious, greedy children. This was the moment when Aeneas' family – which Homer describes as noble, but not of the first rank – began to reveal its vocation for proper guidance: its paternal function toward children and the city's citizens. Laocoon, priest of Neptune and brother of Anchises, was the first to advance and then cried out:

"How can you not see the risk? Only a madman takes gifts from the enemy!"

He then hurled a spear against the wooden statue, which resounded with a sinister noise. The Trojans were about to take heed from Laocoon and the fall of Troy would have been avoided. But a new ruse appeared, and foolish, credulous, childish ears were once again ready to be taken in.

A traitor had been left behind on the beach and he asserted that the horse was a votive offering to Minerva, and had been built on so huge a scale to prevent it from being carried through the gates of Troy and bringing benefit to the city's citizens. He himself had escaped the fate of serving as a sacrifice, to be killed in the vicinity of the horse. At the end of his story, two great serpents rise from the sea and throw themselves on Laocoon's sons, devouring the boys and then tearing apart the father who has run to his children's aid. The monsters thus eliminate the last voice that stood in the way of the ruin of Troy, while also seeming to corroborate the traitor's story: Laocoon appears to have been punished by Minerva for offending the sacred horse. The infantile crowd believes what is easiest to believe: the Greeks have fled, the war is over, the horse is the proof of their victory. To bring it into the city, they demolish a portion of its walls. They feast, sing and drink. They retire to bed and post no sentinels.

Aeneas recounts (II, 270–97): *it was still in the first hours of sleep – the sleep for which men are most grateful to the gods, at the end of a long day, and at the conclusion of ten years of war – when suddenly, in a dream, Hector appeared before me: not the glorious Hector whom all remember and whom we had buried, but the Hector crushed by Achilles, disheveled, encrusted with blood, and with tears falling from his eyes. The unexpected image broke my heart, and crying in turn I asked him:*

– From where, and why do you come to me? What is the meaning of this horrible face you bear?

Hector paid no attention to personal questions, but cried out with a moan:

– Flee Aeneas, flee! Everything is in flames. The enemy already sweeps through the streets, Troy drops from the summit of its towers. We already have done enough for King Priam and our fatherland. It is now too late. If it were possible to defend the fortress, I myself would have done so. Flee! Troy must entrust you with its relics and Penates.

After speaking these words, he gave me the figures and the temple's sacred fire. My anguish was far from over. Though our home stood apart, I heard ever nearer cries. Until the pain awoke me. The dream was finished, but not the nightmare. The noise grew louder, but now was a different noise. The noise of Troy in flames.

The Penates and the sacred relics are of greater importance, here, than any of the persons involved. They connect the fathers to the sons, the Greek world to the Roman world, the city which has been destroyed to the city which remains to be founded.

In general, the Penates have no specific names. They are the divinities that govern the house, the city, the home and the state. The nation, indeed, is an extended family. Though Rome's Penates correspond to the house gods of the Greeks, they came to be worshipped much more intensely in Rome, and were seen as expressions of the power of Roman society and the Roman family at their height. Their central position was shored up by the *Aeneid* itself, the poem of the national religion, while making them in turn the guardians of the city's genealogy: they represent the spiritual as well as material survival of Aeneas' descendants.

The Penates' central position was more than metaphorical. The *penus* was the central and most protected place of both the home and the temple: a small altar with statuettes and other images, dedicated to the divinities that protected the family and the nation's citizens. *Penus* is the root of the verb *to penetrate*, of the term *Penates*, and so forth. Aside from its status as an official religion – and as such it might have been practiced simply by virtue of being prescribed by law – this cult also gave expression to a psychological attitude, both profound and deeply felt. The Penates represented the essence of the group to which one belonged, of the family, of the city: of something so intimate and so thoroughly linked to the feelings, rather than to rationality, as to seem undefinable. The Penates, in fact, as said before, have no specific names. They are the tutelary deities of the relationship between the generations, of the truest, most naked, and therefore most concealed expression of their continuity: their worship took place indoors, unexposed to the light of the sun. Wreathed in obscurity – a lack not only of light, but also of clear definitions – the observance of the cult of the Penates intermingled with the worship of the Lares, and as well with the veneration of the eternally burning fire which was voted to the goddess of intimacy (II, 297): the shy virgin known to the Greeks as Hestia, to the Romans as Vesta, and honored by all. These forms of faith involved a devotion to the fathers which was also religious, in addition to civic; and they also involved a sharp separation between male and female tasks. The Penates, moreover, were not only a Roman myth. Hegel, whose thought has profoundly influenced the whole of the modern Western world, saw them as the universal basis of the family.[2]

The Penates were the seed of the continuity of the Roman family: the source of the feeling of deep reserve that permitted the male's elevation to the status of the father. Our wholly prosaic modern languages show us that a parallel regression has today taken place, a lowering of the father to the status of the male. *Penus* and *Penates* are words which have long been forgotten, and their only remaining trace is found in "penis" and "penetration." The collective imagination that speaks through language has ceased to discover the identity of the male in values of family feeling and continuity (Penates), and sees it instead entirely in terms of sex.

As Troy is consumed by flames, and as hordes of people scatter through its streets, emotions too become fiery and collective. Aeneas forgets his role as a father and regresses to the state of the male who lives the life of a warrior:

I madly grasped my sword, aflame with the desire to fight, and to organize resistance. But I could shape no plan. All I desired was the finest of deaths, with my sword in my hand, fighting in defense of my home and its symbols. I ran through the streets which were lit by fires. Panthus, the priest of Apollo, came toward me, holding the Penates and the sacred relics of Troy.

– Panthus! Where is the center of the fray? Where can we throw up our defenses?

– Ah, Aeneas! There is nothing we can now defend. Troy, the Trojans, and all our city's glory are now a thing of the past. Even the gods are leaving Troy.

In the streets I encountered a group of brave young men.

– Do you want to fight at my side in a hopeless battle? The gods have already fled. We stand in defense of an already fallen city. Our daring lies in the lack of all illusions.

They followed me, and we furiously rushed through the streets of the city, bathing them in Greek blood. But the enemy grew ever more numerous. Panthus met his death. I too sought death where the blood flew thickest. Yet death refused to find me. We reached Priam's palace, where the battle was most furious. In our last defense, we threw down our towers on the enemy. The family of the king gathered around the altar, believing this holy place to be able to save their lives.

This was the moment when Achilles' son appeared, Pyrrus (whom Homer called Neottolemus). And this is a warning. Just as the father holds a benediction which is passed along to his descendants, we are here reminded that the non-paternal male is the seat of a malediction that likewise perpetuates itself. Pyrrus is an engine of war and blood, precisely like Achilles. He pursues Poletes, Priam's son, and kills him before his father's eyes. The old king cries out: *May you be damned by all the gods! You have profaned the face of a father, killing his son within his sight. Even ferocious Achilles respected my supplications.*

(More than the murder, the truly intolerable deed is the profanation of the father.)

Pyrrus replies: *Then go to him. Bear him a message: report to my father on all my cruelty. It is time for you to die.*

He drags Priam to the altar, where the king trembles and slips in his son's blood. Pyrrus' sword slashes his body apart.

Aeneas continues: *Then, suddenly, for the first time, my mind shaped a vision of my father, who was Priam's age.*

(Virgil thus picks up a theme from the *Iliad*, where Achilles, on meeting Priam, was reminded of his own father: the appearance of the father in the mind of the son annuls the warrior and imposes a feeling of compassion.)

Where can Anchises be? My wife Creusa, and Ascanius? As though returning to my senses I looked about: my companions were gone, had been slain or had fled or succumbed to the flames.

I ran towards home through the Trojan night. But Helen, who had hidden in the shadows, suddenly stood before me in the light of a flaring flame. So, was this women for whom we all had lost our lives now to return to Greece as a queen? No. There is no glory in killing a woman, but justice must be done. I turned in her direction.

Suddenly Venus, my mother, appeared:

– My son, why do you lose control of yourself, and as well of the time which rapidly escapes you. The gods themselves, Neptune, Juno, Minerva, and even Jove – and here for a moment she dispelled the smoke of the fires and showed them to me – are destroying Troy, not surely the frivolous Helen. Take flight! Rush to the side of your father, save the lives of your family! (II, 589–620).

(Even if this strikes us as the first sensible and loving intervention on the part of Aeneas' mother, it once again derives from self-interest. Unlike the modern reader, the reader in antiquity immediately understood that Aeneas was to ignore Helen since she was living proof of Venus' egoism. Venus, in fact, had purchased the judgment of Paris: to persuade him to declare that she was the most beautiful of the goddesses, she had promised him the love of the most beautiful woman on earth, who was Helen, the wife of a Greek king; and Helen's abduction had launched the war against Troy.)

Then I saw that Troy was collapsing, like a great tree beneath the blades of axes. I breathlessly ran to my house. But my father, whom I wanted first of all to bring to safety, [II, 35–6] *refused.*

– My place is here, in the dead city, since I myself am already dead. Salvation is for you, who are young.

– Father, how can you think that I might depart without you? If you and the gods desire that this be the place of our death, then death remains the only choice. Let me dress again in my armor, to return to battle with the Greeks.

(II, 660: "You and the gods." The will of the father and the will of the gods lie on the same plane. Destiny demands the death of the son at his father's side: Polites beside Priam, Priam at the altar of the fathers, now Aeneas beside Anchises, Ascanius beside Aeneas.)

Creusa grasped my knees and wept:

– Why do you leave your father, your son and your wife, who depend upon you? First of all defend your house! (II, 674–7).

Creusa's words receive sudden, unexpected aid from a sequence of signs: a light shines on Ascanius' hair, followed by a clap of thunder from the left, as a clear sign from Jove. Anchises, an expert in prodigies, cries out:

– The gods speak to us. They ask for the salvation of my grandson, and through him our people. I abandon my resistance! The whole family shall depart!

I threw a lion's skin across my shoulders, knelt down, and begged him:

– Quickly father, sit around my neck. And carry the Penates and the sacred relics: my hands are filthy with blood, I must not touch them.

With the crippled old man on my shoulders, my son holding my hand, my wife to follow at a distance behind me, I went out once again into the flaming streets.

(The scene is the same as before, the streets running with fire and blood. But Aeneas is now a different person; his nature has reversed. Until only a moment before, the clash of arms inspired him. He ran towards the battle and sought it out. The sight of the Greeks was both hateful and joyful. Crossing swords with the enemy offered redemption to a life that finished in nothingness. Aeneas was Achilles. Now, however, every sound of alarm, every gust of wind, advises prudence or retreat (II, 726–9). Aeneas plans and calculates; Aeneas makes his escape. Aeneas is like Hector in flight. What has happened to him? What has become of his strength and audacity? We have watched him oscillate between two duties: the instinctive duty – immediate, individual and Achillean – of doing battle; and the other more complex duty – extended in time, inclusive of his family and servants, and Hectorean – of saving himself. We have seen him split in two, into the male and the father.)

Charged with my burden, I moved out to beyond the gates of Troy, to the craggy temple of Ceres, where I had told the survivors to meet me. Anchises, Ascanius and the Penates were safe. And Creusa? I turned to look back. Creusa had disappeared. In desperation, I once again put on my armor, returning to the city and its alleys, back to our house which once had been serene. I saw nothing but Greeks, counting their spoils, women and children taken as slaves. Careless of risk, I shouted Creusa's name in the streets. And her spirit appeared before me.

*– Do not despair, Aeneas. There is no point to that. You can do no more for
me. My life is gone. Take heart: I will be no prize of war for a Greek. My spirit
will live here in peace, and has the honor to remain in these lands, close to the
goddess Cybele. You are to save our family, Ascanius, and our love for him: you
will one day have another land, and another spouse* (771–88).

She disappeared, leaving me with useless arms and tears.

*The night that protected me was about to vanish into dawn. I hastened out of
the city, to our place of hiding.*

*I encountered many Trojans who had survived and escaped, and who wanted
to follow me. This surprise gave me strength. Behind us, Troy was closed off by
a circle of Greeks. We had no return, no others might join us. Again I lifted my
father onto my shoulders and went off toward the mountains with the ragged
survivors.*

The second and most dramatic book of the *Aeneid* thus reaches its conclusion. We too should halt for a moment and ask ourselves a number of
questions. Why did Aeneas shift back and forth so rapidly, incapable of stop-
ping and standing firm? Why did Virgil endow him with two such distinct
personalities?

The poet wanted to present two temperaments which were at war with one
another even more fiercely than the Greeks and Trojans: two psychological
attitudes, rigorously male, similar to those already described by Homer in the
mortal conflict between Hector and Achilles, and again in Ulysses' internal
oscillation between two irreconcilable modes of being. But in Virgil's tale –
more conscious, more pedagogical, and less fatalistic – we are already able to
descry intentions, and a possibility of choice.

On the one hand, Aeneas is constantly subject to an impulse for combat. It
can grasp him at any moment, due to no external cause. It constitutes his simplest duty, imposed by the values of the time, by the reader's expectations, by
his own internal judge or super-ego. His account of his adventure constantly
reminds us of it, and he nearly begs pardon for remaining alive: he threw himself into the places of greatest danger, but the gods had decided that his hour
had not yet come. It was a battle in the company of the whole of his nation
against all of their common enemies. Friends and adversaries are only occasionally mentioned by name and have no personal relationship with the teller
of the tale. The hero's actions and his encounters with the other – whether
friend or foe – don't constitute parts of a continuum, and instead are confined to the instant. All relationships are horizontal, within the group, or,
indeed, within the horde.

The group, here, isn't to be understood in the pre-anthropological terms
employed by Freud or Engels. It's a question instead of the psychology of
animal behavior. The group of the warriors is reminiscent of the all-male
bands (which we've seen at work in the apes to which we are closest) that
come together to facilitate the search for food and females, but which are
always ready to fly apart when the occasion actually arises, each ready to

challenge the other. Does the comparison seem far-fetched? Yet still we have seen that the epic cycle of the story of Troy is the mythic metaphor of an enormous primordial brawl among males for the possession of Helen, the female.

Unlike Homer, Virgil adhered to an ideology. He wanted to make a contribution to the power of Roman society. He felt – in many ways accurately – that it was destined to extend its power over the whole world. For Virgil, the impulsive group belonged to the past, and the society of responsible fathers to the future. It was the loom on which Rome had decided to weave its cloth, and the axis of its system of laws. So, in the second book of the *Aeneid*, none of the Greeks abandon the condition that makes them a horde, whereas the Trojans, no matter how disarrayed, give birth to a project and arrange themselves in an orderly way around Aeneas.

In addition to feeling the impulse to go out and do battle, Aeneas is also subject to the impulse to save his family and his people. This drive is much more complex than the first. It has something of the quality of Ulysses' project. It's a goal that never grows immediately clear to him. He has to be persuaded by interventions from Hector, from Venus his mother, and from the spirit of Creusa. We have already seen that fatherhood comes into existence by way of the family and society. Aeneas seems constantly to turn his back on this task, always distracted by the immediate duty to enter into combat. It's rather as though seeking salvation required a mode of reasoning which was too abstract for a mind immersed in fire and blood, and therefore in the grips of animal battle. Though the constructive impulse is surely presented as a highly powerful force, it still remains less than definitive, or somehow not yet mature.

The poet has given a description of an evolutionary shift which is no less decisive than incomplete: in the personality of Aeneas (ontogenetically) but also, since Aeneas was the symbol of a new society, in the founders of Rome (phylogenetically).[3]

This is the development in which we're interested, just as it interested Virgil.

Aeneas has to choose. The final moments of the defense have arrived, and time and energy are running out: he must either do battle against the enemy, or save the tribe. The terms of the conflict are irreconcilable: on the one hand stands a duty so simple as to constitute a simple extension of instinct (the instinct which has led young men throughout the ages to volunteer to rush toward death, and which old men find it comfortable to see as the exercise of free choice); and on the other, we have a duty which can only be constructed by fighting against that instinct. In the second case, the immediate satisfaction of impulse is rejected. Effort is channeled into a composite operation which offers immediate gratification only for a mind with an abstract grasp of adherence to project and intentionality. The rest is deferred.

The mind has no natural readiness to function with such complexity. It has to be prepared by listening to a variety of voices. Aeneas has to hear the words of his mother, of his father, of his wife Creusa, of the ideal model which he sees in Hector. (Whether it's a question of real people or of various interior authorities is of little importance.) Since intention isn't rooted in instinct, it offers no immediate sense of security. Aeneas' feelings when lifting his spear and when lifting his aged father cannot be compared to one another. The first is simple and gratifying. The second depends on the achievement of an act of understanding, by plumbing the depths of the mind. It's only within the mind that the adolescent, horizontal strength of the warrior can mature into the vertical strength of the fathers.

Horizontality is the typical quality of the fighting spirit of the peers in the group of the young lions whose steps stride lightly since they know no weight of responsibility. All of them are handsome and glorious, but none of them is himself; each of them while standing still is the group, and the horde while in running attack. Verticality is found in the force of the tree as it strains up into the sky and sinks down its roots into the earth. The pressure of his father on Aeneas' shoulders is vertical. Verticality is found in the need for understanding which led him to decide to carry that weight. The only thing left of the young lion – of the youthful spirit of combat – is its skin: the symbolic cushion for the burden which the adult has chosen to bear. The son's shoulders support the father who no longer can carry himself. Both of them have the instinct of survival, but only one of them has the strength that makes survival possible. Implicitly, the vertical bond is also hierarchical, and the bearing of the burden brings the compensation of an elevation. Bearing the weight of the other grows out of an awareness of difference and complementarity: it brings about clear liberation from the state of dispersion experienced in the group of the youths, where equality and anonymity are synonymous.

Aeneas the young lion has expired. But Aeneas the man doesn't fall into the gulf, and instead rises to his feet again, taking his place in the chain of the fathers. Anchises above him, his son Ascanius below. The three of them constitute a genealogical tree that makes its way into the future. They are united by the transmission of fatherhood from one generation to the next. They have been united by seed and by birth, which have found their passage through the body of Aeneas. While fleeing from death they are again united by a process of rebirth, by way of Aeneas' hands, which lend their support to both the following and preceding generation.

The image of Aeneas in flight with his father and his son is the central link in the chain of the fathers that held society together. Very few images have ever been so thoroughly charged with a program (Fig. 1).

For ancient Rome, the arms of the hero who had founded the city – the right arm that guides Ascanius, the left arm that steadies Anchises on his shoulders – were symbols of the highest ideals, much as Christians see the open arms of Christ. Statutes, paintings, mosaics and coins (dating back to as far as the sixth century BC, when Rome had just been born and Virgil was still half a millennium away) reveal this image to have been one of the figures

Figure 1 Escape of Aeneas from Troy (photography archives of the Ministry of Culture, Rome).

most frequently employed in antiquity.[4] Augustus, who commissioned the *Aeneid* and consolidated the triumph of the Roman patriarchy, ordered the erection at the center of the Roman Forum of precisely such a statue of Aeneas, in flight with his father and his son.

Why does the apotheosis of the founding hero show him in flight? The answer is clear if we shift our attention away from the story's literal meaning and look instead at the underlying symbolism which excited the interest of both Virgil and Augustus.

The decisive struggle isn't to be found in the brief, circumstantial conflict between Greeks and Trojans (who starting in Book VIII of the *Aeneid* are even allied with one another). It lies instead in the millenary and still undecided conflict between two psychic structures, as found, on one hand, in the male of the horde, and, on the other, in the male who assumes individual responsibility, which is to speak of the male that Roman society wanted to incarnate in the fathers.

The course that Aeneas most truly follows is not the voyage from Troy toward the founding of Rome (which, as we'll see, is of a circular nature, with the voyage returning to its point of departure). It's the question, instead, of forever taking leave of the flames – not only the fiery destruction of Troy, but also the ardent impulses of the horizontal group of the youths – for the purpose of founding non-reversible and vertical commitments, such as genealogy.

Aeneas' generosity was a fortress protected by the walls of his piety. And in the course of their arduous flight, he showed it toward his father, and as a father, with the same daily constancy with which he showed it to the gods. The ancient Mediterranean peoples – not only the Romans – saw these virtues as fundamental. Another legend which was widely diffused in antiquity – Virgil can be imagined to have ignored it since it reduced the heroism of the beginnings of Aeneas' voyage – tells us that Aeneas was seen by the Greeks as he fled with his father and son. They were said to have been so impressed that, even though drunk on victory and the spoils of war, they allowed him alone of the Trojans to escape: indeed, they even permitted him to take his riches with him.[5] Such an episode would count as unique in the history of ancient sackings, and as such reveals the intensity of the classical world's respect for the virtues the scene embodies.

The *Aeneid* has been seen, from its very start, to sketch out the program of Roman society. In doing so, it gives us not only the figure of the father on which that society was grounded, but also a complementary female figure, destined to confirm his role.

Even before addressing the poem, the public was fully aware of its protagonist's origins: his mother, yes, was divine, but utterly alien to any commitment to motherhood. As such, she was precisely the opposite of Anchises, whose assumption of responsibility for Aeneas dated back to what we call the age of latency, and with whom we understand his son's relationship to be much more solid than the fortress of Troy.

The female figures in the *Aeneid* are sharply divided: one group immediately arouses suspicion, whereas those of the other play roles in total support of the males, free of all hint of competing with them.

The beginning of the work is dominated by Juno. In Greek and Roman mythology she is one of the personages who are closest to those of the precedent cultures of the Great Mother Goddess, but here she shows only the devouring, infernal and destructive side of her power. She is in radical conflict with Jove, her spouse, who decrees Aeneas' shining destiny and surveys its realization from above. The king of the gods has lost the adolescent traits that he shows in Greek mythology. He has become more paternal, and ever more clearly differentiated from his female counterpart. Juno, on the other hand, is a degradation of the archetype of woman-as-mother, just as Venus, who is wholly extraneous to motherhood, debases the archetype of woman-as-lover.

We might expect the central female figure to be the protagonist's wife. Creusa is described quite rapidly, but we hear enough to intuit the presence of a woman with a voice of her own, and with complex feelings. But this also means that she might in some way condition Aeneas, the evangelist of the purity of the patriarchy. So, in all the numerous representations of Aeneas in flight with his father and son, it's inevitable for Creusa to be absent, or to appear as a figure that follows behind them (or who even seems to impede their flight).[6] It's also logical for her death to come immediately, at the very beginning of the poem: her function is to voice the demand that Aeneas turn his efforts entirely to the defense of the family, abandoning the fervor of his adolescent impulse to rush to all fronts; and once having done so, she's to offer no obstacle to the further course of destiny, which decrees that the hero is to undertake other adventures and to marry a new and utterly subservient wife.

The figure of the woman is simplified. She isn't allowed the complexity which opens the road to an individual personality. In contrast to the dangerous figures of Juno and Venus, attention is also drawn to two positive female deities who are equally one-sided. It's symbolically significant that they live in the heights, above the city of Troy. That's where we find the ancient temple of Ceres, the goddess of the harvests and a generous mother who has no terrible side. Still higher, on Mount Ida, is the seat of the goddess Cybele, another good mother, who offers a permanent home to Creusa, freeing Aeneas to pursue a new and different life.

The pious, generous father is almost schematically juxtaposed to pernicious or untrustworthy mothers, and the comparison is part of Virgil's implicit program for the civic structure of Roman life. Males are exhorted to develop a complex, individual personality: such men will bear responsibility for the family and the people as a whole. Women, quite to the contrary, are only permitted to be useful and generous, and will otherwise be harmful and destructive: they are condemned to a lack of profundity, which is no less problematic than outright subordination. In comparison with Greece, Rome allowed women more rights. But it vetoed all broader understanding of the psychology of female figures.

The voyage of the fathers grows ever more energetic as Aeneas proceeds along his course in search of his new land: as Virgil saw it, the advance of the Trojan ships was the advance of a new society.

In Book III, the fleet is still led by Anchises. The elder patriarch makes the decisions as to when sails should be raised and sets the ships' course up until his death. But Aeneas is responsible, surprisingly enough, for determining the general direction in which they move. Still, however, his contribution to the progress of the voyage remains indirect and passive.

"Seek out the ancient mother," had said the voice of the god Apollo (III, 96). His prophecy had promised that the Trojans would discover their new land in precisely the place from which Troy's original founders had departed, in highly ancient times. This theme is at once both poetic and psychological, involving the whole of the tribe in the *nostos* – the archetype of difficult, intensely desired return – which characterizes the adventures of Ulysses, Agamemnon and the other major heroes. Anchises believes, on the basis of historical memory, that this place of origin must have been in Crete. So, it's here that the voyagers disembark to construct a new Troy.

Aeneas, however, has a dream. He dreams of the Penates and the sacred relics which the dying, blood-smeared Hector entrusted to him, and which accompany the voyaging exiles. Anchises, as the patriarch, interprets the dream; and since he is obedient to the will of the gods, he recognizes their voice, and sees that it speaks through the visions of his son. The unconscious, archetypal mind of Aeneas is more powerful than the conscious, historical mind of Anchises. This is not the place of the ancient – and new – homeland. They are to travel further westward, all the way to the land which the Greeks called Esperia, or Italy. This, in the most ancient of times, was the place from which Dardanus had departed, the ancestral father of the Trojans. There they will find the city of Corythum.

Aeneas has once again revealed his nature as a prophet and a dreamer. And, as is often the case with visionaries, his emotions strike us as impassioned, but he remains incapable of transforming them into acts of will. Aeneas is completed by his father: Anchises' memory of history is inferior in power to Aeneas' vision, but the old man holds his place at the head of the hierarchy because he's capable of transforming vision into facts.

Corythum is the ancient name of the Tuscan city of Cortona. Virgil places this image in Aeneas' dream since the cult of the founding fathers and the "ancient mother" was for him a true religion. He intensely explored its depths and charged its symbols with complex meanings. Corythum was an Etruscan city, like Mantua, the city where Virgil was born and in which he took such pride, since the Etruscans were an extremely ancient people whom the Romans had assimilated but never canceled out. He was also aware of the legend that the Etruscans had come from the Orient, from Lydia, a land that bordered on the region of Troy and was partly incorporated into it. So the peoples involved were endlessly moving in a circle; destinations and origins repeatedly coincided; the chain of the fathers was the terrestrial expression of something eternal and divine.

This cult, which finds its sacred model in Aeneas, but which clearly came from Virgil, is of particular pertinence to our subject. It takes the form of a religion of descendants who turn their gaze intensely toward those who came before them, or toward the maternal and paternal archetypes. But whereas the chain of the fathers consists of real people who little by little, along its backwards course, become more mythical, until turning into links between the human and the divine, the maternal line is entirely different. It presents us with a rupture rather than a continuity: one immediately encounters a goddess who is concerned with herself alone, or an ancient mother who lacks all personification in figures of real women. The paternal side of the cult expresses devotion towards real fathers. The maternal side is a void.

The endless voyage resumes. Along the coast of the Ionian sea, a stop at the Strophades provides the Trojans with abundant cattle. They prepare offerings to the gods and copious banquets. The Mediterranean seems once again to have become the Great Mother who offers constant nourishment. Female deities appear. But they are the Harpies: women down to their breasts, but rapacious birds below, and with manners that are even more rapacious. The Harpies, always hungry, steal and devour the food. Instead of nourishment, their bodies continually produce its opposite: excrement that makes the air unbreathable, and inedible whatever they have not stolen. They scream a prophecy of hunger at the Trojans. Anchises gives the order to flee from these mothers that spew out famine rather than food, and invokes a benediction from the gods.

The old man continues to guide the ships. But males can also be something other than good fathers who drive away devouring mothers. As Homer had told the Greeks, this was something of which Virgil wanted to remind the Romans. Hidden in the grottos, beyond the sphere of daily life and civilized custom, there still survives a non-paternal and non-redeemable male personality, armed with claws and ready to strike. This backdrop to the *Aeneid* (III, 561–692) is identical to that of the *Odyssey*, which is older by at least six centuries and based, in turn, on a series of tales which were countless centuries older. The duplex nature of the male is an archetype, and as such reappears unchanged in differing places and epochs.

The scene is in Sicily on the flanks of Mount Etna, a place of volcanic fire that spills upwards from the bowels of the earth: an image of visceral impulse that erupts directly into facts and actions, never showing itself to the sky, never passing through the light of day, never exposing itself to the scrutiny of reason or the gaze of the gods. After landing on these beaches, the Trojans encounter a creature so miserable as virtually to have ceased to be human:

Achemenides, a Greek in the company of Ulysses up until the time of the adventure in the cave of Polyphemus. In the haste of their flight, his companions had departed without him. He has ever since led a horrid life, nourishing himself on roots and seeds, and attempting to remain beyond the reach of the blind, groping monster and his hunger for human flesh. Rather than continue to live this life, he prefers to surrender to the Trojan enemies, who may very well put him to death for his part in their city's devastation. But Aeneas takes him in, since a man of piety responds with generosity to suppliants.

These, as least, are the words of the myth. But we can also imagine that Aeneas spares Achemenides as a service to Virgil, who wanted to make a point: he's telling us that the final and decisive battle has nothing to do with Greeks and Trojans and is waged instead between the bestial male and the spirit of paternal piety. Males – whether Roman or barbarian, Greek or Trojan – have to flee from the monstrous adolescent that lives on impulse, unreservedly committing themselves to the father. The father is the shore to which history has to navigate. The infinitely extended voyage – the symbol of a never-completed effort – allows no compromise.

This is the point at which the patriarch dies. Book III closes with Anchises' death.

Book IV tells one of the most momentous love stories ever recorded. If it were anything other than that, Virgil – a poet of the feelings more than of battles – wouldn't have lent it attention. And we, in turn, would have little reason to discuss it. It shows us that even while bowing to the will of the heavens, to the gods, and to destiny, earthly events have an autonomy all their own: and here on earth, faced with Dido, Aeneas makes no display of either courage or generosity.

As night dissolved into dawn, Aeneas had completed his tale; and Dido, while listening, had fallen in love.

Dido is a young widow who had promised to relinquish love, which her dead husband carried off with him. A queen who wields command and the sword, and a woman who delicately receives her guest and passionately loves her companion, Dido is a person who is charged with oscillations, and at least as complex as Aeneas. In the following days, her mind is full of torment. Anna, her sister and confidant, has fewer doubts: why should Dido forever relinquish affection, children and the political advantages of a union with the Trojans? Why make do as a woman alone, in the even greater solitude of the head of a state surrounded by hostile peoples? It is more than a question of constructing a project for the course of her life, as perhaps a man might feel the need to do: a powerful passion has entered Dido's heart. Anna has understood.

The *Aeneid* shows the queen's state of mind to grow ever more excited and febrile. Absorbed in love, she neglects the business of state. Her sister, moreover, isn't the only force that prods her on. Venus fills Dido's fantasies with the memory of Ascanius, so sweet and so similar to his father. Virgil himself is moved while observing the intensity of her womanly feelings. But the patriarchal myths and institutions have already decided how things will work out. The poet treats the story as given fact and makes no attempt to correct the injustice that befalls the queen. Dido is sincere, human and passionate; but the *Aeneid* recounts that she is also possessed. Persons overwhelmed by a passion and by the gods who conceal themselves behind it were considered by the ancients to be "in guilt." Such persons precipitate into tragedy, even in the lack, from our point of view, of evil intentions that merit punishment.

Virgil's description of Dido as she embraces Ascanius (I, 657 ff., 717 ff.; IV, 84–5) allows us to understand that the Roman father's love for his child does not stop with "never leaving the mind at rest." It also sees itself as superior to all other emotions and refuses to be placed on the same level as the love of the mother. The woman's feelings are the fruit of no act of will, no conscious intention, no chosen project. Even caring for her child is a further expression of instinct and passion. Maternal love, as we see it in this episode, can't be distinguished from erotic possession. It's a question of a single, uncontrollable impulse. If the child and the lover are drawn together in a single figure, the feelings involved are themselves a single feeling. Ascanius is a child who intensely resembles his father; and Dido therefore loves him, with no possible distinction to be drawn between maternal affection and erotic passion. The love of a father, as Virgil seems to insist, is a highly different thing, capable of control and of drawing distinctions. Can we imagine a man who grows enflamed with passion because the daughter of the woman he loves sits on his knees? The ancient world would have found such a thing ridiculous. The modern world would find it perverse.

Juno and Venus, in the meantime, vie with one another in the debasement of the dignity of the gods, no less than of human feelings. Juno pretends to desire the marriage of Aeneas and Dido; Venus pretends to believe her and to give consent. Virgil presents the myth in ways that make it seem that the queen's terrible delusion has less to do with Aeneas than with a passionate, capricious female principle. Working together, the two goddesses unleash a storm from which Dido and Aeneas both find refuge in the same cave; by the time they leave it, the queen will have abandoned her fidelity to her dead spouse. She herself adds another moment of feminine guilt to the plot, immediately announcing, without sufficient forethought, that her marriage with Aeneas has been decided.

Father Jove, however, has observed this sequel of caprices and reminds Aeneas of his duty to continue his voyage (IV, 219–78). Anchises, Aeneas' earthly father, then appears in a dream and repeats the warning (IV, 351). Our modern minds can only be amazed by the way in which duty and destiny here coincide with one another. Aeneas has a moral duty not only to his children, but also to descendants who lie in the distant future, not yet born, but *destined* to be born.

Aeneas, suddenly, is once again overwhelmed by doubts. But it's not that he's tempted to remain in Carthage: his anguish revolves around how and when to tell Dido of his decision to depart. In the light of the rectitude and moral consistency usually shown by Aeneas, the drama is exaggerated. Even if indirectly, Virgil is showing us the shadow side of the just and steadfast father. If we take the tale literally, we wonder where the hero who so much fears being scolded by a woman has mislaid his virility. But if we look at it psychologically, we see that the queen's passion can't be understood as alien to the protagonist's psyche; it's also part of his own make-up, and his unconscious mind immediately intuits its dramatic importance. But his way of relating to passion lies in having to reject it.

Dido too holds an image of a descendant in her mind: a future son whom Aeneas might father, and who would totally resemble him[7] (as in a contemporary poem by Catullus, we here see an indirect return of the Greek idea that only the father is consanguineous with the child). But it is also clear that the *Aeneid* doesn't consider these two notions of posterity to lie on the same plane. Aeneas' commitment is grounded in his duties as a founding father, and he bears responsibility to the whole of his society; Dido's hopes rest only on maternal longings and derive from instinct, and as such concern only herself.

Virgil reminds us that love cannot be duped. Dido in fact perceives that the Trojans are preparing to depart. She confronts and reproves Aeneas. She runs away, and reproves herself. She attempts a reconciliation; she attempts to delay the departure. She begins to go mad and voices ever more atrocious accusations. She is sorry not to have murdered her lover and dismembered his body, scattering his limbs across the land, sorry not to have quartered Ascanius and served him to his father as food. She swears eternal hatred to Aeneas and all his descendants, which historians will see as a prophecy of the future wars between Rome and Carthage, but which we can see as a symbol of the enmity between the paternal and maternal worlds, psychologically split apart from one another. And as the wind fills the sails of Aeneas' ships, she throws herself on a sword at the top of a great pyre which she has already seen to preparing for herself, so that even at a distance the Trojans will see it.

In Book V, the voyage continues. Having gone ashore in Sicily on account of unfavorable seas, the Trojans organize games in celebration of the anniversary of Anchises' death. Ascanius has grown, and greatly distinguishes himself: he approaches his father, and the father of his father.

But the ancient world was two worlds. The Trojan women celebrate the anniversary on another beach, apart from the men. They wail, and hope to find a homeland. The terrible Juno doesn't miss the opportunity to work against Aeneas. She summons the goddess Iris and orders her to assume the appearance of a Trojan woman. Iris descends to the beach and seeds dissent among the women.

"Women," she cries "we have traveled now for seven years from one land to another. Have we carried the Penates from Troy only to drag them across the seas? Why can't the new Troy arise right here? Why does the new Troy never arise? Take up these torches!" (V, 618 ff.). And she herself grasped a firebrand.

The Trojan women hesitate. Then, on realizing that a goddess has spoken, they grow excited. The beach teems with obsessed women. They are reminiscent of the ancient bacchantes: but erotic passion for men has here turned into hatred. Howls accompany the torches which the women throw onto the ships: the wooden bodies of a paternal program which is too complex and uncompromising. Hulls begin to go up in flames.

The chain of the fathers must immediately set itself into motion to extinguish the fires of impatience and to reassert the meaning of destiny and project. This time, its action departs from the youngest. Ascanius sees the flames from a distance and is the first to rush to put them out. "Wretched women, here you burn no Greeks, but your own hopes" (V, 670 ff.). Aeneas prays to Jove: "Father, if we still remain dear to you, give us a sign; otherwise, destroy us!" The leader stands on the verge of the loss of both hope and authority. But the celestial father stands firm and summons a rain that douses the flames, both of the fire and of overheated spirits. Most of the ships are saved.

The voyagers have grazed the danger of an irreversible rupture: never before has the distance between the fathers and the mothers been so great. The myth is aware of the danger and excogitates a compromise. Anchises appears to his son in a dream, suggesting that those who desire to construct a city on this site, traveling no further, be allowed to do so. Only Aeneas and the most courageous continue the voyage.

In Book VI, Aeneas keeps his appointment with the world of the dead. He is to visit Anchises and gather his instruction on the voyage. But among the spirits of the dead, he can't avoid an encounter with the spirit of Dido as well. Overwhelmed by feelings of guilt, Aeneas attempts to speak with her. The queen recedes without a word. Even after death, the enmity between their worlds remains complete.

An analysis of the condition that Virgil and the Romans attributed to the dead lies beyond the scope of our discussion, and it's not much different from that of the Greeks. We are interested, however, in understanding that the visit to Anchises and the netherworld itself are metaphysical expressions of the chain of the fathers. Anchises' spirit is indispensable for the completion of the voyage and its program. The voyage moves first of all through genealogical rather than geographic spaces. The old man gives no indication to his still living son on the next ports of call; he shows him the souls which in future centuries are to find incarnation as important Roman figures.

For 130 lines, the *Aeneid* lists the descendants who will render Aeneas' tribe illustrious. And, by now, we won't be surprised to discover that none of them are women.

We thus reach the end of the first half of the poem: the six books dedicated to the voyage. Virgil's intention was to craft a single work that would bring back to life, in current and Roman terms, the two unsurpassed Greek poems: the *Iliad* and the *Odyssey*. The first part of the *Aeneid* constitutes Aeneas' "Odyssey." In the following books, the seventh through the twelfth, the hero has landed in Latium, where the Trojans fight a deadly war, instigated by Juno, with the indigenous populations: the second part of the *Aeneid* can be considered an "Iliad" on Italian soil.

Given its more military spirit, the second part of the *Aeneid* contains fewer references than the first to the myth of the Roman father. We can nonetheless turn our attention to a number of passages.

Here again on the example of the *Iliad*, one of the central motivations for the battle is a woman for whom the men combat. King Latinus has lost his sons. In this land which was traditionally in the power of the Great Mother, Latinus is the symbol of the precarious state of the patriarchy, which to shore itself up awaits the arrival from the Orient of the patriarchal Aeneas. His only heir is the gentle Lavinia: a princess who smiles, cries and blushes, but who never speaks. From a psychological point of view, she's a bit too gentle and remissive, and without – in contrast to Dido – a temperament of her own: rather than a real woman she is a woman-object created by the male fantasy that holds the rudder of the poem and bends the myth it relates to its own purposes. Both the society and the psychology of the individual demanded that the female offer no surprises.

Turnus, king of the Rutulians, wants to marry Lavinia and unite their two kingdoms. A prophecy, however, has told King Latinus to await the arrival of a foreigner. Latinus is a benevolent personage and the reception he offers Aeneas allows the reader immediately to understand that he is preparing to accept him as a son-in-law. An old and benevolent father, a younger and war-like but pious father, and a princess who is always silent and obedient: the premises for the beginning of the Roman patriarchy.

But the times are not yet right, since first the terrible mothers must be confronted. Juno (VII, 293 ff.) sends the Fury Allecto to the earth: in the form of a serpent, she enters the heart of queen Amata, Lavinia's mother, and enflames her with hatred for Aeneas. Amata is a calculating woman: she rejects Aeneas, a landless exile, and prefers Turnus, the king of a solid realm. Then the Fury flies to Turnus, enflaming him as well. The *Aeneid* grasps every opportunity to make it clear that father and mother are enemies: even those of Lavinia, even in the same family. Everything good is paternal, everything malignant is maternal.

In short, a mortal war breaks out between the Trojans and the Italic allies.

The Trojans are inferior in number and are set under siege by Turnus. The situation grows desperate: while the Trojans are entrenched in the battlefield, the Rutulians set fire to their ships, at anchor in the river. But those ships are still trunks of the trees of Mount Ida, and sacred to Cybele. The ancient Mother Goddess refuses to accept their ruin and transforms them into nymphs, who swim freely away. So, the Trojans, when necessary, can still count on the goddess whose woods helped them to construct their ships – a goddess who is one-sidedly good, and deferential to Aeneas – and also on the females hidden in nature – the nymphs – who brought him up as a child.

Aeneas meanwhile has managed to forge an alliance with Evander, the king of a nearby Greek colony, who sends Pallas, his son, with reinforcements. But the war continues, the fight is hard, and the outcome remains uncertain. Pallas is killed by Turnus (X, 480 ff.). Here once again we see Aeneas' penchant for melancholy and his elevated sense of duty: he feels himself to be guilty for the death of Pallas, just as before he had held himself responsible for the death of Dido.

Of all the forces allied with Turnus, the most dangerous are the Amazons, the mythical female warriors (known to the Greeks as the *antianeirai*, which translates as "equal to the men" and also as "enemies of the men": a meaningful ambiguity, since two quite different concepts are the seat of an identical fear of independent femininity). Their leader is the invincible Camilla.

But Camilla too falls victim to a banal caprice. Her death doesn't come from a hero, but from an equally superficial warrior. For the male psychology of the *Aeneid*, her weakness corresponds to a kind of crack in the personality of the warrior: a crack that allows the emergence of female vanity. Camilla pursues a warrior whose arms and ornaments are gilded: she wants them as a trophy. She pays no attention to her own position in the fray, leaves her flank uncovered, and doesn't hear the whistle of a spear until it passes through her breast (XI, 777 ff.).

A revelatory episode. For the mentality of the *Aeneid*, there's a grave danger in the woman who has too much strength, and, symbolically, in an overly powerful femininity in the psyche of the male. Both of these dangers – the external as well as internal danger – have to be eliminated by bending oneself to the superior rationality of the patriarchal mind, and to its ability for obedience to a project. The female mind, on the other hand, loses sight of the whole and of the final goal: it has the butterfly quality of always flitting to the nearest flower.

In the finale of the poem, the Trojan and Rutulian armies are both held in check. Everything depends on a personal duel between Aeneas and Turnus. The duel has various, alternating phases, since Juno and Turnus' sister intervene unfairly. Finally, the Rutulian prince lies on the ground, and Aeneas' sword hovers above him. Turnus begs to be spared: "Think of the pain of my father, who might be yours" (XII, 930 ff.). We have already seen in the *Iliad* that the memory of the fathers evokes a feeling to which one cannot say no.

The pious Aeneas, respectful of suppliants, stops his blade. He looks at the vanquished warrior and begins to feel pity. Suddenly, he sees the belt of the dead Pallas, now worn by Turnus as a trophy. His thoughts turn from Turnus' father to Pallas'. His fury returns, and his sword descends. There can be no compromise in cutting good away from evil. He was about to spare Turnus in memory of a father; he kills him in memory of another father.

As the *Aeneid* concludes, it strived decisively, with its solar paternal program, into the world of clear and distinct categories. Troy's Penates have found their new home. The epic struggle between the opposing forms of masculinity – paternal and non-paternal – seems to reach its conclusion with the *Aeneid*. This time around, the constancy of Hector has defeated Achilles. True and proper epic also reaches its conclusion with the *Aeneid*, since it brings us to the end of the grandiose, profound and tragic polyvalence of Greek myth and opens the road to just but abstract institutions, of which the system of Roman law is a cornerstone.

While separating good from evil, the conclusion of the *Aeneid* does the same with the worlds of the fathers and the mothers. Every form of femininity endowed with personality, like Dido, or with independence, like the Amazons, has been expunged in the course of the poem. The only good mother who survives to its end is Cybele: a willing instrument in the hands of the fathers. She is an object: the wood they bend to their will and their needs. A means – of transportation, and not only of transportation – which Aeneas has brought along with him while leaving his fatherland.

Jove, the father of the gods, and king Latinus have collaborated in the undertaking. Juno, the mother of the gods, has shown opposition with a dogged ferocity that finally – in the passage where Queen Amata and the Fury Allecto are extensions of her hatred – assumes infernal tones.

Such a radical array of triumphant paternal psychology, totally victorious over maternal psychology, could not last. The *Aeneid* is conscious of this, and closes with a compromise. Juno will collaborate in making Aeneas' descendants great, and Jove will allow the defeated Latins, whom Juno defended, to preserve their name and identity as a people. A definitive rupture is avoided both in the heavens and on earth.

Here we find a harbinger of the Roman politics of inclusion. And it's a question, indeed, of a wholly political stratagem. Forced into a few dozen lines at the end of the lengthy poem, it appears artificial. This isn't, however, to say that it isn't credible: in part it was to find its realization. It does, however, have the quality of an abstract intention. It describes nothing profound and is destined to remain artificial, like all compromises on the part of hegemonic power.

A part of the policy of inclusion will be successful and will find expression in the best aspects of Rome: rather than canceled out, defeated peoples will be gradually assimilated. The other part – the part with which we are not concerned – will not be successful. The Great Mother goddess will continue to be oppressed by victorious Jove, and in following centuries by the monotheistic God the Father who will begin to take his place. The female divinities who were worshipped by the Romans pay for that respect with the repression of the principal aspects of the original Great Mother. And though in fact she remained a presence in the minds of the people, she was primarily seen in the company of evil and associated with superstitious fears of regressions that run counter to the course of history.

The Western world has always attempted to avoid the need to come to terms with this profound part of its mythology. The patriarchal consciousness that shapes the culture was to continue to treat the feminine in general and the maternal in particular with the growing simplification that we have seen in the *Aeneid*. A resplendent mother, for as long as light holds sway. A demonic mother, as soon as shadows fall. Beyond all religious or poetic considerations, the figures of Maria and the angelic woman of the *Dolce Stil Novo* became a part of this effort in the simplification of femininity. It thus became inevitable to live in terror of the repressed, infernal female side of things. Witches were to burn on pyres throughout the Middle Ages. And many centuries later, the archetype of female evil was to dominate Mozart's *Magic Flute* in the form of the Queen of the Night.

NOTES

1 Zoja (1995).
2 Hegel, G. W. F. (1821) *Grundlinien der Philosophie des Rechts*, §§ 163, 166, 173, 257.
3 See Derick Williams, R. (1982) "*The Aeneid*," in Kenney, E. J. and Clausen, W. V. (eds), *Cambridge History of Classical Literature*, Vol. II, Book 3, Cambridge, New York and Melbourne: Cambridge University Press, p. 39: "the values of the Augustan world are foreshadowed as Aeneas learns to leave the Trojan world of heroic and impetuous daring and inaugurate the Roman world of *forethought, duty, responsibility (pietas)*" (my italics).
4 See Roscher, W. H. (1884–1937) *Ausfürhliches Lexikon der griechischen und römischen Mythologie*. Reprinted Hildesheim: Olms, 1978, where the simple list of the principal representations occupies three pages, from p. 184 to p. 186.
5 Ibid., p. 164.
6 Ibid., pp. 184, 67.
7 Catullus, 61.

Part III

Towards modern times and decadence

Chapter 13

From the Roman father, to the Son, to the French Revolution

> God hath sent forth the Spirit of his Son into your hearts, crying, Abba, Father. Wherefore thou art no more a servant, but a son . . .
>
> Galatians 4: 6–7

In the centuries of its greatest achievements, which laid the base for the future of European civilization, Rome absorbed as much Greek culture as it could, and the Roman father was another of its continuations. The horizon of Roman mythology lay in Greece, as we have seen with the *Aeneid*. Rome, indeed, wrote the continuation of Greek mythology, just as Christianity added the New Testament to the sacred scriptures of the Jews. It amplified Greece into a vast and complex society, pulling it into a framework of systematic jurisprudence: such things had never been seen before, and in a certain sense were not until recently to be seen again.

Generalizations on the Roman world are hazardous, since it extended across much more than 1000 years and three continents. It is nonetheless clear that the Roman father was the pillar that established and maintained order, both public and private, and as such was quite different from the Greek father, who was relatively absent from the life of his family. The Roman father had the power of life and death over his children, not only until they came of age, but throughout their lives. Only at death did the father relinquish this extraordinary power. It was in the Roman world that the father reached the apex of his authority over his children, though not necessarily over his wife.

Rome's power and complexity are also mirrored by the Roman father figure. Fatherhood was clearly defined in both social and legal terms. One didn't become a father on the basis of biological circumstance, but by virtue of a formal act. Paternity didn't reside in having conceived a child with a woman, but in signaling the desire to be a father: the father publicly raised his son into the air (with a daughter he simply ordered that she be fed) to indicate his assumption of responsibility. Unlike the Greek father, he was also his child's teacher. In this sense, in Rome, all "true" fatherhood was an adoption, whereas simple biological fatherhood did not count.

This father who reveals himself by lifting his son to the skies repeats and continues the gesture that found its formulation with Hector. The importance of this gesture lies not only in the traces it has left on law, and it does not belong exclusively to antiquity. It stands outside of time, and towers above all institutions.

The legal obligation to feed one's offspring wasn't introduced until the second century AD, at a time when mores had grown confused and divorces and illegitimate children abounded.[1] The reform, however, didn't touch the question of recognition and afforded only this minimum of social assistance. It also cut both ways, linking rights to duties: children too became legally obliged to feed their parents. And little by little, enlarging the scope of duties and responsibilities, the obligation was extended to an ever more ample circle of relatives.

The *pater* thus came to be flanked by the *nutritor*, but the functions of the latter were only technical. Whereas the father embodied the collective imagination's most authoritative archetype, the new figure of the *nutritor* was thoroughly abstract and of little psychological significance; the authorities, in fact, were frequently obliged to restate and clarify his duties. So the man whose only connection with his children is the legal obligation to feed them is nothing new: in Rome, as today, it was a partial remedy for a point of weakness in the family. A man was no longer licensed to show complete disinterest in his children. But nothing obliged him to declare himself their *pater*. And fatherhood – not parenthood – remained the important issue. In order to be a father, it was not enough to be a parent, as a participant in the occurrence of a natural event. One had to perform a specific act, actively declaring the will and intention to *become* the father of the child: just as adoption, in our own society, is an act of will.

In Roman law, the event that establishes every single, personal instance of fatherhood is a clear reiteration of what our reconstruction has seen as the beginning in prehistoric times of all human paternity: the act, no matter how simple, but more than simply physical, that signals the male's intention to establish a stable relationship with his children, in addition to having conceived them. We are looking, indeed, at something more than the laws that regulated the Roman family. It's significant that the norm to which we're lending attention was no abstract and arbitrary rule, but a somehow effortless repetition of the prehistoric genesis of the family. The diffusion and durability of Roman family law should themselves be seen as due not solely to Rome's political and military power, but first of all to its reproduction of the highly ancient images that led the human being from animal life to the monogamic family.

The evolution of Roman law was marked by a progressive creation of paternal duties that went hand in hand with the enormous expansion of paternal rights,[2] implying as well an unlimited capacity for love: to the point, finally, of turning the father into a taller, stronger and more monolithic figure than at any other point in history. We see this clearly in Catullus, the lyric voice of Rome's most glorious epoch. To express the intensity of his adoration for the woman he loved, he wrote that he loved her "not as men love lovers, but as a father loves his children" (Catullus 72). The father's love, however, was always a question of freely exercised choice. Our own frame of mind is likely, here, to find a touch of absurdity. If the blood relationship between father and child was felt to be the strongest of the bonds that hold human beings together, the only indestructible bond, what meaning may have lain in the father's right to question it? But from the Roman point of view, this prerogative was a necessary consequence of the father's unquestionable authority.

Since Roman jurisprudence has penetrated into modern times to an extent unequaled by any of the other of antiquity's bodies of law, it's easy to assume that our collective unconscious has continued for millennia to associate this faculty of choice with its image of the father. This is clearly not without consequences.

Suspicere. To hold aloft. This verb was enormously important since the physical act of briefly holding a child aloft meant to elevate that child to a higher social and moral plane: permanently, from birth to death. This father had that choice: whether or not to give his child the gift of social and moral life, which differs highly from the initial gift of physical life received from the mother. All children received the first gift, but not necessarily the second. This model contained a fundamental intuition.

Any child whom the father, at his own discretion, did not choose to elevate, fell into a place outside of the precincts of fatherhood. Our own society finds such an exclusion of guiltless human lives intolerable, since it recognizes a series of birth rights to everyone; but at the time it ran parallel to the logic that decreed that many, equally guiltless, were even born to be slaves. Birth conferred no rights: rights were conferred by those who possessed them. Fatherhood was a right that belonged to the father, not the child. At the cost of paying this price, which Roman society found acceptable, elevation assumed the value of a rite of passage: a psychological dimension which subsequent experiences of fatherhood have lost. From this point of view, the modern model of fatherhood, while doing away with unjust privileges, has grown narrower. It diminishes the cultural importance of parenthood. To establish a fixed and general principle, it returns to physiology, as though we were animals. The father, today, is the male at the start of the child's life, at conception. A limited figure. Then the mother takes over. But from the cultural point of view – not only in the life of the individual child, but also in the history of the invention of the monogamic family – the father's functions come later than the mother's: it's only after that later point that their roles can begin to complete one another.

Human beings distinguish themselves from animals by virtue of the fact that physical birth in every human civilization is followed by the acquisition of a psychological identity by way of rituals of initiation, no matter if religious or secular. For women, nature itself prepares a series of stages in which initiation comes about by way of bodily experience. Conception, pregnancy, giving birth and suckling are the natural, rhythmic scansion of the passage from the woman to the mother. Men, however, in order to experience a process of growth in their relatively simple biological lives, were forced to invent a considerable number of non-natural rituals.

Becoming a father in ancient Rome was at once to perform a juridical act and to consummate a solemn rite: while initiating the child, transforming the child into a son or daughter, which was anything other than guaranteed by birth, the man too accomplished the rite of his own initiation, assuming the condition of fatherhood, which was the apex of private life no less than the axis of social life. Thousands of years before the writings of Margaret Mead, it was understood that fatherhood has to be taught, both individually and culturally.

Centuries later, intending to promote the welfare of children and the stability of the legitimate family, first Justinian and then canon law attempted to discourage births out of wedlock and decreed that husbands would automatically be considered the fathers of the children of their wives. This afforded the family greater economic stability, and also offered it protection from excessive sexual freedom. But it also put an end to a rite that promoted the growth of Rome's male citizens, and extinguished the *via regia* to their assumption of fatherhood.

The Church reconfirmed the solemnity of *matrimony* (a word, in Roman legislation, that indicates the rights of the mother), no less than the solemnity of spiritual birth, as symbolized by baptism, and still other moments of human life were recognized as sacred. Yet accession to the status of fatherhood was deprived of the previous ritual. (The parallel term for the father's rights, *patrimony*, is exclusively concerned with the administration of economic resources.) The Church authorities simply decreed that a man was automatically the father of all children born to his wife and paid scant attention to natural and adopted children. Yet, still today, "father's day" is celebrated on the feast of Saint Joseph, the most eminent of all adoptive fathers, effectively recognizing that the locus of paternity lies not in the generation, but in the adoption of the child.

The rite of elevation gave the mutual reflection of the son in the father and the father in the son – already quite strong in Greece – the body of a single and unique event, in an irreversible moment of individuation: 'You are the son, and I am the father. I have chosen you. You are therefore unique.' Elevation, since the child enjoyed no inborn right to it, was also an act of election. Being chosen by the father made the son unique – a unique individual – no matter if the father were later to have other children. In turn, the father also made himself a unique individual.

Awareness of this gesture has been lost, but still in modern times, in the widest variety of popular images, it is always the father, and never the mother, whom we see in the act of lifting a child into the air. We will discuss this more thoroughly in a subsequent chapter.

What made the Hebrew people unique, if not their having been chosen – and elevated – by God the Father? And what was to make Rome's conquest of Israel so devastating? Why did the Romans find it impossible to assimilate the Jews, unlike other conquered peoples? The likely answer is surely to be found in Rome's demand that the emperor be accorded the honors of a god, as the spiritual father of all: the Jews had already been chosen by a Father, and this choice, unique and eternal, excluded all others.

In Palestine, a tiny province on the periphery of the empire, Jesus of Nazareth had begun to shake the pillar which the fathers represented.

It is true that he advocated obedience to the emperor and faith in the one true God. But the first reduced to respect for civil order and was a harbinger of the secular state, of which the head is no more than the highest-ranking functionary. And his relationship with God was something that Jesus entertained directly, omitting the rabbis' mediation.

This new teacher talked *about* the father because he communicated *with* the father, but he entertained no dialog with his flesh-and-blood representatives. He addressed himself on high to the skies, and inwardly to the depths of his heart (in the terms suggested by our own viewpoint, or, better, by our metaphor of the world). In any case, his attitude to earthly fathers was revolutionary: he had begun to see them as a psychological problem. He didn't, moreover, see his own earthly father, Joseph, as a sufficient embodiment of authority.

Though he made no declaration of anti-paternal designs, and indeed spoke in favor of the virtues of traditional obedience, Jesus nonetheless turned into Christ – which is to speak of the founding of a highly expansive religion – and began to unsettle the patriarchy in ways of which distant Rome could have had no inkling. But it was visible to the people of Israel, and this was one of the factors that led them to reject the new teachings.

The Christian notions of charity and of love for one's neighbor are the precursors of all modern egalitarian thought, and also of the anti-paternal attitudes which historically have gone hand in hand with it. Much the same ideal of non-hierarchical fraternity that challenged the fathers of Israel was in the eighteenth century to animate the American revolution as well as those which took place in Europe. In the twentieth century, its spirit found expression in the uprisings at the Paris and California universities. The fixity of the order of the one true Father was supplanted by the dynamism of conflicting generations. Christ was God and the Son of God at the same time, which is also to say that *the father was no longer the only earthly image of God, and the image of God in heaven was no longer exclusively a father image.* Both realities, earthly and divine, voiced the new and radical notion of equality by placing the son – as an ultimate value, not in terms of a *coup* in the practice of daily life – on the same plane as the father. Since Christ himself never became a father, he halted the turning of the wheel of the generations and left the son at its summit.

This shift is also clear in the new holy scriptures. Inverting the bias of the Old Testament, the text of the father, the Gospels were written from the vantage point of the son. The "scandal" of the new doctrine ("scandal" is the word that was used by Paul, who spread the new faith throughout the ancient world, I Corinthians 1: 23) wasn't only a question of its general orientation, but also of precise affirmations. There would have been nothing new in a sacred text which accused the sons of forgetting their heavenly father. But it was radically new for the son, even in a moment of desperation, to reprove the father for having abandoned him (Matthew 27: 46; Mark 15: 34).

The words of Christ the teacher uphold the Father; but Christ the son as an actual presence diverts attention away from Him.

This antinomy is also found in the Roman Catholic Church. On the one hand, its commitment to paternal principles is so great as to lead it to give its priests the title of *pater*, and to call its head the "pope," which, etymologically, is again the word for "father." But on the other hand, these fathers are not authorized to generate children, and the terms of praise which were ever more predominantly applied to the Church call it the "mother" of all. Liturgically, the Mother of Christ, Mary, was likewise to grow ever more important, to that point, finally, of the proclamation of her assumption into heaven.

In the initial centuries of the new era, Christianity was plagued by heresies. The most distressing was the Arian thesis that saw the Son as subordinate rather than equal to the Father. We can see it as expressing the resistance of the collective unconscious to the notion of placing the son at the same level as the father. In addition to throwing all doors open to Christianity by making it the official religion of the whole Roman Empire, Constantine also came to the aid of the Son's promotion by guiding the Council of Nicea, where Arius was defeated and declared heretical. Theological disputes had not ended, but the inversion of the positions of Father and Son had been decided, even if for centuries it worked in secret in the cellars of history and the laboratories of the theologians.

The authority of the Church reached its culmination in the Middle Ages. Its moral code, canon law and social system spread across the whole of Europe. Sexuality and procreation were largely brought back, at least formally, to within the confines of the family. The sense in which this world was paternal is imprecise and unusual. Its primary orientation was vertical, ascensional: it turned to God, and withdrew, when it could, up into mountain retreats. Horizontal mobility was greatly reduced, and life was lived in restricted spaces and under limited material conditions, to which little attention was paid. Strong, concentric hierarchies – vassal, noble, king, emperor – were regarded with great devotion, but the father of the family was largely overlooked. The poor were numerous and lived as a vast and indiscriminate group. The aristocrats, on the other hand, derived their identity from a much wider entity than the modern family, defining themselves in terms of blood, clan and lineage.

Towards the end of the Middle Ages and the beginning of the Renaissance, the Roman Catholic Church invigorated the figure of the Mother, by way of its emphasis on the figure of Mary. She holds the divine child in her arms. The figurative arts represented that dyad, and little else. The image of the man is the image of a son, in the context, in turn, of the image of his mother.

The Renaissance and the Reformation were to furnish a turning point in the father's situation. The new intellectual curiosity, mobility, urbanization, the new economic activities and the birth of a bourgeoisie created the premises for the modern type of family, not overly extended and characterized by a certain intimacy. The father stood firmly at the head of this relatively new entity, even if precisely assessing his position is difficult. Some observers consider such a family a new phenomenon, and see it to signal a rise in the father's status.[3] Others see it as the growing and ever more concrete expression of a formerly extant but fairly abstract possibility, and the father stood at its head since that was the position foreseen for him by all the already operative codes; and even while assuming it, he continued his slow decline.[4] But these differences in the evaluation of the status of the father also derive from the circumstance that the objects of the various studies are somewhat different from one another. From sociological points of view, the strength of the nuclear patriarchal family continued to increase until late in the nineteenth century, and even into the twentieth (Ariès); and the father's authority within it remained considerable until the French Revolution (Delumeau and Roche). But from the psychological point of view, the image of the father – this image is the celestial star that guides such earthly institutions – rose to its highest point in antiquity and since that time has been interminably on the wane. This is the point of view expressed in these pages.

Just as man is to imitate God (*imitatio Christi*), the son is to imitate the father. The father is the bishop of the family.[5] But the Christian father of the Middle Ages, the Renaissance and the Reformation – unlike the Roman *pater familias* – always remained a son in relation to a divine progenitor. Little by little, he lost terrain to new figures within the family, no less than to the all-embracing figure of God. First the monastic orders (above all the Benedictines) and then the universities silently slipped from beneath his feet the pedestal on which he had stood as a teacher. The program announced by the Son, calling for the destitution of earthly paternal authority, and consigning it instead to the heavens, gradually found its realization: "And call no man your father upon the earth; for one is your Father, which is in heaven" (Matthew 23: 9).

The family and the middle classes were the period's avant gardes and combined with the Reformation into a powerful conclave that marched with ever more rapid strides toward the modern world. Protestantism demanded energy and an active, sober life, driven by a clarity of will: in symbolic terms, its atmosphere was necessarily masculine and paternal. Its ministers could be fathers in the biological sense as well, in contrast to the barrenness (which some also see as metaphoric) of the Catholic clergy. It was the father, moreover, who served as the minister in the family's private religious services: this phenomenon has always been present in Judaism, while always absent from Catholic societies.

The northern world in which the Reformation asserted itself never knew the superabundant images which typify the Mediterranean regions, where the Reformation never found a footing. But we can disregard this adage, turning our attention to no great quantity of images, but to an image which is highly indicative of the period's availability to the father.

Whereas the Italian Renaissance has given us countless versions of the *Pietà*, where Mary holds the dead Christ in her arms, Germany offers a perfect reversal of the scene: a paternal *Pietà* (the sculpture by Tillman Riemenschneider, circa 1515, is now in Berlin at the Kunsthistorisches Museum Preussischer Kulturbesitz, Fig. 2) in which the Father holds the Son in his lap. This is the very same situation that we find with the Mediterranean madonnas. Even if it's true, as has been suggested, that this sculpture was part of a trinity of which the Holy Ghost has been lost, this still says nothing about the relationship it represents. We here, in fact, have a dyad, self-enclosed and self-sufficient. Even if part of a triad, it remains concerned with a direct interaction between the Father and Christ. Why does it so intensely focus on the father's enormous compassion for his son, who, dead, gives nothing in return? Separated by thousands of miles, and without awareness of one another, in the same epoch, the sculptors exalt, with surprising symmetry, two non-symmetrical but complementary emotions: paternal and maternal love. When Riemenschneider carved his wood sculpture, Luther had yet to nail his 95 theses to the door of the Wittenberg Cathedral. But this precisely is the point. The shift of attention toward the father which accompanied the Reformation was neither an abstract construction nor a private invention on the part of Martin Luther: it was a reflection of feelings and images which were already present in the collective unconscious of northern Europe. This psychological premise, which was absent in the south, facilitated the affirmation of the Protestant message.

Throughout their history, the Reformed Churches have leaned in the direction of the father image. Certain developments in the opposite direction – such as the ordination of women to the ministry – are more to be seen as an evolution in civil rights than as a fundamental shift in symbolism: as an evolution within the paternal mentality, to which the administration of law has always belonged.

We seem to face a paradox. If secularization was more rapid and radical in

Figure 2 Pieta – Riemanschneider (Bildarchiv Preussischer Kulturbesitz, Berlin).

the Protestant countries, this partly came about because the Reformation's reliance on the father also brought it beneath the influence of his slow, millenary decline. Among the collective symbols of the Western world of the previous several centuries, the image of the father was destined to grow ever weaker, as compared with the stability of the image of the mother; this is something, indeed, which we might have expected, having seen that the father is a recent, artificial and cultural phenomenon. As well, the father himself, in his role as the guide of the collective conscious, prefers the "progress" of rationality to the stability of symbols. The Protestant churches conformed to the decline of the figure on which, unlike the Catholic Church, they had almost exclusively relied.

Liberalism, activism and a primarily virile ethic have led Protestant Europe and America – America to the greater degree – to promote modernization and the separation of church and state. But in addition to rendering public life more secular, this has also undermined the metaphysical underpinnings of the very same paternal authority in which this process of change found its origins.

The Council of Trent was likewise crucial for the history of Catholicism. The trench that divided the Reformation from the Council of Trent was more than a separation between two bodies of dogma and religious norms. It cut history in two, leaving Europe divided by so dense a curtain of incense as still, five centuries later, to constitute a border: after a period ten times longer than the one which witnessed the birth and destruction of the iron curtain.

The Roman Catholic Church increased its attention to rites and symbols, in contrast with the greater rationality and interior freedom of Protestantism. But despite the triumph of symbols and saints, the role of St Joseph as the adoptive father of Christ largely remained unsung. I have managed, in Italy, to find no more than a single significant image (Fig. 3).

In quantitative terms, veneration of the Virgin Mary was to surpass the worship of God. There are various parts of Italy in which over 90 percent of the churches bear her name, with the remaining percentage divided between Christ, the Holy Ghost and all the other saints. Qualitatively, this cult of the Virgin Mary offered a form of continuity to the goddesses of Greco-Roman polytheism (primarily to Demeter, or Ceres) no less than to the Great Goddess of Mediterranean prehistory. In either case, it's a question of a female figure whose significance lies in her status as a mother, not as a companion, and also of the return of an archaic image which while losing its official forms had never been forgotten. The lands which had once been Roman no longer regarded Aeneas – whom Rome had declared its patron saint – as their paramount symbol: they rediscovered Creusa, who had been "left behind," and her tenacious cult of Cybele. Moreover, the Roman empire itself – which once had been the fortress of the father image – had been absent from Rome for over 1000 years and had been reborn as the Holy Roman Empire of the German Nation, in the land of Martin Luther.

Figure 3 Domenico Piola – Joseph and the Holy Family (the Church of San Donato, Geneva).

Cromwell's revolution in England – a direct continuation of the Reformation – had sounded the alarm for Europe. It encouraged theological dispute. It had questioned the traditional hierarchies. It had reawakened the appetites and revived the rights of the brotherhood of sons. It had forced society to abandon immobility, and had begun to rediscover the principle of merit: the modern equivalent of the eternal zoological struggle between males. Finally, it had killed the king.

The sovereign's power in society and the father's power in the family were to cease to be absolute and became only relative. But rather than marked by sudden upheaval, this process was gradual, step by step, in accord with the temperament of John Locke, the principal mind behind it.

As yet, the insurrection hadn't spread to the continent. But it permanently marked the relationship between England and its American colonies. The colonies were quick to give concrete form to a direct Protestant patriarchy with its basis in the family and in nearby representatives of the people: the authority of a king who was too far away was open to question.

At the beginnings of the modern era, French society embarked on the course of a more radical renewal, and saw its scope as universal. The women of standing in eighteenth-century Paris were undertaking the secularization of motherhood. Children spent years with nurses in country houses while their mothers found deliverance from the one-sided image of Maria and began to enter intellectual life.[6]

The Enlightenment which at first belonged to an elite was to make its way into society at large. For the father, this was still another turning point, and still another loss of power. His teachings, no less than his difficulty in relating to his children, became a subject of discussion and part of a vast public debate.[7] The father who is a curse on his children was a theme that burst into literature with Diderot, Rousseau and Retif de la Bretonne, and into painting with Greuze. After having been repressed for thousands of years behind a one-sided, overly positive image of the good father, there now emerged the demonic figure of the destructive father. The father who turns into a scourge also causes an inversion of imagery: rather than raised toward the heavens, the son is cast into the netherworld. This collective symbol announces an irreparable crisis.

This new mentality questioned all forms of authority, both private and public. It raised doubts about things which had never before been questioned since they had always been considered "innate": conferred either by birth or the grace of God.

The change in the relationship with fathers in the age of the Enlightenment took place at two levels which reciprocally influenced one another. On the one hand, political process changed the laws concerning the father and the family; on the other, the process of political renewal was influenced by private emotions: we all associate authority, and above all the image of the king, with our own family memories, with our personal image of the father. This private, personal side of events cannot be quantified, but it links revolutions which otherwise were different from one another. It was essential to the French Revolution, no less than to the American Revolution which very shortly preceded it.[8] The period's political theories should be read alongside the private biographies of its protagonists.

Their relationship with their fathers was decisive for both of the principal minds who conducted France towards the revolution.

Voltaire (Jean Marie Arouet) combated his father with all possible strength, and attempted to disclaim him.

Here again, an individual becomes a symbol, and personal behavior expresses collective images. Since time immemorial, the father's gift to his children lay in publicly recognizing them; and the father likewise exercised the inverse privilege, of repudiation. Voltaire attempted to establish another and more authentic alternative: if recognition and rejection are options, children too can exercise them. And that was the form of his rebellion against his father. For a psychological no less than historical understanding of modern juvenile revolt, we ought to remember that Voltaire's first work – nearly two centuries before Freud – was an Oedipus drama. His *Oedipe* was damned, but heroic and essentially innocent. It heralded new and different times, and immediately brought its author extraordinary success.

The life of Jean Jacques Rousseau likewise hinged on his father, but in a diametrically different way.

Rousseau's mother died while giving birth to him. His father, a conscientious watchmaker, showed his son great affection and taught him the love of books. These two components of his birthright may perhaps have been so weighty as to make him incapable of drawing them into himself as interdependent parts of a single thing. He opted for books, and expunged the faculty of paternal love. He had five children, and one by one, with terrifying regularity, consigned them to the period's monstrous institutions for abandoned children.[9] Rousseau was obsessed with ideas of education reform, and this offers a paradoxical explanation for his incapacity to lend attention to his own offspring. His paternal faculties were perhaps so thoroughly absorbed by his vision of his task as to leave nothing over for his children in flesh and blood. And the father he himself had known in childhood may perhaps have been so unusually good as to leave him with the feeling of being inadequate ever to be father in his own right: lending his attention to the problems of education would have constituted the route of expiation which his intellect saw as natural.

Voltaire took up battle against his exterior father and threw him off. Rousseau wrestled with the interior father. These background events reveal their common epoch, in which the time had come in any case to look askance at paternal authority.

When *Emile*, Rousseau's treatise on education, appeared in 1762, it brought about the instant collapse of the centuries of development which, starting from a solid Greek foundation, had led to the construction of the Roman fortress of paternal authority. The Greek father had been a powerful presence in society, myth and literature, but nearly absent from his children's education, which he entrusted to tutors. The Roman father had been a powerful presence within the family as well, since he was also his children's teacher. Rousseau suddenly hearkened back to Greece: it was from a stranger that Rousseau's Emile received the education of which he was to be the new paradigm. In the following generations, the creation of the school system was to translate the intuition contained in Rousseau's narrative into practice, forever removing children from absolute family authority. The demise of the absolutism of the father in the home and of the king in the state were to accompany one another.

The French Revolution spread throughout Europe, and attacked its guiding principles. In addition to heads that fell with a thud into baskets, symbols too were decapitated: those symbols which formerly had been the upright axis which ordered the lives of human beings. Psychology was summoned into service as an adjunct of the blade that ended the privileges of the king, and which also removed Anchises from the shoulders of Aeneas.

The machine set in motion by the French Revolution brought down the head of the absolute sovereign from its formerly unreachable height. (Still today, the phrases most frequently directed at authority begin with the words "down with . . .") His power had been synthesized by an image that floated at a mid-way point between heaven and earth, endowed on the one hand with elements of the figure of God, and on the other with elements of the father figure. When the king met his downfall, the first group of elements wasn't restored to God, just as the second didn't return to the father. In the first instance, the churches were losing their power, and secularism advanced; in the latter, the faculties which the father had ceded to the monarch remained the property of the state, which proceeded in fact to remove the education of children from the sphere of family responsibilities. Rather than always in a position of vertical subordination to their fathers, boys were placed horizontally on a par with their classmates at school, just as it also grew ever more customary for young men to be enrolled among their peers in military service. Marriage became understood as a private, secular contract. It was once again publicly admitted that children could be adopted or born out of wedlock. Divorce was introduced as a remedy for such social problems: it's in the nature of contracts to be renegotiable. The father remained at the head of the family, but mothers too, at least in theory, acquired a horizontal mobility since they were able to remarry. Here again, England had been in the forefront: though it was France that opened the road to divorce, the notion of the renegotiable contract was grounded in the thought of John Locke.

Liberté, egalité, fraternité. The new *axis mundi* is horizontal. These words held the force of a great ideal, no less than of a military hurricane that was to sweep across the whole of Europe.

The luminous project of the brotherhood of sons centered on the notion of creating a world which is free from resignation: a world where injustice can be remedied, where justice can be real and not purely metaphysical. Sons no longer expected to be elevated by their fathers: they intended to elevate themselves.[10]

From the material point of view, this is the project we have to thank for the birth and affirmation of modern society, and for whatever justice it furnishes: whether great or small, it's in any case greater than at any point in pre-revolutionary times. From the psychological point of view, the pursuit of this project has resulted in our greater spiritual freedom, and also in general conditions of more widespread instability: because the measure in which justice is achieved is never entirely to our satisfaction; and because the primacy of the father was fixed and stable, free from the fluidity of the equality of the brotherhood of sons. The dark side of the coin of the glittering new ideas was the tempest that followed the guillotining not of the *ancien regime*, but of the father. Others, in the absence of the king, could restore stability to the state. But who was to bring it back into the family? The authoritative father had always been an archetypal image. This wasn't the case with the sons.

This interior desperation, born in France but soon to grow international, can be seen at the Louvre, in the Salon of 1806 (Fig. 4).

The painting by Anne-Louis Girodet de Roussy-Trioson presents a family group that clusters around a father who clearly is in desperate conditions. An old man, the father's father, weighs upon his shoulders: no longer an Anchises who gave life and receives it back in turn, this grandfather has become a plummet stone that is dragging his son into the precipice. The woman – whom the man, in the name of the new equality, holds by the hand, so as to prevent her from suffering the fate of Creusa – seems so closed up in personal suffering as to constitute only an obstacle, even in spite of her muscular body. (One wonders if that is what she intends to be, as was said of Creusa in certain, older versions of the story.) There is no direct contact between the father and the children, whose hands link each to the other's, and finally to the hand of the mother. Unaware of entrusting their frailty to a person who is equally frail, they seem to mime her attitude, consigning themselves to their mother's psychology as well. It would be hard to formulate a more negative image of the mother. She is a body that refuses to save itself, intransigent in passive resistance, hysterical in its concentration entirely upon itself. The father flexes powerful muscles, but his eyes swell with terror: the branch he grasps, like the rock on which his feet are balanced, will not support him for long. Below, a ravine and a swirling inferno of waves. The title announces: *Scene of the Flood* (1806), and it makes no difference if the author was thinking of the destruction of mankind as recorded in the Bible, or of the destruction of the father as inscribed in society, since we know that unconscious motivations can be far more decisive than those of which we are aware.

Figure 4 Scene of the Flood (Louvre Gallery, Paris).

NOTES

1 Mulliez, J. (1990) "La désignation du père," in Delumeau and Roche (eds), *Histoire des pères et de la paternité*, I, Chapter I; Lenzen, D. (1991) *Vaterschaft. Vom Patriarchat zur Alimentation*. Reinbek bei Hamburg: Rowohlt, Chapter 6.
2 Lenzen, ibid.
3 Delumeau and Roche (eds) (1990); Ariès, Ph. (1960) *L'enfant et la vie familiale sous l'ancien régime*. Paris: Plon.
4 Lenzen (1991), Chapters 8 ff.
5 Schindler, A. (1978) "Geistliche Väter und Hausväter in der christlichen Antike," in Tellenbach (ed.), *Das Vaterbild im Abendland*, I.
6 Badinter, E. (1980) *L'amour en plus*. Paris: Flammarion. The book opens with the information that of the 21,000 children born in Paris in 1780, only 1000 were nursed by their mothers, flanked by another 1000 who were fed by a wet-nurse who lived with the family. All the rest were entrusted to wet-nurses who lived at a distance.
7 Bonnet, J.-C. (1990) "De la famille à la patrie," in Delumeau and Roche (eds), *Histoire des pères et de la paternité*, IX.
8 Greven, Ph. (1977) *The Protestant Temperament: Patterns of Child-Rearing, Religious Experience, and the Self in Early America*. Chicago: University of Chicago Press, VIII; Gottlieb, B. (1925) *The Family in the Western World. From the Black Death to the Industrial Age*. New York and Oxford: Oxford University Press, Chapter 11.
9 De Mause, L. (ed.) (1991), *The History of Childhood. The Untold Story of Child Abuse*. London: Bellew, 1991; Lenzen (1991), Chapter 10.
10 "This, then, is the conclusion of the story of fraternal collaboration. We intuit that it doesn't lack affinities with the story of an ascent. Not a progress, but an elevation. . . ." Derrida, J. (1994) *Politiques de l'amitié*. Paris: Galilée, Chapter 10. The text contains a philosophical criticism of fraternal collaboration.

Chapter 14

From the French Revolution to the Industrial Revolution

With the beginning of the Industrial Revolution, the father approached his darkest hour.

Europe, at its base, was a peasant society, and at its summit an aristocracy, with only a small middle class between them. Despite the limits imposed by the state and the introduction of schools, the father remained the model in the families of all three classes. But in order to be a model, he had to be visible to his children. And in order to be visible, he had to do work that didn't take him far from home.

In many European countries, the peasantry accounted for over 90 percent of the population. The rest, aside from the exiguous aristocracy, consisted mainly of craftsmen, of a few professionals, and of many small traders. So the work performed by fathers nearly always took place beneath their children's eyes. Entertainments were few, and peer relationships were limited in both number and quality. In the countryside, work was hard in the good seasons, but reduced in others. Most free time was spent within the family, listening to the tales of parents or grandparents who, in times when books were scarce and illiteracy nearly the norm, preserved the memory of the family and the world. This silent, industrious mode of life preserved the father's authority much more than might have done the laws that formalized it. Human beings, and especially the young, normally look for symbols, not as abstractions, but embodied in other human beings. Without ever being taught to do so, we choose a model and attempt to conform to it, right from the day when, as babies, we begin to copy an adult or an older brother.

In the conditions typical of the era before the Industrial Revolution – until less than two centuries ago in the countries which have most been modernized, and until only three or four decades ago for most of the rest – this manner of patterning oneself on older members of the family continued without interruption from infancy to adulthood, and was a source, at one and the same time, of both identity and education: something which didn't come from the schools, and which even today they find it difficult to impart. (It's enough, for example, to note the ease with which one learns one's mother tongue in the family, as compared with the enormous exertion involved in learning a foreign language at school.)

For the males, it's true, this process underwent an interruption, and could never have been entirely linear. But it's a question of the straits of a passage which all traditional societies have effectively been able to negotiate, and usually with no great problem: after a lengthy period of attachment to their mother, boys passed over into the sphere of their father, following his movements with their eyes, feet and hands, and, to some degree, in thought. This provided their identification with maleness. At the same time, they gradually discovered that they had become adults and also had learned a trade: *the* trade, their father's trade, as demanded by the general rule. Strength, dexterity and professional ability – or, indeed, the lack of them – all derived from the father. This was the function of the father figure, and was seldom questioned. Youngsters were acquainted with nearly no other adults who might have served as alternative models: not even by way of the images of narrative, such as now takes place on thousands of occasions in the course of every day, thanks to the media of mass communication.

This rural economy was a poor economy. A little less so for those who owned a bit of land, extremely so for those who didn't, but most families were in fact self-reliant. The son of the peasant became a peasant: because he was already acquainted with doing such work; because it gave him a lean economic security, and perhaps a more substantial degree of psychological security; because he lacked alternatives. In general, simply, he didn't *imagine* himself at any other kind of work. In order to negotiate important passages – toward marriage, the priesthood or a new professional identity – one first of all needs to increase one's psychological strength by way of mental gymnastics: one must first of all create and exercise an image of oneself in that new condition. This is the function of imagination. Young men discovered the image of themselves as peasants by way of observing their fathers and grandfathers: by way of the images of a patrilocal, patrilinear and patriarchal way of life. Life was a patricentric narrative.

The Industrial Revolution shattered such forms of stability. It disrupted the social relationships. Yet, as time went by, it created new wealth which allowed the correction of many of its new economic injustices. Prosperity was in fact to rise to previously unimaginable levels. But the new way of life also disrupted family relationships; and these were to enter a state of instability from which they have never since exited.

The revolution began at the bottom, among the poorest. The fathers of such families entered the unknown: they had no mental image of their new activities, no way of imagining themselves as factory workers.

The increasing poverty in the countryside and the generalized growth of the population combined with the new opportunities and pushed ever larger numbers of people into the factories. For reasons that belong to the history of economics, the process continued without interruption and also spread to other countries and social classes which previously had remained untouched by it. There was no route of return to rural life, urbanization intensified, and the general conditions of material life grew ever worse in cities which were ever more crowded. The history of this great upheaval fills whole libraries.[1]

At first, especially in England and in activities such as the textiles industry, manufacturers preferred to employ women and children: they worked for lower wages, even if working conditions were excruciating.[2]

The new situation violently disrupted family life, which the father – since this conviction was essential to his sense of identity – had believed to be eternal. It tore his wife and children from the reach of his authority, and consigned them to an outside hierarchy that knew nothing of personal relationships; it appropriated the father's severity, but none of his other qualities. It was possible for the very first time for the earnings of the other members of the family to be higher than his own. He was suddenly robbed of both sovereignty and dignity.

It was only later, little by little, as industrialization expanded, as factory work became the norm, and as the first laws for the protection of workers appeared, that adult male workers were again the majority, as they continued to be until recently. In the United States, as it outstripped Europe as the greatest industrial power, the percentage of women factory workers in the nineteenth century and part of the twentieth was considerably lower (9.7 percent in 1897). Income once again lay mainly in the hands of the father. But the hunt by which he obtained it carried him ever further afield.[3]

This marked the start of the phenomenon that directly interests us, known by the name of "the invisibility of the father."[4]

On the day the peasant farmer laid aside his hoe and passed through the gates of a factory, he also stepped beyond the reach of his children's eyes: both suddenly and radically. The same fate, bit by bit, was to come to be shared by the craftsman, the smith and the carpenter. Their products were forced off the market by others that were cheaper and made by machines. Such fathers were exiled to shops where they worked with wood or iron in the service of machines which in turn served the purposes of impersonal proprietors. They frequently lost all skills, since their tasks were limited and repetitive. They frequently, as well, lost all initiative since they encountered nothing unforeseen and had no other responsibility than the repetition of a particular series of movements. They almost always lost their pride in their profession since they lost their professional expertise; the products they produced were no longer their own, and frequently they didn't even see them. They were certain, however – even if they hadn't lost everything else – to lose authority over their children and the secure place they had always held in their children's hearts and imaginations: their work, their day, their very feelings took place at a distance from their children, and had nothing to do with their children's lives. They supplied a livelihood, but no longer an example, or direct instruction, or initiation into adult life; these are priceless functions for which institutions and organizations can offer no substitute, just as the school master can't supplant the learning of language within the family.

It is clear that this archaic paternal role has also been idealized. Many fathers were cruel, brutal and emotionally estranged from their children's education and initiation. But it is also clear that collective psychology has suffered an irreversible loss, independently of the failings of particular individuals. The equilibrium of society and the family depends on a world of myths and images no less than on personal experiences. The father figure was a symbol, and as such a great deal more than any simple summation of individual fathers. This central image crumbled, and even began to fuse with infernal symbols.

The son in the industrial era neither sees nor has any knowledge of his father's activities. He no longer has an image of his father as an adult and the head of a family that depends on his work for its sustenance, just as the members of Aeneas' family depended on the support of his body. The circumambient world as well is suddenly deprived of both natural qualities and iconography. No figure offers the boy the colors with which to paint a mental picture of the adult man, of the tasks he performs and the strengths he possesses, of the ways he can reflect the qualities which myth has attributed, once and for all, to its heroes.

Industrialization allowed the father to be sucked by day into the factory, and expelled by night into a dormitory shared only with other men, but at a reasonable distance from his workplace. For his children he became a stranger. With time, and at the cost of both material and psychological sacrifice, the family might manage to reunite itself. But rather than the end of a separation, this was likely to signal the end of an illusion. The reconstructed unity is geographic, but no longer psychological.[5] Once absorbed into the movements of the city, the timeless psychology of the rural family was definitively laid to rest.

The family experiences urban life as mobile and precarious, and its absence of natural, secure and pre-established rhythms strike fear into the hearts of children and parents alike. With no need of support from reality, the collective imagination sees the relative stability of the father and the relative stability of rural life as intimately intertwined, since they were lost at the very same time, and came to be regarded with the same nostalgia.

In a phase of industrialization which hasn't yet created prosperity, the life of such a family can't simply be said to be more miserable than it was in the countryside. Its members also experience their first encounter with parameters of comparison that can make them aware of their degradation. Depending on his age, the son wanders through muddy alleys or in his own turn works in a factory. In any case, he makes the acquaintance of other degraded youths who turn him from an imitative personality into a competitive personality, if not into a downright bully. Urban life also makes other adults visible. He encounters all kinds of men, and realizes that his father is far from a perfect model. Some are stronger, others more intelligent, many are richer than his father, and his father in fact stands out, especially the father who is still very new to his urban condition, as a negative model.

The father, in turn – in today's terminology – is chronically depressed. He has lost interest in his work, and has also lost a large part of his relationship with his family. Rural life and a craftsman's trade had followed seasonal changes and rhythms which had left the family with time to spend together. Now, in city life, working hours are always long, in addition, often, to the great amount of time required for reaching the workplace. Even when possible to do so, the father no longer has any desire to return to his squalid hovel, overrunning with a family that's full of constant complaints and to whom he no longer has anything to recount: neither how he broke the earth with his plow, nor how he bent a trunk of wood to his own intentions. His only task is to bring home his wages. But since he no longer has anything truly worth sharing, this too seems meaningless, as cold as dividing numbers, not warm like the sharing of a soup in the fields, or odorous like the pig that lived and was butchered in the farmyard, or cheerful like the wine of the vineyard. The urbanized father begins to hide something away for himself, and spends it on drink. He rediscovers wine, but not the vine, and its solace lasts for as long as he stays in the pub: at home he is ever more a stranger, with few and hostile words. On the following day, he'll come back home even later, having hidden a few more coins and consigned them to a former farm girl, now fallen to work even lower and more repetitive than his own.

Where others have a father image, orphans have a mental gap. But this isn't the case with the son of the man we're talking about.[6] He is different since he can't pretend to be unacquainted with the father whom in fact he has. For the first time in history, the son is *ashamed of his father*. And not sporadically: he is ashamed of *having* a father, and of being that father's son. That was the day that gave birth to the problem of boys who don't want to grow up, which, in turn, is the source of today's society of adults who attempt to be something else.

An unprecedented figure made its appearance in the collective imagination of Western society: *the unwholesome father*. The narratives, illustrations and finally the laws of the nineteenth century began to lend him attention. This corruption of the fabric of the family – partly real, partly the fantasy of a bourgeoisie that was frightened by the surfacing of new unknowns in society no less than in the psyche – encouraged the state to supplant paternal authority in the affairs of daily life, just as the French Revolution had questioned it as a principle. The process was circular, and the notion of paternal order slid downwards like an avalanche. Even while creating the school master – a figure that competed with the father figure – the schools at first had only attempted to offer families the possibility of sending their children to places of education. Now it was to force them to go to school, in the name of freeing them from diseducative fathers: in the name of the rights of children and finally of the state itself.[7]

The poor, urbanized father – deprived of his rural context, of his traditional work, and as well of his identity – had lost his self-respect, no less than the respect of others. He found a new lease on life when the new situation that placed him in horizontal contact with countless others like him gave him the feeling of belonging to a mass, in which momentary sensations of power compensated his permanent impotence. Such compensation lent support to the growth of the trade unions and gradually alleviated poverty. But his poverty as a father was unprecedented, and perhaps he didn't perceive it since he no longer knew the meaning of being a father. His children and his wife no longer understood him, and felt contempt for him. His employer imprisoned his time in the factory, and the factory imprisoned his thoughts in his work; the revolutionaries wanted to enroll him into their movement, but not as a father – a function Marx saw as having been surpassed – since they were already proposing the structures of a state that would replace the father, freeing itself from his growing inadequacy, and relieving him of the illusion of being able to copy the bourgeois family.

But the nature of the problem wasn't entirely material, nor limited to the poor. All were affected, both practically and spiritually. The father's physical absence from the family was to make its way upward from the lower to the higher classes, in tandem with the descent from the upper classes toward the proletariat of his cultural disappearance.

From below, the image of the unwholesome father – the general lack of confidence in fathers, and of fathers in themselves – expanded to other classes. The urban middle class wasn't afflicted by the poverty of the working classes, and heads of families didn't lose prestige and identity in the wake of any loss of lands and professions. Those who stood to inherit an established paternal profession might be imagined to have been interested in doing so: yet the number of Paris merchants who bequeathed their professions to their sons fell from 75 percent in the eighteenth century to little more than a third in the nineteenth century.[8] The flight from the father wasn't confined to poverty-stricken areas: it was rooted not only in economic crisis, but also in a change of epoch. A flight was in course not only from indigence, but also from a symbol which before had been experienced as a blessing, and which meanwhile had come to seem a curse.

Even among the upper classes, fathers were ever less able to remain content with living on earnings from rents and investments. To preserve their positions, they had to engage in ever more complex activities, and to travel ever further and more frequently away from home, thus slipping out of their children's sight and becoming incomprehensible. Loss of relationship was later but no less radical than among the working classes. Families of higher social standing would appear to have been stronger. But they were also more involved in that circulation of ideas which increased the vulnerability of the collective father image and challenged traditional notions of authority. The new culture of horizontal values first found affirmation among cultivated people, and then descended toward the ranks of the desperate. The secularization of society continued without pause. At the philosophical level, the death of God was first discussed at the end of the nineteenth century, by Nietzsche; and this was the final conclusion, in symbolic terms, of the execution of the king: these two events coalesce in the one great metaphor of the demise of the father.

While these questions intertwined with one another, differentiating social groups only then to come to serve as their common denominator, and feeding circularly on one another, still another new event was to make the father's absence much more simple, evident and democratically universal: the conflagration of the two world wars. Separated by barely a generation, they gave a single group of men the experience of being sons abandoned by their fathers, and fathers deprived of their sons.

NOTES

1 Unfortunately, much less is known about its effects on private life, and in particular on the role of the father. Historical analyses are forced to address such subjects rather indirectly. See, for example, Griswold, R. L. (1983) *Fatherhood in America: A History*. New York: Basic Books; Griswold, R. L. (1998) "The history and politics of fatherlessness," in Daniels, C. R. (ed.), *Lost Fathers. The Politics of Fatherlessness in America*. New York: St. Martin's Press.
2 Thompson, E. P. (1963) *The Making of the English Working Class*. New York: Random House, Chapter IX. In 1834 the textiles industry in the United Kingdom employed 191,671 adults, of whom 102,812 were women (sources cited in ibid., pp. 308–9). For child labor, see ibid., Chapter X.
3 Janssens, A. (ed.) (1998) *The Rise and Decline of the Male Breadwinner Family?* International Review of Social History Supplements. Cambridge: Cambridge University Press.
4 Mitscherlich, A. (1963) *Auf den Weg zur Vaterlosen Gesellschaft. Ideen zur Sozialpsychologie*. Munich: Piper, Chapter VII.
5 The condition of the head of the family who moved to the city while leaving his family in the distant countryside was still widespread among Italian farmers, especially from the south, who went to work in the factories of northern Europe in the 1950s and 1960s (now replaced by immigrant workers from Eastern Europe). It was a highly difficult condition, but – when connected to a project of paternal constancy – finally victorious. One of my patients, a cultivated, urban professional, dedicated years of analysis and the discussion of his most significant dreams to his father, who in his childhood had come back home only for the briefest of intervals, with gifts and a few savings, so as one day to be able to purchase a piece of land. (His return was always the occasion for the celebration of a "father's day.") He was a poor, taciturn and nearly invisible peasant farmer, but his son remembers him as invincible. Like Telemachus with Ulysses, my patient managed to turn himself into an adult by way of this almost unknown father. While remaining in Italy, my patient had studied German (which his illiterate father

had never managed to learn) so as to be able on his own to experience his father's voyage and adventure, at least in cultural terms. The emigrant who didn't forget his family and who finally returned was received with honor. The emigrant who asked his family to join him could consume all his hard-earned savings and soon find himself surrounded by children who were strangers to him: educated in another language, rapidly integrated into a modern condition from the height of which they ridiculed him, or members of slothful urban gangs who were the psychological counterweight to his constant and excessive work.

6 Mitscherlich (1963).
7 For France: Delumeau and Roche (eds) (1990) *Histoire des pères et de la paternité*. Paris: Larouse, XIV. For Germany: Lenzen, D. (1991) *Vaterschaft. Von Patriarchat zur Alimentation*. Reinbek bei Hamburg: Rowohlt, Chapter 12.
8 Delumeau and Roche (1990).

Chapter 15

The disenchantment of war

Ac nunc horrentia Martis arma cano . . .
(And now I sing of the horrible arms of Mars . . .)
Aeneid I, D-1

. . . young men's lives which were crushed in the far-flung empire where the
only law is death . . .
From a letter to his family, in August 1917, from D. G., who was
sentenced to prison by the Military Court of the XXIVth Italian
Army Corps for the writing of defamatory correspondence.

Like Ulysses' son, my father had just been born when his father departed for
the Great War. Italy opened hostilities a little later than the other countries,
but the period of post-war instability made demobilization a long-drawn
process. Millions of children had abundant time to find themselves without
fathers. The terrible "Spanish flu" broke out, and my father's father, who
was an officer in the medical corps, remained in the army for a lengthy period
after the signing of the armistice.

When my grandfather finally returned, my father was over four years old
and had been raised among women: his mother, his older sisters, two maids
and the mistress at the nursery school. Both of his grandfathers were dead.
Though a couple of his uncles were alive, they too were in the army: one of
them for countless years, since before declaring war on Austria, Italy had
been at war with Turkey, on the conquest for lands in North Africa.

My father, obviously, was aware of the existence of adult men, but they
were creatures who rapidly passed in the streets, on the other side of a fence.
Normal life was lived in a world of women. And the world of women, combined with bourgeois comforts, was protective and indulgent, also with a
view to making up for his insecurity concerning his father's return. It was
taken for granted that the question of the absence of the head of the family
in many ways centered on him.

But it was the women of the house who made all the commotion when my grandfather actually returned. My father grew bored with such an air of celebration for a stranger. It was only when dinner was served that he too brightened, owing partly to the fact that the table was finally laden with good things to eat, and partly to his need to return to his place at center stage, perhaps as well in hopes of winning a new admirer.

Halfway through the meal he had passed from lively to boisterous, and my grandfather, who was still a man of the nineteenth century and still in military uniform, banned him to the kitchen. Here the child gave vent to protest, since he couldn't understand such treatment. But what first of all burst out with his tears was the question, "Who is that man?" And the maids replied, while making a sign for him to be quiet, "Don't you know? That's the master."

I was told this story by my grandmother, not by my father or my grandfather, both of whom maintained the habit of a spare use of words.

In the history of warfare, the mobilization of the subjects of the realm has always been preferred to the employment of mercenaries. And since the history of warfare is the nearly constant accompaniment to history true and proper, youthful fathers have always been separated from their children and enrolled in the army, perhaps never to return.

But the two world wars inaugurated a whole new chapter in the story of this ancient privation.

Without embarking on a general historical overview, let's reflect on the meaning of the two world wars as experienced in Europe and in Italy, seeing them as still a further link in the chain of developments that led us first from Greece to Rome. Present-day Italian society follows the general path of the Western world, and especially the United States, with a certain delay; but at the beginning of the twentieth century it pioneered a number of phenomena which subsequently left their mark on the rest of Western culture: in terms first of all of the experience of the First World War and the mobilization of the entire society; then later in terms of the lives of the veterans who survived it; and finally in terms of that collective psychic regression which goes by the name of dictatorship and poisoned the history of the twentieth century.

In the modern era, the only former conflicts to have equaled the two world wars in their length of duration and the breadth of their involvement of the civil populations were Europe's Napoleonic wars and the North American War of Secession. And now this new dimension of total involvement was to be combined with a new psychological experience.

On entering the First World War, the populations of the various countries each experienced a profound sensation of nationhood. The summer of 1914 witnessed the birth of a "community of August."[1] The people invaded the streets "in a spirit of brotherhood." Let's not forget these words. The general feeling wasn't concerned with following a particular leader, but with belonging to a great community of brothers.

Awareness of the war took place on new and different terms. On the eve of the First World War, the distribution of newspapers, no less than the level of organization achieved by the political parties, pulled a large part of the population into an unprecedented debate. Public opinion in Italy vivaciously debated on whether or not the country should enter the war, and was split nearly perfectly in two. Support for entering the war came not only from nationalistic and military circles, but also from many intellectuals. "War, the world's only hygiene!" preached the Futurist Manifesto in as early as 1909, the date of its publication in Paris. The movement, founded by F. T. Marinetti, proposed new principles, rooted in action and aesthetics, for the entirety of human life, and its vitalistic dogma found converts well beyond Italy's borders. It anticipated the activation of images which were latent in the European unconscious.

Ordinary people throughout the world had seen most previous wars as comparable to hail storms: as something, if possible, from which to take shelter. And if nothing else was of any avail, one waited until it was finished, and then got on with repairing the damage as soon and as quickly as possible. One didn't, in any case, waste one's time on discussions as to whether or not war was "right," since that did nothing to prevent the damage which inevitably lies in its wake.

Now, however, the war was seen as a people's war, and the people, for the very first time, had the right to voice opinions about it. In Italy, the area of public opinion which was in favor of opening hostilities didn't take the upper hand until the First World War had already been underway for a year. The country entered the war, and, as happens at the start of such things, it seemed that bellicose ardor was the emotion the majority shared.

But the war turned out to be much longer and more destructive than it had ever been touted as likely to be. In 1916, on the French–German front, it began to be rumored that the fighting would last forever.[2] The years of battle continued. The Pope, who had previously been criticized for lending support to the one or the other warring party, or for saying nothing at all, called the conflict a "useless massacre."[3] In Italy, inside their homes, families cursed the war. It also grew hard to control dissent at the front. The military courts dealt out severe sentences for attitudes expressed by soldiers in their conversations and personal mail. But the number of soldiers who refused to charge to the attack continued to grow. This resulted in summary court martial, and executions were performed by the Carabinieri, Italy's military police. In some cases, given the impossibility of punishing a whole unit, the soldiers to be shot were chosen at random. The specter of dying such an anonymous death shattered all personal relationship between the soldier and his superiors. It was impossible for the shards ever to be put back together again, and they become the symbol of this new and different age. Though the firing squads were able to reestablish a semblance of discipline at the front, the notion of heroism was never again to return to its former luster.[4] The war had begun in the name of national solidarity, but it could only be continued by sending Italian soldiers to die beneath the gunfire of other Italian soldiers.

Disobedience was followed by desertion, which passed from a sporadic occurrence to a common, ever-present goal, and finally became an avalanche: 28,000 cases in 1916, and 55,000 in 1917.[5] The individual soldier's perception of interior authority ever more often had nothing to do with the exterior authority of his officers. The disintegration of the father in civil life had found its corollary in military life. The behavior of the herd – in all its aspects, both tragic and ironically apt – was reemerging from the psyche's most ancient strata.

War is imagined to oppose one group of states to another. But it frequently ends up by opposing – without distinction, and in disregard of all battle lines – the brotherhood of sons to their symbolic fathers. In the First World War, the Italian army's officers remained faithful to the king. But the soldiers reached the point of encouraging one another to shoot those officers. Fraternization among the rebels at odds with the paternal order leapt beyond the established borders. Italian and Austrian soldiers exchanged greetings and gifts from the opposing trenches which were so close and so similar to one another. This was the most extreme expression of the existence of a horizontal brotherhood that supplanted all vertical hierarchy. And it was punished with particular severity.[6]

The severity of the punishment for desertion and disobedience in fact led many to consider surrender. But at the risk of their lives. The officers on both sides frequently ordered that fire be opened on surrendering soldiers: on the one hand to discourage surrender, on the other to avoid the bother of taking prisoners. But disgust with the war and with mindless obedience could not be held in check, especially in the countries where the old patriarchal order was about to be overturned. The number of Italian solders who were taken prisoner lay between 530,000 and 600,000. The figure for the Austro-Hungarians was 2.2 million; for the Russians between 2.5 and 3.5 million.[7]

In Russia, the insubordination of the sons culminated in an epoch-making upheaval. The czar, the aristocracy and the old order were done away with: all power passed, at least nominally, to the fatherless masses. The new course found sympathy among the troops of the other armies and enlivened the temptation to definitive rebellion. The hierarchies felt the brunt of a common disavowal. It was no longer a question of any desire to redesign geographic borders, as the wars of the past had always hoped to do. The desire was to establish the outlines of a new interior geography: of a new relationship between the ego and authority.

Disenchantment with war was the most rapid of the processes of disenchantment that forged the modern secular world. War was no longer an inebriating pagan god, but a statistical exercise in the technology of massacre. For the first time, "the fatherland became more alien than any enemy."[8]

Long before Vietnam, the typically modern sentiment of mistrust for war, accompanied by the demise of heroic myths and the rise of a pacifistic counter-mythology, was a part of the First World War: in Italy such feelings were particularly lively and spread with considerable virulence, even though the world of officialdom – at first the military censors, and later the Fascist government – attempted to quash and conceal it. Once peace returned, Hemingway, who had fought on the Italian front, made them the highly powerful subject of *A Farewell to Arms* (1929). The success of this novel and of E. M. Remarque's *All Quiet on the Western Front* (*Im Westen nichts Neues*, 1929) reminds us that negative descriptions of war for the very first time found more terrain and wider diffusion than its praise.

But there was also an unconscious side of the experience of the First World War, and, for our purposes, this is what we find most relevant, since the irrational nature of its criticism of governments and military establishments also ended up by overwhelming the family. Its effects were thus more lasting as well as more personal. Criticizing the governments for the evils which had led to the war soon in fact became an empty exercise. At the end of the First World War, four of the massive empires which had fought in it had ceased to exist, whereas the number of independent countries on the map of Europe had greatly increased. And even where the form of the state remained unchanged, the governments changed. The fathers, on the other hand, who had not been killed, remained in charge, just as my grandfather had intended to make clear.

The tension between the veterans and their sons, between the veterans and the surrounding environment, was at this point wholly unprecedented. Collective symbol had decreed the destitution of the father; but the fathers wanted to hear of no such thing, since at the moment of the decree they had been far away.

It's not only that the fathers were absent for a particularly long period of time, in comparison with previous wars: the unprecedented fact is that they weren't away in a period when values were stable, but precisely at the time when the criticism of all forms of patriarchal authority was at its highest. With no conscious agreement on a program, pedagogy and psychology had done away with the absolute authority of the head of the family while the new political movements were dealing a similar blow to the governments, and all at the very same time that positivism and secularism were demolishing the ascendancy of the celestial Father.

In Italy, the beginning of the twentieth century wasn't celebrated by fireworks, but by the gunshots of Bresci, the anarchist who killed the king in front of Monza's Royal Palace. The great majority of the population was of course outraged by such an event. But that is not the point. The collective imagination was by now in the grips of figures of authority in their death throes, whereas a king, in order to be a king, has to sit there on his throne, unapproachably: he can bend down to touch his subjects, but his subjects are not on their own initiative to reach up and place their hands on him. The same can be said of the patriarch within his family. A king beneath the fire of a pistol, and a father who quarrels to assert his authority, have already been relieved of their names.

Mitscherlich tells us that nineteenth-century fathers gradually moved away from their homes as a result of the Industrial Revolution; and their sons, who no longer saw them at work, were troubled by a gaping psychic void which little by little came to be filled with disturbing fantasies. The world wars can be seen as a repetition of this loss, in a form both sudden and total. Rather than having the character of a problem that gradually takes shape, it assumes the features of a true and proper trauma that can tear up the roots of even a healthy personality. Its disruption of ordinary life, and its quality as total and tragic caused the war to do more than to stimulate the individual imagination. It also gave birth to numberless forms of collective, popular fantasy: true and proper legends of which the content was monstrous and anti-heroic[9] and which functioned as alternatives to the official truths that no longer could be believed. The "regressive" character of these tales and rumors was often quite clear; it was said, for example, that the "no-man's land" between the opposing trenches swarmed with deserters who lived like worms in tunnels. The twentieth century thus saw an unexpected return to spontaneous fabulations and an oral culture that sprang mysteriously across the trenches and spread among opposing armies; this phenomenon was something that the authorities of the warring countries were impotent to control.

These legends were mainly created by soldiers at the front. But the civilian population at home also contributed to them, with the difference, however, that they lacked the ability to measure such tales against the actual reality of the conflict. So, they spun their fantasies with greater freedom and on the basis of more complex motivations. The amalgam created by the mixture of the anti-heroic nature of these unconscious fabulations with the conscious criticism of the authorities responsible for the war was ruinous for the reinsertion of the fathers who returned as veterans: once the official ceremonies were over, their reception was often quite different from what they had expected it to be.

Here we touch a nerve of that paradox of the father to which we have referred from the very start. A soldier's duties are clear. The father who served as a soldier knew what his officers expected. But on going back home, things were much more complicated, since the ways the war had been experienced had grown highly complex. His extensive powers as a parent were met by extensive expectations: in addition to demanding affection, his children demanded that he be a success, as a soldier no less than as the head of the family. The absence of the fathers had been so prolonged as to have reduced their children's stomachs to hunger, and their psychology to a state that resembled Telemachus' depression. Despite the mediation of the mother, which surely played an important role, the father found it difficult to explain to his children that he had abandoned his family because that was what his duty as a soldier had demanded. Unless embodied in powerful images, the notion of duty is a pale abstraction.

Children's needs are psychic as well as material. Fathers whom their children saw as heroes might have been able to offer them mental sustenance, and thus, to a certain degree, to make up for their absence. But the First World War marked a turning point. On the one hand, the collective image of the conflict grew enormously complex, and, for the first time, even openly anti-heroic. Hearing the war criticized at home kept children from seeing their soldier fathers as positive figures; and in the child's unconscious, where the army's commander-in-chief and the simple soldier father are simply two different versions of the same *matrioska*, hostility toward the military command frequently spilled over into hostility toward the father who had participated in its perverse operations. Let's repeat it again: what the father does *objectively* is something his children cannot overlook. In the final analysis, what the child could traditionally *receive* from his or her father in war – an image on which to reflect with pride – was for the first time rejected.

On the other hand, the child's *losses* reached unprecedented proportions. The father's absence was so prolonged as to allow the family's economic distress to grow enormous, and the father to be nearly forgotten. This was also the period in which psychology and pedagogy first reached a wide-scale audience and drew general attention to the ways in which privation of a parent hinders a child's development. The novelty of this point of view lay in its emphasis on the child's position, in disregard of the traditional prerogatives of the head of the family. The ordinary Italian father wasn't laid low by the anarchist Bresci's pistol, but by the writings of Maria Montessori.

The father who went off to war deprived his son of his support in decisively formative years. The father who didn't go off to war had to bear the taint of a more traditional shame, even if his reasons for remaining at home were far from shameful: this, in fact, was the point of view that was universally promoted. An English propaganda poster is perhaps the most effective example (Fig. 5): an obviously bourgeois father has two serene children, but no serenity of his own. The boy is seated on the floor and plays with toy soldiers, and the little girl, seated on her father's knees, inquires, "Daddy, what did *you* do in the Great War?" The guilt feelings in the father's eyes are the symmetrical reversal of the question's innocence, and his silent mouth is the counterpart to the child's expectation of tales of heroism. What makes this poster interesting doesn't lie in its reliance on blackmail, which wouldn't have been anything new for propaganda, but in the fact that its pressure is applied by a child. It is nothing new for a father to be expected to *recount* the war to his children; what's new is his obligation to *give an account of himself* to his child, and thus be *judged* by his child.

While this tumult raged in the psyche, the tumult in the streets was not much different.

Social stability had been shaken throughout Europe. The factory owners (the *padroni*, which derives from *padre*, the word for father) were severely criticized for work conditions which the war had made even worse. Events in

Figure 5 Daddy, what did you do in the Great War? (The imperial War Museum, London).

Russia raised the specter of a possible Communist revolution. Though Italy was one of the victors and had entered the war for the purpose of drawing the Italian population of the regions of Trento and Trieste into the national community, the final result was the definitive expulsion of a far greater number of people: the dead, the invalids, the mutilated and the permanently alienated. The streets were filled with veterans whom it was impossible to restore to civil life.

An able ex-socialist politician who had broken with his party's position and battled in favor of Italy's entering the war confronted both problems together. He founded a movement that mainly attracted the support of the veterans and made it an instrument for suppressing strikes. His success won approval and followers all over Europe, and the support within Italy of the fathers of bourgeois families. He directed his energies into creating a mythology for his group, and raised the torch of the heritage and values of ancient Rome: the supremacy of the Mediterranean in the outside world, the power of the *pater familias* in private life. Anti-heroic feelings didn't disappear, but were swept beneath the carpet by the political censors. The dictatorship functioned primarily in negative terms, issuing prohibitions and restoring a certain order. Its ability to function as a positive authority – to make concrete proposals and to restore ideals to the humiliated fathers – was far more reduced, even if not negligible. In spite of powerful pressures that aimed to revive the Roman presence which had dominated the Mediterranean, only about 100,000 Italians emigrated to North Africa; but millions left for America, which was officially denounced as anti-heroic and materialistic.

One might imagine the irruption of Benito Mussolini into the twentieth century to signal a rise in the power of the father figure. But any such impression is mistaken. Mussolini accelerated the father's decline.

The end of the war revealed the demise of four great empires – the Russian, German, Austro-Hungarian, and Ottoman – as ratified by grandiose public events and presented with unprecedented amplitude by the nascent instruments of mass communication.

But in the highly impressionable collective imagination, not only did the deathless fathers suddenly die. It also witnessed the sudden rise of a new male protagonist who took their place: an anti-paternal figure who remotely but directly descended from Achilles.[10] Even though Mussolini placed himself at unreachable hierarchic heights, he always continued to address his speeches mainly to his *camerati*: the corps of comrades who, in the Fascist imagination, fought at his side, and with respect to whom he was the first among equals. Meanwhile, he set up groups of collaborators and legions of militiamen: a horde of brothers, but subdued to discipline. As the circle little by little grew larger, the masses were subjected to a process of psychological mobilization that aimed to excite a spirit of youthful heroism in all, regardless of age. It caught the bourgeois democracies unprepared, and was then to be imitated throughout the century by totalitarian regimes of both the left and right: in this world of collective images, even Pol Pot – who dubbed himself "the first brother" – descends from Mussolini. But the heroic tale of the revival of Rome was also accompanied, unawares, by the folk tale of Collodi: a fable is autonomous and remains untouched by the words of officialdom, and is also invincible since it constitutes their spontaneous, unconscious completion. The dictatorship hoisted the banners of Caesar's Rome, but it unconsciously issued marching orders to the archetypes of Pinocchio and Lucignolo as well. "Brothers" such as these were destined to slip into erratic and antisocial modes of behavior.

Contributions to the new male model also came from powerful intellectual figures: Gabriele D'Annunzio, the aestheticizing poet and seducer whom Fascism turned into a literary idol; and F. T. Marinetti, the prophet of Futurism. The latter took part, in Milan, in 1919, in the founding of the *Fasci di Combattimento* (the Fascist street squads), thus pushing Futurism far outside the class of traditional groupings of intellectuals. He was among the first to intuit the potential of mass communication and he put it to use for the linking of culture, politics and public life. His provocative proclamations aimed to create a total *movement*. And though the name of the movement appeals to the future, its intention was to do without it, and to live entirely in the present.

His words inaugurate a new man: but a man who is far from unknown to us. Words spoken among the brotherhood of sons:

> The oldest of us are thirty. . . . When we reach forty, let other younger men, more valid than ourselves, throw us into the trash bin, like useless manuscripts! This is what we desire!
>
> (*Futurist Manifesto*, Paris, 20 February, 1909)

These words entered the DNA of the rebellious sons of the whole century, to be repeated, as we know, two generations later by the forces that opposed the war in Vietnam: "Never trust anybody over thirty!" Words inimical to everything feminine: "We want to glorify . . . contempt for women" (*Futurist Manifesto*).

Inimical to peace and every non-destructive form of masculinity:

> The periods . . . that rejected the heroic instinct and which, turning to the past, found self-annihilation in dreams of peace were periods in which femininity was dominant.
>
> We live at the end of one of these periods: *What women as well as men most lack is virility.* . . .
>
> Women are the Erinyes, the Amazons, the warriors who combat more ferociously than men. . . .
>
> (Valentine de Saint-Point, *Manifesto of the Futurist Woman*, Brussels, Paris, Milan, March 1912)

Words inimical to every form of stability. To all lasting relationships between men and women. Words that announce a future in which men and women will relate to each on the terms of machines:

> Terrestrial speed: love of the earth, the woman, dissemination on the body of the world (horizontal lust) = automobilism lovingly caressing the streets, white female curves. . . .
> Speed destroys love, the vice of the sedentary heart, sad coagulation, arterio-sclerosis of humanity-blood.
> (*The New Religion – The Morality of Speed*,
> Futurist Manifesto by F. T. Marinetti, Milan, May 1916)

Words – prophetic words – of contempt for nature (*Futurist Flora and Sculptural Equivalents of Artificial Odors*, "Enough of Natural Flowers!" *Futurist Manifesto* by F. Azari, Milan, November 1924). Words of radical contempt for continuity, fidelity and preservation: even for preserving of one of the world's most unique cities (*Against Venice and the Past*, Manifesto by Boccioni, Carrà, Marinetti, Russolo, Venice, July 1910). Of nausea for stability and coherence even in the field of culture: "We want to destroy the museums, the libraries. . . ." (*Futurist Manifesto*). Words – sincere words – in negation of the existence of the fathers, in favor of the sons as a new breed of heroes who spurn the couple:

> Women . . . bear sons, and among them, in sacrifice to heroism, take up the tasks of destiny. . . .
> Instead of reducing men to the servitude of execrable sentimental needs, push your sons and your men to go beyond themselves.
> You are the ones who make them. You wield all power over them.
> (*Manifesto of the Futurist Woman*)

Words – frightfully consistent words – of the father's relapse to the male whose only task is fecundation: "It's normal for victors, chosen by war, to come to rape in the countries they conquer, in order to recreate life" (*Futurist Manifesto of Lust*, Milan, January 1913).

Many of the follies of the end of our millennium – ecological, environmental, racial – are anticipated here, along with a masculine identity both radically new and tremendously archaic. An identity that lives in the moment, that desires to nullify time. For such a male, *sons, and with them, symbolically, the future, are things that belong exclusively to women.*

The Futurist Manifesto was published in March 1909, and the new male model which Fascism would bequeath to Europe and the whole of the twentieth century appeared in its company, as though issuing from its egg. In November 1916, Emperor Franz Joseph entered his tomb and stepped once and for all out of time – which for him had seemed to stand still – and took the ancient paternal model with him. Less than two years later, the continental empires had expired. The demise of the oldest of the emperors was followed by the disappearance of Europe's oldest imperial state, which saw itself as nothing less than the continuation of Caesar's Rome.

The numerous expressions of regret which today surround them are expressions of nostalgia not for such monarchies, but for a male image that dominated the collective imagination and which now can manage nothing more than uneasy, disorderly tremors in Europe's collective unconscious.[11]

Mania supplanted melancholy. The world of duties which was celebrated by Roth, Werfel and Zweig – Jews who cultivated historical memory and who had felt at home in the era that now was fading – was replaced by the world of the moment and its pleasures, as celebrated by Marinetti and D'Annunzio, who were secular and hedonistic like the century they inaugurated. The only thing that remained was the world of speed – proclaimed, significantly enough, by a *movement* – and the explosion of the emotions, both of which harbingered the century's predilection for heady spectacles, loud noises, drugs and the instantaneous. And both of them supplant the notion of the project and the ideal of self-restraint, which the era of the fathers can perhaps be said to have administered with too much parsimony.

NOTES

1 Leed, E. J. (1979) *No Man's Land. Combat and Identity in World War I.* Cambridge: Cambridge University Press, Chapter II, "The community of August and the escape from modernity"; Ferguson, N. (1999) *The Pity of War.* New York: Basic Books, VII.
2 Fussel, P. (1975) *The Great War and Modern Memory.* Oxford: Oxford University Press, Chapter II.
3 Note to the Heads of State from Pope Benedict XV, 1 August 1917.
4 At the end of the war, which had seen the service of 5,200,000 Italian soldiers, the military tribunals had moved to some 870,000 indictments for crimes that ranged from rebellion to the simple expression of dissent. See Forcella, E. and Monticone, A. (1998) *Plotone di esecuzione. I processi della prima guerra mondiale.* Bari: Laterza.
5 These figures once again refer to the Italian armed forces. The French witnessed tens of thousands of desertions in the months of May and June 1917. In Russia, mutiny swept through the army as the revolution advanced. See Gilbert, M. (1994) *First World War.* Chapters XVII–XIX.
6 The military tribunals inflicted from five to 20 years of imprisonment for small exchanges, such as a piece of bread or cigarettes. Forcella, and Monticone, (1994), p. 33.
7 Ferguson (1999), XIII.
8 Leed (1979), VI.
9 Bloch, M. (1979) *Apologie pour l'histoire ou métier d'historien.* Paris: Armand Colin, III, 2; Fussel (1975), IV; Leed (1979), IV.
10 For a vast study of heroic imagery in fascist Germany, see Theweleit, K. (1980) *Männerphantasien,* II Bd. Reinbek bei Hamburg: Rowohlt.

11 In Friuli – where the schools, as in the rest of Italy, are still in the grip of a nation-alistic rhetoric that views Austria as an atavistic enemy – 17 August sees the solemn celebration, with the participation of representatives of the whole of central Europe, of the birthday of Emperor Franz Joseph. Again in Italy, the vast reception accorded to essays and narratives on the old Austrian Empire counts as one of the phenomena which has most surprised the world of publishing. There are other countries as well in which the reevaluation of the most patriarchal of the empires seems to know no pause, even on the part of scholars in strictly historical disciplines. See, for example: Kann, R. A. (1974) *A History of the Habsburg Empire, 1526–1918*. Berkeley, Los Angeles and London: University of California Press; Michel, B. (1991) *La chute de l'Empire Austro-Hongrois. 1916–1918*. Paris: Laffont; Michel, B. (1995) *Nations et nationalismes en Europe Centrale. XIX–XX siècle*. Paris: Aubier.

Chapter 16

The reversal of the public father

The mother image . . . retains its unchangingness, for it is an embodiment of the everlasting and all-embracing, the healing, sustaining, loving, and saving principle. . . . On the other hand, besides the archetypal figure of the father, the personal father image also has a significance, though it is conditioned less by his individual person than by the character of the culture and the changing cultural values which he represents.

E. Neumann, *Ursprungsgeschichte des Bewusstseins*, 1949

There is a relationship between the feelings that a leader awakens in his country's citizens and those which a father, in the same country and period, awakens in his children. Frequently the process is circular: a sovereign of great prestige encourages families to take the father as a model; in turn, a period of strong expansion of patriarchal power within the family can increase the elevation of the position of the king. The contrary process has also been encountered. The modernized state tends to supplant the father, especially in education. But it is difficult to define the direction in which authority flows, from the public to the private, or vice versa. Their interrelationship belongs to the psychology of symbols, which can't be approached in quantitative terms or reduced to cause and effect.

In Western countries, the father has undergone a long, slow decline: an uncertain decline at the beginning of the modern era, but then more visible in the last two centuries. The figures of state or religious authority that rank as collective metaphors of the father follow a parallel decline.

Yet, the terrors of the twentieth century were spawned by the rise to power of horrific male authorities. If we regarded the relationship between private and public symbols as direct and rigid, we would have to imagine the father suddenly to have reared his head again. Where do the "terrible fathers" come from? How does their devastating power over the masses relate to the psychology of the individual father?

Though a graph of the father's decline would show a steady descent, it would surely be no straight line. In the last 100 years, its fluctuations have been more irregular than ever before, with peaks as sharp as knives. The use of the term "reactionary" as a description of Fascism and the other nationalistic dictatorships which were spawned by its example is quite correct from a psychological point of view. After voicing the concerns of humiliated veterans and a bourgeoisie that was frightened by workers' strikes, Mussolini's movement ever more vigorously exploited the desire for a return to the traditional order of the family: so, it was truly a "reaction" to the disintegration of the patriarchy. In this sense, the word "reactionary" can also be applied to dictatorships of other political origins, such as the dictatorship of Stalin, who was known as "the little father."

Having reached the summit of power, Mussolini prophesied, in Milan, on 25 October 1932, "Within a decade, Europe will be Fascist." Like the trail of mice that followed the Pied Piper, the years lined up behind him and proved him right. Ten years later, the old continent's democracies had been reduced to a scattering of islands in a sea of totalitarianism.

How could Mussolini make such an accurate prediction? Why was he able to foresee that dictatorships would spring from the ground within a short period of time, just as one foresees that mushrooms will appear after a period of rain? It surely had nothing to do with any accurate knowledge of internal conditions in Europe's various countries. When he decided on Italy's entry into the Second World War, he wasn't even fully aware of the situation in his own country, which revealed itself to be unprepared both materially and psychologically.

What can be seen as common to the humiliated micro-Austria, to Italy's disoriented veterans, to the ruinous inflation of the Germany of the Weimar Republic, to Portugal's rural drowsiness, to Hungary's lack of ethnic cohesion? The answer is simple and has partly been furnished by the writings of Reich, Jung and Fromm: a nostalgia for paternal authority, which was universally on the wane. Mussolini was the first to see it, and this turned his prediction into prophecy.

A prophet sees further because his feet don't rest on the ground, but in a slightly higher place. The image of Mussolini was perceived as suspended between earth and sky, like the figure of a secular saint. After mobilizing the community of brothers by assuming the position of the first among them, the dictator erected a place for himself as the semi-divine father of his country. Fascism applied less energy to the construction of a new political and economic regime than to the creation of the exemplary man: it had to set up the paradigm for the raising of all its children, the staff that supported the fathers and which had to stand strong. All free time which these children enjoyed was lifted out of the family's private life and inserted into public life, with its Sunday reunions around the Father of the Nation. The movement born from the veterans – the brotherhood of frequently violent sons who rebelled against the order of the father – undertook a search for stability, amending its original sin and searching out consensus among the confused families who constituted the majority.

Emulation of the Fascist model on the part of other European countries didn't limit itself to recreating the political dictatorship, but also followed the example of this new psychological dictatorship. It allowed the masses to be manipulated more profoundly and at greater speeds, while, reciprocally, it regenerated the functions of political life. This was equivalent to the ubiquitous mobilization of an immense, barbaric process of collective psychotherapy which proceeded in ways which were never clear even to the chieftains who served as the therapists. The need for the father – a flame on which the century was to pour gasoline – was satisfied for millions of children in sudden and dysfunctional ways by the dictators, thus even more thoroughly uprooting the father from the family. This psychological laceration has been even more enduring than the period's heritage of political ills, but still remains to be adequately described.

Why didn't the dictatorships help the father to recover authority within the family, even in the moment of their greatest ascendancy? While paying lip service to the traditional virtues of fathers, Fascism and Nazism in fact preferred to direct the lives of their nations' children entirely on their own.

The biographies of Hitler and Mussolini have received enormous attention. But their personal qualities as fathers can be summed up very easily.

Hitler dedicated his life to politics and renounced having a family and children. Mussolini was a prolific father, but substantially absent. He had five legitimate children, many illegitimate children,[1] and an incalculable number of lovers. The last was shot along with him, and her corpse was publicly exhibited, suspended upside down, beside his own.

Like Chronus, the dictatorship took on the features of the Terrible Father, who in the myths assigns his sons impossible tasks.[2] Like Chronus, it allowed them to be born, but only then to devour them. They were not allowed to grow or to lead autonomous lives: they were only allowed to exist in a state of suffocation within the body of the dictatorship.

Like Polyphemus, such sons had to be strong while remaining semi-barbarous and never becoming adults: they thus assisted the supreme authority in its control of the intermediate hierarchy, no less than of the fathers of families who attempted to preserve some measure of autonomy. The mobilization of the youth against their parents, which was again to be conspicuous in the program of China's Red Guards, is powerfully exemplified in a cartoon that refers to the Third Reich (Fig. 6).

"And this is the stuff for which our father is willing to risk the family reputation," say the children in Nazi uniforms as they discover works by Thomas Mann and Stefan Zweig on their bourgeois father's bookshelves. The situation is clear. Tradition demands that the father nurture his own authority by rising up toward other spiritual fathers and gradually inviting his children to follow him. But the favorite sons of the dictatorship will never grow, since it gives them authorization to judge their parents and to avoid the slow ascent up the trail of genealogy. They appropriate only the most negative side of the

»Und wegen so etwas setzt unser Herr Papa
den guten Ruf der Familie aufs Spiel!«

Figure 6 German cartoon of the father-son relationship in a middle class German family in Nazi times (Kurt Halbritter, Adolf Hitler's Mein Kampf. Gezelchnete Erinnerungen an eine grosse Zeit © 1998 Carl Hanser Verlag, Munich – Vienna).

father – the blackmail notion of reputation – and throw aside all respect for gradual growth, experience and the project of cultural improvement.

Fascism and Nazism further narrowed the father's already shrinking space. On the one hand, the finally victorious anti-fascist movements increasingly assumed an anti-paternal tone, in opposition to the excessive *machismo*, authority and paternalism which characterized the dictatorship. On the other hand, the dictatorship overtly praised the father, but covertly attacked him from the rear, always thwarting the cultural autonomy of the family and its sphere of private feelings.

Fascist paternalism was further perfected in Germany. In Italy, the dictator found it difficult to rally all of the nation's sons around himself, since he had left another collective father in office: the king. Mediterranean tradition also gave mothers a more powerful role. This was part of a more archaic way of experiencing political life: the citizens' identification with the state was limited (as in fact it remains) and in fact subordinate to powerful personal ties with both the church and the family. In this sense, the Italians could more easily withdraw their trust from the new adoptive father, since they had somewhere else to turn: and, even if the date was late, they in fact withdrew it while he was still in office.[3] (Even the way in which they turned to new mass-movement parties is indicative of such archaic allegiances, to the extent that belonging to these parties repeated the age-old model of belonging to the church.)

The situation in Germany was quite different. Hitler's initial function was to fill the void created by an economic crisis unequaled anywhere in the world. He then filled a void of faith which derived from a less stable traditional religious tradition that was fractured into allegiances to various churches. He likewise put an end to that absence of the state – the lack of confidence in the Weimar Republic had few precedents – which had resulted from the collapse of the empire and the disappearance of the emperor. Finally, his field of action lay in a society where it was considerably more difficult for the mother silently to replace the father. For an analysis of the way in which the dictatorships distanced from one another after their initial embrace, these are the kinds of considerations with which to begin, and not with the tautologies that assert that the Germans were more obedient to the dictatorship than the Italians were because they have a more powerful Super-Ego.

We know that Hitler and Mussolini lost the war by throwing themselves into ever more impatient campaigns. Hitler, damning himself in the eyes of the world, opted for the "final solution" in 1942 when the war had barely begun. But fathers think in terms of projects and distribute their energies throughout the course of time. The dictators condemned themselves to ruin since in fact they lacked the father's central quality: they were driven by impatience.

The end of the Second World War opened a final review of the image of the father. The father was held accountable not only for the horrifying scope of the massacres, or for the extent of the devastation, but also for the psychological disaster of the absolute collapse of credible authority. The public father had been so destructive as to drag the private father as well to an unprecedented level of discredit.

This final review took place in all the countries of the Western world: in those which had established the regimes of the terrible father, and also in those which had always fought against them. Sentence was pronounced not only on Fascism and Nazism, which had attracted the censure of the whole world and thus committed a military suicide, but also on Soviet Communism, which was later to effect its own liquidation through an act of economic suicide.

A public death of the father figure is a much more definitive condemnation than might be the case for the mother: the father is more intimately connected with historical circumstances.[4] Like the individual father, the collective father too must come to terms with the demand that he stand victorious. It must also be added that the dictatorships created a radical simplification of what we have termed "the paradox of the father" – the contradictory demand that the father embody fairness and justice, while at same time being a victor in the outside world. Fascism, Nazism and Communism, at least in its Stalinist form, declare that right and wrong are never to be found in any principle, and exclusively derive from objective victory and defeat. So, if their power proves insufficient, they have already passed judgment on themselves.

Manifestations of open nostalgia for terrible dictatorial regimes leave us incredulous. Our surprise, however, lessens when we observe them from a different point of view: not as political phenomena, but as expressions of nostalgia for the father. Such nostalgia played a fundamental role in the birth of those dictatorships and is even more crucial as a source of explosions of nostalgia for them. The absence of fathers and of father figures has now in fact grown much more grave. Even those who declare themselves to have kept their senses since they feel no nostalgia for the terrible fathers are frequently attracted by their negative grandiosity. Just as children find a universal pastime in bantering that "my father is stronger, more powerful, richer, etc. . . . than yours," the hunger for the father is in fact so great that many pursue his omnipotence in terms of destructive power, asking, "Who killed more millions of people, Stalin or Hitler?"

Our collective imagination now attributes a place of prime importance to images of the father who *destroys* life. Since he first became the companion of the mother – who still today gives life – and since the very invention of the word "father," which we have seen to derive from the image of providing nourishment, the inversion is complete. The dominant public image is now the negative one. These murderous fathers arouse an immense degree of collective fascination. No one has ever been the subject of a greater number of biographies than Adolf Hitler. There is no comfort, moreover, in observing that most of their horde of readers, while endlessly consuming descriptions of tyrants, declare them to arouse disgust. Voyeurism is highly comfortable in the garb of moral fervor. A public that experiences sexual excitement while viewing spectacles of sexual violence is something for psychologists to be worried about, even if these spectators are vocally in favor of more severe punishments for such kinds of crimes.

The unique experience of the European countries which lived through the social reality of dictatorship lies in having been visited by the terrible father in flesh, bone and blood: in having been humiliated *also by the collective and historical dimension of the experience of the unwholesome father*, who already a century earlier had begun to pollute private families.

By 1945, Mussolini, the father of the new Rome and of Europe's other tyrants, had already raced to the end of his course. The final events were of greater psychological than political significance, the image more telling than the historical fact.

In an outlying square of the city of Milan – the city from which he had marched less than a generation earlier, on his way to becoming the head of the country's government – he was strung up between the earth and sky, in a parody of the position in which we have seen him at the summit of his success. Everything meanwhile had been inverted: this father is a negative model. As a model of death, he was exhibited in death; as an inverse model, he was strung from a rope upside down, suspended by his feet.[5] As a model no longer to be adulated, he was caressed by clubs, spit and urine; as a prophet of the mystique of blood, he was anchored to a gasoline pump, the fluid that pulses in the veins of the new society. Benito Mussolini had attempted to be a total example in life,[6] and in death achieved that goal in reverse (Fig. 7).

A collective unconscious apparently exists, and was the director of this scene. And if a collective unconscious exists, that image was far more vast than a square in the city of Milan, far more enduring than the spring of 1945, far more significant than historical accounts that distinguish the left from the right. Between 1989 and 1991 we saw the very same fury shatter the statues of Eastern Europe's dictators.

The return of the strong father had depleted itself in only a few decades. And the reversal of the exemplary public father – his literal and symbolic inversion into his very opposite, making him a negative of himself – also inverted the model which had been constructed for the sons, reversing that too into its negative. As precursors of psychological warfare, the Fascist regimes used the inflation of the hero figure as their principal tool for mobilizing the masses: heroism was constantly invoked and no longer had to be sought in exceptional, sacred or towering events; heroism lay in the daily performance of the duties the dictatorship prescribed.[7] Heroism was the brightest of the torches which the fathers were supposed to pass to their sons: but it revealed itself to be a destructive force, rather than positive. If psychology were a question, like accounting, of simple addition and

Figure 7 The hanging of Mussolini in Loreto Square (Olympia Publifoto, Milan and Rome).

subtraction, the elimination of the hero would have been possible. But since the hero is a figure, precisely like the father, which has always been found in all human cultures, he too became a taboo: like the omnipotent father, he was henceforth to live in the darkness of cellars, where he turned into something mysterious and demonic that by virtue of remaining unknown could create new kinds of havoc.

If the terrible father is primarily to be seen from the inside, we have been right to begin with the countries that bore him within themselves, like the heart within the body. This allows the gaze of psychology, which begins necessarily from the inside, to rest on society.

But this imposing phantom by now bedevils the imagination of the whole Western world, even in places where it does not dominate its history. Even the Anglo-Saxon countries, which in terms of concrete politics are those which have remained at the greatest distance from it, perceive its presence at the center of their collective psyche. They know quite well that the image of the supreme leader casts a shadow of potential destruction, and their imagination now calls it up with enormous ease, so much so that their literature and cinema find it a source of endless nourishment; yet, no parallel fantasy has till now given birth to a supreme female leader with the characteristics of a terrible mother.

The graph of the status of the father in the twentieth century is simple. Where the father has been involved in collective political tragedy, the line that describes his collapse is more uneven. Where dictatorship has existed only as an image, as a narrative, the line of his descent is more regular. But its overall movement is the same, since it started out still quite high as the century began and then slumped into a great depression, which is still another image that society borrows from psychology.

America – the *alpha* of the Western world – offers a very clear lesson on the course that things pursue. In the well-established liberal democracies, the collective images aren't subject to the monolithic pressures of a regime, but to the sum of the complex pressures of the means of mass communication. Yet, despite their immense plurality, these means of communication, in the course of the years, were to undergo a common transformation that would culminate in their onslaught against the President of the United States, Richard Nixon. They had once been the voice of the fathers, but had become the voice of the sons.

This isn't to imply that the means of mass communication in liberal societies have utterly done away with the pedestal on which the father stands, as happened beneath the dictatorships. In the midst of the general crisis, such means of communication can re-appropriate their creativity and offer positive stimuli as well as denunciations. Much of the system of information, especially in America, has improved its ability to evaluate authority. It no longer repeats what is taken for granted, but looks at the world with curiosity. The press that once sung the praises of the wars against the Native Americans (the "Indians") began at a certain moment to criticize the war in Vietnam.

We thus discover a further expression of that disenchantment with war which in the early part of the century had asserted itself more radically in Europe than America, thanks to America's distance from the battlefields. In Europe, however, it proceeded by starts and stops, bit by bit as one stumbled over the corpses and debris the war left behind. In America it was more meticulous and became a structural process; and the Puritan code had already prepared a space for it.

This stringent moral code also made it natural to begin to reexamine the wars of the past: what had the fathers' fathers done to the Native Americans? Did they too exterminate women and children? Here again we see the difference between fathers and mothers: since the heritage of the fathers is primarily a cultural heritage, it weighs even at a distance on the sons, like an ancient malediction. The process of moral reevaluation refuses to come to a halt. If war is no longer just, and at most justifiable, this can exonerate the start of a war while directing scrutiny at specific features of its later course. After the sons who in Vietnam refused to be heroes at any price, after the reassessment of the fathers' fathers whose heroism was all too facile in wars against nomadic, stone-age tribes, what was to be said of the heroism of the fathers? Could Vietnam be criticized without lending renewed attention to Hiroshima? Had it been necessary to employ the most destructive arm the world has ever known against houses of wood and paper? Rather than lacerate a generation, America's reevaluation of the father fells the whole genealogical tree.

We can't predict the extent to which this need for historical self-criticism will extend itself to Europe and the rest of the world. But we know that it holds a question: aside from its political aspects, is the attitude of children towards the father – for which we've imagined the fundamental model to be eternal – undergoing a change? If the public father – both political and military – is now truly to be judged on moral terms, and no longer on the basis of the ability to prevail, is this also to say that children as individuals will one day cease to demand that their fathers deliver both profit and rectitude at one and the same time? That Freud will regard his father's hat with more benevolence? In addition to *losing* power, can the father perhaps be said to have *earned* a more authentic relationship with his children? Did the hidden counterweight to his exaggerated power in the past lie in his children's contradictory and likewise exaggerated expectations?

In a particularly significant year – the 1968 of the European student revolt – a new hypothesis appeared in France.[8] It found its point of departure in Freud's *Totem and Taboo* (1912–13) which presents the theory that the primitive forms of religion and the first forms of social life arose from the collaborative efforts of a brotherhood of sons: after murdering the father, they had sought and discovered the ways through which to control their rivalries and their common sense of guilt. Freud continues that in the course of thousands of years the constant introjection of the image of the father allowed the construction, within the personality, of the Super-ego, and of civil and religious institutions in the outside world. Once this had taken place and found consolidation, the world took on a strong paternal imprint, as seen in the monotheistic religions, in patriarchal institutions, and, little by little, in the always more rational and scientific orientation of culture. This is the point, the debt to the father having been paid, at which Mendel hypothesizes the reappearance of an archaic sense of guilt towards the mother, whom he sees as having been identified with the body of nature that was raped and exploited during the construction of the paternal world.

This hypothesis has to be purified of the limits that lie at its origins. Freud's thesis is flawed in its anthropological assumptions; and the revolt of 1968 founded a European youth movement which in Germany and Italy – countries with many wounds that had only partially healed, and intoxicated by feelings of guilt for having permitted the rise of ruinous dictatorships – found its final result in terrorist organizations of sons who fired bullets against the generation of the fathers.

The attempt to interpret historical change as psychological change is far more profound than customary political analysis; and it owes this greater depth precisely to the fact of paying scant attention to short-lived novelties. It looks instead at the extremely lengthy wave that guides the movements of the collective images of the father and the mother. In following years, a return to the Great Mother Earth was predicted even by Toynbee,[9] with the authority of the historian who examines human civilization as a long, single process in symbiosis with the earth itself.

The thinking of the ecological movement of even more recent years has constructed theories that criticize the anthropocentric point of view which God, at the beginning of the book of Genesis, consigned directly to mankind. Its fusion with the feminist criticism of patriarchal institutions results in a combined attack against male, Western rationalism, which sacks the earth, women and all other forms of life.

I believe such new departures to be destined to remain with us, since in fact they're in harmony with history's longer groundswell and are not to be undone by shifting attitudes that find their source in ephemeral, generational phenomena. In contrast, what do the "men's movements" have to offer, aside from the potent nostalgia of old soldiers? In addition to lacking the possibility of finding orientation in a corresponding criticism of matriarchy, they don't even know where to site themselves on the enormous charts of history. History gave us the father, and history is taking him away from us.

In the Christian skies, finally, even God seems to close a similar cycle, as though He too had decided to deprive us of the father.

The vision of the Emperor Constantine gave Christianity its official recognition as a religion, and instantly fused its power with that of the Roman Empire. In Constantine's dream, God consigned him the cross and ordered him to put it on his insignia: victory lay in the sign of the cross (AD 312). This was the first official communication that descended from the skies to the Western world. The most recent occurred in Lourdes. In the period that lies between them, everything had been reversed. Before, God spoke to the Emperor of Rome, who stood at the summit of masculinity. Today, in a remote French hamlet, the skies speak again. But no longer to an emperor; and no longer with the voice of God. The voice from above was the Mother's voice, and she directed it to the ear of a little girl.

NOTES

1 Messina, F. (1998) *Mussolini Latin Lover*. Fiumendinisi: Associazione Culturale "Carmelo Parisi." This text lists at least seven. It was only occasionally that Mussolini furnished them with economic assistance. Any personal interest in these children is hard to find. Benito Albino, born in 1913, was the only one of these children to be recognized by his father, and the only one to receive, at the order of a judge, a regular check. Later, shortly after coming to power, the dictator had the boy's mother confined to an insane asylum, where she died a few months later in unclear circumstances. The boy was interned in an anonymous boarding school. Years later, arbitrarily, Mussolini stripped the child of his surname. Benito Albino died in the navy, during the war unleashed by his father.

2 Neumann, E. (1949) *Ursprungsgeschichte des Bewusstseins*. Zurich: Rascher, Chapter 3; Stein, M. (1973) "The devouring father." In Hillman, J. et al., *Fathers and Mothers*. Zurich: Spring.

3 In the summer of 1943, immediately after the Allied forces had disembarked on Italian soil, Mussolini was deposed by his fellow members of the Gran Consiglio del Fascismo and the population cheered in the streets.

4 See the quote from Neumann at the head of this chapter.

5 Archetypal valences are surely to be seen in the suspension upside down of the corpse of a person who was once an authority. Saint Peter is traditionally recounted to have asked to be crucified upside down, since he considered himself unworthy of the same death that Christ had died.

   In September 1944, the newly liberated Rome witnessed an occurrence which was discussed for quite some time. The mob in the streets took hold of Donato Carretta, the director of the city's prisons during the period of the Nazi occupation, beat him to death and then strung up his corpse by the feet in front of the prison, and before the eyes of his family. Historians have now abandoned a primarily political interpretation of the incident (Carretta was a decent functionary and had secretly aided the anti-fascist opposition) and read it as a "rite" of inversion that was repeated the following year in Milan on the corpse of Mussolini. See Ranzato, G. (1997) *Il linciaggio di Carretta*. Milan: Saggiatore, Chapter 5.

6 Like Christ between the thieves, "the man of Providence" was displayed among other fascists who had been killed. As the mob mocked Christ by crying, "Come down from the cross" (Matthew 27: 40; Mark 15: 29 to 32), the crowd around the corpse of Mussolini screamed "Make your speech!" See Luzzatto, S. (1998) *Il corpo del Duce*. Turin: Einaudi, II, 2.

7 Huizinga, J. (1935) *In de schaduwen van morgen, een diagnose van het geestelijk lijden van onzen tijd*. Haarlem: H. T. Tjeenk Willink & Zoon, Chapter XV.

8 Mendel, G. (1968) *La révolte contre le père. Une introduction à la sociopsychanalyse*. Paris: Payot.

9 Toynbee, A. (1976) *Mankind and Mother Earth*. Oxford: Oxford University Press.

Chapter 17

The voyage of the Joads

John Steinbeck was deeply moved by epic poetry. He knew that the post-classical poets had entered the portals of a progressively narrowing passageway in which the freedoms enjoyed by Homer were forced to move in the ever more limited space of the poet's awareness of his own historical relativity, which has the power to curtail inspiration and grandiose language. The world had thus created poems which were ever less epic: national poems, cantonal poems, provincial poems, poems no longer of epochs, but of generations. They grew ever more distant from the grandeur of the human being, since they rendered the greatness of *that* person at *that* moment; ever more distant from the epic sense of tragedy, since they recounted the victory of a good over an evil, whereas the essence of tragedy lies in the awareness that the human being is always enmeshed in both.

Finally the poets had abandoned epic.

But Steinbeck didn't believe the renunciation to be definitive. What sorts of emotion can be portrayed without a perception of the tragic grandeur of the human being? What sort of literature could be something other than a consolation prize?

The narrowing tunnel sooner or later had to reach an end and an exit. And where could grandeur newly spread its wings, if not in America's great open spaces? Where could tragic paradox once again be seen, if not in the poverty of the world's richest nation, at the time of the great depression.

In true narrative, the language is always new, the story always an archetype. It was necessary to make the masses recount the battles of the *Iliad*, to seat social injustice within the framework of the *Odyssey*.

The grandiosity of epic implies, however, that it can never narrate a single thing, since to do so would make it subservient to a theme and a point of view. Its tragedy implies that it can have no happy end and must always skirt desperation: as it reaches one goal, it has to move away from another.

The time had come for a narrative on poverty, for a siege against the Troy of the poor. But that wasn't enough to make it epic. The odyssey underway in society would not by itself suffice; its program was redemptive and positive: the hopeless on the march could themselves be a source of hope. When

Steinbeck began to write, he knew that remedies were taking shape: the New Deal was reforming the continent, and fearless enterprise – a goddess who has her temple in America as Apollo had his in Delphi – would complete the work. The story of the Oakies' migration toward their promised land had to be accompanied by another tale that had no goal, no Ithaca. Inexpressible while crying out. Secret but not unknown. Intimate and yet so commonplace, so general, that all could see themselves in it. A greater collapse than of Troy, or of a social class, or of one of America's ways of life.

In writing *The Grapes of Wrath*, Steinbeck turned his attention not only to the collapse of rural life, but also to the collapse of the father.

He remembered the tale of an epic voyage that had elevated fathers to the greatest stature they had ever known. His task would be to invert it, following a downward rather than upward voyage. He took the *Aeneid* from his bookshelf, placed it on his desk, and began to rewrite it.

The hero wasn't to remind us of the prince, and instead represents the masses: Tom Joad is the father of a farming family. The realm of Troy is a plot of land in the south central plains. It had once been the property of his grandfather, but had been mortgaged as times grew ever harder. Troy was sieged by the Greeks, these fields by the banks. The harvest can no longer hold its own against their assault. The fortress isn't expunged by the calculations of an astute Ulysses, but by the tables of an anonymous actuary. The wooden horse is a metal tractor, sacred to Minerva as technology has always been. Like the Greek horse, it is manned by a traitor, a pauper on the side of the rich. A courageous attempt is made to take arms and confront him, but manages only to summon an incomprehensible punishment, like the divine reproof that struck down Laocoon.

Like the tragic heroes, the Joads don't understand what destiny so suddenly requires of them. Life, before, had been livable and serene, and now they're forced to choose between hunger and the unknown, between death and flight. Their plight is no chastisement for any error of their own, but a caprice on the part of gods who don't deserve a place on Olympus, since – no less egoistic than the gods of antiquity – they stand on the side of the already strong and victorious.

We know very little about Tom Joad. He is moderately authoritarian, moderately just, moderately loquacious. He loves his land and his family, but is no fanatic.

He has six children. The first three males are extensions of their father, and Steinbeck's apparent intention is to give them the role of Ascanius. But whereas the young Trojan prince is the repository of his father's virtues and will give them new life in a new people, a city, an empire, the three young Joads mirror the faults in their father's character, his immaturity, the fissures he has left on their path to adulthood. Adulthood is something they will never reach since their father's personality is the stairway that would naturally lead to it, and many of its steps are missing.

Papa Joad is the protagonist and emblem of the social ruin that Steinbeck wants his epic tale to recount. To show it to us, he might have turned his attention to Papa Joad alone, analyzing the facets of this character. But that would have left him with a psychological novel, and at a distance from the epic tale of the disinherited masses and the dissolution of the patriarchal family. So, Steinbeck chose to deal with him by way of a kind of chorus. His representation of the father who falls apart exploits the fact that parents transmit parts of themselves to their children: the description of each of his sons thus shows a facet of Tom Joad's character, and of what remains of the failing rural patriarch.

Noah, the first son, isn't especially good at anything. Not that he's actually retarded: he can do arithmetic and perform the work of a farmer. But "perform" is the word. Noah lacks initiative, enthusiasm and feeling. Despite his age, love for a woman is as distant from him as another planet. We can't even imagine that Mamma and Papa Joad made love to conceive him. (In spite of six children, not a line of this lengthy book alludes to anything erotic in Tom Joad, the father. Steinbeck could hardly have made it clearer that he's the perfect antithesis of Venus' son.)

Noah, therefore, offers a good picture of one of his father's central features. A feature that still falls short of depression, since something in depression is also a presence: of melancholy, of intense though crepuscular states of feeling. Noah is an example of renunciation without discouragement, since courage has always been unknown to him. He is even unacquainted with fear. He is likewise an example of renunciation without frustration, since he has never suspected life to have something more to offer.

Noah represents a silent but constant possibility in the psychological history of the male. Its millenary tradition has vitiated his personality. He is conditioned, on the one hand, by millennia of weariness with responsibility; on the other, he finds himself beyond the pale of the millennia of the egoism that discovered its seat in the habit of commanding a family. Millennia flatten things out; the sands, with time, lower even the pyramids. Noah is the male who not only has sloughed off responsibility, but who has even grown incapable of egoism. He no longer knows how to be a father; he no longer knows how to be a companion; at most we can imagine him in bed with a whore.

He is biologically sterile since he will have no children; he is also psychologically sterile. He produces nothing new, no initiative, no will. He is in one of civilization's blind alleys. His reversion from a father back into a simple male prompts the discouraging thought that the millennia have passed in vain. Noah represents his father's failure, and also the failure of fatherhood. It makes us uneasy to learn that his father treats him with more indulgence than he shows his other children: in the language of symbols, Tom Joad does nothing to fight off bankruptcy, and finds it sweet to surrender to it.

But let's look at the background of Tom Joad's failure, since here too there is something to learn. When his wife was about to give birth to Noah, Tom was "alone" in the house. (And why is it put that way? Wasn't his wife a presence for Papa Joad?) The midwife was late. Distressed by the suffering of his wife, no less than by her gaping vulva, Tom Joad had rushed to put a premature end to that intolerable bath of archaic womanhood: nearly averting his eyes, he had inserted his hands into her vagina and forced the exit of his son.

Perhaps the chain of the fathers was refusing to prolong itself, and then was forced to do so. But artificial continuities come at a price. The child had suffered: no wounds were visible on his body, but revealed themselves in the whole of his behavior.

The ancient patriarchs regarded everything feminine with superior detachment. This father at the end of the line maintains a maximum distance from the feminine – he finds the birth revolting – but no detachment. The father who helps his wife give birth, assuming a midwife's functions, represents the patriarch who can no longer live on interest. The depletion of his economic resources is a metaphor of the depletion of his cultural resources. He is asked indelibly to bloody his hands with maternity. Overwhelmed by the current of female life, he assumes the aspects of femininity considered to be the weakest – uncontrolled emotion, hysteria – but not the capacity to entrust oneself to instinct: the result is the birth of a male – Noah – who is mentally and biologically sterile.

The second son is named Tom, like his father. He has talent, and initiative. His head frequently rises above the story's sea of mud, and his intuition and ability to listen make him likable. Tom Junior unexpectedly rejoins the family as they are rolling up their mattresses and about to depart in desperation. He has been away for years, since he too ended up in a blind alley: in a drunken brawl he had killed a man. In self-defense, it is said. After years in a penitentiary, he is now free on parole.

Anyone, they say, would have done the same. The family is on his side, starting with the mother: Tom Junior repays her by giving her the reassuring sensation of having a man in the house who knows how to face up to problems. Without its being declared, one feels the boy's father no longer to give her that sensation: he has been beaten by the economic crisis, and failure for fathers is always a guilt. Tom Junior is clearly his mother's favorite son and they share the understanding of a couple, which too she no longer shares with his father.

Tom Junior is a young man with many positive qualities. Like Ascanius, he begins the voyage by taking his father's hand: indeed, he frequently seems to guide his father. But Ascanius, and every hero's son who desires in turn to become a hero, pays vivid attention to the models of masculinity and is always intent on their interiorization, making them a source of interior authority. Or, in times of upheaval and regicide, the youth who's destined to become a hero carefully observes his father so as better to be able to throw off his code. None of this is found in Tom Junior, who is neither his father's continuation nor a source of revolt against him. He is only the son of de-generation, or of the rupture of the tie of generation. The child of brawls, drunkenness and disorder, by which the generation of the fathers is overwhelmed, as we will see especially in his uncle.

As in many similar cases, his rough and violent exterior also conceals a son who is overly attached to his mother: such an attachment is not unrelated to a lack of development toward paternal qualities. We suspect that the young man's hidden symbiosis with his mother abets his explosions of violence: without being aware of it, and in a primitive way, he is still on the search for a male identity and has never learned to limit himself to the ritual expression of his aggressive impulses.

This character reminds us of the possibility of a "good" form of masculine aggressiveness. But all the same – at the moments when stability and a symbolic transformation of the male into the father are necessary – it can cause expulsion from society. Since he has never constructed an interior authority that corresponds to external authority, this kind of male is unable to transform himself into a complete adult: into the adult male who cannot rest content with a clear conscience and adherence to his own ideals, but who must also achieve, in the name of his family, an objective success which has nothing do with morality.

The third son, Al, can be quickly described. He is bright and has a number of attractive features; he loves to work on machines and busies himself at keeping in repair the old car in which the equally decrepit family travels. But he is also immature. Dazed by the course of events, he finds his only security in regressing to the state of the male animal. His ideal is his awe-inspiring brother, who had been capable of killing. The men's growing fragility in the face of unforeseen developments gives women a chance to emerge. Al is secretly afraid of this. Women are mysterious, and dependence on women is to be feared. His misogynous attempt to reestablish distance from women is the world's most ancient: with big talk and fabulous promises, he aims straight to the point and manages every night to get a new girl into bed, and immediately afterwards abandons her. This splinter of masculinity takes but does not give. The mathematics of the narrative tell us that he will not be able to pay his debts. Al is another symbol of the son who runs aground on the difficulty of proceeding, in turn, to his transformation into a father.

Then comes the first daughter, Rose of Sharon. At first she seems to be a vacuous character: in a still archaic rural world she appears to be a harbinger of the young consumers who always have something to ask for and who never assume responsibility. But this isn't a quality that truly defines her, and it's not a feminine quality: it's a temptation on the path of all the Joads. And of all the Joads in all of us.

Rose of Sharon has just married Connie. They are expecting a child and count on one another. Connie offers his arm and encouragement to Rose of

Sharon, receiving in exchange her ever more complete femininity. He seems to be the only young man who is transforming himself into a father.

The last two children in the Joad family are a boy and a girl. Still too small and free of responsibility, they symbolize the lack of awareness that accompanies the voyage as the necessary condition for going off into adventure.

We have already spoken of Papa Joad, and little remains to be added. He is the protagonist in reverse of the epic tale of the father, and the narrative makes this clear from the start. Tom Joad is a man who knows his duty. He has plowed the fields, and fathered children. But now he has ever less to do. Rural life and the rural family are on the decline.

The mother too does what she has to do: she takes care of housekeeping chores, and when times grow serious she stands a few steps behind the father. When faced with danger, the family seems to regress to animal behavior. As happens when herds of cattle catch the scent of a wolf, the males line up before the females and the young. When the bank manager comes to negotiate the capitulation of the farm, it is still the father, its patriarch, who goes out to meet him. Shortly afterwards, a discussion is held by the family council, which is again a group of men: the father, the grandfather and the uncle.

Steinbeck's inspiration for the grandfather also comes from the *Aeneid*, with the epic model turned inside out. Anchises was wise, noble, just and glorious. Grandfather Joad is small-minded, scheming, delinquent and filthy. Anchises was solemn and eloquent. Grandfather Joad is confused and scurrilous. Anchises had been paralyzed, as a punishment from the gods. The divine punishment for Grandfather Joad lies in being forced continually to hop around, despite his age, like the hyperactive boy who still lives inside him.

In the head of the clan of the Joads, we see a degeneration of paternal attitudes and a forefather lacking in wisdom: not precisely unwholesome, and even perhaps likable, but irreparably alien to depth of character and responsible behavior. In addition to being a figure in which all the paternal values have withered, he has also lost the reserve with which the father held them in custody. He reveals that the father's collapse isn't caused by fissures that now suddenly appear, but by hidden worms in the genealogical tree: by an infirmity which already in earlier times had grown irreversible.

Uncle John is the father's older brother. Perhaps he has more character, more depth than Papa Joad. But he has never managed to become the head of a family. He has no family.

Here too, the failure goes a long way back. The uncle had been married, and perhaps had loved his wife. But arrogance had tiptoed into his home and pulled the rug from beneath his feet. His wife woke up one night with sharp stomach pains and had begged him to call the doctor. The patriarch replied that she shouldn't worry and probably had eaten too much. Various codes had led the uncle to respond as he did. The code of virility, which demands the minimization of pain. The rural code of self-reliance which tells the patriarch to save his money and do everything on his own. The code of the partner, jealous of the possibility that his wife in the midst of the night might call for the assistance of another man and show him her body. On the following morning the aunt was dead. From that time forward, Uncle John was incapable of a relationship with a woman. His life as a depressed bachelor would break down periodically into gluttonous excess. He led an orderly life, but would suddenly roll about in the filthiest brothels and swill the most violent alcohol that crossed his path. The following day would mime the one before: in the opposite direction, but with equal masochism, he would wallow not in vice but shame. He would beat his chest and beg for a forgiveness that no one could give him, since he had offended only himself.

The uncle doesn't want to expiate – he has done that often enough – but to repair the past, to restore it like the shack of which he had once begun to serve as the benevolent patriarch, and to live inside it.

The uncle too shows the anti-paternal fissures which threaten the masculine personality: the propensity to disorder, the repentance that instead of giving expiation plunges constantly forward, turns back against itself, and explodes in a howl of egoism. Of all the disabilities in fatherhood which the family shows, his are the most desperate and despairing: not only because they voice desperation, but because they are directed to the past, to fatherly qualities that might once have come into existence, but now no longer. He begs forgiveness from a wise authority that would be capable of forgiving him. But he cannot turn to the father whom he himself has never been. Nor to his personal father, who in fact exists, but who is anything other than wise. Nor to the collective figure of the strong, good father, which history is obliterating.

The uncle's sensitivity, even though exasperated, is incapable of saving him. It's not enough. Because it's not accompanied by awareness. Awareness not of guilt, but of responsibility, which is something different. The psychology of the adult and the father doesn't allow us to remain in the past. Instead we have to accept the new expenditures – with caution but without reserve – which life demands of us. Only the child, remembering the total protection of infancy or of life inside the womb, strikes out at things that alter a comfortable equilibrium. During the night that tortures his memory, Uncle John refused to pay the psychological price demanded by an illness which was already underway, and by a peace of mind which was already lost. And in subsequently living without his wife, he was unable to pay the psychological price which the change imposed: the acceptance of mourning but also of its reaching an end, of the need to be open to something new, and of the fact that the initial costs of change are even greater than those of mourning.

The uncle reveals important features of the period's masculine personality. Though close to fatherhood – he is the father's older brother and was himself about to become a father – he never attains it, and as well shows traits of "the unwholesome father." Slavery to alcohol and gluttony: it is nearly as though degeneracy were an act of desperation in the face of the lack of renewal; and the lack of renewal the punishment for degeneracy. They constitute the tangles of a vicious circle too complex ever to be resolved, and to which we can only refer as "the complex of the unwholesome father." Aside from its more humiliating aspects, fortunately enclosed in proletarian conditions of life which have largely disappeared, this figure is a metaphor of the permanent sense of guilt which fathers feel for having failed to provide assistance and assume responsibility in their relationship with the world of femininity. Today, as the historical masculine responsibilities are ever more radically questioned, and as masculine feelings of guilt become increasingly conscious, this symbol is painfully up-to-date.

We have grouped the family – or, better, its adult males – around the rickety van to which they are about to entrust their search for a better life. The epoch and the country of technical progress have opened their doors: even a vehicle can be charged with emblems. Born a good while previously as an automobile, it has been transformed, in the hands of Al, into something like a truck. He has fitted it out with a large crate made of planks of wood. The technology that America acquired in the decades between the wars is at the service of all. This vehicle that was made for passengers is now transformed by human hands into a vehicle that transports objects: the family's belongings. People now are at the service of objects. In the course their voyage, the Joads attend to their vehicle every day, because it counts more than they do. They continually lose pieces of their family and put up no opposition, but the van is always essential and must be saved. The dead will be buried in secret to avoid the cost of a funeral, but spare parts for the car are bought at whatever their price.

The Joads are ready. The governing body of the family, the core of the patriarchy – the grandfather, who presides even if he no longer governs, the uncle and Papa Joad – has come together. Around them, in circles, the male sons, the women, the children. At the last moment, an ex-preacher by the name of Casy asks to join them.

Young Tom, giving precedence to being liked, presents the outsider's proposal. Papa Joad, giving precedence to calculations that respect no principles, counts his scant money and the many persons who are about to set out. No one replies to him. All of them prefer to bask today in their generosity than to join the father in his worries about tomorrow. With the voyage still to begin, the father has already lost control of his family's size and has written the opening lines of his letter of resignation.

Casy is taken on board. Papa Joad's hesitation is perhaps explained by his having perceived a new threat to his authority. The ex-preacher is charged with moral fervor and believes in expiation. He has an understanding for Uncle John and much in common with him, since he too has been dragged into sin. But he discovered a path of his own on the day he understood that no path can be prescribed for others. Others are to be helped if they need help. But their path is something they have to find on their own. All the members of the family, however, ignore that "ex-": they treat him as a guide and a *spiritual father*. Such figures are always sought for and constitute an archetype that shines all the brighter when fathers no longer have anything to say.

The addition of Casy to the caravan at the last moment is the symbol of an attempt to effect a substitution which is ever more frequent in the times in which we live. Everyone wants his company at the moment of the great departure. In moments of uncertainty, uprooting ourselves to begin a voyage, a great renewal, we drive a scalpel into our souls, exploring ever further. Not down to the interior authority – the Super-ego, which posts prohibitions – but far deeper, in search of a spiritual father who can talk about what is right and tell us what to do, and not only what not to do: with words for me, that tell me what *I* must do, and not how all should behave.

With the Joads' departure towards the west, the patriarchy's voyage toward the occident, its journey toward the sunset – the occident is the "place of falling," of the falling sun – paternal authority truly begins its descent: it *mellows* and grows accommodating. Yet not in the sense that gentleness is a quality the father might acquire; he's more like the fox who loses strength while striving after grapes beyond his reach. What we observe is a state of loss to which the mother can offer little if any remedy. Partly because authority is at an ebb for all parents; but also because culture – the paternal culture within the maternal culture – can't be rewritten in the space of a few years, as though it were a theoretical treatise. One repairs the void as best one can with fragments of the father: on the one hand, one entrusts oneself to the interior guide of the Super-ego, which abandons us to solitude and tells us only what we are not to do; on the other hand, many embark on the search for a new guide, in the form of a spiritual father who combines authority with affection. From the psychological point of view, the demise of the father doesn't leave us without authority: quite the contrary, it leaves us alone in the company of the Super-ego, which functions as a cage for the Ego. We are left with the authority which is *hostile* to the Ego, but lack the authority which is *friendly* to the Ego, and which offers it nourishing warmth. In contrast with common opinion, what we most tend to lack today is precisely this positive authority – within us, within the psyche – and we combat this void by demanding that it come from someplace else, in the outside world. And demand – when directed to the outside world, which is the world of economics – generates supply, as dictated by the laws of the market. So, there's an ever wealthier market for gurus. While the father grows ever more destitute.

The countryside has been expunged, the surviving Trojans escape towards their Italy: the western plains, California. The van warms its motor, but does not yet depart. Steinbeck lets it idle; and reflects.

Where is Anchises? He is the fathers' ancient heartbeat, and that of the father of the fathers: so, will he allow himself to be torn away from his fatherland?

Will he exchange the pride of dying in the place where he has always lived for the meager advantages of flight? No, the head of the clan of the Joads is Anchises' antithesis in knowledge and authority, but not in pride. Grandfather Joad, despite his constant cynicism, believes in the only true sources of continuity, which are procreation and the land. Like Anchises, he will not depart. Never.

In the *Aeneid*, the old Trojan was persuaded to depart by Jove. In the twentieth-century United States, gods rarely descend to the earth to change the minds of stubborn men. The tale takes recourse to the other members of the family, who arrange an encounter between the old man's stomach and the god Dionysus. Once they have got him good and drunk, the father of the father ceases to oppose resistance. The family is finally able to get him on board and they all depart (Chapter X).

Rattling along, the emigrants advance. And the dog immediately comes to woe, the last link of the family chain, and the only animal that accompanied them. Steinbeck's myth makes it clear that the family's symbols have been destroyed even before the destruction of its economic base. The dog is the link between rural life and nature. He is hit by a car, and we understand that this older form of existence has been crushed by the advancing world of technology.

Again as in the *Aeneid*, the head of the clan dies shortly afterwards. Since Grandfather Joad is Anchises in reverse, his death is likewise antithetical to Anchises' solemn departure. The chorus of celebrations with grandiose games is reduced to a clandestine burial, since the family has no money for a funeral service. Anchises' glorious tomb is replaced by a fruit jar which is laid in the hands of the corpse, containing a note that gives his name and a homely eulogy, as a last scrap of defense against a totally anonymous death.

Casy remarks "Grampa didn' die tonight. He died the minute you took 'im off the place" (Chapter XIII). In the Joads' migration, no faith or prophecy guides Hebrews or Trojans to a promised land. The voyage has been undertaken for purely mundane reasons, guided by material calculations. In flight from poverty, not in search of a destiny. In the name of the lie they repeat to themselves: "Out there, we'll find a better life." Since when, however, are calculations a substitute for faith? Without actually voicing this question, Steinbeck places it between the lines.

The voyage continues. Rose of Sharon complains about all the hardships. She swears she'll abandon the car at the next town, and fills her husband's mind with thoughts of bourgeois comforts: he'll become a mechanic, he'll buy her a refrigerator, they'll live a different life. The men, meanwhile, talk among themselves, resolving technical problems.

An archetype, as the word's etymology announces, flies across the millennia and comes to roost tenaciously unchanged. Let's return on our own to the *Aeneid*. There too the hostile forces were feminine, Juno or the Harpies; there too the women wanted to abandon the journey, set fire to the ships, sabotaged the voyage. Virgil's heroes too had to come to terms with their wives' impatience, with their hunger to settle in new homes. But archetypes wear the garb of the times. Just as the capes of princes have been transformed into rags in this American *Aeneid*, the strength of the heroes likewise fails and the men capitulate, whereas female inconstancy consolidates itself into grandiose stability.

Rose of Sharon does not leave the van. It's rather that masculine strength abandons the father step by step, in the person of the men who, after the grandfather, desert him. The group of the males – the synthesis of a larger father, with many faces and rich with potential – falls apart.

Masculine unity declines along with the patriarchy. It spreads out horizontally and each of its fragments follows a course of its own. The first to leave the group is Noah in Chapter XVIII. The simpleton. The farm boy at the end of his line. The family has reached a small river where it might be possible to survive by fishing. Noah sits down on its banks and goes no further. The others' aspirations – to find work, to create a new life by adapting to the new society which is taking shape – are of no interest to him. He is not interested in living, but in surviving. The eldest son, the steel in the chain of the fathers, no longer belongs to the ranks of the Joads. Not even a makeshift funeral accompanies this departure.

Rose of Sharon complains, and caresses the privilege of her pregnancy. But she doesn't give in. Now we are less surprised when we learn that not she, but Connie – her husband, the new father – leaves the group and runs away.

Meanwhile, in the discussions along the road, the head of the family is ever more accommodating, uncertain, and aligned with the group that decides in disunity. The mother advances from the edges of the circle to its center, first silently, but then letting it be known that when she has something to say she doesn't expect to be contradicted. She's doesn't defend either this or that individual, but the family as a unit, and the unity of the family, which gradually recognizes that this in fact is its strength. The Great Mother – even perhaps the Great Juno – now presides over the voyage.

Steinbeck continues to hold the *Aeneid* in his hand, testing his muscles against its myth, and giving it back to us in reverse.

John Joad drinks and rebels, and refuses to continue the voyage. The sensitive uncle, the oldest member of the family after the grandfather's death, discovers old age not as the vessel of wisdom, but of stubbornness and renunciation: the qualities that had rendered Grandfather Joad an antithetical version of Anchises. Like the grandfather, Uncle John is loaded back into the vehicle against his will.

Casy doesn't announce a desire to leave the group: epic destiny makes that decision for him.

The Trojans reached a land in which the inhabitants chased away all foreigners. The Joads reach California and encounter an external authority, the sheriffs, which resembles the internal authority – the Super-ego – by virtue of performing the function of always saying no. Casy allows himself to be sent to jail in place of Tom. And the loss of Casy completes the regression of the male personality. The preacher represented the element which was capable of filling the void of the father. He knows how to listen, has foresight, and believes in teaching others to set up personal but just rules for themselves. And he does more than believe in it. This is something he actually does. He is convincing. He brings youthful energy to the modes of behavior that the father teaches. And in a youthful way, Tom Junior feels a similar aspiration to justice: but what he actually brings into the world is excess, which lapses necessarily into self-destruction. The preacher who allows himself to be jailed represents the way in which the possibility of being oneself can be placed under lock and key by the Super-ego: and the cry of protest against this closure of the route to maturity is the liberty that Casy consigns to Tom, who embodies generous disorder.

In prison, Casy experiences a rebirth as a preacher: as a preacher of social justice. We also see his release from prison, but for the equilibrium of the psychological narrative he has to disappear. A man can't assume the role of Jove, the god who shows exiles the right road.

The paths of Tom and Casy cross again while Casy is organizing a strike. But reactionaries arrive in the night and leave the preacher dead, his skull caved in, which in turn causes the Joads to lose yet another son: Tom's hand once again takes hold of a club, and to vindicate Casy he again kills a man. He too, moreover, has received the blow of a club in the face and can easily be identified; his situation is hopeless and he can only go into hiding, knowing that returning to his family would damage rather than unite it.

Could the Trojans reestablish their tribe on the distant coasts of Italy without Ascanius? Can the Joads recreate the life of the Joads now that they have no sons, now that only Al remains? Al grows: he confronts the failure of machines with ever greater ability, but knows nothing about fixing the failures of the father.

The voyage is ever more weary. By now the men come together to make decisions only when the women – the mother – force them to do so. Without a spiritual guide and with no destination – no point of arrival decreed by destiny – they shape no goals and can only react to hard material contingencies. But what the father fears most of all – even more than the difficulties, the constrictions – is having to decide: having to say out loud that all the alternatives by now have run out, and that the family has to move again. And from the moment in which he allows that terror to take the upper hand, he ceases to be a father.

We had been warned: a father is a person who teaches a principle of justice, and who gives his family the means with which to take that teaching out into the world. He does not offer ideas or love, if not accompanied by actions. The paradox is that the father was always accustomed to this order of things, and was therefore unconscious of putting it into practice. If his failure now lies in the lack of action, he again remains unaware of it, since the fault is already a part of his soul. He has been blasted psychologically, even before being branded by material circumstances.

Father Joad attempts to shift his failure and to blame the outside world, declaring: "Seems like times is changed. . . . Time was when a man said what we'd do. Seems like women is tellin' now. Seems like it's purty near time to get out a stick." His wife responds, "You get your stick, Pa. . . . Times when they's food an' a place to set, then maybe you can use your stick an' keep your skin whole. But you ain't a-doin' your job, either a-thinkin' or a-workin'. If you was, why, you could use your stick, an' women folks'd sniffle their nose an' creep-mouse aroun'. But you jus' get you a stick now an' you ain't lickin' no woman; you're a fightin', cause I got a stick all laid out too" (Chapter XXVI).

Women, perhaps, once wasted energy in comments and interpretations. Not the father, up until having completed his work. Now he lapses into doubt – he stutters, which amounts to the sound of doubt – bringing time and action out of joint. Finally, he even indulges in the least paternal of all ways of wasting time: he begins to apologize.

The voyage continues a little while longer. Rose of Sharon has ceased to complain. The time has come to give birth to her child. After the assault of so many privations, the baby is born dead.

The Joad family has lost everything. It meets the remains of another ruined family. The father is a middle-aged man, like Papa Joad. In the grips of starvation, and almost dead. His stomach, by now, can hold no solid food. They should buy him something, at least a bit of milk.

This unknown father becomes the corporeal reflection of the point which Papa Joad has reached in spirit. His conditions are terminal. The men would like to do something for him. The women know what to do. The mother leads her daughter to a corner, beside the dying man. Rose of Sharon gives him her breast. She has milk, but no child. The father's last nourishment comes from the mother.

This, then, is *The Grapes of Wrath* (1939), the story of the farmers in the great depression, and of paternal drought.

To give his story epic depth, John Steinbeck turned for inspiration to Virgil's *Aeneid*. Or perhaps that's not exactly the way things went, but it makes no difference. We continue to repeat that unconscious intentions often achieve more profound results than conscious ones, with their tamed and optimistic goals. The simple fact that *The Grapes of Wrath* is one of the century's most famous books – far beyond the confines of the uprooted generation and the country for which it was written – speaks of the profundity it in fact achieves, independently of literary virtues. It is carried less by the choppy waves of an economic cycle in descent than by the age-old groundswell of the demise of the patriarchy. The fact that the attention it provokes has been directed almost entirely to the first means only that the second arouses so much fear as to make us prefer to repress it completely. But the book's ability to capture readers' imaginations in any case derives from its return to the timeless themes of the *Aeneid*: the father, and the voyage.

Steinbeck's story is epic because it describes a universal event that spans many thousands of years. The voyage of the Joads is not only a social but also a psychological migration. Their debasement is something more than the debris of a form of economy and agriculture. It signals definitive departure from the father whose tasks descended from the skies; fathers today look after their bank accounts.

The father today

Chapter 18

The rarefaction of the father

You, get out – you've got no father feasting with us here!
Iliad, XXII, 498

Along with European civilization, it seemed that the father too had conquered the world. But instead, in an alarming number of cases, he has already ceased to exist. The world grows aware of it after it has already happened.

It has been said that the father is becoming a luxury.[1] His traditional psychological functions are exercised to an ever slighter degree. His material tasks are conferred to mothers or institutions. His erosion as a psychological figure is by now accompanied by physical disappearance. How many fathers are unavailable to their children, and for how long? We should now take a look at a few figures.

In the last 100 years, the births and deaths of professions have been more numerous than in all previous history. The collapse in the number of farmers and artisans with respect to the total population seems tantamount to a genocide against the traditional professions, leaving children at a distance from their parents, and above all from their fathers. The disappearance of the traditional head of the family makes one think, in turn, of a mass patricide. Yet fathers have not been abolished: they either are ever more often and further away from their children, or have simply stepped out of their lives.

The pace of this shift has grown ever more rapid and has extended from the West to the other countries of the globe. The father gives ever more money, but ever less time to his children. He counts out money *for* the lives of his children, but he himself counts ever less *within* those lives. American fathers have been calculated to spend an average of seven minutes a day with their children.[2] And all studies reveal, with respect to every period of history, that fathers' participation in the raising of children is drastically inferior to the mothers'.[3]

These few minutes a day are what "life with father" amounts to in the foremost country of the Western world. Many children don't even have this much. In how many cases do children live *without* a father? Statistics told us already in the 1970s that divorces in the United States had increased since the beginning of the century by 700 percent. It followed that four out of every ten children born in that decade were destined to pass a part of their childhood with only one of their parents, which almost always meant with the mother.[4]

The change has not been gradual. In 1900 there were only three divorces for every 1000 marriages, and in 1960 there were only nine.[5] In the 1950s the increase in the average life span had created a situation, at the end of the decade, in which the percentage of children who lived with both their parents had reached the highest point ever recorded.[6] The rarefaction of the father wasn't to overwhelm American society until the 1960s, 1970s and 1980s, with the explosion of divorces and of births out of wedlock.[7] A projection for children born in 1980 foresaw that 70 percent of white children and 94 percent of black children would find themselves with only one parent before reaching the age of eighteen.[8] It was only in the 1990s that a regress or reversal of the tendency was again to be seen.

Nothing before, in any period, had ever caused so great an upheaval in private life: even in the periods after civil wars, epidemics, the plague, or barbarian invasions, the family had always managed a slow return to previous conditions. At the end of the twentieth century, more than half of the children in the United States spent their childhood, either totally or in part, with only one parent,[9] and births out of wedlock had risen to over 30 percent of total births.[10] (The situation in Europe is more varied: births out of wedlock are close to 50 percent in Scandinavia, about a third in France and the United Kingdom, but far fewer in the Mediterranean countries.[11])

According to one study of the explosive 1980s in the United States, more than 50 percent of the children of divorced parents had not seen their fathers for more than a year, whereas only a third saw their fathers at least once a month.[12] Another study of the decade[13] reported that only 20 percent of divorced fathers saw their children at least once a month, and that half of them had interrupted all relationships with their children by the time the children had reached adolescence. One could imagine this spontaneous absence of affection to be a reaction to the laws that force divorced fathers to support their offspring. But the observance of the laws is likewise on the wane: other studies[14] report that at ten years' distance from the divorce, 79 percent of American fathers either don't fulfill their obligations, or have simply disappeared.

In addition to their statistical findings, the texts reveal as well that the researchers are far from unanimous on the guidelines used for their studies. Different studies consider a contact between a divorced father and his child which consists of two week-ends per month and one dinner per week as *"relatively limited"*, *"frequent"* or *"very frequent."*[15] Different studies define the same thing in entirely different ways. And since this "thing" is the relationship with the father, we can only conclude that the relationship with the father belongs to the sphere of ideology, or to individual tenets that cannot be verified. It doesn't manage to present itself as a practical reality to be discussed in practical ways.[16]

As is always the case when revolutions are underway, it's impossible to keep data up to date or to collect it with a constant methodology. The three large volumes by Michael L. Lamb constitute the most complete study of the role of the American father in child development. With respect to the first of these publications (Lamb, 1976), the third (Lamb, 1997) reports a slight but encouraging increase in the level of commitment to their children on the part of the fathers who live with them. This improvement is accompanied, however, by an explosive increase in the number of families from which the father is absent.

A number of highly different situations lie behind this last fact.

In the upper and upper middle classes, the absence of the father is due above all to the decision to put an end to a dissatisfying marriage. In this part of society, divorce has spread with great rapidity, and even if divorce can often be seen to have degenerated into a "consumerism of alternative families" it nonetheless constitutes an expression of freedom and the exercise of a right. While remaining a rejection of fatherhood, this form of non-fatherhood seems to represent a choice.

In the poorer classes the situation is different: the father's absence has less to do with choice than with a lack of alternatives, and nearly exists from the very start. This portion of society is concentrated in the black ghettoes. Extremely young couples with no economic independence, or who don't even live together, fatalistically procreate children without being married, or get married for the occasion: in either case, there's a high probability from the very start that the new mother will remain without her man. She thus continues to live with her own family, or, better, with her mother, or grandmother, and so forth, since this absence of the father repeats itself from one generation to the next. Fatherhood can be missing from the moment of the child's birth, or even conception.

In 1965, D. P. Moynihan published a study which had been commissioned by the United States government: *The Negro Family. The Case for National Action*.[17] The Civil War, in which America spilled more blood than in both world wars together, had been fought for the liberation of the black slaves. A hundred years later, Moynihan's report revealed that the scars of slavery were still quite visible in the Afro-American family and constituted the United States' most impelling future problem.

Half of the black population had by that time reached the middle classes. To gain that achievement, it had given the father even greater importance than found in the traditional white family. This is still further proof of the existence in the West, and particularly in American society, of a relationship between the success of an ethnic group and a strong father figure. The other half of the Afro-American population was on a desperately downwards descent: it had been urbanized; it lived in slums; illegitimate births increased; and the presence of its fathers diminished. In the wake of these problems came delinquency and drug abuse. With reference as well to anthropological findings,[18] Moynihan declared that the roots of the problem came from a long way back.[19]

The role to be played by today's father is taught by the fathers of the preceding generation. As we discussed in this book's first section, Mead postulates the existence of a primary decision, at the beginning of civilization, which marked the moment when the human male first chose to provide food for females and their offspring: this is something male animals, among the mammals, do not do. They expressed an intention which then became a tradition, which is to say that it was transmitted. If there's a lack of insistence on adhering to it, this tradition can also be forgotten. In fact, it has no basis in any instinctive act, such as the mother's nursing: it is a socially established rule, and social rules must be taught. During slavery, the rules were changed: unions between slaves were simply *de facto*, unregulated, and afforded no recognition as families, with the result that pa-ternal responsibilities ("pa-" implies "nutrition") were no longer taught. The slave father didn't necessarily belong to the same owner as the mother; and in any case he could be sold and separated from his children, unlike the mother. Such conditions existed for centuries and weakened the identity of the father. Responsibility for children was left entirely to their mothers.

From a psychological point of view, this amounts to a kind of regression to the conditions of animal life. The slave owners unconsciously encouraged it, and exploited it as a source of confirmation of their own superiority. But the vicinity and reciprocal dependence of slaves and masters made them unconsciously quite similar to one another. Indeed, the white males regressed even more completely to a pre-paternal state: they coupled with the female slaves, and left them pregnant. Once the child was born, not only was the child not recognized, but might be sold by the father-master along with the mother-slave. As in animal society, the child was entirely the concern of its mother.

Moynihan has been criticized, and primarily because of his postulation of a clear causal link between the absence of the father and subsequent marginalization. Others have inverted the relationship, affirming that the impoverishment of the family is the final result of socio-economic poverty.[20] The only thing observed with certainty in the United States is a direct correlation between the two: the frequency with which a group lacks its fathers goes hand in hand with that group's degree of marginalization. In any case, the alarm sounded by the Moynihan report was dramatic; and it had the merit of opening a discourse on the quality of the poverty which the future held, not only on its quantity.

In subsequent years, the problem has grown ever more grave.[21] A survey carried out in 1987 indicated that 85 percent of the black men who became fathers before the age of 20 did not live with their children. The figure for middle-class white men of the same age and in the same situation[22] was 23 percent. Meanwhile, drug abuse and juvenile crime grew dramatically more widespread, and fatherless male adolescents accounted always for the greatest number of offenders. Eighty-five percent of the male population of America's prisons is fatherless.[23] The apprehension aroused by *The Negro Family. The Case for National Action* has proved to have been more than justified.

But there is also a sense in which Moynihan was too optimistic. While denouncing the inhumanity of slavery in the United States, he compared it to slavery in Brazil and spoke of the greater tradition of tolerance in Latin America.[24]

In Brazil, the gravity of the problem of the growing rarity of fathers is clear and unquestionable, but it is difficult to determine the extent to which it is the heritage of slavery. In the metropolitan area of São Paulo, the area where conditions most resemble those of North America's slums, the lowest rung of the social ladder is occupied by fatherless black families. The absence of the father sucks such families into a vicious circle that inevitably influences the next generation. In black families of equal poverty, children who live with their fathers are more likely to go to school, and those whose fathers are absent are more to likely to have to go to work.[25]

Northeast Brazil can in some ways be said to have made the passage from colonial society to present-day slums without ever entering the modern age. In the poorer parts of Recife, the most frequent form the family takes can be described as *matrifocal.*[26] "Matrifocality" refers to family circumstances in which the father is not necessarily absent, but where in any case he is not a decisive factor. The relationship between mother and daughter is very strong, whereas the relationship between father and son is quite weak; the extended family is exclusively the mother's family; all important decisions are made by the women; and so forth.

In Recife's matrifocal families, the father's presence is at best intermittent. At times he is there, at others he disappears. Once inside the walls of the home, he is passive. The house belongs to the women, inclusive of the project that shapes the lives of the people it houses. The lives of the men – no matter their age and with no real questions raised – take place in the outside world, in bumming around in groups, or pursuing sexual adventure. As time goes by the men of any particular generation, and increasingly with the succession of the generations, lose control of both the house and their women: "cuckold" is the most typical insult. Sucked backwards into prehistory, they revert from the condition of fatherhood back into simple males. Finally, when the family's economic situation has grown more stable, and perhaps when the children are already at work and earn an income, the wives throw them out definitively, as bees do with their drones, the parasitic males.

The relationship between marginalization and the absence of the father can here be seen in a different light. Some imagined the absence of the father to be caused by poverty. Yet, even when poverty has been defeated, the father makes no return. Quite to the contrary: his presence is declared to be useless, and he is definitively eliminated. It is almost obvious that the father makes no return because no such thing any longer exists: there are no fathers, only a pack of males. Even if it comes from backward, outlying parts of Brazil, this is an example of a typically *modern* situation. And no other example of our modern situation so clearly reveals the animal precariousness at the base of it, the tragic substitutability of males.

Ulysses' family had to wait ten years for his return, but he did return, and he expunged the parasitic suitors. But if the father remains to reappear after a lapse of hundreds of years, Penelope strikes an alliance with Telemachus and throws out the parasites on her own.

So we know that there is often a general correlation between the poverty of a family and the absence of its father.[27] Now we can attempt to look at Anglo-Saxon North America and Latin America in comparative terms. In North America, the brunt of the problem is primarily felt by the impoverished, urban black population, which accounts for no more than five to six percent of the total population. Until recently, the greater part of the United States was unacquainted with it. The Protestant tradition had given the father figure so great a value as to make it seem invincible.

In Latin America, the combination of marginalization and the absence of the father shows a different set of features which is often even more tragic and of wider scope. The underprivileged constitute a larger percentage of the population and are not so sharply separated from the middle classes, which in turn find it more difficult to reach the stable socio-economic situation which they enjoy in wealthier countries. The father may be absent not because he divorced and went his separate way; his absence often dates from the very birth of his child, if not earlier. The relationship between poverty and the absence of the father is tragically evident. It is not "only" a heritage from slavery, and it isn't limited to the ghettoes.

In Mexico alone, there are 2.8 million families which are headed by women, which amounts to 17.1 percent of the total population. But the most stunning fact is that the average income of families headed by women is only a third of the figure for those headed by men.[28]

From the psychological point of view, the Latin American tendency to seek refuge in the matrifocal family has also been encouraged by the long-standing influence of the Catholic Church, which has never given the father image in general or the father of the family in particular all the weight they have in the Protestant and Jewish traditions. The Roman Catholic Church, obviously enough, has never denied the value of the father, yet it has seldom made a specific attempt to propose him as a model for the child. But this difficult process of education is precisely the factor that cannot be set aside, if we believe, in agreement with Mead, that fatherhood is a cultural institution, rather than a natural given. If a society is to have fathers, they have to be insisted upon, much more than with mothers.

The father figure can also serve as a vantage point from which to view the differences in development that separate North America from Latin America. The gap that holds them apart results not only from political, religious, cultural and environmental differences, but also from the different roles they ascribe to fathers. Neither technology, nor natural resources, nor the level of capital accumulation, nor any of their other cultural phenomena are alone sufficient to account for the distance between the two semi-continents. The Rio Grande is also the frontier of fatherhood. *Without a strong middle class, supported by a strong father, no country or ethnic group seems until now to have fully entered the modern age.*[29] The *Latino* families that manage most easily to integrate themselves into American society and to rise within it are those with stronger father figures and more solid family structures.

Here we encounter a seldom-treated aspect of the division of the continent and the difficult task of modifying the cultural frontier at the Rio Grande. The South and Central American families that successfully enter the United States are frequently those which have a project: families with a strong father figure, in symbolic terms, but also in flesh and blood. The drone-fathers who dedicate their lives to alcohol and the pursuit of sex remain in their native countries. At the cultural level we thus find an unconscious repetition of an economic phenomenon which already has been highly criticized: the world of the rich makes a low-cost purchase of the best of the resources of the world of the poor, while leaving behind its inferior products.

Beyond the enormous differences between North and South America, between Afro-Americans and indigenous Indios, one feels a similar loss of the father, as determined by centuries of pressure from the European immigrants. Possession of a father figure was a precondition for social ascent. But since the middle and upper strata of society were reserved to Europeans, blacks and Indios had no need of fathers; indeed, their lack of fathers was in many ways of service to the social order. Even in the first few centuries of their presence, the European immigrants in both North and South America attempted, though in highly different ways, to monopolize the system of the patriarchal family so as to reinforce their own dominion over the other two principal ethnic groups. The bodies of the males, especially the blacks, had to be kept available for work; the bodies of the females, above all the Indios, had to be kept available not only for work but also for sex.

The sexual exploitation of Indio women in Spanish and Portuguese America was taken for granted for a lengthy period of time, given that at first the European immigrants were disproportionately male. Among the Spanish in sixteenth-century Peru, men outnumbered women on the order of seven or eight to one.[30] Though brutalized and humiliated, the Indio women were finally indispensable to the white man: they also prepared his food, and they also gave him children.[31] As more or less willing concubines, black and native women were allowed a degree of power which the colonists denied to black and native men. Both black and Indio males introjected this state of castration for centuries and lost their self-image as subjects who make choices and assume responsibility; who teach their children the ways of adult life; who function as fathers. A number of historians consider the *machismo* and violent jealously which still today are found among the lower classes to derive directly from the conquest, in which the women too were "conquested" by the Europeans.[32]

Extreme situations such as colonization and frontier life, where the defeated are treated like something intermediate between the human being and the beast, are marked by a certain reversion to animal society. The monogamic contract that regulates civil life by assigning a female to each male is no longer observed. As happens among the primates, a stronger group of males attempts to control the greatest possible number of women, and the weaker are forced to remain content with those it leaves behind.

The patriarchal hierarchy here assumes a curious structure. At the top are the European men. Then the European women. But given their scarcity, they are immediately followed by the black and Indio women. The black and Indio men are the lowest group[33] and are prevented from being fathers to a greater degree than their women are prevented from being mothers. For psychological, sociological and even, unfortunately, for zoological reasons: we have seen that reversion to animal forms of society is always accompanied by a reversal of the institution of fatherhood.

The initial era of colonization in Latin America was followed by a period that reestablished a balance in the numbers of European men and women. For statistical as much as for legal reasons, the violence committed against black and Indio women receded to a lower level. But they were frequently unable to reconstruct true families with the men of their own ethnic groups, who meanwhile had ceased to learn to be fathers. At the lower levels of the social pyramid, this ancient evil has remained; matrifocal families are both a sign of its continued presence and an attempt to do away with it, by doing away with the father altogether.

These brief considerations already provide an image of the growing rarity of the father in the modern world.

A country-by-country survey would serve only to indicate local variations of a world-wide phenomenon. Tellenbach's conferences on the father have been taking place in Germany for years.[34] He notes, moreover, that the father's absence at the two extremes of the social scale is far higher than the norm; this is what he found among schizophrenics from highly disadvantaged circumstances, and also among the leaders of the students' movement of 1968, who came from upper middle class families.[35] This is perfectly in line with the absence of the father which we have already seen at the social extremes of the United States.

It's clear, of course, that it is always artificial, in no matter what country of the world, to establish similarities between the upper and lower poles of society. That's the case here again. In the lower classes, we're more likely to find fathers who are totally absent, and children who become delinquent or psychotic. In the upper and middle classes, children are more likely to be simply maladjusted, and the father's absence is likely to derive from business that keeps him away from home, or from circumstances that accompany divorce. It's the latter situation that threatens to grow worse in the future, and further to propagate itself.

The conditions of the lives of manual workers, who began to experience the disappearance of the father at the beginning of the Industrial Revolution, have meanwhile improved in ways that can give them time to spend with their families. For fathers in more elevated circumstances, nearly the reverse has occurred. Such a father more easily decides to divorce. To what degree do cultural and economic advantages help him to maintain contact with his children?

There was a time when he owned a factory or a rural estate. He could oversee his interests from a nearby home, where he continued to live with his family. His present-day counterpart – whether a CEO, an entrepreneur, a professional or a banker – has a much more complex life. The schedule of his work day has slipped beyond his control. He works at irregular hours, and the social aspects of business relationships consume his leisure time. There are also frequent trips, often unplanned and unforeseeable. Communication with his children is problematic in cultural terms as well, since his family belongs to the strata of society in which change takes place most rapidly. He can't teach them his job, since the professions of his class shift more radically from decade to decade, or even from year to year, than is true of simpler occupations. He likewise finds it impossible to initiate his children into a social group, since another of the results of globalization is an always increasing fluidity of the very society in which he moves; homes are frequently bought and sold as the family moves from one city or country to another; he can't teach values and principles to his children, since these too grow relative in the company of all the other shifts and changes.

These are the sources of the new impulse in the father's disappearance. It has been calculated that close to half of the family units in the major Western cities are by now the result of a change in the initial relationships from which the children were born. In nearly all cases, the children have followed their mother.

The phenomenon of the vanishing father began at the two extremes of society and is now on the march toward its center: it tends gradually to spread into the middle classes. But it enters their lives from above: the middle classes would never dream of miming the behavior of classes below their own. The marginalized portions of the population of the great cities – portions where the nineteenth century's "unwholesome father" still survives – are largely caught up in autonomous patterns of behavior: the dynamic of the forces that shape their lives is a source of no "contagion" for other social groups, and their numbers are unlikely to increase beyond a certain degree. For the average population, they constitute a comforting negative model, and in many cities their numbers are even declining. The rarefaction of the father in the middle classes is primarily abetted by the examples of "freedom" provided by the upper classes.

Taken as a whole, the advance of the absent father pursues this route: from America, to Europe, to the third world; from the major to the smaller cities, and then to rural communities; and, finally, from the upper to the lower reaches of the social scale. There has been no lack of alarmed concern, but a parallel in the world of animals once again comes to mind: it frequently occurs that the endangerment of a species is recognized when it is already too late to undertake measures to assure its survival.

The comparison rings true. As said in the introduction, a psychological history necessarily starts from a long way back. We have seen that the decline of the father began centuries, indeed millennia ago. Most fathers, however, continued to avoid taking notice, until decline gave way to collapse. Perhaps there will seem to be no point in studying a construction as it collapses. But the collapse of an edifice in no way implies the collapse of the history of the erosion that led to it, and it doesn't expunge the history of the building itself: these are things we want to know, not for the purpose of changing the course of history, but in order to transmit the memory of history to our children. To train and inform their memory is also, in fact, to expose them to the true ideal of fatherhood. The gaze of the father is the organ that transmits memory while also transmitting itself. The paternal gaze peers beyond the moment and creates the existence of time. When directed toward the future it formulates projects; when directed toward the past it constructs the meaning of the events of the world which already have taken place and the mode through which to grasp it. Project relates to the future as memory relates to the past.

Our overview can lead to no facile optimism. The phenomena of absent and unwholesome fathers broke out with the impoverishment of the proletariat and the beginning of the Industrial Revolution. But now that the working classes have exited from conditions of poverty, the father continues to be absent, and has yet to recover his nobility.

The next step came with the great twentieth-century wars: their violence inaugurated an even greater distance between fathers and their children. When peace returned, the father didn't return in its company. Even if he survived the war, Ulysses by then was exhausted and didn't survive the homeward voyage. The world wars did a great deal more than to snuff out the lives of the fathers of millions of children. They were also the very first wars in which millions of still-living veterans were taken from their children: veterans who never succeeded in turning themselves back into fathers. For the family, finally, it made little difference: the father didn't die in the war, but at the moment of returning home.

NOTES

1 Guggenbühl, A. (1992) *Vom Guten des Bösen. Über das Paradoxe in der Psychologie*. Zurich: Schweizer Spiegel, Chapter 3.

2 Abramovitch, H. (1994) "Pigmy giants," *San Francisco Jung Institute Library Journal*, 13(3): 43–7. Source not given; French fathers too give their children only few minutes a day: see Delumeau and Roche (eds) (1990), XV.

3 Pleck, J. H. (1997) "Paternal involvement: levels, sources and consequences," in Lamb (ed.), *The Role of the Father in Child Development*.

    Dana Mack (*The Assault on Parenthood*, New York: Simon & Schuster, 1997, Chapter 9) draws comfort from a study that indicates a 5 percent increase in paternal involvement between 1987 and 1991. But given the level of departure, the involvement of American fathers remains extremely low. The same can be said for Europe, and even for the Scandinavian countries. (See note 8, in Chapter 20 of this volume.)

4 Keniston, K. (1977) *All Our Children: the American Family under Pressure*. New York: Harcourt Brace Jovanovich, as quoted by Bloom-Feshbach, J. (1981) "Historical perspectives in the father's role," in Lamb (ed.), *The Role of the Father in Child Development*.

    The records for 1895 show 40,000 divorces and 620,000 marriages. The figures for 1980 show 2,413,000 marriages and 1,182,000 divorces. The shift in the ratio of divorces to marriages is from 6.5 percent to 50 percent (source: National Center for Health Statistics).

5 Dafoe Whitehead, B. (1997) *The Divorce Culture*. New York: Knopf, Introduction and Chapter 1.

6 Coontz, S. (1997) *The Way We Really Are. Coming to Terms with America's Changing Families*. New York: Basic Books, Chapter 2. Popenoe, D. (1996) *Life Without Father*. New York and London: The Free Press, Chapter 1.

7 A fairly complete review of the shift can be found in: Blankenhorn, D. (1995) *Fatherless America. Confronting Our Most Urgent Social Problem*. New York: Harper Perennial, Chapter 1.

8 Hofferth, S. L. (1985) "Updating children's life course," *Journal of Marriage and the Family*, 93–115, 97.

9 Lamb in Lamb (ed.) (1997) *The Role of the Father in Child Development*.

10 Popenoe (1996), Chapter 7.

11 Source: Eurostat, *Newsweek*, CXXIV, 3, 20 January, 1997.

12 Furstenberg, F. et al. (1983) "The life course of children of divorce: marital disruption and parental contact," *American Sociological Review*, 48: 656–68, as quoted by Huntington, D. S. (1986) "Fathers: the forgotten figures of divorce," in Jacobs, J. W. (ed.), *Divorce and Fatherhood: The Struggle for Parental Identity*. Washington: American Psychiatric Press.

13 Osherson, S. (1986) *Finding Our Fathers: The Unfinished Business of Manhood*. New York: Free Press, as quoted by Gordon, B. (1990) "Being a father," in Meth, R. L. and Pasick, R. S., *Men in Therapy*. New York and London: The Guildford Press.

14 Furstenberg et al. (1983); Rosenthal, K. M. and Keshet, H. F. (1981) *Fathers without Partners: A Study of Fathers and the Family after Marital Separation*. Totowa NJ: Rowman and Littlefield, as quoted by Huntington (1986); Blankenhorn (1996), Chapter 7.

15 Fares, V. (1996) *Fathers and Developmental Psychology*. New York: John Wiley & Sons, I, 1.

16 *The New York Review of Books*, XLIV, 19 December 1997, presented a review of

five texts on the problems of the American family. Two of them used the word "really" in their titles. The insistent use of a term that appeals to the notion of reality might seem to symbolize the fear of having lost contact with it.

17 Office of Policy Planning and Research, US Department of Labor, Washington DC. Reprinted by Greenwood Press, Westport CN, 1981.

18 Mead (1949).

19 Moynihan, D. P. (1965) *The Negro Family. The Case for National Action.* Washington DC: Office of Policy Planning and Research, US Department of Labor. See also the reconstruction by Varenne, H. (1986) "Love and liberty, the contemporary American family," in Burguière et al. (eds), *Histoire de la famille*, Vol. II.

20 A recent and fairly complete summary of these various points of view can be found in Daniels, C. R. (ed.) (1998) *Lost Fathers. The Politics of Fatherlessness in America.* New York: St. Martin's Press.

21 Biller, H. B. (1981) "The father and sex role development," in Lamb (ed.), *The Role of the Father in Child Development*; Marsiglio, W. and Cohan, M. (1997) "Young fathers and child development," in Lamb (ed.), *The Role of the Father in Child Development.* Between 1960 and 1990 the overall percentage of black children who lived only with their mothers passed from 19.9 percent to 51.2 percent (an increase of more than 250 percent). Source: Bureau of the Census.

22 Marsiglio, W. (1987) "Adolescent fathers in the United States: their initial living arrangements, marital experience and educational outcomes," *Family Planning Perspectives*, 19: 240–51, as quoted in Marsiglio and Cohan (1997) "Young fathers and child development," in Lamb (ed.), *The Role of the Father in Child Development.*

23 Bly, R. (1996) *The Sibling Society.* Reading MA: Addison Wesley, Chapter 7. Source not given.

24 Moynihan (1965), III.

25 *Famílias Chefiadas por Mulheres*, SEADE (Sistema Estadual de Anàlise de Dados), São Paulo 1994.

26 Scott, R. P., (1990) "O homem na matrifocalidade," in *Cadernos de Pesquisa*, 73: 38–47, São Paulo, May; Smith, R. T. (1973) "The matrifocal family," in Goody, J. (ed.), *The Character of Kinship.* Cambridge: Cambridge University Press.

27 In North and South America, and partly in Europe. In the Scandinavian countries, the absence of the father is a highly common phenomenon, even without being correlated to poverty. See Coontz (1997), Chapter 8. Many Arab countries, on the other hand, are marked by a situation in which poverty coexists with families with at least nominally strong fathers.

28 *Los hogares en Mexico*, INEGI (Instituto Nacional de Estadistica Geografia e Informatica), Aguascalientes, August 1997. The problem, naturally enough, is less visible outside the great cities, and, in general, has grown less virulent with the advance of modernization. But the few available statistics also tell us that in a more traditional country such as Ecuador the percentage of women who are heads of families is at its highest in the classes that earn the least, and lowest in those that earn the most. See *Hogares y pobreza*, INEC, Quito 1994.

29 Even the exception of the Scandinavian societies is only apparent. The high level of prosperity and the extent of the social services today protect unwed mothers from marginalization. But when modernization came about, the fathers were still in their places, in line with a Protestant tradition which is still today reflected in the reliability, sobriety and efficiency of the daily rhythms of Scandinavian life.

30 Bernand, C. and Gruzinski, S. (1986) "I figli dell'apocalisse: la famiglia in Meso-

America e nelle Ande," in Burguière et al. (eds), *Histoire de la famille*, Vol. II.

31 Her role as connecting link between the indigenous population and the immigrants, and as the "founding mother" of present-day Latin America, remains little discussed, even today, and is banished into the unconscious. An exception will be found in the thorough study by Gambini, R. (1988) *O espelho ìndio. Os jesuitas e la destruçâo da alma indìgena*. São Paulo: Editora Espaço e Tempo.

32 Paz, O. (1950/1986) *El laberinto de la soledad*. Mexico DF: Fondo de Cultura Economica, IV; Mirandé, A. (1997) *Hombres y Macho*. Boulder CO: Westview Press, 2.

33 This psychological consideration finds a parallel in economic practices. In the history of slavery, their capacity for reproduction and their usefulness for sexual purposes made female slaves sell at higher prices than males. Deveau, J.-M. (1998) *Femmes esclaves. D'hier à aujourd'hui*. Paris: France Empire.

34 Tellenbach, H. (1976/1978) "Suchen nach dem verlorenen Vater," in Tellenbach, H. (ed.), *Das Vaterbild in Mythos und Geschichte*. Stuttgart: Kohlhammer, I, II.

35 Tellenbach, H., in Tellenbach (ed.) (1976). Specific studies have suggested the possibility that the lack of the father is of greater significance than the lack of the mother among the factors leading to suicide. It's to be noted, moreover, that this finding applies both to Western Germany and to Eastern Germany, before the collapse of the Berlin wall. See: "Die Bedeutung von Elternverlusten in der Kindheit bei depressiven und suizidalen Patienten," *Praxis Kinderpsychologie und Kinderpsychiatrie*, November 1991, 40(9): 322–7; "Eltern-Mutter- oder Vaterverlust in der Kindheit und suizidales Verhalten im Erwachsenenalter," *Psychiatrie Neurologie Medizinische Psychologie* (Leipzig) April 1989, 41(4): 218–23. For similar indications with respect to other Western countries: "Suicidal attempts and ideations among adolescents and young adults: the contribution of the father's and mother's care," *Social Psychiatry and Psychiatric Epidemiology*, October 1993, 28(5): 256–61 (Quebec); "Experience of parental loss and later suicide," *Acta Psychiatrica Scandinavica* May 1989, 79(5): 450–2 (Denmark); "Les facteurs suicidogènes chez l'enfant et chez l'adolescent," *Synapse. Journal de Psychiatrie et Système Nerveux Central*, September 1997, 138: 79–82 (France).

Chapter 19

The abdication of the father: in flight toward the past

Now we'll attempt to look beyond the statistics. The disappearance of the father is a psychological collapse, in the minds of fathers themselves no less than in the collective imagination. It's a source of disorientation even for those whom the patriarchy caused great pain.

Collective psychology found reassurance in the father image, since the collective imagination saw the father to embody responsibility, even if there is no way of knowing how true this might have been in daily life. The rarefaction of the father image provokes confusion and recrimination, since responsibility, by definition, is something from which there can be no release. Bewilderment and criticism then become elements of a vicious circle: the fathers take them as still more reason to distance from their families and shrink from fatherhood. In this era of brutal economics, the father is like a business in crisis: if all forecasts are negative, and no one has anything good to say, share price falls, and then collapses, and creditors insist that all outstanding bills be paid immediately. The bankrupt firm is dissolved and canceled out of existence.

We don't, of course, insist that this is always the way things go. We do suggest that this is the way they tend to go, on the whole, and in the course of time, within the flow of a great, unconscious decline. From the outside, in day to day affairs, observing the process is more difficult. There may also be fathers who play their role successfully and responsibly, and who would therefore reject the notion that fatherhood itself is in decay.

In daily practice, the analyst constantly encounters cases in which the father abdicates his role in ways which are no less unconscious than radical, and which are also a sign of the times. We daily encounter situations in which men revert to animals, and are once again only males, refusing to be fathers and husbands. The male animal's instinct is to fecundate the female, seeking no other relationship with her, and assuming no paternity of the offspring. If cases such as these repeatedly present themselves to analysts – whose clientele is far from large – we are faced with something more than an individual malady. We are dealing with a symptom of the male's much more general flight from civilization. Consumerist promiscuity undermines monogamy, and this also threatens the existence of the fathers who invented it.

One example is found in those men whose sexual desire for their wives disappears when they enter pregnancy. These men become suddenly a mystery to themselves.

The period of gestation brings something new into the sexual life of a couple. But the nature of the novelties for any given couple cannot be foreseen. In some couples, sexuality ebbs; in others it increases. This isn't what interests us here. Once pregnancy has been achieved, we can surmise in most cases that both instinct and the powerful archetypal images of eros push less vigorously towards sexual intercourse, since its principal goal has already been reached. The animal, or what remains of the animal in the human being, would turn attention elsewhere: the female to the protection of the embryo, the male to the insemination of other females. So, the rules of civilization second the instinct of the female, while attempting to inhibit the male's, which threatens to bring disorder into society. The couple is encouraged to pursue its unity entirely on the basis of the maternal and paternal archetypes: on condition that the male continues to recognize himself in the latter.

We imagine this, moreover, to be one of the reasons why tribal civilizations demand that the husband identify with the task of his wife by way of the *couvade*, which drastically distracts him from new sexual interests. In the *couvade*, the man is in a certain sense overwhelmed by his involvement with his child: he suffers all the mother's anxieties and the pains she experiences in giving birth, even to the point of abandoning his daily occupations and passing more time in bed than she does. It can be generally stated that tribal civilizations place the father at a lower level of importance than in the West: so in moments when his identity has to be strengthened, they ask him virtually to immerse himself in the indestructible force of the mother. Though living in conditions which are close to nature, the tribe thus attempts to avert the dangerous vectors of instinct and to reinforce the monogamic contract.

And what allows men of tribal cultures, whose use of the will for the establishment of personal tasks is limited, to succeed in gaining complete control over an impulse as potent as sexual desire? The answer lies in their continuing access to myths and rites which involve them in the world of the archetypes, which wield an even greater power than instinct. Even while living in a world from which myth has been expunged, European and American fathers-to-be likewise enjoyed the protection of a highly potent archetypal figure until only a short while ago: the figure of the father which was charged with unconscious associations with the authority of Hector, Ulysses and Aeneas. This timeless, collective model was able to compensate the inevitable weaknesses of individuals. But since the time in which fatherhood has turned into a source of more feelings of guilt than of pride, such unconscious associations have plunged to depths that render them close to imperceptible.

Clearly enough, there have always been men, in all cultures, who turned their sexual attentions elsewhere as soon as they had fulfilled the "duty" of conceiving a descendant. The disparity between the power of men and women allowed them ample freedom; at times there were also circumstances, as in ancient Greece, in which sexuality and family responsibility were different and separate things. In other times and places, such as eighteenth-century Paris or Venice, wives too could allow themselves sexual freedom. This isn't what we are talking about. We don't want to talk about individuals whose behavior is in harmony with the collective values of the societies in which they live, and who therefore suffer no strident internal conflict. Men in such conditions could betray their wives without any grave discomfort, because they were authorized to do so by their culture, and because they had already identified with fatherhood: they continued to feel civilized.

We have already remarked that the Roman rite of the elevation of the male child served the purpose of the psychic birth of the son as son, *and of the father as father*. But the modern man, even if he intends to commit himself to fatherhood, is still, on the one hand, in the grips of instinct, and, on the other, conducts his life in a civilization from which the rites of fatherhood have disappeared. If such a man's fantasies now turn to other women, *this doesn't take place within the norms of his civilization, but by way of his abdication from his status as a civilized father*. Like a portrait removed from the wall and stripped of its frame, fatherhood is no longer a significant image. The man has conceived biologically, but he hasn't baptized his psyche in the waters of fatherhood.

Without cultural coordinates that guide them toward fatherhood, and frequently with the personal experience of having themselves been deprived of fathers – it's not by chance that many such men had absent fathers, or fathers who were too submissive to the mother – the psyche of these men regresses, and they return to the state of the male animal.

The purely male impulse is to produce another pregnancy like the first: more offspring, but in the absence of fatherhood, with its demand for commitment to the child already conceived, and to the task of providing for the child. Civilization therefore makes highly radical attempts to control this male instinct. So, the man who feels it stir can feel the earth to tremble beneath his feet and shake the pillars of civilization. That sensation, however, comes too late: it's not enough for him to correct his ways, since something is lacking not only in him, but in the whole of society.

Freud tells us that the construction of civilization depends on the repression of the instincts.[1] But the individual cannot construct it alone. The individual needs collective rules and symbolic celebrations. The male's entrance into civilization – the passage from simple fecundation to fatherhood – has likewise always been in need of rituals: the ritual of the *couvade* in tribal cultures, the ritual in Rome of the *pater familias* who held up his son in public, thus announcing, "I not only have conceived this child, but also intend to nourish him." Similar things are found throughout the history of the West, where the father led prayer at the dinner table, broke the bread, and gave the children his blessing.

Such rituals have disappeared – fathers having found their way from authoritative to unwholesome – and the man stands alone. He doesn't succeed in turning himself into a father in the moment in which his wife is about to make him one. He feels himself sucked backwards, towards a pre-civilized condition.

There are various situations in which a man regresses and feels the claws of the beast within himself. Let's now consider another, which is also one of the most universal injustices in the relationship between men and women. It's little discussed, almost as though it were accepted with fatalism.

No human being becomes more attractive with old age. Yet men undergo a slow decline and at times acquire additional seductive features with advancing years. Things stands differently with women, who after middle age quite rapidly lose the capacity to attract a man. The older man, especially if endowed with intelligence and power, can aspire to a young partner; frequently he finds her and leaves a wife of his own age. The opposite is much more rare.

They are various reasons for this lack of symmetry.

On the one hand, there are ancient conventions, primarily connected with the patriarchy. Men have more power than women, and older men more power than younger men. So the male of a certain age stands at the summit of the power structure. Traditionally, he took a younger wife, more attractive and compliant than a woman of his own age, and better suited to giving birth to children. Convention approved, since the custom reinforced the patriarchal structure of society.

On the other hand, we have the fact that the patriarchy itself was not constructed on a void, but on a pedestal prepared by nature. Men, even with decreasing capacity, can procreate up until death, since they continue to produce spermatozoa, whereas women lose the capacity for reproduction in the second half of life, which the insistence of medical science has rendered unnaturally long. The couple that consists of the older man and the younger woman is more frequent than its opposite not only as a result of the historical oppression of women, but also because it takes advantage of this prehistoric asymmetry.

Let's return to an example from analytic practice. A man made the acquaintance of a woman without having seen her, by way of lengthy telephone conversations. He was very much attracted to her. On meeting her, he discovered her advanced age. The attraction remained, but with a brusque shift towards feelings of reverence: the man's fantasy abolished the woman's body and its place was taken by an archetype charged with gentleness. He discussed the relationship in analysis and rejected all feelings of sexual attraction, as though his psyche had ruptured a principle of natural order. This attitude can't be interpreted entirely as a sign of discomfort with a desire for incest with the mother: incest is a cultural taboo, and therefore more complex, and not linked exclusively to the difference in age. Among elderly men who desire a younger woman, the sensation of breaking a natural law is extremely rare.

Biological law is the law that demands procreation, and which therefore rejects the elderly woman. But the existence of a similar "law" doesn't mean that we have to accept it, since to do so would be also to accept a return to intolerance for homosexuality, which is another variant that the state of nature has marginalized since it's not conducive to reproduction. The laws of psychic and cultural life are much more complex than those of biology. Unfortunately, in this regard the foundations of patriarchal custom rest fairly directly on biology. If those foundations begin to crumble, what lies beneath them becomes more visible. This is to say that in situations of fragility – of rapid transformation of the surrounding culture – the attenuation of the rules of civilization can cause the reappearance of the animal "rule": the laws not of ethics but of biological survival. Protection from such a regression can only be found in consciousness. Civilization is in any case based on the repression and redirection of the instincts.

The elderly man of the past who married a younger woman simply made visible the patriarchal hierarchy of society, with no discomfort. The present-day man accepts the equality of men and women, and more frequently marries a woman of his own age. But is he unconditionally satisfied by his more correct behavior?

Let's refer to the case history of a man who had children who were almost grown and a wife his own age. He suddenly became aware of an attraction for a younger woman, and he couldn't understand how precisely such a thing might happen to him: it was something he had never sought – unlike the patriarchs who pawed young girls without embarrassment. He felt guilty towards his wife, who didn't deserve to be rejected and humiliated; he felt vulgar with the young woman, who deserved the delicate attention that he might have given a daughter, and who might indeed have been his daughter; he felt uneasy with his children, by whom he feared to be judged, and compared to the Bible's libidinous old men.

Since he took no pride in the temptation he felt, it caused him enormous suffering and he struggled against it. He did not realize that the reason for his regression also lay in a difficulty with growing older; the dignity of the traditional father had facilitated the process of aging. The finest aspects of the archetypal father were rooted in his moral authority and had little to do with physical prowess or seductiveness. As the family's proxy for the divine father, the image he developed was more likely to be spiritual and an-erotic.

The guilt which caused this man to suffer had less to do with his betrayal of conjugal morality, than with an ontological betrayal of civilization. Without his being aware of it, the absence of the image of the father – in the society around him no less than in his vision of himself – had reawakened the male on the search for fecundation. That male sleeps a very light sleep beneath the millennia which have constructed fatherhood, and it once again directed his gaze toward another woman.

In the closing decades of the twentieth century, the delinquency of gangs of young males has become a major problem. One of its most visible features is group rape. The young "suitors" throw themselves on the body of Penelope, and, as we're told by a non-Homeric version of the myth (see Chapter 10), generate Pan. They generate the symbol of Pan: in postmodern times they once again give visibility to the highly ancient god of rape[2] by allowing its spirit to possess them without restraint. Horizontal laws release the brotherhood of sons from the vertical order of the father. The horde authorizes exit from the monogamic nuclear family along with regression to the functional efficiency of the pack.

It's a mistake to refer to such instances of sexual aggression as "aimless" forms of group delinquency. The unconscious aim is quite precise: the reestablishment of a way of relating to women which is free of all civil responsibility. That goal is achieved. If the male is no longer a father, he must after all become something else. The simplest solution to this radical identity crisis is to return to the condition that preceded the father's invention. Group rape is an initiation into a regressive form of adult masculinity. The individual can associate rape with a sense of guilt. The pack, however, has a culture of its own and functions as a tribe that ritualizes regression: it transforms guilt into a collectively accepted event.

It's not enough to say that rape has always existed, and simply wasn't denounced, as a result of male dominion. Its always having existed is itself the source of a major question. Rape was perhaps a quasi-right of a patriarchal and male-centered world. An infraction frequently tolerated (in silence, or by projecting onto the *responsibilities* of the female who had "provoked" it) when committed by the young future patriarch or by the patriarch himself: a compensation for the *responsibilities* of fatherhood (institutional responsibilities, but originally, in the memory of the collective unconscious, freely chosen). Rape today is no silent act on the part of the patriarch, but a boisterous act of the pack. Its irresponsibility toward the victim, and to the horror's possible offspring, is no compensation for individual responsibilities which have elsewhere been assumed; it is the regression of the whole of a group to a total lack of responsibility for anything and everything that lies outside the present moment. It is a transgressive manifestation not of heterosexual eros, but of the homosexual eros of the excited pack that bonds with itself by way of its victim.

The sense in which such groups are fatherless goes beyond the material fact that its members frequently have no fathers, or have fathers who at best are inert. The group is also fatherless in a cultural and symbolic sense: it has regressed to the pre-paternal rungs of the ladder of evolution.

Let's look for a moment at a particularly disturbing instance of collective sexual violence.

In the last several years, ethnic rape has made its appearance among the horrors that Europe has so creatively furnished to the world. The term refers to a particular version of the sack – given that women are a part of the booty – in which rape is committed with the deliberate goal of increasing the numbers of the victors' ethnic group. Rather than an accident, pregnancy is the goal of the procedure. This crime, however, is nothing new: it's precisely what the Futurists prophesied in the *Futurist Manifesto of Lust* (Chapter 15).

It might be objected that it's even more ancient. That the ancient Greeks carried off the women of defeated Troy, after having massacred their husbands, and conceived children with them. But that's precisely where the difference lies. The children of the Trojan women, even if bastards and inevitably inferior to the Greeks' legitimate offspring, were not abandoned. They were fed in the victors' homes. And the victors knew that they were the fathers of these children, watched them grow up, and, no matter how summarily, provided for them.

Here we're speaking of children who are deliberately conceived without the existence, even for a moment, of a project or a fantasy concerning their future.

The true horror of ethnic rape isn't to be found in its violence and cruelty. It lies in the fact that it instantaneously throws us backward, through hundreds of thousands of years, to a condition in which the law was not the law of fatherhood, but of animal fecundation. The psychological backdrop, not by chance, of such instances of mass regression is the disintegration of the collective image of the father. It is likewise no accident that their geographic backdrop is furnished by disintegrating dictatorships. The death of the terrible fathers continues, and brings to light still further aspects of the maladies afflicting fatherhood.

NOTES

1 Freud, S. (1929) (*Das Unbehagen in der Kultur.* English translation: *Civilization and Its Discontents*). Standard Edition, Vol. XXI.
2 Hillman (1972a).

Chapter 20

The abdication of the father: in flight toward the future

When psychoanalysis appeared, it seemed that the father had found an ally.[1]

Sigmund Freud was deeply attached to his mother, and supposed that all male children felt a similar preference. But as a man of his times, he placed the father at the family's summit. And he was personally inclined to identify with the spiritual teachers of the Hebrew tradition. He thought of the father as the guide who, departing from a still amorphous child, constructed a social being. And by introjecting such a father figure, the child laid the basis of morality; at the end of the period of intense attachment with the mother, the child gave birth to an interior authority (the Super-ego) which referred as an ideal to God the Father, to the personal father, and to other hierarchical figures.

This alliance between psychoanalysis and the father has not only been lost along the road, but has even been supplanted by an indirect hostility to the father.[2] Freud's followers have grown ever more concerned with the relationship between mother and child, and have marginalized the father: while turning their attention to the earliest stages of the life of the individual, they seem unconsciously to move backwards in the life of the species as well, all the way back to the pre-human family which foresaw no true relationship between father and child.

This hasn't been a question of an ideological allegiance. Post-Freudian theory has grown increasingly concerned with the initial phases of life. It therefore found it inevitable to direct attention to the symbiosis of mother and infant. In particular, Melanie Klein[3] has hypothesized that the formation of the Super-ego takes place during the first year of life, within the child's relationship with the body of the mother. The father thus loses his role as the teacher who imparts the sense of morality and social life: the root conceptions of right and wrong, the origins of the perception of the other, and of respect for the other, are seen to go back to a phase in which the child has not yet learned to talk.

The art, literature and culture of the entire twentieth century are neither comprehensible nor would have been possible without psychoanalysis. This is all the more true of our concepts of the family.

The decline of the father, already underway for centuries, thus came to be accelerated by the influence of neo-Freudian research. While shifting emphasis from the father to the mother, psychoanalysis also accentuated the primary relationships rather than the social relationships; corporeal experience came to be seen as the basis of spiritual experience, which was thus reduced to a superstructure. Psychoanalysis began to reflect another major tendency of Western civilization: its disengagement from the social dimension and from community experience, both religious and secular. This disengagement goes hand in hand with the victory of individualism and the sense of the private.

If it finds its roots in the original instincts and in the primary experiences, my psyche has few possibilities of adapting to the demands of society: this seems to be the indirect message of Freudian pessimism, even in spite of the strength of Freud's personal sense of society.[4]

Neo-Freudian and Kleinian research are central to the modern understanding of the human being. But they are concerned with the child's individual development. The picture has to be flanked and completed by an understanding of the social dimension of the human individual as seen through the great collective images that guide our cultural experience. Perception of the link between the personal and the collective unconscious was introduced by the psychology of C. G. Jung.[5] Another characteristic of Jungian psychology lies its interest in the "here and now," as opposed to the patient's remote past.[6]

We can refer to the initial period of growth, the period mainly of corporeal relationships, as primary, and to the successive period as secondary. This is clearly an approximation, but is sufficient for our present purposes. During the primary period, the child is mainly in relationship with one other person (a dyad). The secondary phase sees a shift from the dyad to the triad, the group and the collective. This secondary phase is the object principally studied by Jungian psychology. For a number of reasons: because it corresponds to the "here and now" of the patient who is looking for help; because Jung turns attention to the psyche *per se*, and only circumstantially to corporeal experience; and, finally, because Jungian psychology speaks of a collective as well as of an individual psyche and is therefore directly involved in the pursuit of an understanding of society.

Freudian psychology – especially in its neo-Freudian phases – principally concerns itself with biopsychic experience and the primary; Jungian psychology looks for its basis in the dimension of cultural experience and the secondary. From our point of view, post-Freudian psychology bears an indirect responsibility in the global advance of individualism: its attention to instinct and the pre-social phases of life pays scant attention to the possibilities of influencing the collective dimension; it thus encourages fatalism. The favorable reception often accorded to Jungian psychology on the part of persons of culture derives precisely from the role it attributes to the variability of culture as opposed to biological determinism, and as well from the ways in which its collective dimension can function as a restraint on individualism.

So, neo-Freudian psychoanalysis has accelerated the father's decline. But, as we know by now, it only threw wide an already open door.

Let's follow the course of events with the aid of a few images.

While looking at the illustrations in the books on the family and the father which were published in the nineteenth century, and also at the start of the twentieth, we immediately grasp a series of elements which remain independent of differences in class and nationality, and which underline the "collective quality of the father." The father is never a part of a dyad. He is almost always shown with the whole the family, and generally at its center. In a furnished living-room, which in turn we can suppose to be the center of the home. The father is a person who exercises a profession and belongs to a social class: he is highly defended, highly dressed, highly defined by his role (Fig. 8), even in the cases of working class fathers or of fathers who are farmers (Fig. 9). In every epoch and part of the world, the father wears Hector's armor.

Even if he dresses in clothing, exercises a profession, and conducts a life which no longer hold places in our memories, we immediately grasp the social and cultural geography in which he moves. The gaze these fathers direct at us immediately tells us who they are: craftsmen, nobles, farmers. Their images vary with their social status more than is true of the images of the mothers, since they allow us to glimpse the society that stands behind them, as filtered to a lesser or greater degree through the painter's or photographer's prejudices. The father is the obligatory route through which the family enters the surrounding society.

Such portraits remained nearly unchanging, century after century. But in the course of the twentieth century, indeed within the space of the last few generations – no more than the tiniest fraction of the history of fatherhood – things changed quite radically.

The image of the group, the family portrait, has virtually ceased to exist. The father seems to have lost his function as the link between the family and society. The group has disappeared. The background context has disappeared. The father's profession and social status have ceased to be visible. A previously unknown dyad appears: the father with a small child.

In the extreme – but frequent – case we want to examine here, the images captioned *the new father* present us in fact with a *new stereotype*.

The fathers are all young, handsome and half naked. They all wears jeans, below a bare chest. Publishing companies all across the world might appear to have signed a secret pact. In more or less tedious images, the father is reduced to a body.

The phenomenon, moreover, isn't confined to advertising and weekly magazines in which sentimental images obviously aim to impress the simplest reader. The truly striking fact is that even serious texts appropriate such images. They let it be known that the new fathers bare their chests, reject the world of society,

Figure 8 The Werburn Family (Simon Meister).

and immerse themselves in a dyadic and presumably symbiotic relationship with the child (Figs 10, 11 and 12). It's worth nothing that the last, even though stripped of his clothing and turned into an image for a tourist brochure, tosses his son into the air, unconsciously repeating the gesture of Hector.

As the male body has been reduced to an object – in much the same banal and exploitative ways which women have battled against in their struggle to be seen as individuals and not as stereotypes – the role of the father seems to be marked by a passage to primary custody of the child. In turn, this makes the man in question appear unreal and one-sided, like so many of the images of the Madonna which were produced by the minor artists of the Renaissance. It also seems to imply a "breast envy." It has been justly observed that these chests are usually hairless.[7]

Figure 9 A German agricultural family (Ingebor Weber-Kellerman (1976) *Die Familie.* Frankfurt: Insel Verlag).

Such an image of the father seems insincere in comparison with the openness of the nineteenth-century reproductions that substantially showed him as the patriarch he was. The modern image has an exiguous relationship with reality. The primary care of children on the part of their fathers remains, according to the point of view, a noble ideal or a hypocritical fantasy. We have seen that in practice it still continues to occur very rarely.[8] Even when it does occur, it is nearly always a simply auxiliary to the care provided by the mother.

How has this regression in our stock of collective images been able to take place? Are we to imagine a program of propaganda? Of books which exhort the fathers who read them to a specific mode of behavior?

The texts which furnish these illustrations come from authors and publishers who cannot be suspected of such a thing. They haven't provided us with propaganda leaflets, but with scholarly investigations that aim to describe the historical circumstances of fatherhood. And even if they aspired to proselytism, why would they give it the dated garb of a Fascist, Nazi or Soviet rhetoric – the eternal sentimentality of bare chests and babies being kissed – which has regularly proved to obtain the opposite of whatever it attempts to propose?

Figure 10 Father and son (Petit Format, Pascale Roche).

Figure 11 Father and son (Urban & Fischer Verlag).

Figure 12 Father and son (© "Life", Jan Saudek, Prague).

Does the father – or better, the father's body – truly know how to give something new by taking care of the body of the child? Doubtless, he has finally learned to be of assistance to his partner. But that, precisely, is the point. We are looking here at *the new partner*, but at no true image of a new father. In addition to lacking breasts, he also lacks any other specific relationship with the act of providing nourishment. Even those who claim that men are better cooks than women will know that they're talking about men as restaurateurs and not about men as fathers: they're speaking about certain men's capacities for a professional relationship with food, and not about its use as the language of dialog with the child, as it is for the mother. Paternal nurture has no specificity, and is only a copy of what mothers do.

It's clear that the rush to the "ever more primary" – the frenetic need to plant what counts into ever more precocious phases of infancy – is more than an evolution on the part of post-Freudian research, and reflects as well an involution on the part of our whole society. It synchronizes with a tendency to subtract ourselves from the social dimension, each of us taking refuge in our own private corner: in individualism or in the "relationship" to which we refer as symbiosis, where two subjectivities nearly blend into one.

If we continued to remain faithful to the traditional image of the father as the person who introduces his child into society, the father would become ever more irrelevant, since as such he would be extraneous to this highly privileged dimension of private life.

But the fact that our notion of the father is a cultural construction, and therefore modifiable, allows various authors[9] to run ever more vigorously toward the primary stage, carrying the father with them, and exploring his role in the life of the new-born infant. The father becomes impossible to grasp, because he in fact becomes maternized.[10]

In many men, such an interest is unconsciously encouraged by feelings of guilt which modern culture in general and feminism in particular are bringing to the surface. It represents what they would like to be (surrounding them with an *aspirational atmosphere*[11]) in order to put themselves at ease with their conscience. A father who changes his baby's diapers strikes them as difficult to criticize, and can secretly subtract himself from the thankless subsequent role of the educator-castrator, as assigned to him by Freud. One aspires to a finally gentle father, finally only positive: as pure as the most insipid Madonnas. There are also men who have no desire to make such a role their own, but who nonetheless encourage it, with the unconscious hope that it will mitigate male competition and make "real men" like themselves more rare and more sought out. And many women, finally, look at it kindly since it ought to lead – and here again, the word is "finally" – to a collaboration on the part of men. And so forth. The "primary father" seems to be accompanied by a flood of advancing consensus.

Yet, at the speed with which patterns of male behavior actually change, it is hard to see when the primary father might realistically come into existence, just as we can shape no clear idea of the specific functions that would differentiate him from the mother.[12] It's not clear if such a father is to result from the encouragement of an instinct or from the imposition of a new duty. For the moment,[13] the primary father who is dedicated to the *natural custody* of his child is mainly a *cultural fantasy*, a flight toward the future and a hopefully better male.

Yet, the image of the primary father is less a question of moving toward something new than of fleeing from something ancient. The father, like Jehovah, has been incapable for millennia of being anything other than good and terrible at the same time. The assumption of an identity as a primary custodian holds out the hope of a simplification of such a complex and conflict-ridden condition, but it also risks making the father unreal and one-sided. This is something which has always afflicted women. The description of the world, in words or images, was male. Thus, the image of Jehovah, in all his complexity, as generous and cruel was true. The image of Maria, on the other hand, in her one-sided tenderness, was frequently unreal. It is this last which the primary father emulates, thus creating a man who in turn has little credibility. In addition to eschewing his relationship with the heavens, the image of the new father seems as well to reject his relationship with society. The father as he appeared in those older representations was always a part of his family, his class and his professional corporation: a part of a collective world. He had to make choices: which is also to say he had to do evil, and not only good. He had to function in the world: he had to be able to dirty his hands. Now, finally – the fantasy of the primary father seems to say – his hands are clean. The father can relax into the incomparable wholeness of symbiosis, where all cumbersome complexity is superfluous.

Images from every period of the past tell us that the father, even when he wasn't in society, *was not alone with his child*. He was involved in the maintenance of links between the generations, as well as with the supernatural: Aeneas while leading Ascanius in the sight of Anchises; Abraham while sacrificing Isaac in the sight of Jehovah.

The new father removes his clothes, the garments placed on his back by society, metaphysics and history. He proceeds towards a nudity as free, intimate and oceanic as symbiosis. Society has decided to undress Hector to keep him from frightening his child. This child will have no fear, but will he still have a father?

On the one hand, the elimination of Hector's armor can render the father truly superfluous, insofar as he is indistinguishably similar to the mother. On the other, the facts tell us that in cases such as these the son will look for other male figures who continue to tout their arms. Perhaps there is no solution to the contradiction of the father: the father's contradictions may hold his most profound identity. The father has to remove his armor in order for his son to recognize him. But he can't remove it without first wearing it. Once again, the God closest to the human being is the God of the Old Testament, both just and terrible; and Hector remains the most appropriate father, complete by virtue of his complexity.

We have now made use of different words, but they once again formulate the "paradox of the father" with which we began. This is one of the father's specific characteristics: he must be capable of being a father and also of being a warrior. Unlike the mother, he cannot be only one of these two things: the child who sees him only in his armature will be unable to recognize him; the child who never sees him in arms will be unable to recognize him as a father.

All human beings have to be able to make use of aggressiveness. They must all be able to defend themselves. Society foresees that children are to learn the qualities of combativeness primarily by way of an identification with the father. As said before, this isn't because the nature of the father is necessarily aggressive, but because the specialization of aggressiveness has always been entrusted to males, making it a nearly inalterable image of the collective unconscious.

Culture and society are only indirectly concerned with the primary stage of development. The secondary stage is marked by a further phase of development, and by a second birth that makes it possible to offset lacunae in the first. For the pre-modern civilizations, this second birth was initiation, a passage which mainly took place beneath the aegis of the authority of the fathers, or of proxies for the fathers. The parents' tasks were clear. The mother gave physical life and took care of the child in the first years of its life. The secondary phase was primarily guided by the father, as least insofar as male children were concerned.

Even though initiation has gradually been lost by the wayside, this separation of tasks can in general be said to have continued up until the twentieth century.

Like the functions of their parents, the destinies of children were also highly different. Among a large majority of the primitive peoples, and even more so among the peoples of the West, the lives of males are more complete than those of females. Access to society, to spiritual life, and thus to the process of initiation was more or less limited for females. The great renewals of the secondary phase of growth were largely reserved to males and took the form of interactions between them.

The changes which mark the twentieth century have led us to leave behind these two distinctions: the clear separation of the tasks of the parents, and the difference between the possibilities of sons and daughters. All the same, the effort to eliminate the privileges of fathers and male sons has unconsciously proceeded in the same direction pursued by post-Freudian psychoanalysis: it has diminished the importance of the second phase of development, while increasingly turning attention to the primary phase. In order to strip young males of anachronistic advantages in secondary development, one has not proceeded towards an equal level of socialization and initiation for daughters:

one has taken it away from the boys. While relieving the fathers – and their male substitutes, such as priests and spiritual fathers – of the monopoly they held in socialization and initiation, there has been no attempt to pass these functions along to the mothers as well: they have simply been gradually eliminated.

The rush towards the primary seems victorious. It is only superficially surprising to note that males have been the first to encourage it. Initiation caused suffering, but conferred identity. Today, all identity has ceased to be certain, whereas we could hardly have grown more clearly accustomed to avoiding suffering: out of ideological conviction even more than for reasons of convenience.

Our unbridled consumer society is a planetary exercise in the replication of primary needs. We know this repeated receiving of the breast, with no need to give anything in exchange, to be indispensable in the first phase of development, since the human infant is the least autonomous of all newborn creatures. But as adolescents and adults, our desire immediately to enjoy all possible comforts and to distance from all possible pains holds us entrapped in the condition of psychic sucklings: we remain without an initiation into that balanced alternation of giving and receiving which is the precondition for moral growth.

Here, at the psychic level, we encounter a dramatic manifestation of the neoteny of the human being. We have already seen[14] that the human body resembles the body of a mammal that's incapable of completing its growth. It's much the same with the psyche. We imagine children to envy adults. In the bottom of their hearts, it's the adults who envy the child.

Today we want the father and the mother finally to stand on the same plane. The first must not be exclusively – or better, must not be necessarily – an agent of aggression that frightens the child and disrupts its symbiosis with the mother, and which thus is the foe of the stage of primary development and the force that initiates the secondary. But the ideal cannot be symbiosis, indistinctly for both father and mother, without an image that favors distinction, individuation and entrance into society.

If the rigidity with which the primary was assigned to the mother has disappeared, and the secondary to the father, the final goal must not be allowed to present itself as an unconscious fantasy of an absolute primary. While refusing to predetermine the tasks of each of the parents, given the rapidity with which modes of behavior change, the system of the family must in any case distribute the tasks that arise and which have to be fulfilled with respect to the following stages. Can we reprove adolescents for not wanting to become adults, if adults prefer to forget the adolescents and to concern themselves mainly with infancy?

We have also remarked[15] that the devoted, dependent gaze which children direct toward their mothers is natural and timeless. It derives from the facts of birth and nursing, and even perhaps from the stage of life within the mother's body. In any case, it requires no mediation from a third party. The mother herself, on the other hand, almost always has to function as a mediator in shifting the gaze of the child from herself to its father. This is something we often overlook, since we observe the family *after* this passage – initial and fundamental – from the dyad to the triad.

Today, as a result of the criticism of the patriarchy, if not as direct revenge for the father's absence, mothers take advantage of their power as mediators and refuse to exercise it, no longer attempting to bring father and child together. The father, desirous of existing in the eyes of his child, therefore goes straight to the source, seeking out the gaze of the child and the original, physical, maternal embrace: the dyadic embrace.

It has often been pointed out that male development, unlike female development, depends upon a caesura. The girl child who has had a good primary relationship with her mother can retain her as a model, continuing her psychic development without interruption. The case with the male child is different. At birth, and then in the general course of the decisive primary phase, he mainly relates to his mother; but sooner or later he must shift his gaze toward the father or another male figure.

This theme has been most insistently raised by Kleinian analysis (the school of object relations), which directs its attention to the study of very precocious phases of development. It has also been challenged by feminist authors, since its concentration on a psychological disadvantage of male children has led it to overlook the historical advantage they enjoy in society.[16]

Let's take a brief look at this disadvantage not from the perspective of the primary phase, but in terms of the following phases of development.

We noted in our opening chapters that evolution, above all with the appearance of the mammals, rendered the relationship between mother and infant ever more complex, thus permitting the mothers to construct an embryo of culture, and marginalizing the males. The invention of the monogamic family and of continuous paternal commitment were in a certain sense the male response to this exclusion, and they gradually proved victorious, to the point of making civilization and the patriarchy nearly synonymous.

But the victory of the fathers was far from complete. The civilization the fathers constructed, and in which they dominated, also confronted them with an unexpected problem.

In natural conditions, among the mammals, it is the mother who prolongs the functions of caring for the newborn infant, extending them throughout the whole of the period in which the offspring is not yet autonomous. But the animal cub, even if a male, doesn't remain disadvantaged by having had only a female model since this situation reaches its end long before puberty. This rule, moreover, will be seen to hold even for species which are highly evolved and which don't entirely rely on instinct, flanking it as well with rudiments of education.

It is only among human beings that culture has even further prolonged the length of the child's dependence and thus of the period of parental care. The human being's lack of autonomy and education can continue until the age of thirty (which, in natural conditions, is nearly equivalent to the average life span). In this perspective, initiation may have been invented and administered by males, and primarily destined to young males, since the males were the individuals who felt the need for it.

Schools, of course, didn't appear until much later. But since the early years of schooling present themselves as extensions of the primary biological function, while also being difficult and of little gratification, it was natural to entrust them mainly to women. The result was the construction of a cultural apparatus that continued to copy the patterns of nature. Subsequently, as has also occurred in most professions as general living conditions have slowly improved, the higher levels of education likewise began to open themselves to ever greater numbers of women. Males were content to remain a majority only at the very top, at the level for example of the university careers where power and money are concentrated. In the final analysis, both the laziness of adult males and the structural characteristics of Western civilization, which is far more concerned with efficiency than with questions of psychology, were finally to put young men in the position of encountering few male figures along their path toward adulthood.

This too may be one of the factors that make it so difficult for young males to negotiate their passage to adulthood; it may also be one of the reasons for which all the countries of the world see more delinquency and drug abuse among young men than among young women.

NOTES

1 Krüll (1979), 4.
2 Blos (1985), 1; Fthenakis (1985), I, 2.2; Samuels (1993), 6.
3 Klein, M. (1975) *The Writings of Melanie Klein*, Vol. I: *Love, Guilt and Reparation and Other Works*. London: The Hogarth Press.
4 Freud, S. (1929) (*Das Unbehagen in der Kultur*). *Civilization and Its Discontents*, Standard Edition, Vol. 1.
5 See also, for example, Jung, C. G. (1943) *Ueber die Psychologie des Unbewussten*, in *Collected Works*, Vol. XXI.
6 See, for example (in the light of the largely non-systematic nature of Jung's presentation of his thoughts) *Some Aspects of Modern Psychotherapy* (1930) in *Collected Works*, Vol. XVI.
7 Samuels (1993), 8, p.179.
8 Pleck (1997), in Lamb (ed.), *The Role of the Father in Child Development*.
   Figure 12 is found in Gaunt, D. and Gaunt, L., "The Scandinavian model", in Burguière et al. (1986), Vol. II. The essay reports that in Sweden the time spent by fathers with their children is not even a fourth of that of the mothers. And Sweden holds first place throughout the world for the paternal care of children. (See also Popenoe (1996), Chapter 6.)

Figure 13 comes from Chapter XV of Delumeau and Roche (1990): this chapter of the book also informs us that the direct participation of French fathers in the lives of their children remains extremely low, in spite of the revolution in behavior in the period from 1975 to 1985, which resulted in an increase of *a few minutes a day*.

9 Male authors, such as Blos (1985) and Fthenakis (1985).

10 Cremerius is a sharp observer and has underlined that maternization has had an effect not only on the theory but also on the practice of post-Freudian psychoanalysis:

> When authors such as Winnicott, Mahler, and above all Kohut began to become well known in Germany, many colleagues changed their working techniques – at times quite suddenly – in the sense that they showed the desire to be good, generous, pre-oedipal mothers. The facility with which they were able to transform their clinical activities into an exploration of the new concepts was quite surprising. From the very first session, they proposed a fantasized mother-child world as the terrain of communication, and did not note that their attitudes, discourse, and choice of words and images included a whole series of signals that invited the patient to regress to this level. In the cases in which the colleagues brought tape recordings to the supervisions and had me listen to parts of their sessions, the change was even more clearly to be grasped. In the course of the refurbishment their concepts, even their tones of voice underwent a change. . . . I frequently had the impression that they were changing the very shapes of their bodies into those of a mother.

Cremerius, J. (1981) "Ueber die Schwierigkeiten, Natur und Funktion von Phantasie und Abwehrmechanismen psychoanalytisch zu erforschen und zu definieren," in *Vom Handwerk des Psychoanalytikers: Das Werkzeug der psychoanalytischen Technik*. Stuttgart: Frommann-Holzboog, 1990, Band II, 11.

11 Samuels (1993) 8, p. 180.

12 See also the various articles in Lamb (1997).

13 See chapter 18.

14 See chapter 4.

15 Ibid.

16 See, for example, Segal, L. (1990) *Slow Motion. Changing Masculinities, Changing Men*. New Brunswick, NJ: Rutgers University Press, Chapter 3.

Chapter 21

The disappearance of elevation

and raising his son [Hector] kissed him, lifting a prayer to Zeus . . .
Iliad, VI, 474–5

In the period between the end of the eighteenth century and the beginning of the twentieth, France rediscovered the image of the father who lifts his child into the air.[1] A century earlier, that image would have been blasphemous: the only child to be raised toward the skies was Christ, concealed in the elevation of the host.

Such images, however, indicate no return toward the authority of the Roman *pater familias*. It's true that the Revolution, in the name of progress, of the triumph of will over nature, rediscovered the Roman notion of adoption. And if every true fatherhood is an adoption – a choice – that active, voluntary choice is summed up in the gesture of the father who lifts his child into the air. But trust in the father was no longer the same as in Roman times, and these images make this clear. They are often rhetorical and sentimental: at times, they were commissioned by the political powers in the attempt to lend fresh vigor to the family, which little by little was growing weaker as the state assumed functions which once had been domestic. Others are caricatures of the family's condition. Others again are propaganda posters or even commercial advertisements.

The return of that gesture signifies that the relationship between father and child lay again at the center of attention. But the relationship was tense and dramatic.

It is a sacred gesture. But the sacred, as the word originally indicated, can be either divine or demonic. The gesture reappeared in reproductions and in literature as a description of the new relationship between father and child. Words spoken between fathers and children are likewise sacred, and can likewise be blessings or curses. After the beheading of the king and the birth of the Republic, the relationship between father and child was once again central.

What became of this gesture and as well of the father's words in the course of the twentieth century?

Elevation and benediction are bodily and discursive expressions of the same paternal attitude. The elevation, benediction and initiation of the child are the legal, theological and anthropological expressions of the same need to endow the child with life.

The male – who in nature has no capacity for giving life and can make no more than an animal's donation of sperm – can accomplish an upwards leap, toward the spiritual dimension: he turns his thoughts to his child and authors rites that render his intentions concrete, irreversible and publicly shared. If the appearance of the father coincided with the birth of the project that unfolds in time, then elevation, benediction and initiation hold the father's project with respect to his child: the second gush, but this time of spiritual sperm.

It may very well be that every body of earthly ritual is a subspecies of this fundamental need which establishes an equality among the fathers of all times and all cultures while setting them apart from the beast. This is so for simple tribal groups, where every rite centers on initiation, and no less so for the colossal Catholic Church, where in any case it is always a father – from the "padre" with which one address the simple priest to the "pope," which means the same thing – who directs holy words to a congregation of spiritual children.

If there is sense in speaking of the death of the father, it's a question of something more than his growing statistical rarity. His demise lies first of all in the fact that the rites of which his existence consisted have ceased to be celebrated.

That gesture has an unbroken continuity from Hector to the Roman *pater familias* to the Jacobean father and up to our very own times: at one and the very same time it is the father's recognition of his child, his reflection of himself in the eyes of his child, a prayer and a prolongation of the self in the project he entrusts to his child.

Today, Robert Bly attacks that "sibling society"[2] to which the Futurist prophets, nearly a century ago, entrusted the future of masculinity. The models and the learning that count for today's young men come first of all from other young men: the significant bond – the direction in which they direct their gaze – is horizontal. Bly and those others who are nostalgic for fatherhood would counter this horizontality by proposing a return to the vertical gaze which links children to their fathers and their ancestors. But this vertical gaze and sense of order are those of Hector who, while lifting up Astyanax, asked the gods to make him stronger than himself; of Aeneas who walked with his father on his shoulders and holding his son by the hand; of the Roman father who raised his son into the air as a sign of having recognized him. The unbroken line of the fathers passes from Greece into recent American essays, confirming its current as well as archetypal importance.

This gesture, all the same, requires a capacity for symbolic and transpersonal thinking, like every rite to which we entrust our deepest feelings.

Otherwise, the Roman image might lead us to think that the father is placing his child on a high chair; or on hearing Hector's prayer that Astyanax grow up to be a stronger man than himself, we might imagine him to hope that his son will have a future as an athlete. If we stop at the literal, material content of the words, we lose the meaning of the father. The material world holds no sufficient justification for his existence. The mother has been taking care of that since time immemorial, better than he can (let's not forget that "mother" and "matter" – *mater* and *materia* – have the same linguistic roots).

Unfortunately, our epoch stands at considerable distance from any respect for symbols, prayer and rite as self-sufficient values, and we immediately attempt to interpret them, or clearly to define their content. Having amassed a wealth of objects, while growing psychologically impoverished, we do not comprehend that a mystery can make more sense and be charged with more intensity than its solution.

Men have resigned from paternity precisely by way of the rejection of symbol. Rather than being forgotten, Hector's gesture and prayer have been taken literally. The father wants to "elevate" his children in society, and does all he can to guide them towards positions more comfortable than his own. Instead of investing the lives of his children with his symbols, he invests his money in funds that will help them to climb the social ladder.

Following the last world war, a whole generation of European and American fathers began to push their children toward "better" professions than their own.[3] Unfortunately, however, the goals they furthered were frequently an expression of a low level of self-esteem and gave vent to a sense of a rupture between themselves and their descendants, instead of representing the formulation of a true and proper project that voiced an understanding of their children's true dimension. An entire generation of working-class fathers took the bread from their mouths in order to send their children to colleges and universities. In present-day Italy, for example, the demand for various varieties of manual expertise is high and remains unsatisfied, whereas many doctors are unemployed, or employed at levels inferior to their education: neither society as a whole nor the children as individuals have reaped the benefits which that ocean of sacrifices was intended to create. This alone, however, would leave little to complain about, since a general improvement in their material lives has in any case taken place.

The unforeseen novelty lies in the fact that social advance has ever more frequently shattered the link between the generations. Children with degrees are ashamed of their uncultured working-class father; children who adhere to standard speech criticize their father's broken grammar; children who are competent in several languages are embarrassed by the father who can't exchange greetings with a foreigner, and so on and so forth.

It is not enough to appeal to tautology and to accuse children of ingratitude. Why should they have been grateful yesterday and ingrates today, after having been given so much more? We have to draw a distinction. Today's youth have been given more in material terms. But the money of which they have had the benefit was a substitute for elevation, benediction and initiation: the world of symbols, the realm of the spirit, and continuity from one to the next generation. These are things which a father has to give by way of rituals; money, even if it comes from him, can be withdrawn at a bank with a slip of paper.

Sons know that their father wanted them to be comfortable. They do not know that he wanted them to be men. They have their doubts. He didn't give them the model of an adult man: wanting them to be different from himself, he denied himself as such. Yet, he continues to assert that it's possible to become a true adult. Either the father is lying, or he's hiding an essential secret. Either way, he doesn't deserve their respect.

A study of the father's blessing[4] clearly reveals it to constitute an archetypal need not only on the part of the child, but also on the part of the father. Like all the psychic needs that seem so ancient, universal and self-contained as to merit designation as archetypes, the father's blessing presents itself as a self-justifying rite, charged with a life of its own. In the Bible – and even though the Bible teaches the distinction between right and wrong – the father's blessing always and in any case has an effect, independently of the good or evil intentions of those involved in it; its power is even independent of the person to whom it is imparted.

As the firstborn son, Esau had the right to receive the benediction of his father Isaac. To prepare us for the fact that he will not receive it, the Bible describes him as having a non-paternal temperament: unsuitable to continue the tradition of the father in the course of the generations. Esau in fact prefers immediate gratification to the pursuit of any project. In a famous Biblical story we see him sell his birthright for a bowl of soup (Genesis 25: 29–34).

Isaac desired at a later moment to confer his blessing upon Esau, but his age and blindness allowed him to be deceived, and instead he gave his blessing to Jacob. The blessing had its effect all the same. Jacob, the younger brother, received his father's spiritual heritage, and Esau, the firstborn, was henceforth to be his brother's servant (Genesis 27).

This a highly important episode for Jews and Christians alike, and it leads to a number of essential observations on the father figure:

- The actions of the father are an objective fact for his child, independently of the father's intentions. Good intentions are not enough. This is the root of the "paradox of the father."
- The rite of the blessing has a life of its own, again independently of the father's intentions. Intentions, in fact, are subjective and contingent. The rite is absolute and eternal.
- Since this rite is absolute, unconditioned and charged with power, it is a necessity in the psychic life not only of the son but also of the father.

- Just as the blessing is one of life's essentials, rather than one of its possible trimmings, it ranks not only as good (the term "bene-diction" is reductive) but is also terrible, like life itself. Terrible for the son who does not receive it, tremendous as well for the son who does. A little further on in the Old Testament, Jacob will be assailed by a figure who appears in the night, will be wounded, and will wrestle with him until daybreak. Only at that point does he learn that he has encountered an angel of the Lord, and will receive his blessing. The angel (messenger) of the Father wounds and blesses at one and the same time. The blessing and the wound are inseparable. As a font of affection and fear, the father's blessing has been a part of the history of the West in the form of family prayer, under the guidance of the father of the family.
- If the rite of the blessing has a self-sufficient, independent and pre-existent form with respect to the individual who in any given instance imparts it, then every child will at some time feel the need for it, even if the father has shown no intention of imparting it. Our own terminology calls the father's blessing archetypal. If the need remains unsatisfied, the son will feel a privation at the core of his own identity, which Kuder refers to as the "Esau complex."

The Esau complex is currently of great importance: on condition, once again, that we refrain from seeing it in literal or individual terms. Today's children don't have to confront the cunning of a brother who can subtract a blessing and turn it to his own advantage, but must hold their own against the collapse of the rites of passage that subtracts it forever from everyone.

The father had to project himself and his child into the future. With Esau, who sells his future for the immediate advantage of sitting down to a meal, the Bible shows that this project can be threatened by immaturity. Limited horizons and the temptation to relax in satiety are the true brother-enemy from whom children must protect themselves.

When Esau learns that his father's blessing has been stolen from him, he is furious and seeks out Jacob, intending to kill him (Genesis 27: 41). Just as we have seen in the course of the last 100 years, the demise of the paternal project arouses aggression among the brothers.

Like Esau, all of today's adolescents obscurely feel that they haven't received an essential gift from their fathers. They can't however, be jealous of a brother, who likewise didn't receive it. They can only be jealous of their fathers, and of the whole chain of fathers. They have been led to believe that the generations flow one into the other in solemn and harmonious succession; and they deduce, not mistakenly, that for them the rite of passage has been missing. This suspicion, which constantly grows since it's never clarified, can turn into an unconscious fantasy: there is something of great value which their fathers have deliberately denied them. The homicidal fury of the Esau complex, which should address itself horizontally to the brother, thus moves in an unexpected vertical direction. This shift of hostility toward the father is complementary to the shift of admiration towards the "brothers." In fact, if role models are not sought among the fathers, but horizontally among other young men, the peer group can no longer be the scene for the manifestation of rivalries, which instead appear in the vertical relationship with parents.

This upheaval along the axis of the relationship between the generations has taken place in the course of a very few decades, leaving us unprepared, incredulous and unconscious of what has truly happened. In extreme cases, its manifestations have been brutally criminal. In my own country, Italy, which is known for its families' relative stability, there have been various cases of adolescents – sons of families which had offered them every material satisfaction – who have murdered their parents so as to come into possession of whatever they had kept for themselves. Having lost the ability to move within the world of rites and symbols, the father has ceased to be a source of benediction and instead reduces to a benefactor; rather than offerings of sacred words, he makes gifts of worldly objects. And this, we imagine, is precisely the point at which the son's unconscious fantasy effects its entry; the father is to be both punished and expropriated, since he has hidden a treasure which he ought to have passed along.

The image of the father's blessing – along with the other two figures of accompanying the child, which are elevation and initiation – offers symbolic terms which can help us to grasp the interior void experienced by today's adolescents.

Let's now take an example from ordinary life, far from the extremes of homicidal fury.

The father is absent as an image, even more than as an individual; *the absent father* is itself the present-day father image. Unlike Ulysses, his absence isn't explained by his having gone off to do battle in a war, but by his refusal to do battle within his relationships. Often the father is no longer there even if he hasn't divorced and continues to share a house with his children. More than for what he has done, today's father stands accused for what he has *not* done. For what he has not said, more than for words he has spoken.

The silence of fathers deafens the analyst's studio. Every day, patients reprove their fathers for not having expressed themselves, even for not having defended themselves; for not having explained and defended their own points of view; for having been present but silent, for having offered no response to children or mothers; and so forth.

Above all, they stand accused of having kept silence in front of achievements their children attained with great effort and sacrifice, struggling not for the achievement itself, but for their father's praise. The fathers' inability to give ritual celebration to their children's symbolic passages has been one of the most tragic impoverishments of twentieth-century private life. While able to purchase expensive merchandise, we no longer know how to offer joys that cost nothing. We have to imagine the general run of fathers to suffer from an "Isaac complex": culturally too old and psychologically blind like Isaac the patriarch, they no longer know the sacred words of benediction or approval, or they don't know how to say them at the right moment or to the right person.

How great a surprise it can be, what an incredulous leap the heart can make, and how much nostalgia can at the very same time arise for an unattainable good, when children suddenly learn – from a relatively meaningless third person or from even more casual circumstances – that their father's habitual conversation is nearly entirely about them, and sings their praises! The celebration had taken place, but in secrecy.

At times it's an office colleague who tells the story of how everyone smilingly avoided the father at coffee breaks, since they could bear no more of his tales of his daughter's prodigious success at university. At other times, an old box spews out newspaper clippings: the father's religiously ordered record of the praises of his son's achievements as an athlete. (Why had he kept them under lock and key? And why had he only grumbled, "You're wasting too much time on tennis! You've got studies to think about too!"?) At times it's even that woman whom the son had never really liked and with whom his divorced father had gone to live, who reveals that after the great step of deciding to share her bed, he didn't in the night lie down beside her to do the things that men and women do together, but to talk about the prizes his son had won in school contests.

At times such information is the beginning of a dialog. At others it's the beginning of nothing at all since by now the child has learned in turn to maintain silence. Frequently it is only the beginning of a song of regret, since the scene of the revelation is the father's funeral.

These scraps of a joy that never took place, all the same, like all relics, speak. They recount the tale of an Isaac complex: the need to celebrate his descendance has entered the father's heart, without reaching its goal in the heart of the child. Secular society has put an end to the rite, but not to the need which lay at its origins. It's not always necessary to attribute a father's silence to faulty intentions; it's more likely a question of a lack of awareness as to what is expected of him. To an enormous, irrational sense of reserve. To an anxious and uncontrollable need for secrecy.

This form of self-protection which was typical of the sense of paternal dignity has slipped out of control, and often grows to enormous proportions. Things that should simply have been defended and preserved for moments of solemnity find themselves finally relegated into places from which they can never reappear. This all-obscuring cloud bears a paradoxical resemblance to Hector's armor, yet darkens precisely those private spaces which his shield was designed to keep vital and alive.

If the psyche is an organ, like the bodily organs, that seeks equilibrium by correcting excesses, such overwhelming reserve can be seen as an act of unconscious compensation.

Traditionally, patriarchal society allowed male competition to flourish in war; and the excessive violence released by war may perhaps have permitted the fathers to maintain civil behavior in private life. War, fortunately, no longer holds such a central place among the activities of the Western world. The competition that rages within the mammoth commercial apparatus in which we are immersed today is its extension, on an apparently less destructive plane. In this new breed of war, however, consumerism and the means of mass communication have reached a level of shamelessness unequaled in all history. Television and the press, which as entrepreneurial activities still remain predominantly in the hands of the fathers, need ever more broadly to sell themselves, and turn, like global prostitutes, to proffering scandals and intimacies that ever more beat back the limits of modesty and reserve. They cancel out a highly ancient psychological law: rather than the mark of an absence of truth, secrecy signals the presence of respect for something sacred.

The mother's unconscious is less affected by the infamy of this stock of collective images, since women still feel the need to free themselves from having been forced for centuries into attitudes of excessive reserve.

For the fathers, the discomfort is more profound, even if equally unconscious. They witness the violation of intimacy and the loss of secrecy which mass communication inflicts upon famous personalities, and they unconsciously shudder at the possibility that something similar might happen to themselves. Their own responsibilities in this commercial drift of the world also provoke a silent feeling of guilt. Their daily lives in the workplace expose them to public scrutiny, and they therefore feel a particular need for privacy. They don't know how to deal with these interior pressures. Reserve and the shrouding of sexuality have been taught throughout the centuries to women, but not to them. They are likewise less adept than the mothers in the expression of their feelings.

The need to compensate for society's lack of reserve, their inexperience in the governing of intimate feelings, and their ignorance of the value of secrecy cause an unexpected return of the repressed. The fathers become obsessed with hiding their feelings; their affective reserve grows no less enormous than embarrassed, unconscious and uncontrollable. The reserve which was once a positive quality becomes a prison cell.

Our simplification of the significance of initiation has been intentional. After physical birth, the human being experiences a need for a second, spiritual birth. Initiation is the ritual route of access to a new stage of life, superior to the one before it, and more complete. According to Mircea Eliade, initiation is the line of demarcation between two worlds of history and anthropology. Where it exists, we find ourselves in the pre-modern world; when it disappears, we enter the modern world.

In its most typical form, initiation was the route of access to adult life for young men. Beneath the ritual guide of masculine figures that belong to the order of fatherhood, the adolescent males of tribal cultures were thrown into a radically new dimension that exposed them to existential risk and death. This exposure, again, was both material – in many traditional cultures a boy became a man through a great act of courage, for example by facing a ferocious animal – and symbolic: to reach his new identity, the child, the incomplete being, dies in order to be reborn.

The example of initiation is further proof that rites which are ancient and universal do not easily disappear. We believe them to have been forgotten and surpassed: but in fact they leave behind residues which are unconscious and uncontrollable, and therefore much more dangerous than the original rites from which they stem. And since fatherhood, compared to motherhood, has a greater need to be culturally constructed, distancing from initiation and distancing from the father strike us as complementary elements of something our culture is forgetting.[5]

Motorcycle duels and "surfing" on the roofs of trains can almost too easily be spoken of as ways in which adolescent males return to the practice of initiation ordeals, but no longer in the presence of adult guides or of rules that set limitations. The disappearance of initiation can't properly be said to be the *cause* of such new and dangerous games. They do, however, insert themselves into the psychological void which its disappearance has left behind, and they are used to satisfy needs for growth which have remained unsatisfied.[6]

A frequent trait of today's "men's movement" lies precisely in the reproposal of initiation. But whereas an author or an intellectual tendency can surely inaugurate an *abstract philosophy*, it's doubtful that the same can be true of a *rite*. In order truly to fulfill its function, a rite must follow a tradition: it has to be practiced by the whole of a society and find roots in the surrounding culture.

We have far too little awareness today of the values of rite, and likewise lack sufficient awareness of the functions which males embody and absolve. In the course of the centuries, the widest variety of societies have felt males to be the seat of primordial energies which have to be tamed and ritually channeled. It thus became possible to use those forces for the organization of the family and the process of accrual that results in civilization.

These energies today seem again to find their outlet in regressive forms of expression: forms we might nearly see as the final degeneration of the Futurist lust for adventure. They find their manifestation in duels between young males who want to win the favors of the females and who unconsciously desire "promotion to adulthood" (or initiation). Rather than being directed into a process of accumulation, masculine energies are squandered in games that have no winners, or even in purely destructive games where everybody loses. At this point, it seems nearly that the typical features of men, as opposed to those of women, are entirely negative, which encourages the more aggressive wings of feminism. Men in turn grow concerned about the destructive potential of feminism, but find it difficult to understand the destructiveness of anti-paternal, youth-centered male regression.

Today's father lacks the power and prestige that made him the ideal and irreplaceable model for his son. He can function as authority and guide only indirectly, by denying his son something he might otherwise give. When the son refuses to grow up, the father *denies him his respect*. Indeed, unconsciously and indirectly, the father feels *contempt* for the male son who doesn't know how to make the leap from adolescence to manhood. But the father's lack of respect can also be read as the absence of the ritual figure – the priest – with whom to celebrate initiation. The son perceives this absence, and the father who is no longer a patriarch is seen as the ancient figure of the castrating authority, with none of the qualities of the good authority. Father and son are caught up in a vicious circle, fueled by contempt and the lack of respect.

One of the curses for students of the theme of the father lies in the difficult task of defining his psychological characteristics independently of the customs of any specific time: what is truly the father's specialization, with respect to the mother? If we answer that the father is the person who teaches his child to ride the bicycle, we may have a valid metaphor for a good part of today's middle classes in Europe and America, but not for times and places that were unacquainted with bicycles. We'll therefore attempt to say, in agreement with Samuels,[7] that the father's specific characteristic lies in the promotion of differentiation: the unfolding of the child, in the child's actions, and in the child's mind. This links with our hypothesis that the invention of the father was contemporaneous with the birth of the capacity for the formulation of projects: the project here is concerned with the development not of material things (which economic development pursues) but of the human potential of the next generation. Full and complete differentiation is the form of initiation – no longer modeled *a priori* – that can bring a son or daughter into today's complex and pluralistic society. Whereas the father's task was once above all to accompany his child through certain obligatory straits, today's father must be more concerned with his child's individuality: he promotes his child's specificity. But the task is so complex as to discourage many men from being fathers.

Even while having disappeared as a social and religious ritual, paternal initiation in fact survived until recent times within the context of many professions. Craftsmen, farmers and land owners primarily learned their skills directly from their fathers.

All of this, however, was possible in a stable world, but not in a world condemned to progress. The contemporary world obliterates this reassuring passage of batons from one generation to the next.

First of all, education and even professional training have abandoned the home and tend to take place in those impersonal institutions to which we refer as schools.

In the second place, when the principal imperative is progress, fathers no longer desire their children to continue to pursue their profession. They want their children to "rise" to better professions.

Finally, even when the father's profession can be taught and learned at home, and even when the father desires his child to continue in his line of work, it may very well be that changes which occur within the space of a generation will leave him with nothing worth teaching, since technical progress day by day makes his professional skills obsolete.

Just as the father's role as the initiator who guides his children's education and future professional life has irreversibly disappeared, his children's leisure time has likewise ceased to hold a place for him. The socialization, entertainments and various other interests of his children no longer have anything to do with him. For thousands of years, fathers taught their children how to ride a horse, and then, for a couple of generations, how to ride a bicycle. Today the father has no authority when it comes to dealing with electronic games, and even his computer is different from those of his children. He belongs to a different world.

The distance between the generations continually increases: the period of learning grows ever longer, and parents have children ever later in life. Above all, the cultural gap grows enormous. The speed with which the behavior patterns of the young evolve is even superior to the speeds of technology. The adolescents influence one another. The males often seek out a homeopathic substitute for the paternal authority which their fathers no longer represent and look up to a friend who's a little older, a little bigger, a little tougher: Pinocchio's Lucignolo. They rapidly model themselves on each other. They learn from other youngsters whom they see on the TV screen or in magazines: they form a closely-knit group, even while living at considerable distances from one another. They thus tend to grow homogeneous in an endless global city of peers, living in an indistinct everywhere where the only constant is the latest passing fashion. They come to lose that sense of geographic localization and historical continuity which has always helped us answer the question: "Who am I?"

The horizontal learning which typifies adolescence is not only the learning that takes place in destructive gangs; and it has the advantage of being fast. Its inadequacy almost always lies in being neither individual nor a part of an experience of initiation. It satisfies the need for instruction but not the need for growth, and it nourishes a constant compulsion to the repetition of the same experiences with only minor variations; such repetition holds the secret expectation that one will finally make the leap into a life which is full and complete.

But the father too lacks consciousness: at times he simply makes no attempt to maintain a relationship with his child, at others he is gripped by anxiety and fears that his child will abandon him. Behaving as though he were the person who risks exclusion, he attempts in turn to insert himself into the adolescent world of horizontal communication. This is what lies behind those studies which tell us that the "activity" which fathers most often perform with their children lies in watching television.[8] It also explains a new phenomenon which has appeared in any number of countries within the last few decades: children who address their father by his first name. If I no longer ask my child to call me "daddy," the relationship may very well lose the uniqueness which made it sacred. Yet the use of the word alone can mean very little if the whole of the culture that created it has disappeared. The father feels that there is a greater degree of dialog when his children address him in the way they address their friends, since it strikes him that the network of relationships with friends is the only one that remains.

When the relationship has been inverted, it's the father who seeks the approval – the blessing, the initiation – of his children. But this often leads to the very reverse and provokes his children's censure: though they may never have known him to be anything different from what he is, they nonetheless know within themselves what they want their father to be.

Already today, this situation is much more common than one might be likely to imagine. Up until not too long ago, meals were the family's moment of self-celebration. The father dismissed his child from the table as a form of solemn punishment. Now, however, the dining-room table is an instrument which the young employ to punish or reward their fathers. Youngsters come home late and find every possible excuse for not sitting down to eat with father. This also gives them additional power, since it gives them a way of making him a gift. For their father's birthday they might just remain at home, while their friends all go to McDonalds, the temple of the rites of the community of the young.

NOTES

1 Delumeau and Roche (1990), XIII.
2 Bly, R. (1996) *The Sibling Society*. Reading, MA: Addison Wesley.
3 Mitscherlich (1963), VII; Wurzbacher, G. (1954) *Leitbilder gegenwärtigen deutschen Familienlebens*. Stuttgart.
4 Kuder, M. (1994) *Das Ringen des Sohnes um den Segen des Vaters*, a thesis presented at the C. G. Jung Institute, Zurich.
5 For a wide-ranging study of the need for initiation in modern society, see Henderson, J. L. (1967) *Thresholds of Initiation*. Middletown CT: Wesleyan University Press.
6 The author has had occasion to study the tremendous quantity of drugs consumed by young males in an unconscious attempt to achieve initiation and to reconstruct those rites of initiation which have disappeared: Zoja (1985).
7 Samuels (1993), 6.
8 Hosley, C. H. and Montemayor, R. (1997) "Fathers of children with special needs," in Lamb (ed.), *The Role of the Father in Child Development*; Hite (1994), III.

Chapter 22

The breadwinner

When we speak of "laws," we can be speaking of any number of different things: the laws of the state, or moral, religious, scientific or economic laws. Different, but not unrelated. Max Weber has revealed a strict correlation between Protestantism and economic development: in the sight of both God and the marketplace, initiative and personal sacrifice bear fruit. The United States has guided the economic development of the West not only because of its vast resources and the size of its internal market: when those resources still remained to be exploited, and the population of the American colonies was smaller than that of the mother country, Europe had already exported its most inflexible Protestant minds, preparing a secondary destiny for itself.

Patriarchal structures and the Protestant temperament, in various degrees of severity, went hand in hand with one another in the America of the founding fathers.[1] The father's principal task in relation to his children lay in the *teaching of values.* A substantially religious function. It was held, with religious fervor, that the father alone, in spite of his obligations in the workplace, and not the mother, was able to educate a child. Thus, in the infrequent cases of separations, the children were entrusted to their father.[2]

The nineteenth century brought a great change. The Industrial Revolution forced many fathers to be away from their families for ever more extended periods of time in order to be able to follow their work and led to the rise of a new mentality. Men encountered previously unheard-of opportunities for self-affirmation and the accumulation of wealth. The Protestant attitude and the great mobility of American society allowed them to exploit this new situation to a greater degree than took place in Europe. With the advance of the twentieth century, the transformation became complete. The father's principal task no longer lay in teaching values, and instead he had become a "breadwinner."[3]

The rapid cultural shifts of the last few decades have produced still other ideals of fatherhood.[4] In particular, we have witnessed the appearance of the image of the *new father* who shares household work with the mother (the co-partner). This figure has already been discussed.[5] It contains a great ideal of justice and equality within the couple. But we also know it to remain at considerable distance from reality. In this chapter we can leave it aside – just as one can leave aside the classless society of Marx, which was likewise a noble ideal – and turn our attention to actually extant conditions.

The twentieth century has consolidated the figure of the breadwinner both in Europe and America. This seems, objectively, to be the model of the father that now prevails in the West, and it has also been exported to the developing countries.[6] It is encouraged by market economies and leaves little space for the demands of psychology and feminism. Such a father spends very little time with his children, but generally feels no guilt about it; he is much more likely to experience feelings of guilt if he loses an opportunity for economic gain, even if the loss results from no fault or lack of initiative of his own.

The ideal of the breadwinner is in a certain sense regressive and leads quite a way back in time. As though reminiscent of the first human societies of hunter-gatherers, the father leaves his home and family for ever longer periods of time and concerns himself with bringing back the greatest possible quantity of food. On doing so, he has fulfilled his duties. But when the modern breadwinner reappears, he doesn't light the fires of the rites and evoke the images of the hunt: rather than a bloody deer, he drops his dirty laundry on the threshold. Without the benefit of those archaic images, the child's only way of evaluating his father lies in rationality – the abstract graph of how much he has bought or sold – and the child doesn't experience the emotion of the father's return.

We can here refer back to the "paradox of the father" which we presented at the beginning of this book. We saw that a father has to win his children's affection by displaying strength. The child looks up to the man nearly as if he were a part of a bevy of animals in which the males compete with one another. The father is expected, more than the mother, to be acquainted with society and to understand it – society and its rules of the jungle – and he is taught that he is not to succumb to it, and not only to be good and just. Similar expectations are as old as the world itself: but this image today is the child's equivalent to the father's ideal of himself as a breadwinner. The child wants a victorious father, and the father wants to make himself a winner in the universal games of the marketplace. The attitudes are complementary, and reciprocally bolster one another. The affirmation of the ideal of the breadwinner has reinforced the paradoxicality of the father's situation.

Why do we call it "paradoxical"? Because fathers are a product of civilization and do not exist in the world of animals, yet their children demand their adherence to a model of animal behavior.

For as long as the father's function lay mainly in teaching values, the education he gave his children could subordinate the principle of earthly might to the greater principle of divine justice. When the father becomes a breadwinner, things change.

The father's identity is ever more dependent on his success in the marketplace. Objective success seems ever more pertinent than moral integrity. It's not by chance that the unwholesome father who made his appearance with the Industrial Revolution was more a social than an ethical failure: the European worker who lapsed into drink, and later the unemployed father in America's black ghettos. They were the first heads of families to abdicate, losing not only the respect of society but their self-respect as well, along the course of a vicious circle.

The contemporary family identifies with the new life-style and as well with the new mentality.

The position of mothers in the hierarchy was once intermediate between those of the father and the children. She had no right to judge the father, and, if any such case arose, the criteria to which she appealed were moral rather than concerned with success. In the majority of today's American families, she too has become a breadwinner. In Europe this phenomenon is not so broad, but not because the ideal is any less widespread: the difference lies in Europe's higher levels of unemployment. Europe's conversion to the new values is already complete. The mother too, naturally enough, can at this point lose the respect of her children as a result of a lack of success. But this doesn't reflect a shift in the ways in which the maternal function is evaluated; its occurrence, quite to the contrary, reflects the mother's assumption of paternal functions. We are dealing in cases like these with a mother who is also a father. She too is a hunter, even if the booty is an income. She too is a hunter, even if, breaking with tradition, she is a woman.

We know that the anxieties of parents influence their children even if not directly expressed. So, children in turn withdraw their respect and affection from a father whose lack of success robs him of respect and affection for himself. Traditional ethical principles wane as society becomes more secular, whereas the ethic of the breadwinner is self-sustaining. It is linked to the economy and develops in accord with economic development: it reinforces the "paradox of the father" and turns against him, ironically so, since he was the person who first brought it into the family. Its connection with the market causes it to respond to market cycles more than to moral values. In the wake of globalization, it is exported from the West towards the developing countries, where it seemed that the father's moral role might have continued to survive for longer.

The father who found his function in the transmission of values almost never lost his children's respect: he was answerable only to God, and only God could withdraw respect from him. The present-day father is answerable to society and to society's criteria of measurement, which even adolescents know how to use. Today's father can be judged by his children at any and every moment: history has never before been acquainted with such a situation. This new "moral" law, which derives from the laws of economics, depletes the image of the father more than any law of the state might deprive him of rights and prerogatives. All fathers once held an authority that came directly from the heavens. Today they have to earn it by combating among themselves, with some acquiring it by taking it away from others. Even the law of the fathers has ceased to be vertical and is now horizontal.

The passage from teacher to breadwinner isn't simply a question of the replacement of one function by another, and the difference for the child lies in something more than the fact that this new function keeps the father far from home. In existential terms, the two kinds of fathers stand on different planes. They are separated by that philosophical revolution which appeared in the nineteenth century and to which we refer as the death of God. Previous to that revolution the father was a spiritual and metaphysical fact; in its wake he is only material fact and offers only material care: that's true of the breadwinner who supplies his adolescent children with money, and no less true of the "new father" who concerns himself with the bodily needs of the earlier phases of his children's lives.

After the death of God, the father is no longer the vicar of the Father; he is no longer the initial link in a rising chain that connects earthly life to the great beyond. He lives only on the earth, and the earth is a scene of competition with the other fathers, with the mother, with his children as well. The values he represents are no longer "transcendent" but economic: the terrestrial and quotidian values that belong to the very same world which the child inhabits, and we remember that this is the world above which the child was once to be elevated. The father is no longer an image of the spirit. His image is no longer austere. The father as an ideal has grown clouded, and one only sees fathers in flesh and blood. And as time goes by the absence of a father image with a stable place in children's imaginations transforms itself – since archetypal needs can never dispense with images – into the image of the absent father.

Can fathers whose existence is entirely material reprove their children for having lost respect for authority and returning to the pack? Such criticisms remind us of the story of the wolf who while drinking from further upstream accused the lamb downstream of muddying his water. Just as a river flows from above to below, things pass on from parents to children. In obedience to the economic circumstances of a society in the course of its modernization, it was the fathers – well before their children – who first took up positions on the terrain of peer competition. Their public confrontation of one another is what allows them in turn to be confronted by their children: having ceased to be given and sacred, hierarchy is established *ad hoc*, whenever the case demands it, by comparing bottom lines. Adolescent males so easily return to the pack since their fathers, more silently, have already done the same. The young men primarily compete to be able to choose their women; the fathers compete to support the women they have already chosen and the children those women have given them.

When seen from such a point of view, the novel developments of the last half century take on greater complexity.

In generational terms, the revolts of the students of Europe and America were uprisings against the father's authority on the part of the horde of sons. But in terms of the archetypal images to which these revolts referred, they attempted first of all to subvert the ideal which sees economic competition as the dominant social principle. This is to say that they finally amounted to a rejection of the image of the herd that seeks no orientation in a superior order and that resorts to battle for the constant reinvention of its hierarchy. Those rebellions expressed a nostalgia for a society anchored to metaphysical values, and as such were opposed to our contemporary society where the fathers' task is to relate to each other less as fathers than as wolves. From this point of view, it was the sons and daughters – even if in ways which were frequently unconscious, violent and vulgar – who embodied the need to express opposition to the horizontal modes of relationship that were taking control of Europe and America.

In the last few decades, the young have maintained silence. They too, as they entered maturity, became part of the society that functions horizontally and that replaces moral values with principles of objectively measurable success: the society already inhabited by their fathers. And they have not been followed by new generations in revolt.

As Freud observed, the interior authority that we call the Super-ego should represent morality, but secretly tends to respect the law of the victor: if my actions are successful, it accosts me with little reproof, even if they have not been moral; if I fail, it can lead me to depression and feelings of guilt even if my actions have been moral. Supported by this unconscious bias, the new "paternal" law of objective success has spread on the basis of its own objective success and has found its historical vindication in the fall of the Berlin wall.

The rise of Reagan and Thatcher and the collapse of Communism as the result of Eastern Europe's conversion to the principles of market-economy competition are psychological as well as political events: global ratification that the fathers' mission on earth lies in the role of the breadwinner. States by now have the task of duplicating the commitment of the fathers on a vaster scale, making themselves the framework and arbiter for the countless fathers in battle.

In the post-modern era of the great, civilized and basically democratic West, the most archaic of crimes has been repeated millions of times: not the crime of Cain against Abel – who were brothers in spite of being different – but the much more ferocious crime of Achilles against Hector. The assassination of the one brother left the other a survivor; the assassination of Hector, the hero of fatherhood, finds its only survivor in the competitive, pre-paternal male.

Is the father a father by virtue of having an income, or by virtue of having children? He knows that success is the basis on which he is judged, both as a worker and a parent. Much can be learned in this regard from the situation of divorced fathers, who now are nearly half the total and could soon become the majority.

Divorce ordinarily deprives them of their children. The father for whom this loss results in no great suffering once again throws himself into the role of the breadwinner: so as to be able to meet his new expenses, and also to create a new life for himself and to reap the benefits of his new freedom. But the father who is deeply involved with his children may also behave in the same way: he needs more money to ingratiate himself with his ex-wife, through whom his connection with his children now has to pass, and also to maintain his children's respect. The role of the breadwinner becomes his way of softening the feelings of guilt which are intertwined with his affection for them.

Studies of divorce most usually direct their attention to the problems it creates for children. But observers have also recorded – though not, unfortunately, in the context of exhaustive studies – the psychic suffering which often afflicts the father who suddenly finds himself without them: the *involuntary child absence syndrome.*[7]

This affliction appears primarily as depression. Its most conspicuous characteristic is the degree to which it remains unconscious: the father, often, may even be unaware that the lack of his children is the cause of his depression; in other cases, he perceives the link, but makes no attempt to remedy the situation by intensifying contact with his children. We are dealing here with a new situation: once it was the son, like Telemachus, who sought his distant father. So there are no rites and traditions that might orient fathers in search of their children. The individual father either discovers a way of his own, or represses the problem.

The loss of a significant relationship is always a source of suffering. But to see things in broader terms, we can also ask if the surrounding world doesn't intensify the pain of the separation. If the dominant values are those of success, the divorced father who is deeply connected to his children – and these, inevitably, are the fathers who are most inclined to experience conspicuous guilt feelings – superstitiously introjects them (whether or not he subjects such values to rational criticism makes no difference) and adapts to them, thus reinforcing the reproof he hears from the Super-Ego "You didn't know how to deserve your children: this is why you have lost them." The father's crisis in self-esteem finds corroboration in objective fact. The father who has lost his children doesn't feel punished for having committed a moral error, which might be redeemed, but for a personal incapacity.

This interior accusation signals two things to the father. It reminds him that carnal procreation isn't enough for him: his responsibility is to choose his child, to continue to combat for his child. It also reminds him that our competitive culture never accepts anything as irreversible: one can merit one's child, or lose one's child.

The psychic discomfort of the divorced father becomes part of a vicious circle. And he finds it difficult to break free of this circle since in addition to feeding on his personal circumstances, it is also reinforced by two phenomena which mark the whole of our epoch: the general collapse of the father, of which his drama forms a part; and the general hegemony of values that substantiate material success rather than ethics. This father now feels humiliated, on seeing his obligations reduced primarily to financial support. He hasn't understood that even his life before divorce – and basically the lives of all fathers – had ever more centered on the question of financial support, as though it were the highest outcrop of an island that in any case was sinking.

So the first rejection of ascendant values can't be ascribed to the new horde of the young. This new development was placed on their path by history: directly so by the Industrial Revolution, and indirectly by the American and French Revolutions which preceded it, even in spite of their having taken place in the name of justice and brotherhood. In part, it was a question of one of the elements of progress, which is something we are not to regret for as long as we eat its fruits. The release of human beings from a superior but excessive authority – father, king, God – placed them all on the same plane and conferred them equal rights, yet also unleashed rivalries which before would have had no chance to exist.

The pack distinguishes itself from the community since the pack consists of coequals all on the run, with no superior authority, no father. It too requires a hierarchy, to keep it from self-destructing in the rivalries between its members. But its hierarchy has no base in any true authority, such as we found in the relationship between generations; its order is simply a question of progressive levels of strength: the ranks rise from the weakest individual and go up to the alpha male. Each is a little stronger than the one before. These strengths are not deployed within the group, but cumulatively directed to the outside.

We are not interested here in the zoological nature of the true pack; we only want to discern the elements that lead to the alliance of two fatherless sons, like Pinocchio and Lucignolo. In this classic children's story,[8] Pinocchio is an incomplete son. On the one hand, he has no mother: a fairy becomes his adoptive mother only at a later point in the tale, and remains of little importance. On the other, he has no father: Geppetto, clearly enough, would like him to be his son – he chooses him as a father has to do – but manages only to make him out of wood, without being able to make him a real boy. He is a poor carpenter, with no true authority over his son, since he is powerless and has no money.

Pinocchio stubbornly refuses to go to school, and rejects all duty and authority, until meeting up with a boy who is a little bigger and older, more rebellious, and more sure of himself: Lucignolo. He falls immediately beneath his sway. Lucignolo has no authoritative knowledge or experience through which to protect him: he transmits no teaching, no figure which might be introjected for the purpose of constructing an interior authority. Pinocchio and Lucignolo will live through a series of exciting adventures, drunk with the sensation of their cumulative strength. Their road can lead only to perdition, and they suffer a highly symbolic punishment: they are transformed into animals, and not into animals that run in freedom. They are turned into donkeys, which at the time were the most exploited of all the beasts.

Peter Härtling, a German writer, tells a similar story, but modern, true and autobiographical.[9] As a child he felt contempt for his father, who was a mildly mannered and soft-spoken lawyer; he preferred the example of the older and more aggressive boys of the Hitler Youth, and his ideal father was Hitler himself. At the end of the war, his father was captured by the Red Army, and never returned. Posthumous research, which the writer conducted with increasing intensity as the memory of his father slipped ever further away, led to the discovery that his habitual clients had been Jews and opponents of Nazism, whom the timid lawyer had defended at the risk of his life. This anti-heroic bourgeois gentleman was the hero the boy had been seeking but had never managed to find, if not while mourning his loss. As said before, Nazism and Fascism were not only reactionary and paternalistic ideologies. They were also movements that enrolled whole herds of Lucignolos and directed their aggressiveness against their fathers.[10]

Pinocchio and Lucignolo strike our imagination since they represent the happy, purposeless and improvised alliance of two fatherless boys. We can't explain the unending success of this simple story of the wooden puppet by remarking only on the growth of the length of his nose. We might wonder as well if this story doesn't hold a remarkable harbinger of the condition of today's young men, which is one of our most pressing concerns.

NOTES

1 Greven, Ph. (1977) *The Protestant Temperament: Patterns of Child-rearing, Religious Experience and the Self in Early America.* Chicago: University of Chicago Press.
2 Pleck, E. H. and Pleck, J. H.(1997) "Fatherhood ideals in the United States: historical dimensions," in Lamb (ed.), *The Role of the Father in Child Development.*
3 Ibid.; Griswold, R. (1993) *Fatherhood in America: A History.* New York: Basic Books.
4 Pleck and Pleck (1997).
5 See Chapter 20.
6 See Chapter 14.
7 Jacobs (1986). See also Delumeau and Roche (1990), XV; Feldman, L. B. (1990) "Fathers and fathering," in Meth, R. L. and Pasick, R. S., *Men in Therapy. The Challenge of Change.* New York: The Guilford Press; Fthenakis (1985), 10.
   Other studies have shown, even in cases where the couple does not divorce, that the decline of a marriage causes more psychic suffering to fathers than to mothers. Cummings, E. M. and O'Reilly, A. W. (1997) "Fathers in family context: effects of marital quality on child adjustment," in Lamb (ed.), *The Role of the Father in Child Development.*
8 See Introduction.
9 Härtling, P. (1995) *Nachgetragene Liebe.* Köln: Verlag Kiepenheur & Witsch.
10 See Chapter 16 and Figure 6.

Chapter 23

The search for the father

But, you must know, your father lost a father;
That father lost, lost his, and the survivor bound
In filial obligation for some term
To do obsequious sorrow . . .

Hamlet, I, 2 (89–92)

At this point, our research *on* the father must recognize that it is also a search *for* the father. It addresses a reader who is interested in both. Books on the mother don't have to be so ambiguous.

We can't conclude our narrative on the father without lending attention to the child who is on the quest for him. So, now we'll invert our gaze and look at things through the eyes of a son. This isn't however a point of view which differs from the father's. It's precisely the form in which his gaze would like one day to survive.

In the course of his quest, the son wants a number of different things. He's looking for his father. He wants to know him from the inside, just as once he knew him from the outside. He wants to make the acquaintance of "the father" who lives within him: he wants to become an adult.

In its simplest form, this quest is a voyage.

Ever since Telemachus entered the opening cantos of the *Odyssey* in pursuit of Ulysses, the search for the father has been a central theme of Western literature.

Telemachus must find Ulysses not only because he needs his help in his struggle against the invading suitors, but also – as he himself explains (I, 215–16) – because a son on his own has no way of knowing what father authored his life, and it's insufficient to receive this information from his mother.

When they recognize one another, Ulysses warns Telemachus to show no reaction if the suitors insult and humiliate the father he has finally found (XVI, 274–7). He is to harbor no doubts about ultimate victory.

In the development of the narrative, this suggestion is a preparation for their assault against the suitors, but it also holds a more ample meaning. It nearly contains a prophecy, and this may be the reason for which the conclusion of the *Odyssey* remains so up to date.

In recent history the father has been attacked and humiliated by the movements which have fought against the abuse of authority, and against male abuse. History has indeed succeeded in limiting the excesses of fathers, but not of the males. It has subdued the arrogant paternalism of the God the Father, of the king-god and of the father-god. But it has not subdued male arrogance. The father has in fact been displaced by arrogant males who resemble the suitors in the *Odyssey*, and the father himself shows the tendency to regress to the state of the male animal.

Humility – and humiliation if necessary – is an experience through which the father has to pass in order for his authority to be purified. The patient Ulysses is humble, and knows how to postpone victory until the opportune moment: humble to the point, on one occasion, of adopting the name of "Nobody." His patience and humility contrast with the suitors' superfluous violence. If his qualities win the day, they will bring about the restitution of the potency of the father, free of all male arrogance. If they fail, we have only the violent male, and lose the necessary principle of authority. The *Odyssey* is a prophecy of this risk and of this possibility. This is why Telemachus' voyage and Ulysses' return still today speak of a world which is not at all alien to us.

The son's voyage doesn't always take place in the geography of the outside world. His peregrinations can also be symbolic. They can present themselves as a search for a relationship that allows the father his proper place and renders him justice.

Hamlet is perhaps the best-known example. We can also note that its references to the university seem to harbinger the anguish of the fatherless students who are typical of the twentieth century. At the beginning of the story, the protagonist, like Telemachus, is a son imprisoned in a passive nostalgia for his father, who had suddenly died. Hamlet the elder then appears to his son as a ghost, demanding revenge. Hamlet wants to give him satisfaction. But to do so, he must first of all understand his father, and, by understanding him, internally make himself a father. Hamlet has to reestablish contact with the students of the University of Wittenberg, which at the time was one of the first dens of free thinkers. Like the students of Berkeley and the Sorbonne in the mid-twentieth century, his restless companions believed themselves to have left the father behind them, whereas in fact they were searching for him. All of them are anxiously seeking a truth and an authority that they no longer find in the outside world. Hamlet has to return into their midst, to dialog with them, in order to overcome their one-sidedness and their desperation as fatherless sons.

The quest for the father is an ancient and archetypal theme, which symbolically tells both society and the individual that a father is an always continuing effort that never reaches a definitive end. A father: whether being one or having one makes no difference; it makes no difference if the point of view is the father's or the son's. The quest contains an unconscious residue of phylogenetic memory, and retells the story of the father's always precarious status. Both the Old and New Testaments can also be seen as an endless search for the father, who is found only to be lost once again. The tale they tell has left the whole of the Western world with a subterranean anxiety: the anxiety that lies in the knowledge, as we have repeated from the start, that the father – both the personal father and the principle that allows the son to become a father – is not a natural given.

Even the symbolic quest for the father which Härtling recounts[1] begins with an image of trying to find him in the outside world. One of the author's earliest memories is of his father's leaving home every morning in his automobile to go to his office. At about four years old, Härtling ran away from home one day on his tricycle and was found in the midst of the city traffic while traveling through the streets in hopes of joining him.

Little by little as the times come closer to our own, the father moves further into the distance and the search grows more desperate. When Albert Camus was killed in an automobile crash, still at an early age, the wreckage of the car was found to contain 144 manuscript pages on his search for his father.[2] Camus' father also died quite young. To make his father's acquaintance, the writer had combed through record bureaus in various parts of Algeria; he had placed great hopes in this new autobiographical novel.[3]

The precocious loss of his father is the event that tortures Homer's model son, and much the same takes place today. Even cinema – a form of expression that risks abandoning archetypes in the name of ephemeral novelties and spectacular success – is overwhelmed by the search for the father, in every possible form. It's a highly dramatic story in Marta Meszaros' trilogy *Diary for my Children* (Hungary, 1993); a delicate story in Giuseppe Tornatore's *Nuovo cinema Paradiso* (Italy, 1988). Remembering the success of *Bambi* (1942), Walt Disney (USA) produced *Lion King* (1994). With *Smoke Signals* (1998), the search for the father even makes its appearance in the cinematic saga of America's native peoples. Alan Parker's *Pink Floyd – The Wall* (UK, 1982) gives us the songs of the rock group as they scream out the pain of the loss of the father. Theo Anghelopoulos develops a discourse on the absent father in *Landscape in the Fog* (Greece/France, 1988), as again can be said of the German director Wim Wenders, with *Alice in den Stätten* (Germany, 1973)[4] and *Paris, Texas* (USA, 1984). And the two great cycles by Edgar Reitz – *Heimat* (Germany, 1984) and *Die zweite Heimat* (Germany, 1992) – are more or less directly dedicated to the two generations of Germans who lost their fathers in the world wars. This theme, moreover, is no luxury for the exclusive consumption of the prosperous. The cinema of impoverished countries likewise bewails the father with whom no contact can be re-established: Walter Salles' *Central do Brasil* (Brazil, 1998), Idriffa Idrissa Ouédraogo's *Le cri du coeur* (Burkina Faso, 1994), Rachid Bouchareb's *Poussières de vie* (Algeria/ Vietnam, 1994). But Luís Buñuel's *Los olvidados* (Mexico, 1950) remains the first and most tragic.

Throughout antiquity and up until the threshold of modern times, such tales were concerned with the timeless archetype: they unconsciously told the story of the father's inherently precarious condition. Today they speak as well of something which is much more conscious, more precise, and more urgent. They speak of the need to rediscover a father who is ever more frequently absent.

If there is any sense in offering an intuitive judgment on such a vast phenomenon, we feel the profusion of these researches to be a reassuring sign: today's father may have forgotten his children, but his children have not forgotten him. If fatherhood, as Mead remarked, has to be taught in order not to go lost, the next generation may find itself composed of sons and daughters who still have a father figure because they have managed to continue to imagine one: because they have managed to teach fatherhood to themselves.

We can't believe that only writers and film directors are capable of this feat of imagination; their creativity gives voice to a general and unconscious nostalgia. Let's take an example from daily life.

Paola is a young woman who's about to finish her university degree. She is both intelligent and exuberant. She can be highly communicative about sad events, but in a slightly boisterous way, as though she were accustomed to staying as far away as she can from being downhearted.

She grew up in a matrifocal family, like those we have encountered in Latin America, but of a very different social status. Her mother is cultivated, active and positive, and her daughter has inherited her personality. The father comes from an old, wealthy family, but would seem never to have become an individual. Indecision more than dishonesty had allowed him to become embroiled in financial scandals, and he had lost a considerable portion of his wealth.

For as long as she can remember, Paola's father had always been a drinker, and cheerless even when drunk.

"When he'd had too much to drink, he'd ask: 'Do you love me?' He always considered me his favorite child. I was close to him, and didn't pass judgment on him. I think I helped him. This is something else I learned from my mother: even though he never really paid her back, she always helped him; it was only a couple of years ago, when my sister and I were already nearly grown, that she finally decided to leave him."

But Paola's parents still remained in touch with one another, and her father continued to be dependent on her mother. Now, however, he was more aggressive; and this allowed Paola to view him more critically, and to criticize her mother for having allowed him to remain a baby.

A short while previously, her father had carefully taped all the cracks around the doors and windows of his house, had swallowed a bottle of sleeping pills, and had turned on the gas. He was discovered and saved by chance.

He spent a long period in the hospital, always complaining like a spoiled child and with no apparent memory of why he was there.

"The doctors and the police couldn't believe he was still alive: he had organized things so well. I know, because I looked into everything very carefully, read all the medical and police reports, and tried to listen in to what was being said when people thought I couldn't hear them. I was doing my best to learn everything I could about what might have turned out to be the last few minutes of my father's life: those minutes that he himself now knows nothing about. I think I've learned everything I can.

"I didn't find it hard to imagine that he might have tried to kill himself. By itself, his attempted suicide probably wouldn't have been enough to make me enter analysis.

"Perhaps I didn't have a father, but didn't realize it. There were ways in which it seemed to be the other way around, that he was my son, and this made us very close to each other. He had often remarked, 'If it wasn't for you and your sister I'd just give up.' But we were there.

"The suicide attempt took place in the morning. A perfectly ordinary morning. I discovered that he had just finished breakfast. I thought, 'You kill yourself in the evening, or in the middle of a sleepless night, after drinking a bottle of whisky; not at eight o'clock in the morning, after finishing up your coffee.' Then I learned that he had made a number of telephone calls and canceled his appointments for the day. I began to imagine that even a normal morning could be the time you choose to put an end to your life. But something was missing.

"He said that he only lived for us, so how could he possibly leave us like that, in such a perfectly orderly way, but without a word of good-bye to his children, or at least to me. A letter, a tape recording, at least a note. There had to be at least that much. While he was in the hospital I searched through every corner of his house; even the bathroom, even the garage. Like a treasure hunter, or a dedicated archaeologist. I kept it up even after it grew clear to me that there was nothing to be found. Maybe I'd have kept it up forever. But they released him from the hospital. His house belonged to him again, and for me it was once again a place with no particular meaning.

"It's clear to me now that I couldn't give up, just as you don't give up when a person you love is missing, even after the point when it's clear that they're no longer alive. My father, now, is physically alive, and it's only natural to be happy about that. But for me, after trying so hard to find a letter, and being so sure that it had to exist, the fact of never having found it means remaining without a father. Or better, the fact that this letter never existed was like reaching the realization that I had never had a father at all. Now it's nearly obvious that I entered analysis to continue that search."

Article 30 of the Constitution of the Italian Republic – born from the ruins of Fascism – proclaims: "The law dictates the norms and limits for the attempt to establish paternity." It's surprising to think of the search for the father – with which we are now familiar as a mythic theme – as a subject of modern laws. History clearly amuses itself at retracing the outlines of eternal symbols, even with the use of seasonal instruments.

Despite the efforts of legislators since times as early as ancient Rome, the number of children abandoned by their parents has always been enormous, in every period of history.[5] Owing to traditional privileges, a lesser degree of physical involvement, and, basically, to incivility, abandonment has been immeasurably more frequent on the part of the male parent (whom we intentionally avoid referring to as "the father").

We know that the search for the father is more than a material necessity: it is also a universal psychological need. All of us, like Telemachus, want to know whose child we are. Adopted children sooner or later attempt to discover their biological parents, even when their adoptive parents have given them as much as possible. The above-mentioned article makes no reference to maternity, but only to paternity, since the male parent can disappear without having been identified. The laws are only interested in the correction of a social injustice, not in responding to a psychological need. But we also see the modern legislation on the search for the father as symbolic. Its goal is to discover the father who is no longer there. And today's father, unlike the fathers of former times, is often psychologically absent even when his identity is known. We therefore see the laws on the subject primarily as a symbol of a much more general vacuum that charges our times with anxiety. All societies create metaphoric heroes who voice the values in which they believe: the epic values of classical antiquity, the Christian values of the Middle Ages, the juridical values of the modern secular state. Present-day Italy finds its only heroes in the judges.

The fact that a man can father a child and then flee from the task of *being* a father is one of the most frequent and insidious crimes of all times. It's insidious by virtue of contravening justice on a scale far different, for example, than theft: theft is fully remedied when the stolen object or an equivalent one returns into our hands; the absence of a father bears consequences throughout the whole of a life, and even for the following generation. Technological progress in this particular field has silently enacted one of the greatest revolutions of all times. A simple sampling of blood and the analysis of its DNA today make it possible for paternity to be determined with absolute certainty. The abandonment of millions of children on the part of their fathers in every corner of the civilized Western world is a different but no less flagrant crime than the injustice suffered by America's slaves or Russia's serfs. It's therefore stunning to be able to defeat this crime by way of a simple laboratory test, without the rivers of blood of the War of Secession or the massacres waged by the White and Red Armies.

Technology can suddenly and forever overturn a highly ancient predicament. We experience this development as psychologically overwhelming since we haven't had time to adjust to it: a novel departure is abruptly at work in an ancient cultural situation.

Reducing a complex train of events to its minimum terms, we can say that the human male has always had the power to choose whether or not to have sexual relationships, and with what precautions; and then, in the case of a pregnancy, to choose whether or not to recognize his child. Unlike the woman, he could also think of the two events as separate and independent. In a certain sense, the entirety of patriarchal society found its original base in this freedom which differentiates the father from the mother and which furnishes the truest content of the father's relationship with his child: this relationship is based on the male's *faculty of choice*. If affirmatively exercised, it transformed him into a father; if negatively, it made him a being who returned to animal behavior. Today, at least as a principle adopted by the laws of my own particular country, this "threshold of reversibility" for the act of procreation has shifted. The greater area of choice has even come to be assigned to women.

Motherhood is made reversible for women by way of the interruption of a pregnancy; and after the birth of a child, a woman can declare her unwillingness to be its mother, and thus offer the child for adoption. The male, on the other hand, no longer has the possibility, from the very moment of a fecund sexual relationship, of subtracting himself from a "paternity test" at any moment in the rest of his life. The child can point a finger at his presumed father and drag him into court at any age. In fact, the right to identify the father and to advance financial claims never comes to an end: here there is no such thing as a statute of limitation, which in Italian jurisprudence exists even for homicide.

Italy is a country where the mass mentality is still highly charged with *machismo*, and men are psychologically unprepared to confront this revolution. In a cultural context where a critique of the father has been underway for quite some time, the new paternity tests have been known to cause males a paranoid feeling of persecution, even if the problem of the father's identity is as old as the world itself, and even though the new technology has only simplified it. If men feel persecuted, this is once again due to the mistake of taking things too literally. The new technology, in itself, brings only clarity. And the technology alone is one-sided. The search for the father is a great deal more than his physical identification. It's an enormous myth that no longer has access to the language of myths, and which therefore attempts, by way of juridical formulas and genetic codes, to survive in "myths" which are still accepted: the myths of civil law and of secular science. The individual father is impotent in the face of the disappearance of a timeless myth, and this obscure awareness throws him into consternation.

We observe once again that materialism, the predominant force in the rational thought of the society in which we live, can lead too far from symbolic thinking, which remains the center of gravity for all true and proper psychology.

The problem of the search for the father can never be exclusively legal, statistical or economic: having found the absconded father, one can force him to furnish his child with economic assistance; but he can't be forced to confer the paternal blessing of which his child is equally in need. The search for the father is not only a personal problem: it's a torment for the whole of society, which attempts to make the fathers prevail over the males of the pack. This is a struggle in which civilization itself is at stake: victory on the part of civilization can be said today to continue to remain in the distance, and meanwhile the regression toward the irresponsible male seems to have risen to levels which have never been seen before.

We are convinced that the voyage toward the father, the quest for the father on the part of the child, is essential to the identities of both; and we reach that conclusion for a very simple reason. If the father, as an expression of the culture from which he derives, feels that the condition of fatherhood is necessarily intentional, then the child too, within the terms of that very same culture, must hold some corresponding conviction.

If biological procreation isn't in itself enough to make a man a father, and if it's necessary in any case for the man to adopt his child, then the child too must find it insufficient simply to have been given a physical life. Even if less directly and more unconsciously than the father, the child too must signal the desire for adoption, selecting his or her father. The reasons for the search for the father don't simply lie in his frequently being at a distance from his child, at work or at war, periodically or forever. Just as adopted children sooner or later seek out their biological mothers, all children must at some point make the attempt to seek out their father, even if they have always lived with him. The situation is nearly reversed. Sensitive children understand that their fathers are in fact their fathers as the result of the making of a choice: of having chosen to be a father and of having chosen them to be his children. Fatherhood is always a cultural fact, and the simply biological father is not enough for them. So the child must in any case "search out" the father; and even though the father whom the child rediscovers is once again the biological father, the child must return his gesture, choosing him in turn. Otherwise, the child will turn attention toward a paternal figure who can function as a guide to initiation, toward a mentor assigned by his or her personal history. In symbolic terms, however, the need which fuels the search is always one and the same.

Humanity has always been acquainted with the absence of the father, and in this sense our own epoch is no exception. A novelty which could prove to be even more grave than the absence of the father would be the absence of the search for the father.

NOTES

1 Härtling (1995). See Chapter 22.
2 Todd, O. (1996) *Albert Camus. Une vie.* Paris: Gallimard, Chapter 50.
3 Now published: Camus, A. (1994) *Le Premier Homme.* Paris: Gallimard.
4 Starting from a chance encounter between a man and a woman, the director offers a riveting description, in the relationship between the man and the woman's daughter, of the anxieties of a daughter without a father, and of a "father" who has no children. The man is unaware of his need for a child, whereas the girl knows very well that she wants a father, that she wants him to be respected, and that people should know that she is his daughter.
5 In past centuries, the Ospedale della Pietà, in Venice, like many similiar institutions, took in abandoned children. Next to it stands the Chiesa della Pietà. Tourists who note its façade while strolling beside the Grand Canal should turn for a moment into the narrow Calle della Pietà which runs to the right of the building. A few steps forwards will then reveal this tablet on the side of the church:

> *The Lord God shall fulminate with malediction and excomunication against all who send or permit their sons and daughers to be sent, whether legitimate or natural, into this Hospice of Piety while possessing the means and faculty to raise them, they likewise being obliged to repayment of all damages and all costs incurred for such children; nor can they be absolved if this obligation remains unsatisfied, as clearly appears in the bull of our Lord the Pope Paul III.*
>
> On the day of November 12
> In the year of Our Lord 1548

Part V

A final reflection

Chapter 24

A final reflection

Our approach throughout this book has been psychological. It's a good rule for the psychoanalyst to refrain from offering advice to individual patients: so what could be said of offering advice to the whole of society? Jungian analysts propose no standard cure. They presume that people in psychic pain are in need above all of *individuation*, which is to say that the patients' task is to overcome interior contradictions, to understand their particular needs, and as completely as possible to become themselves. What they offer their patients is no previously given or ideal solution but a *search*. Thus, in speaking of the father figure, we shouldn't say: "The father should be like this." Instead we say, "Look for him, no matter if within yourself or in the outside world."

We feel it useful to reaffirm that the father figure is no easily retrievable or ready-made image. Those who desire to have a father must look for him; and those who want to be a father must also undertake a quest. While looking for the father, just as in the rest of the process of individuation, one has to be honest with oneself.

Honesty demands, first of all, that we ask ourselves if the discovery of the father is truly what we want. The ample forms of the search for him sometimes conceal a different purpose: laziness and self-indulgence.

The ideal father should favor his children's growth, autonomy and differentiation. But in a moment of history that's characterized by the absent father, the search for the father can also be suspected of concealing a rejection of individuation, or an ingenuous attempt to entrust oneself to an outside force.

Such a rejection of personal responsibility might constitute a duplication, in a less political key, of the process which rendered the twentieth century the womb of tyranny, the beast in the bosom of history. After the end of the First World War and the collapse of the empires, Europe faced two possibilities: an era of new insecurity or new freedom. Events, as we know, were to take the more ruinous direction since the greater part of human beings find the limitation of insecurity to be more important that the active use of freedom. We are not to be surprised that many have bartered the latter for the former.

The twentieth-century dictatorships didn't arise for exclusively political reasons; they also gave expression to personal needs.[1] The ever more conspicuous absence of the fathers and the continuing decline of paternal authority abetted the projection of the search for security onto public institutions. The need for vigorous politics concealed the need for a vigorous father.

Things seem to stand differently today. The need for the father comes to expression as a search for something, not as an act of flight. And the discussion centers on the structure of the private family, not on society's political apparatus. But the movements of the psyche always participate in something unconscious; and we have no right to feel ourselves to be necessarily more conscious than the people, two or three generations ago, who opened the road to the dictatorships: they too were most certainly convinced of being more conscious than the people of a few generations previously, and they held that belief mistakenly. So, just as their hunger for the father led them on a search for dictatorship, we can't be sure that our search for the father does not find its base in a secret nostalgia for dictatorship. The sense of insecurity that now leads us to search for the father is in any case a psychic cousin of the insecurity that led to the appearance of the tyrants. In terms of the psychology of the unconscious, we can offer no definitive reply and must continue to doubt our motivations.

It follows, on the one hand, that while pursuing our need for father figures we must also keep sharp psychological vigil over new political developments, especially with respect to emerging political personalities. It would be bitterly ironic for the Western world, while entering the twenty-first century, to confront what counts as perhaps its greatest problem by turning to figures of "the father of the country": figures born in the nineteenth century, and which flourished, degenerated and apparently expired in the twentieth century.

On the other hand, in the private sphere, we have to see that this need also finds an outlet in the search for gurus and psychotherapists. If the notion of the transference and the figure of the analyst continue to be meaningful, people who need to confront this problem might largely be expected to turn to analysis. But the world in which such people live will be a "maternal" world: not so much as a question of the statistical predominance of mothers, but because the daily facts of economics and technology are "maternal," or ever more inclined toward the immediate, oral satisfactions of consumerism, always more conditioned by the desire for quick results. The situation will grow paradoxical: the search for the father will lead people to look for therapeutic help, but their lack of acquaintance with the paternal notions of the development of projects and the acceptance of deferral will lead them to seek out briefer therapies, in hope of virtually instantaneous results.

In its rush towards the primary stage of development, psychoanalysis has nourished the obesity of the sphere of the mother and of private life while helping to consign the sphere of the father and of social life to anorexia. Now it must return to the father, as Freud did at the beginning; and it must deal with him as a social and historical problem, since society and history have been the home in which the father has resided since the darkness at the beginning of time. But there is also another reason why this shift has to come about.

If the twentieth century is the century of the dictators – the terrible fathers – it is also the century of psychoanalysis. Freud, Jung and its other great teachers rendered the culture of the Western world quite different from what it was before: literature, art and even politics, as here we've had occasion to observe, can no longer be properly understood without the use of the tools of psychoanalysis; there are also times when it has to be seen as one of the forces that influenced them. There is no way of knowing if this improved the century; but we know it to have created conditions which no previous century would find recognizable. There can be no doubt that the individual experience of analysis – its strictly clinical application – has transformed the lives of many people. But they remain a limited group. As never foreseen by the solitary Viennese neurologist who created it in the nineteenth century, psychoanalysis in the twentieth century found its principal application in the understanding of history and society. This is the way we've continued to use it in our study of the father: we have been less concerned with the psychology of the father as an individual than with the psychology of the history of the father figure and of the culture that surrounds it.

The absence of the father in the present-day world holds only one certainty: the need to continue to discuss it, and to search for him. Words, of course, will not bring him back; and words which grow too insistent will perhaps one day grow tedious. So, let's make it clear that this tedium too is what we want. The most pernicious psychic disorders derive less from the way one confronts a problem than from remaining unconscious of it. And if the unconscious need for the father led, among other things, to the twentieth century's tyrants, discourse on the father that grows so abundant as to fill us with nausea can only be welcomed. If the discourse on the father fills us with nausea, we'll likewise feel that nausea for the degenerate forms of politics which attempt to exploit it: our nausea will thus have been pressed into the service of the prevention of tyranny.

We began by observing that the growing body of literature seems less to offer a comprehensive analysis of the father than to show us the extent of the nostalgia he excites. Nothing similar takes place with studies of mothers. The father has so thoroughly defended himself from the feelings as to cause their unconscious reappearance in the melancholy tone of the discourse which has taken him as its subject.

This nostalgia is a psychological dilemma. It perhaps finds aesthetic sublimation, but no social solution. The father will never again return to the place in society which he used to hold. How could we possibly reconstruct him and consign him again to the pack that longs for his authority and to the children who miss his affection? We can track down and bring back a person who has just turned the corner. But the father began to disappear countless ages ago, starting even perhaps at the time when Christianity first placed the accent on the son's point of view.

So, this is another question to which we have to respond: are we conducting an honest research or are we only looking for what we immediately would like to find? We can't conduct a search for the father while assuming the psychology of the person who's looking for something that lies just around the corner, such as we find in so much literature where solutions seem immediately at hand. The father is the figure who least of all could find himself reflected in such a procedure, since he speaks through the voice of the project that develops in time and of the ability to defer the satisfaction of immediate needs. At times, the disappearance of the fathers is attributed to the psychological pressures that come from feminism, to the revolts of the youthful population, and to other developments of the last few generations; fathers are imagined to have been put to flight by contemporary phenomena that disparage their functions and activate feelings of guilt. Such arguments have little more weight than the paper on which they are written, since the absence of the father as we experience it today is the final product of a series of reversals which have taken place in the course of thousands of years. Fathers who address such accusations to their children and companions seem to give rein to persecutory projections. It's true that the father thus seems finally to realize that he has problems with the more feminine and adolescent parts of his personality, which is ever less unified. But in the majority of cases, he continues to project those problems onto the outside world, toward those whom he now believes to be his major adversaries.

There is also something more to be said: these recent projections and psychological splits superimpose themselves on others which are highly ancient. Men who function at deficient levels of psychological differentiation have always reduced women to two figures that can't be reconciled with one another: the mother and the lover. But our reconstruction of the psychology of the father in the course of time has made it clear that this fractured attitude to women is based on a precedent problem that concerns the male. It is in fact the male who contains within himself two identities which are far from having been reconciled by natural evolution, and which as well have never been united by the course of the development of history and culture: on the one hand the father, on the other the male who is only a donor of sperm. If men throughout history have assigned two separate archetypes to women – the woman who is sexually available and the woman who cares for the children – the reason lies in their own inability to unify the two corresponding male identities. By projecting his most ancient problem onto his companion, the male declares his incapacity to assume a unified identity by making himself wholly and definitively a father.

In the present-day Western world, the carefree spirit of male adolescence is more dominant than the paternal notion of the pursuance of projects. It's in much the same way, in the course of the centuries, that the spiritual satiety of the monotheism which sees the messiah as already having arrived came to prevail over the nervous patience of its forebear which continues to wait for his future coming. First in the heavens and then on earth, the Son has cornered the Father.

The history of the father in the Western world follows the line of an extremely lengthy decline, occasionally interrupted by a momentary upward rise. Proposals that envision his return either rank as self-deception or provide the occasion for a brief reprieve. The patriarchy is over and done with: never again will the father be a metaphor for the order that prevails at the apex of society.

We can imagine the historical patriarchy, as embodied by real historical individuals, to resemble certain "evolutionary" phases of social development in which despotic regimes seem finally to have furnished a necessary route to the greater affirmation of democracy. The fathers would seem to have invented civilization, at least in the patriarchal forms in which we know it in the West. In part they were later to hamper its further evolution, and in part to accelerate it, sparking the explosion of new departures such as the Renaissance or the French Revolution. Such dramatic developments in fact took place well before the existence of a true and proper feminism which effectively demanded them.

In the Middle Ages, even free thinkers thought of God as a literally extant entity. After struggling to allow him to maintain that status – after the Renaissance, the Age of Enlightenment and Nietzsche – most of Western culture today accepts the notion that God is a metaphor, and that God as a metaphor held in our hearts can inspire our lives to no lesser degree than a personal being who sits on a heavenly throne.

It's much the same for the Father who fills us with nostalgia: the archetype that's spelled with a capital letter. It's hard to imagine that he will ever again find an incarnation in real human beings. He will continue to survive as an inspiration, as the psychological principle that asks for order, project and the ability to defer the satisfaction of immediate needs. The difference lies in the way we respond to his voice: there can no longer be any question of responding with spoken words to a voice that comes from outside of us; from this point forward we reply psychologically to an interior voice. This too is one of the components of history. History doesn't exclusively consist of men and civilizations that are born and then that die, frequently leaving us with memories that teach a great deal more than their material presence was ever able to formulate. It also consists of symbols which seem at times to discover an incarnation, and at others entirely to disappear; but their wake is always charged with guiding metaphors. The father is such a symbol, and the metaphors he leaves behind can offer orientation to all – even to mothers – who choose to seek and accept it.

Mothers will gradually begin to show various paternal qualities as well, and not only for the reason that the whole of society feels the absence of the father and therefore insists that such qualities must not go lost. It is easier for the mother to assume the psychological attitude of the father than vice versa. The father, after all, is an entirely cultural construction. He is a product of society, and society – albeit at a very slow pace – can modify him or change the forms in which he appears. Today's mother – obviously enough – is also a product of civilization, but on the basis of a biological groundwork. Though hidden beneath the deposits of history where surely it can't be directly perceived, this groundwork would nonetheless be difficult to emulate.

The gradual assumption of paternal qualities on the part of the mother has limits of another type. Within the nucleus of the family and up until its children's adolescence, the obstacles are moderate. We know[2] that the family with a single parent – almost always the mother – is not inherently pathogenic. At worst it encounters difficulties that derive from a lower degree of organizational agility, from more limited financial resources, and also from the prejudiced points of view that consider it to be less educative. But when the children enter adolescence – which is also the moment, in situations where the social fabric is not intact, when they begin to group into gangs – even the mother with paternal qualities may find her tasks insurmountable.

Gangs, in fact, even when mixed, have a crude and regressive masculine psychology. While reviewing the course of evolution back to the primeval horde and beyond, we likewise find that packs of animals are ordered by a masculine hierarchy.

One of the principal unconscious functions of gangs is to challenge the father, and this challenge conceals a need for initiation into adult life, which few are able to supply. In some cases, this ability is still possessed by Catholic priests who are also committed to secular and social activities. In some Italian communities, such priests may indeed be the last true barrier that keeps young men from becoming involved with the Mafia. A crude mentality that has little experience or ability in the elaboration of symbols, and which therefore thinks in entirely literal terms, usually leads the gang to seek out true and proper tests of strength with other masculine figures. The men to whom these challenges are directed find it highly difficult to withstand the confrontation and to demand respect; policemen, social workers and similar public figures find themselves in roles which demand that they too function in literal terms when in fact they are faced with situations which are potentially symbolic and psychological.

In the groups into which many adolescents transplant the lives they previously led within their families, the laws are more simple and existence less individual. The group reduces the level of the intelligence of its individual members and makes them an easy prey for stereotypes. It is more difficult for a woman to control such adolescents than it is for a man, since there is always a delay in the adjustment of collective unconscious values to the new situations of the times in which they are in fact immersed. To a large degree the fathers are already absent, but the surrounding culture – and especially that simpler culture which absorbs the lives of many adolescents as soon as they exit from their families – remains at considerable distance from a true adaptation to this new reality and insistently constructs its concepts on simple dualisms like father–mother, man–woman. A mother with no male partner can supplant him through the activation of her own paternal qualities for as long as her children live mainly at home, and for as long as friends and teachers don't display prejudices that cripple the situation. Later, however, in the period of competitive conflicts between young males, the psychological situation finds it easy to regress and to demand more material and less psychological distinctions: it thus insists on siting the paternal and maternal poles no longer within a single person, but respectively in a man and a woman.

If psychology is truly to return to a discussion of the father, it will see his slow, insidious regression toward the pre-paternal male as an immense, collective psychopathology.

   This constitutes a retreat from civilization on the part of a whole epoch. More than simply an enormous rip in the fabric of civic order, it is a true and proper regression toward a state which we thought to have left behind us. Despite its discontinuous movement and its cooling of relationships between human beings, Western society has been characterized by a growing respect for reciprocal rights and responsibilities. Its origins lie in the commitment of fathers to their families and children. Now, however, the responsibility of fathers, when it does not completely vanish, tends to reduce to purely economic terms, and the psychology of the father inclines to wither into that of the simple male. Such a retreat results in an interruption of the flow of civilization, much as was caused by the twentieth century's dictatorships. The "terrible fathers" were themselves a special manifestation of the crisis of the father, insofar as they attempted to alleviate it by turning themselves into powerful, tyrannical national fathers. Those regressions toward father-dictators came to an end and met political, military and economic defeat. But the end of the father's decadence as a principle of responsibility has not yet come into sight. Even if the female half of humanity were to prove itself capable of filling this void at the family level, society as a whole would nonetheless be deeply troubled by an evil which had fallen so sharply on its masculine half.

   We saw at the beginning of our study that in nature every female has a function. Most males, on the other hand, found their only significance as a part of the process of natural selection: their constant combat for the right to couple with the females led to the exclusive transmission of the genetic traits of the strongest. It was only with the human invention of paternity and the monogamic family that males acquired meaning as individuals.

We seem today to witness a return to the pre-human state of life: there are ever fewer fathers, and an ever larger horde of males who are always ready to battle one another. But the monogamic family has not been abolished, and the group of the males hasn't formally returned to open combat for the favors of the females. This is why women – and all women, not only the feminists – frequently find the whole of the masculine world to fill them with a feeling of desolation, of emptiness, as though perceiving it to be utterly void of meaningful subjectivities. It is as though most of the males were in excess: while having lost their individuality by abdicating from paternal responsibility, they haven't even returned to the collective function of working in the service of genetic selection.

We have seen the retreat of the fathers to take place on two planes. Materially, fathers are ever less present. Symbolically, their ritual functions – the elevation, blessing and initiation of their children – are no longer enacted. Mothers can fill the first void, but will find it difficult to fill the second. It has more to do with the general disappearance of rites than with their distribution between men and women.

So, the ability of mothers to take on the role of fathers is not unlimited. Basically, this is what they have always done when the fathers were away at war or on voyages. But in cases such as these, the man deposited an enduring memory at home, a bed carved into a tree, a myth of Ulysses. He remained a psychic presence. Today, the victory has been won by consumerism and a life lived day by day; the notions of the project and of persistence in time have nearly been defeated. Still more than the physical father, the paternal spirit is missing, which also means that mothers and children are without a way to appropriate or express it.

The retreat of the father has been rendered irreversible by the death of rites and myths. This has nothing to do with patriarchy or with matriarchy, but mainly with modernization. The material disappearance of the fathers also depends to a large degree on divorce and the dissolution of couples: on a freedom which in turn is part of the modern condition. And the modern condition is not reversible.

We close with a sense of the weight of having no suggestions to offer. There is one thing, however, of which these pages convince us: that memory is not useless. We began with the feeling that not only the present, but also the history of the father has been abandoned to a tragic obscurity, thus leaving children with the sensation of having been orphaned since a time that can't be defined.

To abandon the knowledge of the history of the father would be to give up the sense of continuity that overcomes time. We have spoken of this sense of continuity as a "paternal" function, and our one great hope is for someone to be able to continue to exercise it: today the mother, tomorrow the child, the day after tomorrow someone else. Our memories tell us that history and continuity are paternal. We cannot give them up, and precisely for the reason that we ever more entrust ourselves only to the world of consumer objects, which is the world of the eternal present. In this sense, even the worries expressed by environmentalists on the future of the planet – within a body of thought which has been described as a return of the myth of the Great Mother Earth – can be characterized as paternal.

We are also our history, and if we do not know our history, we give up the knowledge of a part of ourselves. We have an identity, but if we are fathers who have no knowledge of the history of fatherhood, our identity as fathers will be even more insecure than the one our times have already prepared for us. A father who knows nothing of the father's past is like an American who is ignorant of the Native Americans or George Washington; like a Frenchman who knows nothing of the Franks or Napoleon. Such a life is surely possible, but the persons who live it have no idea as to why they belong today to this community and not to some other one. They know nothing of the nature of the people of which they in any case form a part. Such a father will be likewise insecure, and even while being a member of it will know nothing of the world of the fathers. History, of course, as we speak of it here has nothing to do with battles and treaties, but with attitudes and customs, images and myths. And a knowledge of these things is more than theoretical if it permits a father to look at his child while asking himself the question which the history of fatherhood has consigned to him: "This is my child, but due to the act of procreation, or to the fact of my having chosen this child?"

A psychological history of the father is also necessary for our children, who will one day desire to exit from the dimension of timelessness; and on entering the dimension of time they will raise the question as to who are the people whose lives they continue. Though unaware of advancing a demand, they expect that story to be told. They expect that someone will be able to awaken them from the sleep of unconsidered actions, that someone will flex Ulysses' bow and put an end to the night of the suitors.

NOTES

1 Fromm, E. (1941) *Escape from Freedom* New York: Holt, Rinehart and Winston.
2 Lamb (1997); Samuels (1995).

References

Classics and other well known works which are available in various editions are quoted in the text without being mentioned either in the footnotes or in the bibliography. The title of such works appears in *italics*, and the date of first publication, where possible, is indicated after the title. For example: *Iliad*, IV; Rousseau, J. J., *Emile* (1776); Hemingway, E., *A Farewell to Arms* (1929).

Abramovitch, H. (1994) "Pigmy Giants." *San Francisco Jung Institute Library Journal*, 13(3): 143–7.

American Museum of Natural History (1993) *The First Humans*. San Francisco: Harper.

Ariès, Ph. (1960) *L'enfant et la vie familiale sous l'ancien régime*. Paris: Plon.

Bachofen, J. J. (1861) *Das Mutterrecht*.

Badinter, E. (1980) *L'amour en plus*. Paris: Flammarion.

Badinter, E. (1986) *L'un et l'autre*. Paris: Odile Jacob.

Beauvoir, S. de (1976) *Le deuxième sexe* (1949) Paris: Gallimard.

Benveniste, E. (1966) *Problèmes de linguistique générale*, Vol. I. Paris: Gallimard.

Benveniste, E. (1969) *Le vocabulaire des institutions indo-européennes*, 2 vols. Paris: Les Editions de Minuit.

Bernal, M. (1987) *Black Athena. The Afro-asiatic Roots of Classic Civilization*. London: Free Association Books.

Bernard, C. and Gruzinski, S. (1986) "I figli dell'apocalisse: la famiglia in Meso-America e nelle Ande," in Burguière et al. (eds), *Histoire de la famille*.

Biller, H. B. (1981) "The father and sex role development," in Lamb (ed.), *The Role of the Father in Child Development*.

Bischof, N. (1985) *Das Rätsel Oedipus. Die biologischen Wurzeln des Urkonfliktes von Intimität und Autonomie*. Munich: Piper.

Blankenhorn, D. (1995) *Fatherless America. Confronting Our Most Urgent Social Problem*. New York: Harper Perennial.

Bly, R. (1996) *The Sibling Society*. Reading MA: Addison Wesley.

Bloch, M. (1949) *Apologie pour l'histoire ou métier d'historien*. Paris: Armand Colin.

Bloom-Feshbach, J. (1981) "Historical perspectives in the father's role," in Lamb (ed.), *The Role of the Father in Child Development*.

Blos, P. (1985) *Son and Father*. New York: Free Press.

Bolck, L. (1926) *Das Problem der Menschwerdung*. Jena: Gustav Fischer.

Bonnet, J.-C. (1990) "De la famille à la patrie," in Delumeau and Roche (eds), *Histoire des pères et de la paternité*.

Burguière, A., Klapisch-Zuber, C., Segalen, M. and Zonabend, F. (eds) (1986) *Histoire de la famille*. Paris: Armand Colin.

Burkert, W. (1972) *Homo Necans*. Berlin: de Gruyter.

Burkert, W. (1987) *Ancient Mystery Cults*. Cambridge, MA: Harvard University Press.

Camus, A. (1994) *Le Premier Homme*. Paris: Gallimard.

Cavalli-Sforza, L. L. (2001) *Genes, People and Languages* (Seielstad, M., Tans.) Berkeley: University of California Press.

Cohen, M. N. and Bennet, S. (1993) "Skeletal evidence for sex roles and gender hierarchies in prehistory," in Miller (ed.), *Sex and Gender Hierarchies*.

Collodi, C. (1981) *Le avventure di Pinocchio. Storia di un burattino* (1883). Milan: Mondadori.

Coontz, S. (1997) *The Way We Really Are. Coming to Terms with America's Changing Families*. New York: Basic Books.

Cremerius, J. (1990) *Vom Handwerk des Psychoanalytikers: Das Werkzeug des psychoanalytischen Technik*, Band 2. Stuttgart: Frommann-Holzboog.

Cummings, E. M. and O'Reilly, A. W. (1997) "Fathers in family context: effects of marital quality on child adjustment," in Lamb (ed.), *The Role of the Father in Child Development*.

Dafoe Whitehead, B. (1997) *The Divorce Culture*. New York: Knopf.

Daniels, C. R. (ed.) (1998) *Lost Fathers. The Politics of Fatherlessness in America*. New York: St. Martin's Press.

Darmon, P. (1979) *Le mythe de la procréation à l'âge baroque*. Paris: Seuil.

Dawkins, R. (1976) *The Selfish Gene*. Oxford: Oxford University Press.

Delaisi de Perceval, G. (1981) *La part du père*. Paris: Seuil.

Delumeau, J. and Roche D. (eds) (1990) *Histoire des pères et de la paternité*. Paris: Larousse.

Derick Williams, R. (1982) "*The Aeneid*," in Kenney, E. J. and Clausen, W. V. (eds), *Cambridge History of Classical Literature*. Cambridge, New York and Melbourne: Cambridge University Press, II, 3.

Derrida, J. (1994) *Politiques de l'amitié*. Paris: Galilée.

Detienne, M. (1986) *Dionysus à ciel ouvert*. Paris: Hachette.

Deveau, J.-M. (1998) *Femmes esclaves. D'hier à aujourd'hui*. Paris: France Empire.

Di Lorenzo, S. (1996) *La Grande Madre Mafia*. Milan: Pratiche.

Dodds, E. R. (1951) *The Greeks and the Irrational*. Berkeley: University of California Press and London: Cambridge University Press.

Dunbar, R. I. M. (1988) *Primate Social System*. London and Sydney: Croom Helm.

Dupuis, J. (1987) *Au nom du père. Une histoire de la paternité*. Paris: Le Rocher.

Eibl-Eibesfeldt, I. (1976) *Liebe und Hass* (1970). Munich: Piper.

Eibl-Eibesfeldt, I. (1986) *Die Biologie des menschlichen Verhaltens. Grundrisse der Humanethologie* (1984). Munich: Piper.

Eibl-Eibesfeldt, I. (1987) *Grundrisse der vergleichenden Verhaltensforschung* (1967). Munich: Piper.

Eliade, M. (1975) *Histoire des croyances et des idées religieuses*, I. Paris: Payot.

Engels, F. (1884) *Der Ursprung der Familie, des Privateigentums und des Staats*. Zurich: Hottingen.

Evans-Pritchard, E. E. (1965) *The Position of Women in Primitive Societies and Other Essays in Social Antropology*. London: Faber & Faber.

Familias Chefiadas por Mulheres (1994). São Paulo: SEADE (Sistema Estadual de Anàlise de Dados).

Fares, V. (1996) *Fathers and Developmental Psychology.* New York: John Wiley & Sons.

Feldmand, L. B. (1990) "Fathers and fathering," in Meth and Pasick, *Men in Therapy. The Challenge of Change.*

Ferguson, N. (1999) *The Pity of War.* New York: Basic Books.

Fisher, H. E. (1982) *The Sex Contract. The Evolution of Human Behaviour.* New York: William Morrow.

Fisher, H. E. (1992) *Anatomy of Love. The Natural History of Monogamy, Adultery and Divorce.* Collingdale, PA: Diane Publishing Company.

Forcella, E. and Monticone, A. (1998) *Plotone di esecuzione. I processi della prima guerra mondiale* (1968). Bari: Laterza.

Fossey, D. (1986) *Gorillas in the Mist.* Boston: Houghton Mifflin.

Fox, R. (1967) *Kinship and Marriage. An Anthropological Perspective.* Cambridge: Cambridge University Press.

Freud, S. (1900) *The Interpretation of Dreams,* in *The Standard Edition of the Complete Psychological Works of Sigmund Freud,* 24 volumes, ed. James Strachey. London: The Hogarth Press 1953–74, Vols IV–V. (Original: *Die Traumdeutung.*)

Freud, S. (1912–13) *Totem and Tabu,* in *Standard Edition,* Vol. XIII. (Original: *Totem und Tabu. Einige Übereinstimmungen im Seelenleben der Wilden und der Neurotiker.*)

Freud, S. (1929) *Civilization and its Discontents,* in *Standard Edition,* Vol. XXI. (Original: *Das Unbehagen in der Kultur.*)

Fromm, E. (1941) *Escape from Freedom.* New York: Holt, Reinhart and Winston.

Fthenakis, W. E. (1985) *Väter,* 2Bd. Munich: Urban & Schwarzenberg.

Furstenberg, F. et al. (1983) "The life course of children of divorce: marital disruption and parental contact," *American Sociological Review,* 48.

Fussel, P. (1975) *The Great War and Modern Memory.* Oxford: Oxford University Press.

Gadamer, H.-G. (1976) "Das Vaterbild im griechischen Denken," in Tellenbach, (ed.), *Das Vaterbild in Mythos und Geschichte.*

Gambini, R. (1988) *O espelho ìndio. Os Jesuitas e la destruçâo da alma indìgena.* São Paulo: Editora Espaço e tempo.

Georgoudi, S. and Vernant, J.-P. (1996) *Mythes grecs au figuré.* Paris: Gallimard.

Giegerich, W. (1994) *Tötungen. Gewalt aus der Seele,* Frankfurt a. M.: Peter Lang.

Gilbert, M. (1994) *First World War.* London: Weidenfeld & Nicholson.

Gimbutas, M. (1989) *The Language of the Goddess.* New York: Harper & Row.

Goodhall, J. (1986) *The Chimpanzees of Gombe. Patterns of Behaviour.* Cambridge MA and London: Belkanp, Harvard University Press.

Goody, J. (ed.) (1973) *The Character of Kinship.* Cambridge: Cambridge University Press.

Gordon, B. (1990) "Being a father," in Meth and Pasick, *Men in Therapy.*

Gottlieb, B. (1993) *The Family in the Western World. From the Black Death to the Industrial Age.* New York and Oxford: Oxford University Press.

Greven, Ph. (1977) *The Protestant Temperament: Patterns of Child-Rearing, Religious Experience, and the Self in Early America.* Chicago: University of Chicago Press.

Griswold, R. (1993) *Fatherhood in America: A History.* New York: Basic Books.

Griswold, R. (1998) "The history and politics of fatheressness," in Daniels (ed.), *Lost*

Fathers. The Politics of Fatherlessness in America.

Guggenbühl, A. (1992) *Vom Gutes des Bösen. Über das Paradoxe in der Psychologie.* Zurich: Schweizer Spiegel.

Handke, P. (1998) *Kindergeschichte.* Frankfurt: Surhkamp.

Hartland, E. S. (1894) *The Legend of Perseus,* 3 vols.

Hartland, E. S. (1909) *Primitive Paternity,* 2 vols.

Härtling, P. (1995) *Nachgetragene Liebe.* Köhn: Kiepenheur & Witsch.

Henderson, J. L. (1967) *Thresholds of Initiation.* Middletown CT: Wesleyan University Press.

Hewlett, B. S. (1991) *Intimate Fathers: The Nature and Context of Aka Pigmy Paternal Infant Care.* Ann Arbor: University of Michigan Press.

Hillman, J. (1972a) "An Essay on Pan," in Hillman and Roscher, *Pan and the Nightmare.*

Hillman, J. (1972b) *The Myth of Analysis. Three Essays in Archetypal Psychology,* Evanston IL: Northwestern University Press.

Hillman, J. and Roscher, W. H. (1974) *Pan and the Nightmare.* New York and Zurich: Spring.

Hillman, J. et al. (1973) *Fathers and Mothers.* Zurich: Spring.

Hite, S. (1994) *The Hite Report on the Family.* London: Bloomsbury.

Hofferth, S. L. (1985) "Updating children's life course," *Journal of Marriage and the Family,* 47: 95–115.

Hogares y pobreza (1994). Quito: INEC.

Hogenson, G. B. (1998) "Response to Pietikinen and Stevens," *Journal of Analytical Psychology,* 43: 357–72.

Hosley, C. H. and Montemayor, R. (1997) "Fathers and Children with Special Needs," in Lamb (ed.), *The Role of the Father in Child Development.*

Hua, C. (1997) *Une société sans père ni mari. Les Na de Chine.* Paris: PUF.

Huizinga, J. (1935) *In de schaduwen van morgen, een diagnose van het geestelijk lijden van onzen tijd.* Haarlem: H. T. Tjeenk Willink & Zoon.

Huntington, D. S. (1986) "Fathers: the forgotten figures of divorce," in Jacobs (ed.), *Divorce and Fatherhood: The Struggle for Parental Identity.*

Jacobs, J. W. (ed.) (1986) *Divorce and Fatherhood: The Struggle for Parental Identity.* Washington: American Psychiatric Press.

Jäger, W. (1944) *Paideia. Die Formung des griechischen Menschen.* Berlin and Leipzig: de Gruyter.

Janssens, A. (ed.) (1998) *The Rise and Decline of the Male Breadwinner Family?* International Review of Social History Supplements. Cambridge: Cambridge University Press.

Jones, E. (1953–7) *Sigmund Freud. Life and Work.* London: Basic Books.

Jung, C. G. (1917–43) *The Psychology of the Unconscious,* in *Collected Works,* Vol. VII. (Original: *Über die Psychologie des Unbewussten.*)

Jung, C. G. (1921) *Psychological Types,* in *The Collected Works of C. G. Jung* (1953–79) 20 vols. London: Routledge and Kegan Paul. (Original: *Psychologische Typen.*)

Jung, C. G. (1930) *Some Aspects of Modern Psychotherapy,* in *Collected Works,* Vol. XVI.

Kann, R. A. (1974) *A History of the Habsburg Empire, 1526–1918.* Berkeley, Los Angeles and London: University of California Press.

Katz, M. M. and Konner, M. J. (1981) "The role of the father. An anthropological perspective," in Lamb (ed.), *The Role of the Father in Child Development.*

Kawai, M. (1975) "Newly acquired pre-cultural. behavior of the natural troop of Japanese monkeys in Koshima Island," *Primates*, 1: 1–30.

Keniston, K. (1977) *All Our Children: The American Family Under Pressure*. New York: Harcourt Brace Jovanovich.

Kerényi, K. (1976) *Dionysos. Urbild des unzerstörbares Lebens*. Albert Langen – George Müller Verlag s.d. Also Manheim, R. (trans.). Princeton: Princeton University Press.

Klein, M. (1975) *Love, Guilt and Reparation and Other Works*, in *The Writings of Melanie Klein*, Vol. I. London: The Hogarth Press.

Krüll, M. (1992) *Freud und Sein Vater. Die Entstehung der Psychoanalyse und Freuds ungelöste Vaterbindung* (1979). Frankfurt: Fischer.

Kuder, M. (1994) *Das Ringen des Sohnes um den Segen des Vaters*. Diploma Thesis for the C. G. Jung Institut, Zurich.

Lamb, M. E. (ed.) (1976) *The Role of the Father in Child Development*. New York: Wiley.

Lamb, M. E. (ed.) (1981) *The Role of the Father in Child Development*. New York: Wiley.

Lamb, M. E. (ed.) (1997) *The Role of the Father in Child Development*. New York: Wiley.

Leed, E. J. (1979) *No Man's Land. Combat and Identity in World War I*. Cambridge: Cambridge University Press.

Lekatsas, P. (1971) *Dionysos*. Athine: Idryma Moraiti.

Lemke, W. (1978) "Das Vaterbild in der Dichtung Griechenlands," in Tellenbach, (ed.), *Das Vaterbild im Abendland*, Vol. I.

Lenzen, D. (1991) *Vaterschaft. Vom Patriarchat zur Alimentation*. Reinbek bei Hamburg: Rowohlt.

Leroi-Gourhan, A. (1964a) *Le geste et la parole. Technique et langage*. Paris: Albin Michel.

Leroi-Gourhan, A. (1964b) *Les religions de la préhistoire. Paleolithique*. Paris: PUF.

Leroi-Gourhan, A. (1983) *Le fil du temp. Ethnologie et préhistoire*. Paris: Fayard.

Lévi-Strauss, C. (1948) "La vie familiale et sociale des Indiens Nambikwara," *Journal de la Société des américanistes*, 37: 61–127.

Lévi-Strauss, C. (1949) *Les structures élémentaires de la parentée*. Paris: PUF.

Lévi-Strauss, C. (1956) "The family," in Shapiro, H. L. (ed.), *Man, Culture and Society*. Oxford: Oxford University Press.

Lévi-Strauss, C. (1973) "Race et Histoire," (1952) in *Antropologie structurale deux*. Paris: Plon.

Lévi-Strauss, C. (1983) *Le regard éloigné*. Paris: Plon.

Lorenz, K. (1984) *Das sogenannte Böse. Zur Naturgeschichte der Aggression* (1963). München: Piper.

Lorenz, K. (1967) *Über tierisches und menschliches Verhalten* (1965). Berlin Dormstadt and Wien: Deutsche Buch Gemeinschaft.

Lo Russo, G. (1995) *Uomini e padri. L'oscura questione maschile*. Rome: Borla.

Los hogares en Mexico (1997). INEGI (Instituto Nacional de Estadistica Geografia e Informatica), Aguascalientes, Ags.

Luzzatto, S. (1998) *Il corpo del Duce*. Turin: Einaudi.

Mack, D. (1997) *The Assault on Parenthood*. New York: Simon & Schuster.

Magli, I. (1978) *Matriarcato e potere alle donne*. Milan: Feltrinelli.

Malinowski, B. (1927) *The Father in Primitive Psychology*. New York: Norton & Co.

Malinowski, B. (1929) *The Sexual Life of Savages in North-Western Melanesia*. London: Routledge & Kegan Paul.

Marsiglio, W. (1987) "Adolescent fathers in the United States: their initial living arrangements, marital experience and educational outcomes," *Family Planning Perspectives*, 19: 240–51.

Marsiglio, W. and Cohan, M. (1997) "Young fathers and child development," in Lamb (ed.), *The Role of the Father in Child Development*.

Masset, C. (1986) "Preistoria della famiglia," in Burguière et al. (eds), *Histoire de la Famille*.

Mause, L. de (ed.) (1991) *The History of Childhood. The Untold Story of Child Abuse* (1974). London: Bellew.

Mead, M. (1949) *Male and Female*. New York: William Morrow.

Meier-Seethaler, C. (1988) *Ursprünge und Befreiungen. Eine dissidente Kulturtheorie*. Zurich: Arche.

Mendel, G. (1968) *La révolte contre le père. Une introduction à la sociopsychanalyse*. Paris: Payot.

Messina, F. (1998) *Mussolini Latin Lover*. Fiumendinisi: Associazione Culturale "Carmelo Parisi".

Meth, R. L. and Pasick, R. S. (1990) *Men in Therapy. The Challenge of Change*. New York and London: The Guildford Press.

Michel, B. (1991) *La chute de l'Empire Austro-Hongrois. 1916–1918*. Paris: Laffont.

Michel, B. (1995) *Nations et nationalismes en Europe Centrale. XIX–XX siècle*. Paris: Aubier.

Miller, B. D. (ed.) (1993) *Sex and Gender Hierarchies*. Cambridge: Cambridge University Press.

Mirandé, A. (1997) *Hombres y Machos*. Boulder CO: Westview Press.

Mitscherlich, A. (1963) *Auf denWeg zur Vaterlosen Gesellschaft. Ideen zur Sozialpsychologie*. Munich: Piper.

Montagu, A. (1989) *Growing Young* (1981). Westport CT and London: Bergin & Garvey.

Morgan, H. L. (1851) *The League of Iroquis*.

Morgan, H. L. (1871) *Systems of Consanguinity and Affinity of the Human Family*.

Morgan, H. L. (1877) *Ancient Society*.

Morin, E. (1977) *Le paradigme perdu: la nature humaine*. Paris: Seuil.

Morris, D. (1984) *The Naked Ape* (1967). New York: Bantam Doubleday Dell.

Mossé, C. (1983) *La femme dans la Grèce antique*. Paris: Albin Michel.

Moynihan, D. P. (1965) *The Negro Family. The Case for National Action*. Washington DC: Office of Policy Planning and Research, U.S. Department of Labor. Reprint Westport CT: Greenwood Press, 1981.

Müller-Karpe, H. (1974) *Geschichte der Steinzeit*. Munich: Oskar Beck.

Mulliez, J. (1990) "La désignation du père," in Delumeau and Roche (eds), *Histoire des pères et de la paternité*.

New York Review of Books, XLIV, 19 December 1997.

Neumann, E. (1949) *Ursprungsgeschichte des Bewusstseins*. Zurich: Rascher.

Neumann, E. (1974) *Die Grosse Mutter* (1956). Olten: Walter.

Osherson, S. (1986) *Finding our Fathers: The Unfinished Business of Manhood*. New York: Free Press.

Paz, O. (1986) *El laberinto de la soledad* (1950). Mexico DF: Fondo de Cultura Economica.

Pinto-Correia, C. (1997) *The Ovary of Eve. Egg and Sperm and Preformation*. Chicago and London: University of Chicago Press.

Pleck, J. H. (1997) "Paternal involvement: levels, sources and consequences," in Lamb (ed.) *The Role of the Father in Child Development*.

Pleck, E. H. and Pleck, J. H. (1997) "Fatherhood ideals in the United States: historical dimensions," in Lamb (ed.) *The Role of the Father in Child Development*.

Popenoe, D. (1996) *Life Without Father*. New York and London: The Free Press.

Ranzato, G. (1997) *Il linciaggio di Carretta*. Milan: Il Saggiatore.

Ricoeur, P. (1985) *De l'interpretation. Essai sur Freud*. Paris: Seuil.

Roazen, P. (1975) *Freud and His Followers*. New York: Knopf.

Romilly, J. (1997) *Hector*. Paris: Fallois.

Roscher, W. H. (1884–1937) *Ausführliches Lexikon der griechischen und römischen Mythologie*. Reprint Hildesheim: Olms, 1978.

Rosenthal, K. M. and Keshet, H. F. (1981) *Fathers without Partners: A Study of Fathers and the Family after Marital Separation*. Totowa NJ: Rowman and Littlefield.

Samuels, A. (1993) *The Political Psyche*. London: Routledge.

Samuels, A. (1995) "The good-enough father of whatever sex," *Feminism and Psychology*, 5(4): 510–30.

Schindler, A. (1978) "Geistliche Väter und Hausväter in der christlichen Antike," in Tellenbach (ed.), *Das Vaterbild im Abendland*, I.

Schultz, H. (ed.) (1984) *Vatersein*. Munich: DTV.

Scott, R. P. (1990) "O homem na matrifocalidade," *Cadernos de Pesquisa*, 73: 38–47, São Paulo, May.

Segal, L. (1990) *Slow Motion. Changing Masculinities, Changing Men*. New Brunswick NJ: Rutgers University Press.

Shapiro, J. L. (1994) "Letting dads be dads," *Parents*, 69: 168.

Silk, J. B. (1993) "Primatological perspectives on gender hierarchies," in Miller (ed.), *Sex and Gender Hierarchies*.

Smith, R. T. (1973) "The matrifocal family," in Goody (ed.), *The Character of Kinship*.

Stein, M. (1973) "The devouring father," in Hillman et al., *Fathers and Mothers*.

Stevens, A. and Price, J. (1996) *Evolutionary Psychiatry: A New Beginning*. London: Routledge.

Tellenbach, H. (ed.) (1976) *Das Vaterbild in Mythos und Geschichte*. Stuttgart: Kohlhammer.

Tellenbach, H. (ed.) (1978) *Das Vaterbild in Abendland*, Band I u. II. Stuttgart: Kohlhammer.

Theweleit, K. (1980) *Männerphantasien*, II Bd. (1977–8). Reinbek bei Hamburg: Rowohlt.

This, B. (1980) *Le Père: acte de naissance*. Paris: Seuil.

Thompson, E. P. (1963) *The Making of the English Working Class*. New York: Random House.

Tinbergen, N. (1989) *The Study of Instinct* (1951). Oxford: Oxford University Press.

Todd, O. (1996) *Albert Camus. Une vie*. Paris: Gallimard.

Toynbee, A. (1959) *Hellenism. The History of a Civilization*. London: Oxford University Press.

Toynbee, A. (1976) *Mankind and Mother Earth*. Oxford: Oxford University Press.

Varenne, H. (1986) "Love and liberty, the contemporary American family," in

Burguière et al. (eds), *Histoire de la Famille.*

Vogel, C., Voland, E. and Winter, M. (1979) *Geschlechttypische Verhaltensentwicklung bei nicht Menschlichen Primaten.* In Degenhardt, A. and Trautner, H. M. (eds.), *Geschlechtstypisches Verhalten.* Munich, Beck.

Waal, F. de and Lanting, F. (1997) *Bonobo. The Forgotten Ape.* Berkeley, Los Angeles and London: University of California Press.

Wickler, W. (1969) *Sind wir Sünder? Naturgesetze der Ehe.* Munich and Zurich: Droemer Knaur.

Wickler, W. and Seibt, U. (1977) *Das Prinzip Eigennutz.* Munich: Piper.

Wickler, W. and Seibt, U. (1983) *Männlich weiblich. Der grosse Unterschied und seine Folgen.* Munich: Piper.

Wilkinson, S. and Kitzinger, C. (eds) (1995) Feminism and Discourse: Psychological perspectives. London: Sage.

Wright, P. C. (1993) "Variations in male female dominance and offspring care in non-human primates," in Miller (ed.) *Sex and Gender Hierarchies.*

Wurzbacher, G. (1954) *Leitbilder gegenwärtigen deutschen Familienlebens.* Stuttgart: Enke.

Zihlman, A. L. (1993) "Sex differences and gender hieriarchies among primates: an evolutionary perspective," in Miller (ed.) *Sex and Gender Hierarchies.*

Zoja, L. (1985) *Nascere non basta.* Milan: Cortina. English translation: *Drugs, addiction, initiation*, 2nd edn. (2000) Einsiedeln, CH: Daimon.

Zoja, L. (1989) "Il mito di una madre gelosa," in Galliano, T .G. (ed.) *Le grandi madri.* Milan: Feltrinelli.

Zoja, L. (1995) *Growth and Guilt. Psychology and the Limits of Development.* London and New York: Routledge.

Zoja, L. (1997) "Individuation and *Paideia*," *Journal of Analytical Psychology.* 42: 481–505.

Zonabend, F. (1986) "La Famiglia. Sguardo etnologico sulla parentela e la famiglia." In Burguière, A., Klapisch-Zuber, C., Segalen, M. and Zonabend, F., *Histoire de la famille.* Paris: Armand Colin.

Index